HEALING THE EARTH

HEALING THE EARTH

A Theocentric Perspective on Environmental Problems and Their Solutions

RICHARD A. YOUNG

Broadman & Holman Publishers

Nashville, Tennessee

Libray of Congress Cataloging-in-Publication Data

Young, Richard A., 1944-
    Healing the earth : a theocentric perspective on environ-
mental problems and their solutions / Richard A. Young.
        p.   cm.
    ISBN 0-8054-1038-4
    1. Human ecology—Religious aspects—Christianity. 2.
Human ecology—Moral and ethical aspects. 3. Christian ethics. 4. Religion and sciences—1946-   I. Title.
BT695.5.Y68   1993
261.8'362—dc20   92-39093
                                                          CIP

Contents

Introduction 7

The Case Against Christianity: Fact or Fable? 9

The Historical Quest: Roots or Causes? 28

The Nature of Reality: Fragmented or Holistic? 51

The Value of Nature: Sacred, Utilitarian, or Intrinsic? 75

The God of Creation: Transcendent or Immanent? 99

The Biblical Perspective: Anthropocentric, Biocentric,
    or Theocentric? 115

The Course and Destiny of Ecohistory: Doomsday, Utopia,
    or Kingdom? 134

The Dominion Mandate: Exploitation or Stewardship? 160

A Realistic Portrait of Humanity: Depraved or Capable? 181

The Ethical Dilemma: Human Rights, Nature's Rights,
    or God's Rights? 207

The Christian Stance Toward the World: Renunciation
    or Affirmation? 237

Epilogue: A Christian Environmental Agenda 260

Appendix A 283

Notes 285

Bibiliography 313

Biographical Index 325

Subject Index 327

Scripture Index 329

INTRODUCTION

Is Christian environmentalism a valid category? For many the terms are mutually exclusive. The ranks of environmentalism have been so infiltrated with pantheistic thought that to be an environmentalist is to embrace some form of pantheism, or so it seems. It is without question that the ecological crisis has given impetus to the rise and expansion of pantheistic thought in the West. Does this imply that Christianity is ecologically bankrupt or involvement spells compromise with New Age globalism?

Upon careful reading of the Christian Scriptures, one finds a wealth of ecological wisdom previously overlooked by the dominant Protestant tradition in the West. The theological and philosophical implications of this material offer sufficient grounds for a sustained environmental involvement by the Christian community. This should not be surprising, for whatever passes for truth must correspond to reality, and that reality must include the environment. Any philosophical system that fails to correspond should be held suspect as a potential truth claim. What we are witnessing today with the environmental crisis is a worldview test of immense proportions. It is becoming obvious that the secular worldview with its materialism, fragmentism, and egoism is losing cogency due to its inability to cope with environmental problems. What most do not realize is that pantheism, which is rapidly gaining popularity, is equally destitute of ecological hope. My contention is that the Christian Scriptures, when interpreted through a theocentric framework, offer the most plausible alternative to analyze and resolve the environmental crisis.

This book is structured around major religious and philosophical issues that pertain to the environmental crisis, issues such as the valuation of nature, anthropocentrism, the interpretation of the Genesis dominion passage, conferring rights on nature, and the dilemma of dualistic systems. Each issue is discussed in light of Scripture, interpreted through a theocentric framework that recognizes the integrity of creation, and then, whenever possible, compared with other major worldviews. This book is addressed to all who are seriously interested in how the Christian Scriptures relate to the environmental crisis.

I owe a debt of gratitude to those who have written previously on the religious aspects of the ecological crisis. Many of their thoughts have become the basis for my own discussions or have spurred my thinking into new areas. I am also indebted to Wim Rietkerk, whose lecture entitled "Pollution and the Christian View of Nature" at the July 1989 Atlanta L'Abri Conference, challenged me to put my thoughts in print. Finally, the book could not have become a reality without the assistance of my wife, Laura, whose twenty years experience as a reference librarian greatly lessened the task of tracking down source materials.

1

THE CASE AGAINST CHRISTIANITY: FACT OR FABLE?

The blame for the present ecological crisis has often been cast upon Christianity. Some hold that Christianity has spawned a negative attitude toward the environment which has led to its devaluation, domination, and exploitation. Christianity's influence on Western society is beyond question, from painting, sculpture, literature, music, architecture, law, and social reforms. We live in a Christian, or at least a post-Christian, culture with the influence of Christianity still embedded in the basic fabric of our society. But what about the prevailing Christian attitude of indifference toward the environment? Has God's command to "subdue" the earth and "have dominion" over it affected all of Western society? Is the modern utilitarian view of nature a child or outcome of Christian beliefs? If so, then Christianity could very well be the cause of the ecological crisis and would stand in need of repentance and reformation. This in a nutshell is what many environmentalists are saying. Christianity and the biblical tradition are to blame, either entirely or in part, for the deplorable state of the environment.

The Critics

The present wave of criticism stems from a 1966 address by Lynn White, Jr., delivered to the American Association for the Advancement of Science and later published in the March 10, 1967, issue of *Science*. In his influential and often reprinted article, "The Historical Roots of Our Ecologic Crisis," White charged that "Christianity bears a huge burden of guilt" for the degradation of the environment because of the attitude toward nature it has spawned throughout Western society. "What people do about their ecology," White reasoned, "depends on what they think about themselves in relation to things around them. Human ecology is deeply conditioned by beliefs about our nature and destiny—that is, by religion."[1]

White's arguments against Christianity could be summarized as: (1) Christianity's victory over pagan animism desacralized nature and thereby removed the restraints that prevented people from mistreating nature. (2) God's only purpose for nature, according to Genesis, was to serve human needs. (3) Human transcendence over nature gives human beings the right to manipulate and exploit it to suit their own interests. White contended that human transcendence over nature has contributed to the rise of modern science and technology which in turn has devastated nature and threatens our very existence. For White, these destructive beliefs are Christianity's legacy to the post-Christian world. Before environmental progress can be made, these negative views must be discarded. This prompted White to remark, "More science and more technology are not going to get us out of the present ecologic crisis until we find a new religion, or rethink our old one."[2]

White's seminal article has provoked numerous responses by Christian theologians and apologists, giving the impression that Christian scholars have laid his charges to rest.[3] This is hardly the case. Criticisms are still being leveled against the church, although neither as frequently nor as widespread as they were two decades ago. Many today are looking to religion for help and are even recognizing value in the biblical themes of stewardship and God's ownership. The present wave of criticism is more directed against the conservative sector because of its clinging to traditional beliefs and practices that threaten our ability to respond effectively to the ecological crisis. Besides being indifferent or hostile against environmentalism, much of the conservative right is firmly set in its ways and beliefs and rather resistant to change of any kind.

This new criticism comes from three quarters: (1) ardent anti-Christian ecoactivists, usually of a pantheistic persuasion who are out to debunk Christianity and use it as a scapegoat for the present situation, (2) radical theologians who are using White's arguments to justify restructuring the basic Christian message, and (3) dedicated Christians who see some truth in what White and others have said but recognize that the problem lies with the church's interpretation and practice rather than the Scriptures. The latter contend that the church has failed to respond to the truth contained in the charges, thereby blocking the widespread involvement necessary to bring substantial healing. The present sentiment appears to be that certain Christian beliefs are not so much the cause of the problem as they are a serious impediment to the solution. Even White views himself as a concerned churchman who laments the environmentally menacing way his own tradition has acted and desires that the Christian community rethink its relation with nature and provide leadership for renewal. He did not intend his thoughts to be used to debunk Christianity.

White is not alone in his accusations. John Passmore stated:

> What can properly be argued . . . is that Christianity encouraged certain special attitudes to nature: that it exists primarily as a resource rather than as something to be contemplated with enjoyment, that man has the *right* to use it as he will, that it is not sacred, that man's relationships with it are not governed by moral principles.[4]

Passmore did not find the source of these destructive attitudes in the Old Testament, as do other critics, but in the influence of Greek thought on early Christian writers. "Christianity has encouraged man to think of himself as nature's absolute master, for whom everything that exists was designed. They are wrong only in supposing that this is also the Hebrew teaching; it originates with the Greeks."[5] Passmore argued that traces of this Greek influence can be observed in the New Testament documents.

Arnold Toynbee, another vehement critic, asserted, "According to the Bible, God had created the World; the World was his to do what he liked with it; he had chosen to license Adam and Eve to do what *they* liked with it; and their license was not cancelled by the Fall." Toynbee's thesis is similar to White's, that Christianity's desacralization of nature allowed people freedom to exploit "Mother Earth" for their own greedy interests.[6]

According to landscape designer Ian McHarg:

> The Biblical creation story of the first chapter of Genesis . . .
> not only fails to correspond to reality as we observe it, but in
> its insistence upon dominion and subjugation of nature,
> encourages the most exploitative and destructive instincts
> in man rather than those that are deferential and creative.
> Indeed, if one seeks license for those who would increase
> radioactivity, create canals and harbors with atomic bombs,
> employ poisons without constraint, or give consent to the
> bulldozer mentality, there could be no better injunction
> than this text. Here can be found the sanction and injunc-
> tion to conquer nature—the enemy, the threat to Jehovah.[7]

Among more recent voices are Joseph Campbell, Matthew Fox,
Ralph Metzner, Wendell Berry, and Thomas Berry.

The Objections

The following is a summary and brief exposition of the charges
made against Christianity. Much of the rest of the book will be
an interaction with these charges. There is some validity to the
objections, but as usual the truth is mingled with misinterpreta-
tions, misconceptions, and generalizations that need to be clarified. Our task is not to refute the critics in everything they say
but to interact with them in a positive manner.

License to Subdue the Earth

The most common charge against Christianity is that God's
injunction in Genesis 1:28 to subdue the earth and have dominion over it gives humankind a divine sanction to plunder the
environment for selfish interests. Joseph Campbell said that the
idea of human dominance over nature is "not simply a characteristic of modern Americans." It is rather "the biblical condemnation of nature which they inherited from their own religion and
brought with them, mainly from England. God is separate from
nature, and nature is condemned of God. It's right there in Genesis: we are to be masters of the world."[8] Some even charge that
this divine command is immoral. "The injunction to 'subdue,'
which modern man has taken as his directive," asserted Toynbee, "is surely immoral, impracticable, and disastrous."[9] Critics
claim that this injunction encourages people to exercise unrestrained dominion and has caused what White called "Christian
arrogance toward nature."[10] Leo Marx claimed that Judeo-Christian thought has fostered an "aggressive, man-centered attitude
toward the environment . . . everything in nature, living or inorganic, exists to serve man."[11]

Cultural geographer Clarence J. Glacken attributed part of
Western culture's aggressive attitude against nature to the bibli-

cal account of creation. Glacken wrote, "The acts of man ranging from deforestation to air pollution and nuclear warfare and the multiplication of man have given dramatic proof of his obedience to the orders of God for all life to multiply and for human life, in addition to multiplying, to have dominion over the rest of creation."[12]

Encouragement to Overpopulate the Earth

Another criticism is that Christianity does not restrain population growth. According to Genesis 1:28, God commanded Adam to "be fruitful and increase in number; fill the earth and subdue it." The Roman Catholic Church has used this injunction and Genesis 38:7-10 as justification for their edicts against birth control devices. Most people believe that if the Genesis command were literally observed, the earth would become so overpopulated that nature would die altogether. One writer remarked, "We are on a collision course with our environment. Eco-catastrophe [sic] is predictable and it is made of three elements: people, resources, and pollution—too many of the first using too much of the second causing too much of the third."[13]

Anthropocentric View of Creation

Anthropocentrism is the belief that humanity is the central fact and final aim of the universe, that everything exists for human benefit and humans have, therefore, the natural right to exercise unrestrained dominion over the natural order. As supreme ruler of the natural order, humans have the right to assign values on the various aspects of nature and to use or destroy them as they wish. If they are useful or can return a profit, they are of value; if not, then they are of no value and not worth preserving.

Many find the roots of Western anthropocentrism in Christian theology. Throughout the history of the church, there has been a strong tradition that emphasizes the divine-human relationship rather than the divine-human-nature relationship. It seems that God is only interested with the salvation and conduct of humanity and not overly concerned with anything else He created. The bulk of the preaching and moralizing of the church focuses on one's relation to God or one another, not to the rest of creation. This observation led Lynn White to remark, "Especially in its Western form, Christianity is the most anthropocentric religion the world has seen."[14]

Gerald Barney, who directed the "Global 2000" study on the environment for the Carter administration, remarked that Christian theology teaches because people were created in God's image, they are thus superior to the rest of creation. He maintained that the "whole business" of God's commanding humans to subdue the earth "is going to have to be reconsidered." For Barney, Christianity "is a way of thought that is so anthropomorphic and separated from the rest of creation that it will never provide the guidance we need."[15]

Environmentalists perceive Christian anthropocentrism to be a major obstacle in their war for preservation of wilderness areas, animal rights, pollution control, and resource conservation. How can there be any progress if we persist with the notion that we occupy the preeminent place in creation with absolute rights over the rest of the natural order? Surely the rest of nature will be sacrificed to satisfy our needs and endless wants.

Desacralization of Nature

Pantheistic-minded environmentalists criticize Christianity's victory over pagan animism because it has resulted in the desacralization of nature, the separation of divinity from the physical universe. In pagan animistic cults the natural world is looked upon as divine, a sort of mother goddess who mysteriously has given birth to all living things and then feeds her offspring. Nature is not looked upon as a reservoir of resources for exploitation but as a divinity who bestows her fruit in response to the ritualistic worship of her children. This belief is not limited to primitive tribal peoples, but it is also found in civilized cultures, such as ancient Greece and modern America.

In pagan nature religions, every animal, tree, mountain, and river was the domicile of a divine spirit. Before anyone disrupted the natural order, say by cutting a tree, the residing spirit had to be placated. Toynbee argued that "monotheism, as enunciated in the Book of Genesis, has removed the age-old restraint that was once placed on man's greed by his awe. Man's greedy impulse to exploit nature used to be held in check by his pious worship of nature. This primitive inhibition has been removed by the rise and spread of monotheism."[16] Thus the destruction of animism, critics claim, lifted all religious taboos and allowed the rape of Mother Earth to go unhindered.

The belief that nature is divine was shattered by Judeo-Christian monotheism. Hebrew and Christian thought separated God from creation. "By destroying pagan animism, Christianity made it possible to exploit nature in a mood of indifference to the feelings of natural objects."[17] Lynn White continued, "To a Christian a tree can be no more than a physical fact. The whole concept of the sacred grove is alien to Christianity and to the ethos of the West. For nearly 2 millennia Christian missionaries have been chopping down sacred groves, which are idolatrous because they assume spirit in nature."[18]

This same general theme is echoed in Harvey Cox's *The Secular City*. Cox argued that the "disenchantment of nature" makes nature "available for man's use."[19] Toynbee concurred. "When the Graeco-Roman World was converted to Christianity, the divinity was drained out of nature and was concentrated in one unique transcendent God."[20] He argued that this led to a loss of the sacredness in nature and in turn caused "some of the major maladies of the present-day world—for instance the recklessly extravagant consumption of nature's irreplaceable treasures, and the pollution of those of them that man has not already devoured." Toynbee added that these evils "can be traced back in the last analysis to a religious cause, and that this cause is the rise of monotheism."[21]

Many see the solution in the remarriage of God, humanity, and nature and call upon the services of Eastern thought to perform the ceremony, so that nature once again becomes sacred and something to be reverenced. Paul Ehrlich, for example, suggested that there needs to be a basic change in the way people think, perhaps by following the hippie movement and adopting most of our "religious ideas from the non-Christian East" to correct our deviant attitudes toward the environment.[22] Lynn White sought a solution within the Christian tradition. He turned to Francis of Assisi, whom he nominated patron saint for ecologists,[23] as an exemplar for a reverent attitude toward nature. Francis spoke of Brother Sun, Sister Moon, Brother Wind, and Sister Earth as fellow creatures, each of whom praised the Creator in its own way.[24]

Foundation for Science and Technology

Some charge Christianity with providing a conducive cultural milieu for the birth of modern science and technology and sanctioning their unrestrained conquest of nature. The desacralization of nature and the subject/object dichotomy inherent in the Judeo-Christian Scriptures are considered foundational for the development of modern science. With previous restraints removed, it was no longer sacrilegious to study nature, learn how it operates, and then use that knowledge as power to manipulate it for the betterment of humanity. For example, Stanley Jaki contended that Christianity's belief that the world was designed and created by a free act of God furnished the ideal setting for modern science to develop, because it meant that the world was ordered and coherent and therefore accessible to the human mind.[25]

Others are more cautious, noting that science did flourish in China and ancient Greece and that modern science and technology did not develop in cultures influenced by the Eastern Orthodox branch of Christianity. Jacques Ellul observed that Christian influence in Russia "gave rise to a mystical civilization which was indifferent to material life and had no technical drive and no interest in economic exploitation. . . . Here, then, indifference to technique would appear to be a question of temperament and not of religion."[26] Many critics recognize the complexity of the problem in assigning a direct cause for the rise of science. White, for example, suggested that Christianity has been a major influence on modern science and technology but carefully avoided making an exclusive cause/effect relation between the two.

There is a growing awareness that science and technology are morally neutral.Technology is a mere tool that can be used for good or evil. Although science and technology have unleashed incredible power and have the potential for permanently destroying the earth's ecosphere, they can also be used to help bring healing to the planet. The uncontrolled use of technology admittedly is a major cause in the degradation of the environment, but critics today realize that it is the word *uncontrolled* that is the problem, not the word *technology*.

The charge that Christianity sanctioned or at least condoned the indiscreet use of science and technology by remaining silent is a more justifiable argument. The dominion mandate in Genesis 1:28 seemed to authorize the ravaging of nature, and the church's silence lent credence to this misconception. The church has had a fairly good track record of crying out against moral evils and social injustices, but for some reason it did not speak out in protest against the unrestrained conquest of nature by the misuse of science and technology.

Dualistic View of Reality

There has always been a tradition within the church that encourages a contempt for and a devaluation of the physical. Some look upon the physical world as corrupted with evil or even as demonic. One can easily understand how a dualism between the material and spiritual could arise when Satan is fashioned as the god of this world (2 Cor. 4:4, KJV) and when friendship with the world is enmity against God (Jas. 4:4, KJV). True spirituality is achieved only by escaping from the physical and finding refuge in the spiritual, because only that which is detached from this world of things can be holy. This dualism is also seen in the idea of human salvation. When a person is saved, it is the soul that is saved, not the body, because at death the redeemed soul goes home to be with the Lord, and the body rots in the grave. These beliefs led Ludwig Feuerbach to remark, "Nature, the world, has no value, no interest for Christians. The Christian thinks only of himself and the salvation of his soul."[27] This otherworldliness fails to cultivate a sense of responsibility toward nature or society; the only responsibility before God seems to be saving souls and living a spiritual life.

Environmentalists consider this dualism to be a major obstacle in their attempt to formulate an environmental ethic. If the physical world is not perceived to be of any significance by a large segment of our society, then how can any environmental ethic possibly be effective? The criticism is quite common. Theologian Thomas Berry condemned Christianity for being preoccupied with "redemption out of this world through a personal Savior relationship that eclipses all concerns with cosmic order and process."[28] In *The Coming of the Cosmic Christ* Matthew Fox also argued that a fall-redemption theology, or a preoccupation with human salvation, has contributed to matricide (the killing of Mother Earth) in Western societies.[29]

Another recent voice in accord with this accusation is Michael Zimmerman, who wrote:

> Because of their soul-matter dualism, early Christians tended to dissociate themselves from creation and to seek an other-worldly home. This dissociation, when combined with the doctrine that humanity had been given "dominion" over creation, helped to justify modern exploitation of the natural world. Such exploitation was spurred on by Reformation doctrines regarding the necessity of "developing" one's talents and the Earth through industry. Indeed, the quest to create a technological-industrial "paradise" on Earth can be regarded as a secular version of the Judeo-Christian promise of a New Jerusalem.[30]

Indifference Due to Eschatological Expectations

Many perceive that Christian apathy toward the environment is directly linked to the belief in a literal second coming of Christ. This charge is primarily directed toward fundamental, dispensational, and premillennial branches of the church. The belief that God will remove believers from the world and then utterly destroy it seemingly negates any basis for environmental concern. The world is considered as the devil's playpen. It has been contaminated by human sin, placed under a divine curse, and is awaiting predestined annihilation. This scenario implies that the physical world is evil, transitory, and therefore of little value.

Since the world will perish anyway, why bother taking care of it? For many Christians it is difficult to reconcile their eschatological expectations with sustained environmental concern.

Furthermore, why campaign against the depletion of resources or the pollution of the environment when the Bible predicts that sin and corruption will intensify as the end draws near? The degradation of the environment is a cause of rejoicing for some Christians, since it is another "sign" that Christ's coming is at hand. Some would even say that God has enough resources to last to the end of the age for the church to use in the propagation of the gospel. When the resources run out, the Lord will return.

This way of viewing the Christian eschatological hope contradicts any effort toward social or environmental improvement. Wendell Berry observed, "The human or earthly problem has always been one of behavior, or morality: How should a man live in this world? Our institutional Christianity has usually tended to give a non-answer to this question: He should live for the next world."[31] Berry continued:

> Some varieties of Christianity have held that one should despise the things of this world—which made it all but mandatory that they should be neglected as well. In that way men of conscience—or men who might reasonably have been expected to be men of conscience—have been led to abandon the world, and their own posterity, to the exploiters and ruiners. So, exclusively focused on the hereafter, they have been neither here nor there.[32]

Such criticism comes not only from non-Christian critics but also from nondispensational Christian environmentalists.[33]

There has been increasing activity within theological circles in the past two decades to construct a theology of nature as a basis for Christian environmental action.[34] Responses within Christendom have been of two types, which I will call the reframers and the reformers. Both agree, either entirely or in part, with the objections of the anti-Christian critics and have taken up White's challenge to rethink Christianity. The reframers work outside the bounds of orthodox Christianity while the reformers work within it.

The Reframers

The focus of the reframers has not been to give an apologetic for traditional Christianity, or to develop a theology of nature within the confines of reformational thought, but rather to recast Christianity into a completely new mold, thereby offering a viable

"Christian" alternative. They are rather antagonistic toward traditional Christian theology and contend that it stands in need of a complete renovation that includes a new framework to interpret the text and drastic reworkings of basic beliefs. Only then can Christianity avoid the attacks of the critics and offer a basis for environmental concern. It is obvious from their continued presence on the theological scene that the basic objections of White, Toynbee, and others are not dead issues.

Several avenues of thought have emerged from this camp of radical "Christian" critics: There are the process thinkers following the thought of Alfred North Whitehead, such as John B. Cobb, Jr., Charles Birch, Ian Barbour, and Harold K. Schilling; second, Catholic theologians, such as Matthew Fox, who are attempting to revive medieval mystical tradition with its Christological panentheism; and third, those, such as Thomas Berry, who are attempting to integrate all faiths, with an emphasis on Eastern elements, into a deep ecumenical theology of nature. Other approaches include those, represented by Conrad Bonifazi, who apply the teachings of Teilhard de Chardin to environmental concerns, and the theologians of hope, particularly Jürgen Moltmann, who reinterpret theology in light of the eschaton. In many ways the theology of hope is orthodox; yet there are problems, such as with future judgment and condemnation.

Process Theology

Process theologians draw on the philosophy of Whitehead in an attempt to construct a new framework for the divine-human-nature relationship and provide an environmentally relevant Christian theology. Whitehead attempted to formulate an organic philosophy that would unify all components of the world and correspond to quantum physics in which everything appears interdependent.[35] The themes of organic unity and interdependence are very pertinent to ecological discussions.

Process theologians describe their view as either pantheistic or panpsychic. God is present in nature in that He incorporates the entire universe within His life, yet not in a panentheistic sense that completely identifies God with nature. All reality (including God) is viewed as a single, interdependent, and inter-related organism, made up of individual psychic entities, bound together by a mutual feeling of love. "Such a view," said Ian Barbour, "not only recognizes man's dependence on the natural order but encourages respect for all forms of life. It leads to a respect for life that would nurture an ecological conscience."[36]

An individual has complete freedom to act apart from any other individual, including God. According to process theologians, God can only know the present and past, not the future. God cannot control the course of history as in Calvinist doctrine, but He can influence it by creatively and lovingly participating with the world in the continuing process of becoming. This continuing and creative process of becoming involves the entire community, including God, for everything constitutes a single organic entity which is always in a process of change. In fact, individuals can only be known by their evolving relationship with the rest of the environment, not by their characteristics, because these are always in a state of flux. John Cobb reasoned that "every entity is relational in its most fundamental nature. It is constituted by its relations. Even in thought it cannot be abstracted from them."[37]

The potential of process thought for environmental discourse is striking in that it rejects dualism and sees everything as an interconnected whole. Nevertheless, there are significant departures from basic orthodox Christian beliefs. Perhaps the most glaring difference is that process theology views God as limited. Christian theism teaches that God is omnipotent and triumphs over evil, omniscient in the strongest sense, immutable, independent, and characterized by substance. Process theology teaches that God is not omnipotent and cannot prevent evil, does not know the future, is constantly changing, depends on the world in which He is intimately involved for His own becoming, and is characterized by relations rather than by attributes.[38]

Creation Spirituality

Matthew Fox is a Dominican priest and the founder of the Institute in Culture and Creation Spirituality, an organization that promotes Christian mysticism, feminism, and environmentalism. In December 1988, the Dominican Order, acting under pressure from the Vatican, sentenced Fox to a year of public silence because of his radical views on creation spirituality. He advocates a return to the teaching of medieval creation mystics, such as Hildegard of Bingen and Meister Eckhart. Fox argues that theologians should abandon the quest for the historical Jesus and embark on the quest for the Cosmic Christ, the Christ of cosmology and mysticism. Rediscovery of the Cosmic Christ can heal the pain caused by the crucifixion of Mother Earth by patriarchal religions, such as Christian fundamentalism.

> Religious fundamentalism exemplifies identification with the oppressor—the very hatred of mother that caused it is

embraced and intensified by fundamentalism. Fundamentalism is patriarchy gone berserk. It is banishment of the mother in us all and in our traditions. It results from mysticism repressed and denied, and it always leads to scapegoating—the projected hatred of others. It occurs when the mother principle is rendered a shadow, that is, a repressed part of the personal or collective psyche.[39]

According to Fox, the killing of Mother Earth is the foremost *"ethical, spiritual, and human issue of our planet."*[40] The only hope for saving Mother Earth from matricide is a spiritual and mystical awakening. Mysticism leads to the awareness of the interconnection of all things, breaks down dualisms (especially the religious dualism that separates Creator from the creature), and engenders peace. A mystical awakening on a planetary scale must precede global healing. This involves a cultural awakening to a living cosmology that recognizes the Cosmic Christ in everything.

Fox reduces Jesus to one of many enlightened mystics who have incarnated the Cosmic Christ,[41] claims that Jesus taught panentheism,[42] says that the good news Jesus preached was not the forgiveness of individual sins but the healing and salvation of the cosmos,[43] decries individual salvation as a heresy,[44] and remarks that Jesus died a tragic, untimely death.[45] Fox's teachings are best depicted as mystical panentheism.

Deep Ecumenism

Former Fordham University professor and Catholic monk Thomas Berry is one of today's better known ecotheologians. He is an authority on Eastern religions and a student of the teachings of Teilhard de Chardin. Berry essentially agrees with Lynn White's assessment of Christianity's guilt for the present ecological crisis. He wrote:

> This most urgent theological issue, so far as I know, has never been dealt with in any effective manner, although the accusation has been made by Lynn White, Jr., that Christianity bears "an immense burden of guilt" for the present ecological crisis. Many answers have been written, a few by theologians, but mostly brief articles not entirely convincing because of their inadequate consideration of those dark or limited aspects of Christianity that made our Western society liable to act so harshly toward the natural world.[46]

Berry went on to say that the entire Christian system of beliefs "provide a basis for understanding how so much planetary destruction has been possible in our Western tradition. We are radically oriented away from the natural world. It has no rights; it exists for human utility, even if for spiritual utility."[47]

Berry believes that what is needed is a "new story of the universe" or a new myth of cosmic origins to give solidarity to the awakening environmental consciousness, a creation story that everyone can accept, religious or not. The "new story" goes beyond cultural and religious traditions to the "genetic imperative from which human cultures emerge originally."[48] To arrive at this genetic coding, Berry draws from the basic insights of all religions. The resulting common denominator of religious beliefs, however, appears to be influenced more by Teihardian thought and pantheism than by Christianity. For example, the notion that "the evolutionary process is from the beginning a spiritual as well as a physical process" shows traces of Teillhardian thought.[49] Also, the source for guidance and values is ourselves and the earth, "for the earth carries the psychic structure . . . of every living being upon the planet."[50] As such, Berry argues for a biocentric basis for environmental values, deriving values from the cosmos rather than from a transcendent, personal God.

Another aspect of Berry's cosmology is the sacred character of the natural world. Berry comments:

> The ecological age fosters the deep awareness of the sacred presence within each reality of the universe. There is an awe and reverence due to the stars in the heavens, the sun, and all heavenly bodies; to the seas and the continents; to all living forms of trees and flowers; to the myriad expressions of life in the sea; to the animals of the forests and the birds of the air.[51]

Although biblical Christianity affirms that God can be seen through His works in nature, as the hand of the artist is seen in his or her paintings, and that God is actively involved in nature, it rejects the divine presence within nature as Berry suggests.

Berry's thinking is indicative of a growing movement that attempts to unleash the ecological wisdom of all world religions.[52] Some synthesize their findings into a common core of beliefs, such as Berry's new story, while others borrow ideas from other faiths to incorporate into their own tradition. In summary, reframers seek to revolutionize the basic teachings of Christianity by proposing radically new interpretative frameworks that lack any precedent in Christian thought.

The Reformers

A second group of critics within Christendom, whom I will call the reformers, are more friendly to traditional Christian beliefs.

They seek to preserve the framework of traditional Christian theism but recognize a disparity between the practice of the church and what the biblical text actually says. The reformers acknowledge that much of what White and others have said is true as long as it is understood as pertaining to the misguided practices and beliefs of the church rather than to the Bible. They point to the encroachment of secular thought and cultural norms into the church as the culprit that caused the church's practice to deviate from scriptural teaching.

If there is, as the reformers maintain, an inconsistency between what the Bible teaches and what the church has taught and practiced, then the church stands in need of an ecological reformation. This would entail the painful task of listening to the critics, culling out elements of truth, and modifying teachings and practices to represent adequately biblical truth. The reformers contend that the Christian Scriptures are not responsible for the ecological crisis and will, when interpreted properly, offer an accurate assessment of the current problem and a basis for Christian involvement. They recognize that the practices and attitudes of Christendom have made a significant impact on the present situation and are partially at fault for the present crisis. As the authors of *Earthkeeping* said, "Those who call themselves Christians have been guided at times by principles other than Christian."[53] It is in this sense that we can agree with Lynn White that much of Christendom has displayed a rather deplorable attitude and conduct toward nature.

Even Lynn White recognized that there could be a difference between what Christians practice and what the Scriptures say. White approached the problem as a historian, not as a theologian. He reported on how the church has acted toward nature, not what the Scriptures actually teach. White noted that Christians in various ages differ regarding what they believed the Scriptures teach about humanity's relation to the environment. "So, if one points to the fact that historically Latin Christians have generally been arrogant toward nature, this does not mean that Scripture read with twentieth-century eyes will breed the same attitude."[54] Therefore, White's statement that it is a "Christian axiom that nature has no reason for existence save to serve man"[55] should be interpreted as how Christians in general have interpreted the Genesis passage. Thus White recognized the possibility that it is not the Scriptures but our interpretation that might be faulty.

White desired to find within the Christian tradition something which may engender ecological reform. However, many have questioned his suggestion of reviving the mystical, panpsychism of Saint Francis. Nevertheless, the idea of reexamining the Christian Scriptures and tradition has found fertile ground with many orthodox theologians. They are attempting to recapture a relevant theology of nature to inspire environmental concern within the church. Among the more prominent theologians working within the framework of traditional Christian beliefs and biblical theology are H. Paul Santmire, Walter Brueggemann, Loren Wilkinson, and Wesley Granberg-Michaelson. The present work continues this same quest.

A Needed Response

The ecological crisis has presented a significant challenge to traditional Christianity. There are several reasons for a positive Christian response. First, there is still a need to vindicate Christianity and the Scriptures from misguided accusations. Many ecoactivists have generalized White's objections and have fashioned them into a dogmatized set of indictments against the Christian faith. Christianity is still being represented as opposed to nature and as the cause of the present ecological crisis. Believers should be able to repudiate such notions and demonstrate by a transformed life that Christianity is not a threat to the environment.

Second, the common perception that Christians are insensitive to the environment can very well hamper a Christian testimony and cause many to refuse to listen to the gospel message. Unless there is an environmental involvement by evangelical Christians, the gospel will simply become irrelevant to the masses. This action must flow from a genuine compassion for what God is concerned about rather than from a pragmatic attempt to enhance evangelism.

The credibility of Christianity is at stake. If the church remains silent regarding ecological issues, it could be interpreted two ways: Lynn White's premise is true, and Christianity is at fault, and/or Christianity has nothing to offer by way of help. Either way the credibility of Christianity is shattered. The credibility of a worldview is contingent on its ability to relate to daily life in a meaningful way. There must be correspondence between a religious belief and reality before the truth claim of that system can be taken seriously.

One of the alluring features of New Age pantheism is its involvement in ecological programs. The modern reinterpretation of ancient paganism and pantheistic systems is providing a fresh basis for ecological action, something that is lacking in conservative Christianity. Our pragmatic age evaluates almost everything, including religious movements, on the basis of its capacity to meet current needs. The ability of New Age pantheism to confront the ecological crisis lends considerable credibility to this rapidly growing movement. The reverse is also true. Christianity's lack of involvement communicates the message that it is incapable of meeting one of humanity's greatest crises and therefore that it is not a credible option. Unless Christians articulate a theology of nature and resolve their dilemma whether ecological involvement is legitimate in its own right, the impact of Christianity will be severely crippled in the coming decades.

Third, a slumbering church needs to be awakened to its environmental responsibility before God. Without a theological basis, however, a sustained commitment is unlikely, especially from the conservative Christian community. This particular segment of the church has always placed more weight on biblical and theological justification than on merely trying to be relevant by involving itself in faddish movements of the day. Very few books have been addressed to the evangelical community to awaken its environmental conscience. It is not any surprise therefore that the church continues in its apathy to environmental concerns and sometimes even equates all environmental action with nature worship or New Age globalism.

Granberg-Michaelson recounts a study conducted by Stephen Kellert, Associate Professor of Forestry at Yale, which showed that a correspondence exists between church attendance and attitude toward the environment. Those who attended services frequently often had a negative attitude toward nature, whereas those who rarely attended usually had a positive attitude.[56] Ronald Shaiko has analyzed data from various studies with similar results. He found that 90 percent of the general public in the United States professes the Judeo-Christian faiths, whereas only 51 percent of those belonging to environmental groups do. This disparity again underscores the general apathy to environmental issues by those of the Judeo-Christian faiths. Shaiko also noted that of those belonging to environmental groups, 91.4 percent with no religious affiliation disagreed with the statement, "I believe that plants and animals exist primarily for man's use," whereas only 75.4 percent of Protestant and 69.2 percent of Catholics disagreed with it. Surprisingly, 91.3 percent of the Jews disagreed.[57] It appears that the attitude of mastery over nature is propagated within the Protestant and Catholic traditions.[58]

Finally, Western society needs a cosmology to interpret humanity's relation to the world; that is, a system of beliefs about the makeup of the universe that is relevant to modern culture, that provides a holistic framework depicting the interrelationship of all things, and that offers a sustainable model for environmental ethics. It is our contention that secular and pantheistic models will not fill the void in this human quest. There is a genuine need for a Christian response that interacts with the present concerns regarding the environment, but the response must be more than words. For it to be intellectually credible, it must be demonstrated in the life of the church. It is only then that the Christian view of reality will be recognized as a plausible option to provide a sustainable environmental agenda.

The above four reasons for a Christian response underscore the need to develop a theology of nature that can legitimize and define Christian involvement.[59] The Scriptures must be reexamined from a theocentric and ecological framework to reformulate the proper role of humanity and nature in God's creation. In essence, the theological task is to uncover the larger relational or ecological paradigm that includes nature in the divine-human structure of Western theology. This is perhaps one of the most pressing responsibilities facing the church.[60]

A theology of nature differs radically from natural theology. Natural theology begins with God's revelation in nature and proceeds to construct a knowledge of God. It assumes that contemplation of the natural order will bring one to realize that the universe must have had a cause exterior to itself, and then on further examination to appreciate and understand the mind of the Creator. A theology of nature, on the other hand, begins with the revelation of God in Scripture and from it constructs an understanding of nature. Natural theology is atomistic, beginning with the parts and working to the unifying principle. A theology of nature is holistic, beginning with Christian theism and integrating all the parts. As Jürgen Moltmann said, "The aim of our investigation is not what nature can contribute to our knowledge of God, but what the concept of God contributes to our knowledge of nature."[61]

It is my contention that a plausible integrative perspective can only be found in a theocentric approach, where God is the Source and center of all meaning, values, ethics, and purpose. A theology of nature that does not revolve around God as the ultimate crucible of truth cannot rightly be called a theology of nature. We cannot begin from nature or any segment of the created order and hope to create a theology of anything. A theology of any particular must begin with the concept of God and then impart that knowledge to the particular in question. Second, a theology of nature must be biblically based; otherwise, it could hardly be called Christian. Third, a theology of nature cannot echo any received tradition as if it were the exemplar of truth, but must rely on a fresh reading of Scripture. Traditions often deviate from scriptural norms. Fourth, any contemporary theology of nature must be developed within the contemporary matrix of interaction with and differentiation from nonbiblical environmental movements, such as deep ecology, process theology, creation spirituality, pantheism, and deep ecumenism.

George Hendry noted that theologians have virtually ignored nature, having been preoccupied with other issues, such as justification by faith.[62] He gave two reasons nature was dropped from the theological agenda: the population shift from country to city and the destructive criticism of natural theology at the hands of Hume and Kant. With the demise of natural theology comes the demise of a theology of nature.[63] Theologians and philosophers have left nature to the hands of the scientists, believing that they were more competent to interpret it. The approach of science, however, also being atomistic, has left in its path a fragmented and disoriented world. Humans are estranged not only from the environment but from God, each other, and from themselves. Nature itself has been left in a fractured array of pieces. What is desperately needed in our age is a Christian theology that can provide a holistic framework by which all things are seen as interrelated.

To construct such a theology of nature, one must not rely on contemporary theology, Eastern philosophy, or church traditions, although each may offer glimmers of truth. Instead, one must turn to the Judeo-Christian Scripture and interpret it according to its own plane of reference. The Bible must be the final authority for Christian theology and the ultimate source to discern truth regarding the place of nature in God's order of things.[64]

2

THE HISTORICAL QUEST: ROOTS OR CAUSES?

The general thesis of White and others is that Christianity introduced into Western culture an unprecedented attitude toward the environment that has led to the present ecological crisis. White, however, was cautious about assigning direct causes, noting that historians seldom use the word *cause* because of the complex multiplicity of interacting factors. He preferred to use the more general term *roots*. Just as a tree has a network of roots, so does the present ecological crisis. White argued that "no sensible person could maintain that all ecologic damage is, or has been, rooted in religious attitudes."[1] Nevertheless, religion remained for White a primary "source for historical explanations." White was somewhat more cautious than some of his followers who look upon Christianity as the sole cause. A brief history of ecological attitudes and practices among those of diverse religious beliefs quickly dissipates such ideas. This is not to say that Christians by their unbiblical beliefs and practices have not contributed to the problem. Christians are not any more innocent than the rest of society of which they are a part, as the following historical sketch will show.

Some disdain the entire quest to find causes, for it tends to generate a defensive attitude that blocks positive interaction and

28

borrowing from other traditions.[2] How can we quibble over beliefs when the stakes are so high? White's effort, however, is the only feasible direction to pursue, for unless specific root causes are isolated, effective solutions will not be found. Those who advocate moving beyond the Lynn White debate into the area of comparative religions, such as Eugene Hargrove, fail to realize the importance of a holistic response. Granted, there will be partial improvement as each religious tradition seeks its own environmental response or borrows positive elements from others. Yet the root causes will not have been isolated and responded to in a uniform fashion, for a unified view of the whole would still be lacking. This fragmentary response is somewhat antithetical to the whole ecological movement and will not be much better than the piecemeal solutions of our pragmatic secular society.

Pre-Christian Era

It is well documented that the degradation of the environment began long before the Christian era. Since problems have arisen in cultures not influenced by Christianity, it is obvious that the root cause must lie elsewhere. To substantiate the thesis that the modern destructive ecological attitude stems from the Judeo-Christian tradition requires that no other tradition has ever produced such an attitude, an assumption that cannot be demonstrated. The observation that there are variations within Christian cultures regarding attitude toward nature also argues against this thesis, as a later section will explore.

Primitive Animistic Peoples

One would not expect to find examples of ecological abuse and degradation among primitive animistic cultures, whose people lived in close harmony with the rhythms of nature and believed that divine spirits inhabit trees and mountains. Societies that live close to nature appreciate the relationships between humanity and nature much more than modern industrialized societies. Yet, as we will discover, neither rustic life-styles nor religious beliefs prevented primitive peoples from desecrating the land.[3]

The use of fire, for example, was common among primitive peoples to drive wild animals into areas suitable for the kill. The fires, however, had severe consequences for the environment. Not only were forests and ground cover burned off, allowing for soil erosion, but the natural habitats of countless animals were destroyed. Most notable were the fires set by the Native Americans and the Australian aborigines.[4] Native Americans were also guilty of irresponsible hunting methods as they killed eagles merely to make headdresses and "drove herds of buffalo over cliffs and then only ate their tongues." Some scholars believe that they eventually would have exterminated the buffalo, even without the help of white people.[5]

Despite their reverence for nature, primitive peoples still manipulated the environment to suit their own interests without considering the consequences. As Dubos said,

> The gods of early man were intimately connected with the earth and belief in them generated veneration and respect for it. But respect does not imply a passive attitude; early man obviously manipulated the earth and used its resources. Primitive religion in fact was always linked with magic, which was an attempt to manage nature and life through the occult influences that were assumed to lurk in the invisible world.[6]

Mircea Eliade has also noticed a pervasive theme in primitive cultures to manipulate nature. The task was to improve nature to better suit human needs and fulfill the divine intention.[7]

Primitive belief in animism did not sufficiently curb humanity's bent on exploiting the resources beyond what people needed for sustenance, nor did it prevent people from destructive and irresponsible practices against the environment. As in every generation and culture, human interests prevailed over anything religion might offer as a restraint. Some environmentalists suggest that we must return to animism to establish grounds for respecting nature. Yet, as F. B. Welbourn said, "Respect for nature does not depend on animism."[8] Furthermore, what one believes or knows will never be adequate to restrain the propensity to manipulate nature for selfish purposes, for there is an element of human nature that no ideology by itself can completely eradicate.

Early Near Eastern Cultures

Hebrew monotheism marked a drastic break from the animism of the Canaanite peoples. Hebrew prophets declared that God did not reside in trees and mountains and ordered that the sacred groves be chopped down. This did not engender a destructive attitude toward the environment, as Toynbee and others have suggested.[9] Animism was replaced with respect for Yahweh's property and obedience to His injunctions regarding how His property was to be treated.[10] The major ecological motifs in the Old Testament convey a healthy concern for the natural order; we are to take care of the Lord's creation as responsible stewards, not as irresponsible materialists. Warnings against land misuse are abundant throughout the Old Testament. Whenever the people departed from God's injunctions and devastated the land, they incurred God's displeasure (for example, Jer. 2:7; 3:2).

Although not the dominant position in Jewish writings, there are traces of a utilitarian view of nature, such as in 2 Esdras 8:44: "The son of man who has been fashioned with thine own hands, and is made like thine own image, for whose sake thou hast fashioned all things."[11] A prime example of exploitation was the massive clearing of the cedars of Lebanon. Many nations, including Israel, Egypt, Assyria, Babylon, and Greece, had part in the pillage over the centuries (compare 1 Kings 5:6-7,13-14; Isa. 37:24; and Ezek. 27:5). Today the region is barren, except for a few majestic cedars that "stand as a living testimony to the ruthless exploitation through the ages by state and individual of the magnificent coniferous forests of Lebanon."[12]

Ancient Egypt, Assyria, and Babylon also engaged in irresponsible practices that either destroyed their environment or wantonly exploited their resources. Dubos mentioned that the pharaohs of Egypt commanded their people to drive large numbers of wild animals into enclosures and then shoot them with arrows and that the Assyrians viciously destroyed lions and elephants in like manner as they butchered people.[13] One of the first ecological disasters occurred with rich alluvial soils of the Mesopotamian delta region. The fertile land was transformed into an infertile desert by faulty irrigation practices that led to excessive salinization in the soil. Irrigation can be successful if there is a means of getting rid of the buildup of salt. One way is to allow the land to remain fallow every other year. Continued irrigation, year after year, eventually led to the end of the Sumerian civilization.[14] Today the area is a barren desert.

Early China

Pantheistic beliefs of ancient China did not prevent massive deforestation and soil erosion by clear cutting, burning, and overgrazing. These practices destroyed the soil's ability to hold moisture, allowing the rains to erode the land and flood the Yangtze River. The washing away of the topsoil into the ocean occurred on such a massive scale that the ocean around the mouth of the river was named the Yellow Sea. According to the Tang and Sung poetry, the barren hills that characterize most of China today had been heavily forested in earlier periods. Yi-Fu Tuan noted several reasons for the deforestation of China, all of which are anthropocentric: (1) to destroy potential havens near settlements for dangerous wild animals, (2) to destroy hiding places for bandits, (3) to make more grazing and agricultural land available, (4) to provide timber for palaces, cities, and ships, (5) to provide fuel for domestic and industrial uses, and (6) to make paper.[15]

Regarding science and technology, China far outdistanced Western cultures until the Age of Enlightenment. This observation casts doubt on the common assumption that science and technology could only have originated within a Christian matrix and, therefore, that Christianity is responsible for the destructive arsenal of modern technology. Long before the Christian era, China used technology on a "massive and often destructive scale."[16] The only difference between the Chinese misuse of technology and that of today is that ours is potentially more destructive and there are more people using it.

The Chinese respect for nature most likely resulted as a reaction to the abuse of earlier periods. Perhaps the same cause-effect sequence is happening in Western society today. Yi-Fu Tuan mentioned that an old tradition of concern for the forests existed in China, but

> it is clear that the concern arose in response to damages that had already occurred, even in antiquity. Animistic belief and Taoist nature philosophy lie at the back of an adaptive attitude to environment; alone these might have produced a sequestered utopia. But China, with her gardens and temple compounds, was also a vast bureaucracy, a civilization, and an empire. Opposed to the attitude of passivity was the "male" principle of dominance. One of the greatest culture heroes of China was the semilegendary Yu, whose fame lay not in his precepts but in his acts—his feats of engineering.[17]

One may argue that the deforestation by ancient peoples was done in ignorance of the consequences and that now we know better, but this is not quite true. We do not know the environmental impact of many of our technological "improvements," yet we forge ahead anyway. There is no substantial difference between our wanton actions and those of primitive peoples. Both moderns and ancients advanced against nature despite being ignorant of the consequences. Ignorance most assuredly has caused many of our problems, both past and present, but only when linked with humanity's predilection for self, progress, expansion, and conquest. Benét's description of Americans on the move is an apt description of humankind in general: "We don't know where we're going, but we're on our way!"[18] Progress is by no means a modern idea, as some suggest.[19] Aeschylus, in *Prometheus Bound*, extolled the idea of progress, by which is meant the controlling of nature for the relief of humanity.[20] Blind faith in progress is much more detrimental to the environment than mere ignorance.

Classical Greek Culture

There are several passages from the middle period of Greek literature that depict humanity as having a rightful dominion over nature. Sophocles in a chorus of the play, *Antigone*, depicted humans relishing in their powers over nature and their exploitation of its resources:

> Wonders are many, and none is more wonderful than man; . . . and Earth, the eldest of the gods, the immortal, the unwearied, doth he wear, turning the soil with the offspring of horses, as the ploughs go to and fro from year to year. And the light-hearted race of birds, and the tribes of savage beasts, and the sea-brood of the deep, he snares in the meshes of his woven toils, he leads captive, man excellent in wit. And he masters by his arts the beast whose lair is in the wilds, who roams the hills; he tames the horse of shaggy mane, he puts the yoke upon its neck, he tames the tireless mountain bull.[21]

Clarence Glacken pointed out that ancient peoples were often enraptured by technology and the exploitation of natural resources for economic gain. He referred to such practices as mining, canal building, and drainage of wetlands.[22]

In the often cited *Critias*, Plato has Critias lament the devastating erosion of the once fertile land of Attica, which he described as having had the best soil in the world. Centuries of deforestation and overgrazing had caused the topsoil to wash away into the sea:

> The consequence, is that in comparison of what then was, there are remaining only the bones of the wasted body, as they may be called, as in the case of small islands, all the richer and softer parts of the soil having fallen away, and the mere skeleton of the land being left. . . . Moreover, the land reaped the benefit of the annual rainfall, not as now losing the water which flows off the bare earth into the sea.[23]

Concerning the deforestation and erosion of southern Europe, Dubos remarked, "Early men, aided especially by that most useful and most noxious of all animals, the Mediterranean goat, were probably responsible for more deforestation and erosion than all the bulldozers of the Judeo-Christian world."[24]

Aristotle held that humans are the masters of nature and that animals were made for human use. He wrote, "Animals exist for the sake of man, the tame for use and food, the wild, if not all, at least the greater part of them, for food, and for the provision of clothing and various instruments."[25] The notion that nature was made for human use, however, was debated among Greek philosophers. The Stoics, in contradiction to the Epicureans, argued that nature was made for human use and that humanity had a divine right to exercise dominion over it. The Latin poet Lucretius, following the philosophy of Epicurus, said that it was sheer folly to assume that the gods created the world for human use.[26]

Biologist Richard Wright remarked, "Clearly, it is myopic to focus on exploitation and misuse of the earth by Western societies alone. The evidence indicates that there is a common denominator for exploitation that is independent of geography and religion."[27] The link between religious beliefs and environmental behavior is not as clear-cut as many would like to imagine. The religious tradition of Japan, for example, did not prevent vast pollution of the Japanese land, water, and air by modern technology.[28]

Lynn White understood that one's attitude toward the environment was conditioned by religious beliefs, or by one's worldview. In this, White was correct as long as we understand that the religion or worldview of most individuals is a synergistic blend of the religion they participate in, the preoccupations of the culture in which they live, their innate dispositions, and their own life experiences. People do act according to their worldview, but their worldview is hardly ever based solely on the religion that they profess. An often overlooked element that colors one's individual worldview is the inclination to think of self first, to grasp all one can with little concern for others. Therefore, we concur that people do act according to their religious beliefs, but individual religious beliefs are a hodgepodge of internal and external influences affecting one's perception of life and one's place in the universe. Changes in external ideologies will to a certain extent bring about environmental reform, but one must not be overly optimistic regarding changing those deep-seated and highly resistant elements of human nature that seem to play the most havoc with nature.

Christian Era Until the Enlightenment

Christianity's victory over paganism did not bring any significant change in the area of humanity's treatment of the environment. There are examples of both proper management and abuse before and after the Christian era.

Early Christian and Jewish Writers

Santmire observed that throughout its history the church has given forth an ambiguous statement regarding humanity's relation to the environment.[29] This was even true in the formative period of Christian theology. Perhaps this ambiguity is due to the apparent confusion in Scripture itself; the Old Testament underscores humanity's ecological relation to the land, whereas the New Testament concentrates more on humanity's spiritual relation to God. This dual emphasis has led to two contradictory theological motifs in Christian thought, one world affirming and the other world denying. The first views the entire natural order as a unity, believes that it is a spiritual act to care for God's creation, and holds that redemption pertains to both human and nonhuman elements of creation. The second emphasizes withdrawal from the world, believing that to be spiritual one must be consumed with things on a spiritual plane and seek otherworldly fulfillment rather than fulfillment in this world.

Classic representations of the world-denying motif are found in various forms of asceticism and monasticism throughout church history. Milder forms pervade many conservative churches today. Santmire traced the emphasis on otherworldliness to postbiblical Christian thinkers in the formative years of Christian theology who were influenced by Neoplatonism and adopted their concept of the great chain of being.[30] This hierarchical concept of reality led to a value structure that gave priority to the spiritual and fostered a quest to attain higher levels of being.

In his epistle to the church at Corinth (ca. A.D. 96), Clement of Rome spoke of the harmony of the original created order, "All these things did the great Creator and Master of the universe ordain to be in peace and concord." He appealed to the creation order for the basis for peace and harmony among believers.[31] The oldest Christian writing devoted to nature is that of Dionysius the Great (A.D. 200-265), bishop of Alexandria during the third century, *Concerning Nature*. It exists as a fragment preserved in Eusebius and was part of a work against the Epicureans. Dionysius stressed the solidarity of the entire natural order as created by God and that all God's creatures, including humans, share a common home; "All are eager to sojourn together in one domicile." There is no hint of an arrogant anthropocentrism in his writing.[32] Arnobius (A.D. about 300) echoed the same thought in *Against the Heathens*. He argued against a man-centered arrogance toward nature in which everything was made for human use. Arnobius says that the things of nature "are not brought about in favour of a part, but have regard to the interest of the whole."[33]

Origen (ca. A.D. 185-254) was highly anthropocentric in his views about the purpose of nature. In attempting to support his contention that everything was made for human use, Origen had to draw from Stoic philosophy, not from the Old Testament. When combating the pagan Celsus, Origen remarked that the Stoics are correct, who "place man in the foremost rank, and rational nature in general before irrational animals, and who maintain that Providence created all things mainly on account of rational nature."[34] Tertullian (ca. A.D. 160-230) concurred, saying, "For the creatures which were made were inferior to him for whom they were made; and they were made for man, to whom they were afterwards made subject by God."[35] Early apologists made use of Stoicism's emphasis on the reality of the natural world in their fight against Gnostic dualism. Although the church rejected much of Stoicism because of its pantheistic tendencies, Passmore argued that it did find congenial Stoicism's idea that nature existed solely for the sake of humanity and that this "Greco-Christian arrogance" continued down through the centuries as the official Christian stance.[36] Perhaps the Christian reinforcement of some of these classical ideas is one of the reasons they have continued to have influence on modern society.

Philo's writings also reflect an anthropocentric, utilitarian view of nature. Commenting on Genesis 1:28, Philo stated that God "made ready for him [humankind] before hand all things in the world."[37] In his *Questions and Answers on Genesis*, he mentioned that beasts were made "for the sake of men and for their service."[38] The rationale behind Philo's utilitarian view seems to be humanity's superior endowments, "For the other living creatures in whose souls the mind, the element set apart for liberty, has no place, have been committed under yoke and bridle to the service of men, as slaves to a master."[39] Jobling traced this influence in Philo to Greek thought, yet noted biblical themes in which human dominion must be seen in subordination to God's supreme dominion over all.[40]

It might appear that Augustine had a negative view of the physical realm with his emphasis in *The City of God* on the rivalry of the earthly and heavenly cities. In *Soliloquies* Augustine remarked that he desired to know nothing besides God and the soul.[41] This appears to place Augustine in the world-denying camp. Yet Santmire found in Augustine a struggle with the concept of nature. At first he accepted the views of Plotinus. He then moved more toward a biblical framework, while keeping and modifying certain elements such as the great chain of being.

Augustine did not believe that God was some holy other completely removed from His creation. He also realized that nature has a purpose quite apart from fulfilling human need: "Therefore it is not with respect to our convenience or discomfort, but with respect to their own nature that the creatures are glorifying their Artificer."[42] Augustine remarked that man exercises dominion over all things "by the understanding of his mind, whereby he perceiveth the things 'of the Spirit of God.'"[43] Selfish domination is considered sinful. The mature Augustine, Santmire concluded, does not convey an arrogant anthropocentric view of nature, but stands in the ecological motif of Christian thought.[44]

The Jewish philosopher Moses Maimonides (A.D. 1135-1204) in his early commentary on the Mishnah set forth a utilitarian view of nature. He wrote, "In general it is necessary to know that all things in the sublunary world exist only for the sake of man; likewise all species of animals—some of them for food, like sheep, oxen, etc., others for a use other than food."[45] He continued by saying that there is a human use for every animal and plant species, even poisonous plants, even though we do not understand what it is. Later, however, he reversed his position:

> I consider therefore the following opinion as most correct according to the teaching of the Bible, and best in accordance with the results of philosophy; namely, that the Universe does not exist for man's sake, but that each being exists for its own sake, and not because of some other thing.[46]

Passmore commented that "this is the more typically Jewish attitude."[47]

Eastern Orthodox Christianity

The Eastern Orthodox branch of Christianity held that humans are part of nature and they should humbly exercise compassion toward other forms of life. There was a kindhearted attitude among Greek fathers toward animals. Saint Basil prayed for the salvation of animals, most likely based on Romans 8:20-21. The Eastern church has always embraced a cosmic view of redemption that includes more than merely humans, maintaining that the purpose of the incarnation was to restore the entire creation from the effects of the fall. Chrysostom encouraged people to treat animals with compassion, "Surely we ought to show them great kindness and gentleness for many reasons, but, above all, because they are of the same origin as ourselves."[48]

An example of the Eastern church's concern for nature is the statement of Saint Isaac the Syrian in the seventh century that a charitable heart

> is a heart which is burning with charity for the whole of creation, for men, for the birds, for the beasts, for the demons—for all creatures. He who has such a heart cannot see or call to mind a creature without his eyes becoming filled with tears by reason of the immense compassion which seizes his heart; a heart which is softened and can no longer bear to see or learn from others of any suffering, even the smallest pain, being inflicted upon a creature. This is why such a man never ceases to pray also for the animals, for the enemies of Truth, and for those who do him evil, that they may be preserved and purified. He will pray even for the reptiles, moved by the infinite pity which reigns in the hearts of those who are becoming united to God.[49]

This reflects a cosmic or holistic view of redemption which "gathers together in his love the whole cosmos disordered by sin, that it may be at last transfigured by grace."[50]

Perhaps mystic elements in the Eastern church prevented favorable conditions for the development of science and technology. Science did flourish in Western Europe as well as in the non-Christian cultures of ancient China, Greece, and medieval Islam, but not in countries influenced by the Eastern Orthodox church. Consequently, Eastern Orthodoxy was not tainted with scientific materialism and, very likely, has preserved a more primitive Christian attitude toward creation.

Western Medieval Church

There are traces of the world-affirming motif in the Western church, despite its emphasis on the otherworldly aspects of spirituality. Francis of Assisi in the famous "Canticle of Brother Sun" celebrates the entire creation as one family, referring to brothers Sun, Wind, and Fire with sisters Moon, Water, and Mother Earth. His reverent and worshipful attitude toward creation has been held up by many as the ideal for modern society:

> Be praised, my Lord, for all your creatures.
> In the first place for the blessed Brother Sun,
> Who gives us the day and enlightens us through you.
> He is beautiful and radiant with great splendor,
> Giving witness of thee, Most Omnipotent One.
>
> Be praised, my Lord, for Sister Moon and the stars,
> Formed by you so bright, precious, and beautiful.
>
> . . . .

> Be praised, my Lord, for our sister, Mother Earth,
> Who nourishes and watches us
> While bringing forth abundance of fruits with
> colored flowers and herbs.[51]

Eloi Leclerc in his analysis of the canticle commented, "By speaking of the subhuman realities of the world as our 'brothers and sisters' we are at once introduced to a way of being present in the world wholly different from that which is marked by the will to dominate and possess things."[52] Francis did not separate reconciliation with God from reconciliation with nature. This view of reconciliation cannot accommodate any notion of conquest and dominion. In Francis the attitude of kinship with other creatures coalesced with that of stewardship.[53] Furthermore, since Francis distinguished between Creator and creation and taught the total dependence of creation on God, one cannot construe his words in a pantheistic sense.[54]

Francis' thoughts of brotherhood with the rest of creation continued in Saint Bonaventure, but they probably had no lasting influence on the church. Passmore noted:

> The Franciscan philosophers accepted the traditional Aristotelian-Stoic view of the relationship between man and animals. Pius IX refused to sanction the setting up of a Society for the Prevention of Cruelty to Animals in Rome, on the ground that it would suggest that men had duties to the animal kingdom.[55]

Lynn White's nomination of Saint Francis as "a patron saint for ecologists"[56] stems from his belief that animism can offer a needed corrective to humanity's exploitative attitude and that Francis' notion of reverence and brotherhood of all creation is a viable Christian alternative to animism. Although there are dangers in reviving his mystical and panpsychic tendencies,[57] Francis does offer positive elements that correspond to biblical teachings, such as renouncing materialism (but not to the extent of loving poverty), imitating Christ, recognizing the kinship of all creation, acknowledging a divine purpose in creation apart from human use (that of praise), and practicing a nonexploitative attitude toward nature.

Helpful insights can also be found in the views of Saint Benedict. Réne Dubos suggested that Saint Benedict would make a better patron saint than Saint Francis.[58] The Benedictine monks managed the land in a creative, harmonious, self-sufficient way that retained the productivity and fertility of the soil. Their relation with nature was not a passive, mystical reverence but an active, creative management. The Benedictine monks represent the epitome of wise stewardship under God. "Dubos's extolling of Benedict as the patron of the ecology movement . . . suggests a major criterion for Christian ecological responsibility: mere love of nature without active care is inadequate."[59]

Thomas Aquinas held an anthropocentric, utilitarian view of nature. In reference to the natural order of things Aquinas stated, "Thus the imperfect are for the use of the perfect; as the plants make use of the earth for their nourishment, and animals make use of plants, and man makes use of both plants and animals. Therefore it is in keeping with the order of nature, that man should be master over animals."[60] His utilitarian view of nature led Aquinas to teach that cruelty to animals was wrong, not because of any inherent value or rights of the animals, but because mistreatment might cause the person to be cruel to people as well or because it might lead to loss of property.[61] Thus, as Passmore observed, "There was nothing wrong with cruelty to animals *in itself.*"[62] This view was shared by Kant and others.

Christianity During the Reformation

The Reformers seemed to teach stewardship mixed with anthropocentric utilitarianism. John Calvin, for example, held that stewardship extended to all creation. Commenting on Genesis 2:15, Calvin wrote:

> The custody of the garden was given in charge to Adam, to show that we possess the things which God has committed to our hands, on the condition, that being content with a frugal and moderate use of them, we should take care of what shall remain. Let him who possesses a field, so partake of its yearly fruits, that he may not suffer the ground to be injured by his negligence; but let him endeavor to hand it down to posterity as he received it, or even better cultivated. Let him so feed on its fruits, that he neither dissipates it by luxury, nor permits to be marred or ruined by neglect. . . . Let every one regard himself as the steward of God in all things which he possesses.[63]

Calvin's stewardship theme, however, was mixed with strong anthropocentric teleology, "We know that it was chiefly for the sake of mankind that the world was made, we must look to this as the end which God has in view in the government of it."[64]

In the seventeenth century the English lawyer Sir Matthew Hale concluded:

> The End of Man's Creation was, that he should be the Viceroy of the great God of Heaven and Earth in this inferior World; his Steward, *Villicus*, Bayliff or Farmer of this goodly Farm of the lower World. . . . And hereby Man was invested

> with power, authority, right, dominion, trust, and care, to correct and abridge the excesses and cruelties of the fiercer Animals, to give protection and defence to the mansuete and useful, to preserve the *Species* of divers *Vegetables*, to improve them and others, to correct the redundance of unprofitable *Vegetables*, to preserve the face of the Earth in beauty, usefulness, and fruitfulness.[65]

Hale not only stressed stewardship but also the intrinsic worth of nonhuman creatures. There does, however, seem to be a tinge of utilitarianism in his statement.

Luther also held a utilitarian view of nature. In commenting on Genesis 1:28, Luther questioned what use animals could possibly have had to Adam before the fall since Adam was a vegetarian. He concluded that Adam "would have made use of the creatures only for the admiration of God and for a holy joy." It seems as if Luther was pressed to find some human utility in animals; if they were not for human food, then they were human aids to worship.[66]

Even though Reformation theology still viewed nature as being made for human use, it is not as ecologically bankrupt as some would imagine. Yet, as Santmire noted, "The Reformers' preoccupation with human salvation helped to set the stage for—one is well-advised here *not* to say that it *caused*—further developments in Western thought which resulted in what we can call the secularization of nature."[67] Their focus on justification by faith and God's grace in providing human salvation renewed the church's emphasis on what Santmire called "the metaphor of ascent," or the otherworldly quest for God. This emphasis diminished the church's interest in creation and relinquished any claim to be the interpreter of nature.[68] Science soon took over as the sole interpreter of nature. "All in all, however, the Reformers never really resolved the tension in their thought between the soteriological-anthropocentric focal point and the ecological-theocentric circumference. Perhaps they were never aware of it."[69] The same could be said of much of conservative Christianity today.

Post-Christian Era

The modern period is marked by progressive secularization. The transition from a biblical focus during the Reformation to deism, in which God was partially removed from the context of human thinking, and then to modern atheism has left society without a basis for values and ethics and has stripped it of any hope to integrate all life into a unified, meaningful whole. This progression has led to the arrogant anthropocentrism that extols humanity's powers and triumphs over nature. When God is removed from the conscious life of a society, that society will inevitably deify itself. If God does not exist, then there is no source of values, ethics, and direction other than humanity. Faith becomes directed toward human beings and their technological prowess. These thoughts are epitomized by Julian Huxley in the concluding remarks of *Religion without Revelation,* "My faith," said Huxley, "is in the possibilities of man."[70]

Granberg-Michaelson rightly contended that the roots of humanity's improper relationship to nature are

> found largely in understanding the impact of the Enlightenment and the scientific revolution on how we all think about, and relate to, nature. The secularization of nature has its roots not in the Bible, but in the evolution of modern thinking, according to which humanity removed itself from nature in order to objectively observe, understand, and ultimately control it.[71]

What we are seeing today is symptomatic of a greater problem. The human race has left its mooring and now finds itself adrift in a cosmic septic tank of its own making without any hope of recourse to spiritual values for help. The race stands in need of the spiritual resources Christianity has to offer but—for the most part—is not predisposed to listen, preferring rather to continue its pillage of the environment and the building of its materialistic empire.

The Enlightenment

The Enlightenment refers to the life and thought of Western Europe during the seventeenth and eighteenth centuries. The characterizing feature of the Enlightenment was the growing belief that critical reasoning could lead humanity to true knowledge and happiness in life, apart from divine revelation. It was seen as a liberating movement in which correct reasoning could free minds from bondage to unfounded presuppositions and religious dogma. Enlightenment thought proceeded from the notion of a mathematically ordered universe, the laws of which could be discovered through scientific empirical investigation. The regularity of nature became the channel to discover true knowledge. Aquinas had previously argued that since the orderliness of nature was due to an intelligent designer, one could reverse the process and, by applying reason, learn the truth of the designer through nature. Hence, Aquinas taught that there were two avenues to truth, through divine law and through natural law. There was no conflict between the two laws in Aquinas' thinking.

With the coming of the Renaissance, the focus shifted to the primacy of humanity and its competence in all fields of endeavor. Thus a shift began taking place as to the authority of truth. The seeds were planted that humans could arrive at true knowledge on their own through the study of natural law.

The new faith in reason was bolstered by advances in science and the empirical method. With every triumph in explaining the natural world, the gap widened between ascertaining truth through revelation and ascertaining truth through rationalism. Copernicus shook the security of the church with the discovery that the earth was not the center of the solar system, Bacon and Descartes reduced the universe to a machine that could be understood through the scientific method, Newton explained the working of the universe by reducing the law of gravity to mathematical terms, and Locke abolished the notion of innate knowledge with his concept that all ideas resulted from sensations being inscribed on a blank slate of mind. At every turn, the authority of the church as the guardian of truth was being challenged. The Enlightenment provided the seedbed for the eventual secularization of nature and a mechanical view of reality. The movement embraced both atheists and deists, as well as liberal Christians.

Deism

Although deists and atheists differed on the need for God to explain the ordered universe, they were in virtual agreement on the use of critical reason to discover truth and on the rejection of divine revelation. In addition, deists eliminated the need of God's immanence in sustaining the natural order. God had set in motion the laws of nature and then departed to allow His creation to run on its own accord. God became a transcendent, absentee landlord, who was needed only to account for the orderliness and grandeur of nature and its laws. Everything works by mathematically predictable laws which God established and with which He would never interfere. Since God does not intrude into the affairs of this realm, the belief in a special divine revelation was replaced with revelation through nature. Deism in effect removed God halfway from one's conscious understanding of the universe and threatened to abolish Him altogether.

Since deism's belief in God was based on purely rational grounds, it was easy prey for the attack of David Hume, who argued against the possibility of true knowledge and the existence of God. Some, such as Kant, tried to salvage God from the "debris" left by Hume, but only by appealing to nonrational means. Kant taught that practical reason suggests the possibility of a *summum bonum*, although such an idea cannot be known or understood through empirical methods. Earlier Pascal, anticipating the rationalistic attack against God, had echoed the same idea, saying, "The heart has its reasons, which reason does not know."[72]

Kant accepted the deists' mechanical view of the cosmos and their separation of God from nature. But Kant took this dualism further, saying that God is not an object of knowledge but a subjective necessity to make sense out of our existence. The reduction of God to a transcendent idea, the concept that nature was a "self-subsisting whole," and the transcendence of humanity over nature led to the theanthropological themes of later Protestant theology, as with Barth, in which God and humanity would be viewed apart from nature.[73]

The Scientific Method

Natural science got off to a slow start in Europe because of "the persistence in popular piety of a dread of nature as a realm of sinister and malignant forces, which it was dangerous to inquire into."[74] Hendry remarked that "the quest for the knowledge of nature was not only a distraction from the main purpose of life, which was the salvation of the soul through the knowledge and grace of God; it was a dangerous threat to man's salvation, since it involved him in an ominous traffic with the enemies of God."[75] Bacon, however, set forth an interpretation of the fall that implicated only moral creatures, not amoral nature. This meant that nature was not evil, and it was not wrong to give oneself to its study.[76] He concurred with Aquinas that both nature and Scripture were channels of divine revelation.[77]

With the development of the scientific method by Bacon (*Novum Organum*, 1620) and J. S. Mill (*System of Logic*, 1843), nature became an object to be examined, understood, and then controlled and exploited. Knowledge of an object and how it worked brought power to manipulate and control it. As objectivism advanced, humanity, the observer, became detached from nature, the object. This detachment of humanity from nature, along with the progressive secularization of the age, eventually left nature at the mercy of human exploitation. There was no longer any notion of a community of creation or a sense of responsibility to the divine owner.

The development of the economic-technological structure of Western society only tended to confirm this emerging human-nature divorce. Neither the science of Bacon or Newton nor the economics of Adam Smith could offer any reason not to look upon nature as mere resources for human pleasure and betterment. There is no intrinsic value in nature as nature; its value is measured only in utilitarian and economic terms, a posture toward nature that has dominated Western thinking for the past three centuries.

Bacon and Descartes taught that knowledge could give humans power to control the environment; the more knowledge one has, the more power can be exerted over nature. Bacon remarked, "Knowledge and human power are synonymous."[78] For Bacon, knowledge leads to mastery over nature, a mastery which partially regains humanity's dominion. Although Bacon advocated human mastery over nature and interpreted human dominion in a manipulative sense, he recognized that human rights were not absolute. He wrote, "Only let mankind regain their rights over nature, assigned to them by the gift of God, and obtain that power, whose exercise will be governed by right reason and true religion."[79] Thus humans do not have absolute rights over nature, for their rights are tempered by the rights of the Creator. Bacon held that there were moral restraints in the use of power over nature, teaching that humans should use their knowledge in charity rather than to enlarge their power, something Bacon thought was vulgar.[80] Nevertheless, one cannot escape Bacon's perception that science was the means to reestablish humanity's dominion over nature. "The empire of man over things is founded on the arts and sciences alone, for nature is only to be commanded by obeying her."[81]

Descartes reduced everything that exists in time into two categories, the human mind (*cogitatio*) and physical things (*extensio*), the perceiver and the perceived. The entire natural world, including animals, which could neither reason nor feel, was reduced to mere objects to manipulate and parts of the vast machinery of nature. As noted earlier, this dualism between humanity and nature had its roots in both Greek philosophy and Christian theology. Descartes, however, took these ideas to the extreme, adapting them for the current scientific milieu. Descartes reasoned that knowledge of the natural order is "very useful in life" and can "render ourselves the masters and possessors of nature." Yet this mastery of nature was always conditioned by his concern for "the general good of all mankind."[82]

In summary, both Bacon and Descartes believed that the idea of God is necessary to account for the physical world and that nature exists for human betterment. People had the right to modify and improve nature to serve the well-being of the human race, which in Bacon's mind fulfilled God's intent. The effort to ameliorate the plight of humanity by enhancing the arts and sciences linked the concept of progress with control over nature.[83] Both the dualism of Descartes and the scientific method of Bacon left their impact on modern attitudes toward nature.

Secularization

The impact of the Enlightenment on the present ecological crisis cannot be underestimated.[84] Modern Western society is the child of the secularism spawned during the Enlightenment. The Enlightenment essentially removed God from the frame of reference in human thought and life. Everything, including one's understanding of nature, was perceived without reference to a transcendent God. Without the restraining influence of a divine being to whom people are accountable, nature became nothing more than an object for scientific investigation and a commodity for economic exploitation. With no transcendent source of values and ethics, society was free to construct its own system of ethics, a shift that left nature at the mercy of the insatiable human race. The secularization of nature, more than any other factor, has led to the present destructive attitudes toward the environment. Pascal once said that what we make natural, we destroy.[85]

Secularization takes place when the universe is perceived through a nontheistic framework, constructed from naturalistic presuppositions.[86] Ultimate reality becomes matter or energy, not a personal and transcendent being. For a secular society, God is essentially dead. No longer does the concept of a personal God control society's thought about values, ethics, relationships, or life in general. Everything has been emancipated from metaphysical constraints and understanding. With no God, people are free to do anything they wish—and people, being what they are, driven by the demon impulse within for things and power, have devastated their environment and are threatening their own existence.

Although Christianity might have contributed to this destructive attitude toward nature, it was not the major influence. The secularizing influence of the Enlightenment has had much more impact on the present conditions.[87] Glacken wrote, "Observers, especially non-Western ones, have cited the Genesis passages as criticism of Western civilization and its great preoccupation with man and his struggle against nature. I think this analysis is in error because the matter is much more complex. . . . In my opinion," Glacken continued:

> The historic juxtaposition of man against nature depends much more on modern thought and on more secular ideas. Without ascribing origins to them . . . I would cite three thinkers of the sixteenth and seventeenth centuries who

> expressed this concept at a time when it was more creative than it is at present: Bacon, Réne Descartes, and Gottfried Wilhelm von Leibnitz.[88]

The secularizing influence of the Enlightenment was antithetical to the basic core of Christian theism, for it held that nature could be studied and controlled apart from considering God and solely for the exultation of human glory and power.

In conclusion, the arrogant attitude toward nature that Lynn White spoke of stems more from the secularization of nature than it does from the desacralization of nature. It is much more devastating to the environment to say that God does not exist than to say that there is a God who exists apart from nature. James Barr commented,

> I would say that the great modern exploitation of nature has taken place under the reign of a liberal humanism in which man no longer conceives of himself as being under a creator, and in which therefore his place of dominance in the universe and his right to dispose of nature for his own ends is, unlike the situation in the Bible, unlimited.[89]

There is a growing awareness today that something is amiss in the prevailing worldview. The assumptions that went unquestioned for centuries are now being challenged. The modern secular worldview seemingly fails to correspond to reality and to provide any basis for lasting environmental solutions. It is obvious that the further society persists in this mind-set, the deeper it will become entangled in the polluted monstrosity it is creating. There is an emerging consensus that for any permanent change to take place, the underlying beliefs of the modern establishment must be questioned.

Modern Science and Technology

Many have alluded to technology as the cause of the present crisis. Some assume that the technology that got us into trouble can get us out. Faith in technological fixes is rather naive, for it ignores the obvious fact that people cannot know the consequences of everything they do. Instead of solving problems, technology often multiplies them. Furthermore, it is highly unlikely that technology and the industrial revolution are the primary sources of our problems. Science and technology are neutral tools of a culture. Like a knife in the hands of a skilled physician or woodcarver, it can be very beneficial; but in the wrong hands, it can become a weapon of destruction.

The quest to find the historical roots of our ecological crisis in the origins of modern science and technology is a bit misplaced.

White argued that because science and technology sprang out of a Christian cultural matrix, Christianity "bears a huge burden of guilt."[90] This assertion is faulty on several points. First, it erroneously assumes that science and technology could not have developed in any other cultural matrix. Second, it is an oversimplification to attribute the rise of science and technology to a single religious context when a multiplicity of complex factors were obviously involved. Third, it cannot answer why science and technology did not flourish in Eastern Christianity. Fourth, it falsely assumes that Christianity is morally liable for the present predicament because it (supposedly) gave birth to a destructive tool. Parents cannot always be blamed for the deviant behavior of a child just because they gave birth to it. Fifth, it ignores the historical observation that primitive peoples have devastated the environment without the aid of modern technology. Finally, it assumes that technology is in some way responsible. However, as noted above, technology is a morally neutral tool, which in the hands of a godless society, more often than not, becomes a destructive weapon against nature. The focus of our quest should be on uncovering the source of humanity's deviant attitude rather than the roots that led to the development of science and technology.[91]

If we are ever to attain a sustainable environment, it will not be from science and technology but from a transformation at the deepest level of human consciousness and character. Technological fixes are designed to treat symptoms, not causes. If all we do is treat symptoms, the problem will never be resolved.

Protestant Theology and Present-day Christendom

Because of Christianity's dual inheritance from the Reformation (that is, the emphasis on human salvation and the ambiguous stance toward the environment), the church virtually relinquished any platform for defensible environmental dialogue and left itself open to accept the prevailing attitude of the day regarding the human-nature relationship. The silence of the church is a perplexing problem and indirectly one of the varied roots of the present crisis. Indeed, Thomas Berry wondered how "the industrial assault on the earth" and "the degradation of its life systems" could have developed "in a civilization that emerged out of a biblical-Christian matrix" without a "sustained religious protest or moral judgment."[92]

The focus of Protestant theology during the past several centuries has been on the divine-human relationship; that is, the paradigm by which the church has interpreted God's order in creation has not been theocentric, anthropocentric, or biocentric, but rather theanthropocentric. Barth's theology of creation, for example, is highly theanthropocentric.[93] For both Barth and Brunner, nature was a mere stage for the drama of human redemption.[94] Brunner commented, "The cosmic element in the whole Bible is never anything more than the 'scenery' in which the history of mankind takes place."[95] In Barth's thinking, creation has no inherent value or purpose apart from serving humanity. Such theanthropocentric thinking has permeated the evangelical and fundamental sectors of Christianity. Modern Protestant theology, whether conservative or liberal, has, as a result, become "ecologically bankrupt."[96] Santmire commented that what ecological dimension the Reformation tradition had was lost as "nature was thus handed over by default to the forces of secularism."[97]

Consequently, the church adopted secular modes of thought when it comes to the environment. Instead of challenging the economic and utilitarian value system of secular society, the church uncritically accepted it with hardly a murmur.

Conclusion

Since the environmental crisis is basically a religious, moral, and spiritual problem, the church is desperately needed to respond and articulate sound biblical principles relating to proper care of creation. If there is to be any hope for a lasting change, society must turn to religion, not technology. Paul Sears, a former professor at Yale, said,

> To this let me add that several decades of study of environment and of man so inseparably bound to it have made clear to me that hope lies not in device but in design, not in technique but in the realm of the intangibles—the values and sanctions of our culture. If ever the custodians of religious faith have been challenged, they are challenged today.[98]

Even Carl Sagan recognized the need of religion to help solve the environmental crisis.

> The environmental crisis requires radical changes not only in public policy, but also in individual behavior. The historical record makes clear that religious teaching, example, and leadership are powerfully able to influence personal conduct and commitment. . . . There is a vital role for both religion and science.[99]

Yet, as noted in the previous discussions, there has always been a skewing between religious beliefs and environmental behavior. Religion alone is not enough. No culture has been entirely free of a self-seeking, secular tendency that invokes environmental chaos. During the Enlightenment, this tendency broke the bonds of religious restraint and emerged into public acceptance. Today the secular mind-set appears to be securely locked into place by the economic structure upon which our society is built. Lying underneath this seemingly impregnable edifice is a highly anthropocentric, secular worldview that separates humans from nature, worships the GNP and unrestrained progress, and enthrones humanity as the absolute, autonomous despot of the natural order. The driving force behind the present economic structure and its underlying worldview is the destructive, innate human disposition toward self, greed, autonomy, and materialism. Modern society has freed itself from religious restraints, only to find itself locked in its own prison of pollution and chaos.

THE NATURE OF REALITY: FRAGMENTED OR HOLISTIC?

The ecological awakening in the past twenty years has called attention to the interconnectedness and interdependence of everything in the natural world, both organic (such as humans, animals, and plants) and inorganic (such as rocks, water, air). The life-support system of every living organism depends on maintaining harmony with everything else. This foundational truth of existence has been virtually neglected as we turn our rivers into sewers, our lakes into septic tanks, our atmosphere into gas chambers, and our land into toxic waste dumps, all in the name of progress. As a result, the dynamic and complex structure of interrelationships that support life on the planet is being threatened.

The Science of Ecology

Ecology is a rather recent discipline that could be defined as the study of the relationships that exist between all animate and inanimate forms in a particular ecosystem.[1] The word is derived from the Greek *oikos* meaning "house" or "household." The choice of this root to designate the study of relationships in nature suggests that the diverse forms in the environment constitute one large household. Ecology differs from most other sci-

51

ences in that it is holistic rather than fragmentary. It seeks to understand the harmony and interrelationships within a system, rather than to study a single organism isolated from its habitat.

The environmental crisis has brought ecology to the forefront in modern thought. First, it encourages us to view life holistically and to challenge worldviews that cannot easily accommodate such thinking. Second, it has graphically demonstrated that we are part of the web of life and that what we do to the environment often has adverse repercussions on our well-being. Most environmental problems stem from the failure to realize that we are integral parts of a larger whole.

The Laws of Ecology

In his book, *The Closing Circle*, Barry Commoner outlines four basic laws of ecology:[2]

1. *Everything Is Connected to Everything Else*. The first law depicts the interrelatedness and interdependence of all components within an environmental system. When one component of the ecosystem is altered, it affects other components. The notion that all things are interrelated is somewhat difficult to comprehend. How can something we do affect life on the opposite side of the planet? Many links have been established between remote and seemingly unconnected organisms, such as finding DDT and other pesticide residues from agricultural applications in aquatic birds and ocean fish. "All of nature is joined together like a huge, multi-dimensional net in which any break or tear, regardless of how innocuous or insignificant it may seem, weakens the entire ecological fabric of life."[3]

2. *Everything Must Go Somewhere*. The second law emphasizes that the earth's ecosystem is a closed system. Everything on earth must either be recycled or trashed. Nothing escapes. "In nature," Commoner remarked, "there is no such thing as 'waste.'"[4] Although much of the refuse we produce can be recycled, it is usually emitted into the atmosphere, poured into rivers, or dumped in landfills. Such pollutants are misplaced resources, and their being out of place could bring adverse effects on an environmental system.

3. *Nature Knows Best*. Commoner explained, "Any major man-made change in a natural system is likely to be *detrimental* to that system."[5] Nature does not synthesize organic substances "unless there is provision for its degradation; recycling is thus enforced."[6] Some of the substances we synthesize, however, cannot decompose naturally and therefore tend to accumulate in nature. Many of these substances are very toxic.

4. *There Is No Such Thing as a Free Lunch.* Commoner explains the fourth point by saying, "Because the global ecosystem is a connected whole, in which nothing can be gained or lost and which is not subject to over-all improvement, anything extracted from it by human effort must be replaced. Payment of this price cannot be avoided; it can only be delayed."[7] A farmer, for example, cannot deplete the organic matter in the soil by raising crops year after year without replenishing it; otherwise, the soil will die. The way nature functions places restrictions on how natural resources are used, restrictions which challenge the status quo of our economic structure. Counting production costs takes on new proportions when its ecological dimensions are considered. The price of any product we purchase costs more than the expense of extraction, production, distribution, and profits raked in by entrepreneurs. There is also the expense of renewal of the resource base, reclaiming the landscape, recycling wastes, controlling pollution, and research into more appropriate technology.

The Balance of Nature

Most organisms live within a narrow range of tolerance of physical factors (such as light, moisture, temperature, wind, air, soil conditions) and biological factors (such as interrelationships between animals, plants, insects, microbes). When these are altered, the life of the organism is threatened. This not only applies to individual organisms, it applies to ecosystems as well.

An ecosystem can be defined as "the sum total of the living and nonliving parts that support a chain of life within a given area."[8] Ecosystems are composed of a community of organisms that thrive in a particular set of conditions. There are marshland ecosystems, desert ecosystems, aquatic ecosystems, and the like. Within each ecosystem, there is a mutual dependency between the various organic and inorganic components that form complex food chains and life-support systems. Although these particular relationships are not fully understood, we do know that life within the ecosystem becomes endangered when the range of tolerance of that ecosystem is exceeded. It is becoming increasingly obvious that the entire earth, including humanity, constitutes one large ecosystem, which will continue to support life as we know it only if the "balance of nature" is maintained or kept within a certain range of tolerance.

One must not perceive this "balance of nature" as a static, ideal state. Ecosystems are amazingly dynamic and resilient. The idea of a perfect state of equilibrium or balance of nature is somewhat of a myth.[9] Ecosystems are constantly changing through natural processes even without human intervention. Nevertheless, they do exhibit a certain range of tolerance to these changes within which they can continue to exist and respond to disturbances. Perfect equilibrium is never reached before being upset by another disturbance.

When the range of tolerance is exceeded, a new ecosystem will emerge where the previous one had been destroyed. This process often occurs in nature. For example, when a natural catastrophe strikes, such as volcanic eruption, a succession of communities occupies the area until a more or less stable ecosystem is once again achieved. It may not be the same ecosystem as before the catastrophe, nor does it ever reach perfect equilibrium, but it is nevertheless stable and bustling once again with life. This suggests that there seems to be a self-healing mechanism in nature.

It is rather unsettling to discover that we have been altering the earth's ecosystem by our technological achievements in such a way and to such an extent that, if continued, it may result in irreversible changes on a colossal scale. The problem is not that nature cannot recover and form a new ecosystem but that the new ecosystem which might emerge from the ashes of our tenure on earth may not be conducive to human life. Our efforts to improve life may backfire and turn out to be totally self-destructive. There is therefore, from a human (or anthropocentric) perspective, an impending ecological crisis. The real crisis, however, viewing the predicament from a theocentric perspective, is that this new ecosystem may not be in harmony with God's original design and may not support the life He intended.

The impending crisis is teaching us that we must learn to work within nature's range of tolerance. This does not mean that we should not make changes. Change is a perfectly natural occurrence. All forms of life, from termites to elephants, modify their environment. The changes made by non-human organisms, however, are usually within the range of tolerance of their ecosystem and always within the structure designed by God. As one engages in agricultural and other activities, the environment is altered, often to the point of creating a new ecosystem. This cannot be considered wrong, nor does it necessarily result in an artificial ecosystem. The observation that the human presence exerts a modifying influence on the environment should be accepted as perfectly natural. It is a myth to believe that humanity must fit into the harmony of nature if this is understood as the absence of change. Nor must society forsake technology and return to primitive conditions before an ideal balance of nature is obtained. We are part of a dynamic, ever changing, global ecosystem. To lament the end of nature, as Bill McKibben does, is somewhat odd, for nature is always changing.[10]

What is wrong is that the methods we use to invoke change are often contrary to the way nature operates. That is, our ways and nature's ways are at war. We normally gain the initial victory but ironically suffer the consequences. Most synthetic substances we introduce into the environment, besides being impossible to decompose naturally, often prove to be counterproductive to a healthy planet. The use of chemical pesticides, for example, kills not only harmful insects but also beneficial insects and microbes in the soil. The elimination of the microbes hinders the breakdown of organic matter, which destroys soil structure and fertility and forces dependency on chemical fertilizers. The elimination of beneficial insects forces dependency on more chemical pesticides. Chemical farming practices cripple the way nature works and locks the farmer into a chemical habit. The chemicals then leach into aquifers and poison our drinking water. The problem is that our powers exceed our knowledge. We exert more influence than any other creature but never know for sure what kind of effect our influence will have. It is imperative that we learn to live more in harmony with the working of nature.

Metaphysical Connections

The Quest for Meaning

The course of human history could be depicted in terms of the quest to discover some universal reference point or unifying principle to interpret the meaning of life. The notion of a unifying principle and the feeling of estrangement from it lie deep within the human psyche. Without such concepts in place, people are sick, life is empty, and everything is absurd. This soul sickness or dread that existence is absurd is amplified by skeptical worldviews that deny the possibility of universals. The common denominator of all religions is to heal this soul sickness by finding a unifying principle and entering into harmony with it. In one sense, the religious quest is an ecological quest. The basic law of ecology is that everything is related to everything else and that harmony brings healing. Throughout history, this basic law has been expressed in religious terms, whether in pantheistic religions, animistic tribal religions, contemplative mystical traditions, primitive shamanism, or even classical Judaism and Christianity.

Humans, however, have been led away from this ancient awareness or primordial instinct of the unity of creation by the modern secular, atomistic worldview. The quest for the meaning of reality has been reductionist and somewhat self-defeating since the Enlightenment. Meaning cannot exist apart from wholes, and the modern scientific worldview is anything but holistic. By its atomistic approach and its objectifying nature, science has given many benefits to society, but these achievements have been "purchased at the price of an alienation of man from nature, which has been accompanied by a loss of reality as a whole and an increasing immurement of man in the subjectivity of his own mind."[11] We will never come to grips with the meaning of life as long as we persist with a fragmented, broken, and incomplete picture of the universe.

The growing sensitivity to the environment is helping revive a holistic view of the universe. If nothing else, the eoclogical crisis has jolted the human race to its senses, which have been deadened by two hundred years of piecemeal thinking, to recognize an innate sense of unity in the natural order, a unity that includes humanity as well. This emerging awareness is spurring countless individuals into religious territory as they seek a unifying principle for all life. One might even say that ecological awareness is the beginning of spiritual pilgrimage, bringing people a step closer on their journey to a meaningful existence.

What we are observing today, therefore, runs deeper than a faddist movement of returning to the land and to a simple rustic life. It may be the dawning of a new era of human existence, an era that has definite religious overtones. We are finally recognizing that we have alienated ourselves from a vital relationship with our environment and that the cause of this alienation probably has caused other dislocations as well. The quest for wholeness, community, meaning, and the healing of estrangements simply cannot be confined to the physical realm.

If we define religion as that which relates human beings to the whole, then what we are observing is a religious awakening. Incidentally, the word *religion* is derived from the Latin *religio* (reverence for the gods), the equivalent of *religare* (to bind back, to connect, to fasten). Restoring relations with nature may very well be the first step in restoring relations with the Creator—for renewed concern for the land will invariably invoke wonder at the mystery of it all. Unless we find a coherent holistic framework to interpret reality and follow it to its logical end, we will continue down our suicidal path to destruction, taking nature and everything else with us. There is, however, a danger in following the quest through nature, since one may detour to positions that lack the consistency and coherence demanded for a truth claim (see Deut. 4:19).

The Lure of Monism

There seems to be a growing consensus among the ecologically minded that Eastern traditions offer a more promising outlook on nature than Western traditions. It is commonly held that all Western thought (secular and Christian) pits humanity against nature and turns nature into an object for exploitation.[12] Because the West has been unable to present an ecologically relevant worldview, the door has been opened for some form of Eastern monism to fill the void and provide a sense of unity and harmony with nature. The flight Eastward, however, has a deeper significance than merely finding a basis for ecological harmony. The quest for unity is symptomatic of the spiritual malaise of secular scientific reductionism, which is, by its very nature, destitute of a unifying principle and therefore utterly untenable.

Monism is the belief that all reality is an interconnected, undifferentiated oneness in which individual identities are impossible. It is not to be confused with the belief in a single unifying principle to explain all the particulars of life. There are two forms of monism: (1) Substantival monism says that there is but *one substance* in the universe and that this substance exists on its own right, independent of anything else. Any perceived dichotomy of substances is therefore unreal. This view is represented by the Dutch philosopher Spinoza as well as by Hinduism and Buddhism. Spinoza identified God and the whole of nature as aspects of the single substance. There may be a plurality of kinds in Spinoza's thinking, but only one substance. As Spinoza progressed into monism and then pantheism, he rejected the God of his Jewish tradition as a crude anthropomorphism. In Hinduism, any perceived dichotomy is an illusion or *maya*. (2) Attributive monism says there is but *one kind* of thing, such as the material or the mental. This could allow for a plurality of substances within the one category. Materialistic monism says that the only kind of thing is material (Bertrand Russell and Thomas Hobbs), whereas idealistic monism says that the only kind of thing is mental (G. W. Leibniz and George Berkeley). We are more concerned with substantival monism. All monisms deny that both material and immaterial realms can exist, it is either one or the other.

Monism is correct in asserting that something must exist independently and that all reality is somehow interrelated. The three major problems of monism are (1) the inability to resolve conflicts of interest, (2) the denial of individuality, and (3) the contingency of this realm. The first weakness is that monism fails to provide a basis to adjudicate conflicts of interest regarding the use of nature. The logical inference of monism is that everything is of equal value. If there is only one substance, then there cannot be anything of greater or lesser value; otherwise, there would be more than one, and the system self-destructs. This leveling of all values may sound appealing, but it has serious implications for constructing an environmental ethic and resolving conflicts of interest. If all is equally divine, who is to be the judge and what will be the basis of arbitration? Are rats and cows to be permitted to eat up the grain needed for human survival? Without an authority that transcends the physical, values are either biased toward human interests or completely leveled. Neither option is healthy for the environment. This discussion of conflict resolution will be resumed in chapter 6.

Second, some forms of monism destroy the notion of individual identity. They promote unity at the cost of individuality and as such represent the antithesis of modern secular thought. The pendulum has swung to the opposite extreme. One common form of pantheistic monism teaches that there is only one level of existence, the spiritual, and only one entity on that plane, the Cosmic Soul (or whatever). This Cosmic Soul pervades the universe and constitutes the basic fabric of everything. Nothing exists except this Cosmic Soul, which not only is ultimate reality, he, or rather it, is reality; there is nothing else. The physical realm is merely the projection or emanation of the divine spirit. Thus everything is part of the divine or ultimate reality. The identity of this ultimate reality is somewhat of an enigma. According to Hindu tradition, God can neither be known by the intellect or be explained by the tongue. It can only be experienced. To experience the dissolution of all distinctions and one's soul merging with the over-soul of the universe in a meditative session is to achieve God consciousness or cosmic consciousness. Both are the same thing, for this undifferentiated oneness is God. In emphasizing the ontological identity of all things, pantheistic monism ends up destroying individual identity. This notion of unity at the expense of diversity runs contrary to common human experience and contrary to our understanding of the science of ecology where individual organisms exist in the context of mutual interrelationships.

Third, the first two laws of thermodynamics strongly suggest that this realm is contingent and does not exist on its own right. The first law, or the law of conservation, states that the total amount of energy and matter in the universe remains constant. The second law is the law of entropy. According to this law, the total amount of usable energy is becoming less and less. In any process some energy will be changed into less usable forms such as heat loss due to friction. This is why perpetual motion machines fail. They lose energy due to friction, energy that cannot be reclaimed to keep the machines operating. The implication of these two laws is that the universe will run down. Less and less usable energy is available to keep it going and to sustain molecular order. Eventually, the universe will die of "heat death."

A universe that is in a perpetual state of entropy cannot possibly be eternal. The only thing that can qualify to be eternal (both in time past and future) is that which is self-sustaining and not part of the decaying universe. The logic is simple. If the universe is running down, then it is neither self-sustaining or eternal. If it is neither self-sustaining or eternal, then the most reasonable conclusion is that it cannot be deity in the fullest sense, a sense that is absolutely crucial for most monistic systems.

To identify God with this universe not only confines God to this realm but also subjects deity to the laws of thermodynamics. The inferences are rather devastating to any notion of God. The pantheist god, for example, must have had a beginning and must be in a state of constant degeneration. The pantheistic god is therefore contingent, dependent, and not self-sustaining; in other words, the pantheistic god is finite. A finite god is simply not an adequate base to be the infinite reference point on which to hang an entire philosophical system and to provide a framework for building a sustainable environment.

The only responses open for a pantheist would be (1) to debunk the law of entropy, (2) to posit that their god arose out of nothing by its own accord, or (3) to find something that overrides the law of entropy. The first is scientifically unlikely, and the second is an utter absurdity. The only option to save God from oblivion is to find something that counters entropy. Buckminster Fuller has popularized the idea of syntropy as a possible anti-entropic principle of the universe.[13] Syntropy is a delightful New Age idea where one plus one equals two plus. That is, when organisms pool their energies together, the resulting energy is greater than the total energy of the individual organisms. Teilhard de Chardin poses a different view. He maintains that there are two different kinds of energy: radial (inner psychic) energy that is increasing in complexity, and tangential (physical) energy that holds the elements together and governs physical relations. The latter is subject to the laws of thermodynamics, the first is not.[14] Neither option is convincing.

The Christian alternative offers a much more viable solution. The universe is running down and will eventually need to be rejuvenated, but the God of the universe cannot run down, for

He is eternal and self-sustaining (Heb. 1:10-12). The universe can only be sustained if it is in harmony with a transcendent, self-sustaining, and nondependent God. It is only by positing such a God that the dilemma of monism can be avoided and ecological recovery of our ailing planet has any hope. The biblical distinction between the Creator and His creation is therefore an ecological necessity.

The Gaia Hypothesis

A popular way among New Age enthusiasts to perceive the interrelatedness of the natural order is the Gaia hypothesis. The Gaia hypothesis as formulated by the British scientist James Lovelock depicts the earth as behaving like one gigantic organism. The word *Gaia* is derived from the name of the earth goddess of Greek mythology. Lovelock's interest in the functioning of the earth led him to observe that the earth's self-regulating mechanisms are similar to those of living organisms. He rejected the idea common among some advocates of the hypothesis that there is a global mind governing the planet's self-regulating processes, saying rather that the process is accomplished through a complex set of cause-effect feedback relations. Thus the earth is not a living organism, it only behaves like one. Although scientists debate the validity of some points of the hypothesis, the general outline seems to correspond with the basic operation of ecosystems.

New Age writers have taken the Gaia hypothesis much further than the purely scientific level that Lovelock proposed and given it mystical connotations. The earth not only behaves like a living organism, it is a living organism. Some add that Gaia is a conscious organism with which people can communicate. One example would be the communications of the Findhord community with the Devas.[15] The idea that the earth is a living, conscious organism is found among many native peoples, who communicate with the rivers and mountains. In *Minding the Earth*, Joseph Meeker refrains from using the term *Gaia* because it implies that the universe is personal, as the goddess' name suggests. Nevertheless Meeker contends that we can "enter into conversation with it."[16]

A third level of Gaia interpretation, a natural step from the second level, is to attribute divinity to the earth. Shamanic cultures affirm that the earth is a sacred being, the body of deity, and something to be worshiped. Most think of it as a female deity, a mother that has given birth to all life. Biblical prophets vehemently denounced such pagan nature worship. The idea of a divine cosmos cannot be reconciled with the Judeo-Christian God who created the cosmos and exists apart from it.

But in what sense, if at all, can the earth be considered a living organism? Just because it supports individual life forms or even a global ecosystem does not warrant its being termed a living organism any more than the homes in which we live can be called living beings because they are "alive" with creatures within. If the earth were a living being, it must be of a higher, more complex order than humans, and yet the simple observation remains that the earth is not a sentient being; it does not have intelligence, feelings, or volition. Furthermore, if the earth were a living organism, it should be able to reproduce itself as other living organisms do. The observation that the earth's processes respond in a cause-effect manner to stimuli does not imply that it is a self-conscious organism any more than billiard balls responding when they are struck suggest that they are alive.

The most we can say is that the earth behaves like a living organism, that it is alive in the sense of being "alive" with living creatures, or that it constitutes an environment supportive of life. Daniel Botkin wrote:

> We are accustomed to thinking of life as a characteristic of individual organisms. Individuals are alive, but an individual cannot sustain life. Life is sustained only by a group of organisms of many species—not simply a horde or mob, but a certain kind of system composed of many individuals of different species—and their environment, making together a network of living and nonliving parts that can maintain the flow of energy and the cycling of chemical elements that, in turn, support life.[17]

In this sense we could expand the concept of life to the entire earth, without calling the earth a living organism. The Gaia hypothesis is actually counterproductive to environmentalism, for if Gaia were truly self-healing, then there would be no need for human intervention to try to correct the imbalances.

Biblical Basis for a Holistic View of Life

The Scriptures contain a wealth of resources to substantiate the idea that all reality is interrelated and forms one integrated ecosystem. The biblical view that living organisms are individual, interrelated, and dependent on proper relations within an ecosystem is perfectly compatible with the modern scientific understanding of ecology and the four laws of ecology expressed by Barry Commoner. The biblical view, moreover, expands the concept of interrelatedness to include the spiritual dimension. Just as trees cannot exist apart from their ecosystem, nor humanity apart from nature, neither can either one exist apart from God. God created the entire natural order as a complex interrelated ecosystem that cannot exist in isolation from His sustaining influence.[18]

The Cosmic Community

The unity and interrelatedness of all creation can best be explained in terms of a single Creator. If there were two or more gods, or no God at all, then there would be the possibility of divergent ecological structures in different parts of the earth. Yet there is only one structure or one set of principles governing ecological processes. The observation that the universe is a single interlocking network of life forms in which one part cannot exist independently of the rest argues for the existence of a single Creator. If everything has been set in motion by a single Creator, a Creator who cannot act contrary to His nature as a harmonious triune God, then everything at its conception must reflect the Creator and constitute a single harmonious cosmic community with singleness of design and structure. When everything is perceived as cocreatures and coinhabitants of a cosmic community, we can echo the canticle of Saint Francis and speak of Brother Sun and Sister Moon. It is only within this cosmic community, which has God as its head, that we will find full realization of ourselves as social beings.[19]

The Integrity of Creation

A term often employed to designate the unity and harmony of the created realm within Christian circles is "integrity of creation." The term "signifies an attempt to rediscover a sense of the wholeness of the creation in relation to God and the need for ethical imperatives towards renewal and at-oneness."[20] These ethical imperatives are based on the functional structure of the universe, which in turn is based on the very character of the Creator. In this sense we can speak of the creation as an extension of the Creator. Everything works in harmony when it works by the moral and ecological laws established by God. When these laws are broken, the relations between parts are severed, and the whole ceases to function as God intended. One's quest must be to find those laws that govern relationships. Finding these laws will produce wholeness and health not only to the environment but to the individual and society as well. The healing web of relationships, however, must extend beyond the physical to the spiritual and include a proper relationship with God.

Relational Terminology

The Bible is preeminently a book about relationships. This is evident from the use of relational terms and themes throughout Scripture, terms such as *covenant, love, hate, sin, grace, faith, hope, redemption, salvation,* and *reconciliation.* Sittler noted that "each of these is a term that points to the establishment of a relationship, or the breaking of a relationship, or the perversion of a relationship; and each one points to the promise of blessedness as the reestablishment of a relationship."[21] *Sin* is the primary negative relational term in Scripture. Other negative relational terms such as *anger, hatred, greed,* and *fornication* are subsumed under *sin,* for all tend to sever relations. These relational terms apply to nature as well as humanity.

The biblical concept of salvation suggests wholeness and healing. It refers to the restoring of peace and harmony through the person and work of Christ. It is a healing of broken relations, first between God and humanity, then between humans, and finally between humanity and nature. We are called on to participate in the healing of our broken and fragmented world (2 Cor. 5:18-20) and to work out our salvation in all aspects of life (Phil. 2:12). The biblical notion of salvation is an ecological concept that pertains to the restoration of all relationships that were severed at the fall. That the whole cosmos is included in this salvation is evident from Romans 8:21 where creation itself is to be "liberated from its bondage to decay and brought into the glorious freedom of the children of God."

The Ecological Triangle

The relationships between God, humanity, and nature could be conceived as a triangle.[22] When one side of the ecological triangle is broken, it shatters the other sides as well, for the triangle will function properly only if it remains whole. For example, when we rebel against God, it severs our relation with nature, since we will ignore God's injunction to care for the earth, and nature's relation with God, since God will judge the disobedient through nature, as witnessed by the deluge. Although God is able to heal all these relations, He will do so only in response to our choice. The relations were broken by humanity and cannot be fully restored in the present era without our choosing to return to God, the Creator and Sustainer of all life.

Within the larger spectrum of biblical ecology, we cannot say that everything that exists is interdependent, for this would include God. The Scriptures make a necessary distinction between the Creator and the creation, setting God apart as infinite, self-sustaining, and not dependent on anything else (see

Heb. 9:11). The entire created realm is finite, contingent, and thus dependent for its continued existence on something other than itself. The chain of dependencies reaches up to the Apex, or to the self-sustaining Fountainhead of all life, but does not include Him in the network of interdependencies. If God were included in a cosmic web of interdependencies, then He would be the finite god of process theology and not the infinite God of the Scriptures. The ecological triangle is therefore a triangle of relationships, not a triangle of interdependencies.

The Divine-Human Relation. The link of the ecological triangle which lies at the core of the Christian message is the divine-human relationship. This at the surface may sound rather provincial but not when our relation with God is understood as being crucial to the harmony of creation. It was our rebellion against God that threw the entire cosmos into disorder, a disorder that cannot be fully corrected until that primary relation is restored. The church has focused on human salvation to an extent that it has failed to see the totality of salvation and its involving a triad of relations. True salvation or healing does not take place until the whole is in harmony. To confess faith in the Christian message and then to abuse one another or nature is a woefully deficient notion of salvation.

The Divine-Nature Relation. Ecological relationships must be expanded into the spiritual sphere and include the relation between God and His creation. God not only created the universe and endowed the earth with life but also lovingly cares for and upholds His creation. Creation is totally dependent on the sustaining power of God and cannot in any sense be thought of as an autonomous self-sustaining entity. The quest to find a sustainable environment cannot ignore God. Scriptures depict God as being in control of the forces of nature (Job 9:5-7; 38:12-35; Ps. 147:16-18) and sustaining nature (Neh. 9:6; Ps. 36:6; Col. 1:17; and Heb. 1:3). God even upholds the regularity of nature (Gen. 8:22). The psalmist placed both humanity and nature on the same level of dependency before God, looking to the Creator for daily sustenance (Ps. 104:27-30). Jesus mentioned that God even cares for the birds of the air and the lilies of the field (Matt. 6:26, 28).

The relation between God and nature is affected by human sin. Sometimes God causes drought or other ecological disturbances as a form of judgment. Such environmental retribution may be scorned by secular men and women, but it is entirely feasible in a theistic universe.[23] God does not judge nature, for nature is amoral, cannot sin, and did not fall. God's judgment is on disobedient humanity, a judgment which, at times, implicates nature. Of course, not all natural catastrophes should be attributed to a direct action of God. Since our existence is vitally linked with nature, one way to chastise us would be to affect the world in which we live. Nature's healing is, therefore, contingent on the healing of the divine-human relationship.

The Old Testament clearly teaches that nature is one of the channels through which God blesses or judges His people. God has the power and prerogative to sustain the created order, enabling it to produce an abundance of produce, or to withhold His hand, allowing nature to languish. When we obey God, nature rejoices (Isa. 44:22-23), and when we disobey God, nature mourns (Isa. 24:1-6; Hos. 4:1-3). This mourning of nature is due to God's chastening us by controlling the forces of nature or indirectly by letting the consequence of our ways affect natural processes, such as sickness and disease resulting from toxic pollution.

The Human-Nature Relation. The Scriptures depict humans as living in tension. We are both part of nature and separate from it; both immanent and transcendent. One aspect of this polarity cannot be stressed over the other without resulting in an unbalanced view of our place in the cosmos and our responsibility for the environment. If our transcendence is stressed, the result tends toward humanistic anthropocentrism. If our immanence is stressed, the result tends toward pantheistic biocentrism. With either option, human responsibility before God for taking care of the environment is weakened. The first promotes arrogant autonomy with the belief that we have the right to exploit nature for our own ends. The second encourages a flattened hierarchical system that negates conflict resolution and environmental imperatives. The first looks to humanity for direction, the second to nature; neither looks to God as the source of value and meaning. The tension between our immanence and transcendence is resolved in the biblical concepts of Eden and restoration in which states we exist in perfect subjection to God and thus in perfect harmony with the rest of what God made.

A consistent theme in Scripture often overlooked is that humans are inextricably linked with nature and cannot survive apart from it. We are not, however, part of nature in a mystical, pantheistic sense and are not to be ontologically identified with it, anymore than a wood cabinet is with the tree from which it came. We may be composed of the same material, but this does not mean that we cease to be distinct entities. The entire cosmic community is composed of individual entities each one ecologically bound to the rest of creation. Scripture sometimes uses the term *creation* to denote the entire created realm, associating humanity with the rest of the created order as part of one indivisible whole (Rom. 1:20; 2 Pet. 3:4; Rev. 3:14). The following points provide biblical support for humans being part of nature:

(1) Humans are part of nature in regard to origins. We, like everything else, were created by God, even sharing the sixth day of creation with land animals (Gen. 1:24-31; see Job 40:15).

(2) Humans are part of nature in regard to kind of material. People, animals, and plants were all formed from the dust of the earth, from which also came trees and other vegetation. Being made of the same material as animals and plants establishes a relation between every living organism and between those organisms and the earth. In other words, everything on the earth, whether organic or inorganic, is related in terms of the stuff they are made of.

In Genesis 2:7 we see where people were not created *ex nihilo* but from previously existing material, "The Lord God formed the man from the dust of the ground." The Hebrew word for "ground" (*adamah*) is a cognate of the word for "humankind" (*adam*, see Gen. 1:27; 5:2). The Hebrew *adam* was not only used for "mankind" but also for the adult male of the species and for the proper name *Adam*. It is not certain that *adam* refers to the name of the patriarch until Genesis 5:3. The play on words is evident in Genesis 2:5, "There was no man [*adam*] to work the ground [*adamah*]." This could be expressed in English by saying that there were no humans to work the humus. The play on words also occurs in Genesis 2:7 where we could translate, "God made humans from humus."[24] In addition, God formed "the beasts of the field and all the birds of the air" from the ground (*adamah*, Gen. 2:19), from which also trees came forth (Gen. 2:9). That we are composed of earthly materials is reiterated in Genesis 3:19 and 23 where at death Adam would return to the dust of the ground from which he was taken. Speaking of both human beings and animals, the Bible said, "All come from dust, and to dust all return" (Eccl. 3:20). The creation of humans from the dust of the earth is a familiar Old Testament theme (Job 4:19; 10:8-9; Pss. 103:14; 104:29; 146:4; and Isa. 29:16).

(3) Humans and animals both share the breath of life, or the life principle (Eccl. 3:18-21). This life principle is a special endowment from the living God (Ps. 104:29-30). Genesis 2:7 reads, "The Lord God formed the man from the dust of the ground and breathed into his nostrils the breath of life, and man became a living being." The *King James Version* translates the last clause: "and man became a living soul." The words *living being* (NIV) or *living soul* (KJV) in the Hebrew is *nephesh*. All this means is that God animated the lifeless matter He used to make

the body by imparting a life principle. It does not mean that we are merely living souls that happen to be imprisoned in bodies of flesh, nor does it necessarily imply that we have a soul which animals do not have. In Genesis 1:30 all the creatures of the earth and birds of the air have the "breath of life" or simply "life" as the *King James Version* reads. Again the word is *nephesh*. In Genesis 1:20-21 sea creatures also are said to have *nephesh*, suggesting that the word is not to be restricted to air-breathing animals but rather to the life principle of the animal kingdom.[25] If by *soul* we mean the life principle, then animals have souls.

(4) Humans share the planet with other life forms and thus have a common home. This is typified by the ark in which salvation from chaos is represented by all creatures living in harmony under one roof.

(5) Humans share a common table with animals in that both partake of the same vegetarian diet (Gen. 1:29-30). With 90 percent of the corn, barley, oats, and soybeans going to feed livestock for meat-hungry Americans while millions of people in the world are starving, many are being awakened to the divine wisdom of a vegetarian diet. Cattle are the least efficient animals in the conversion of plant protein into animal protein, consuming an average of sixteen pounds of grain and soybeans to produce one pound of beef. Every hungry person in the world could easily be fed enough on the wasted plant protein that is not converted into animal protein.[26] To eat beans and rice in place of meat is simply unthinkable for most people, but it is better management of God's resources. But how can Americans possibly forgo their beloved hamburgers? The problem is not a shortage of agricultural lands but rather misplaced values. Increasingly, people are advocating a vegetarian diet as part of the redeemed life-style that brings healing to the poor and hungry as well as to overworked agricultural lands. God does permit the eating of meat but in neither the prelapsarian nor restored states (see Isa. 11:6-9). Our lives should reflect a redeemed life-style and be channels of redemptive healing for an ailing world, and perhaps this includes restructuring our diet.

The order of creation suggests a chain of dependency, with latter forms dependent on earlier forms for survival. Animals, for instance, could not have been created before plant life, for they need the plant life for food. Since human beings were the last to be created, they are dependent on everything else to sustain life. We are, therefore, part of nature, and our well-being is contingent on maintaining a proper relationship with the rest of creation. As Joranson and Butigan said, "No one of us lives apart from the natural world."[27]

(6) Humans share a common destiny with the cosmos. Human redemption is linked with the redemption of the cosmos; what happens to one happens to the other (Isa. 11:6-9; 41:17-20; 43:18-21; 65:17; 66:22; Hos. 2:18-20; Rom. 8:18-23; and Col. 1:20). Both man and beast are mortal and suffer the same fate (Ps. 49:12, 20; Eccl. 3:18-20; Isa. 40:6-8). Carl Henry remarked, "Man in his totality, psychic and physical, belongs to the created universe."[28]

Humans, on the other hand, are not simply part of the processes of nature. Genesis depicts us as being unique with abilities that raise us above the rest of creation. This superiority over nature is a self-evident truth that is verified every day by common human experience. Just as God is distinct from the created order and not to be ontologically identified with it so is the human race. Our distinction from nature need not imply despotism anymore than God's distinction from nature implies that God is a despot or that He exploits creation for His own pleasure.

Our uniqueness is such that it enables us to stand apart from nature as either a destroyer or a caretaker. This uniqueness is an obvious fact of existence and cannot be dismissed as easily as some pantheistic-minded ecocritics would like. Instead of ignoring it, we need to confront the moral problems involved and turn it into a positive force. This is exactly what is done in the Scriptures. The Scriptures not only affirm human uniqueness but offer a framework for viewing it in an environmentally healthy manner.

First, only human beings are said to have been created in the image of God, not animals, plants, or any other part of the created order (Gen. 1:27). Instead of giving us the absolute right to ransack nature to satisfy our greed, the divine image furnishes us with unique gifts to manage God's creation in a responsible manner. To be like God engenders a sobering responsibility, not an arrogant autonomy. We do have godlike powers to transform and create, but these are not intended to be employed apart from an awareness of the Authority who gave us those abilities and delegated to us responsibility to properly use them.

Second, only human beings have been given the responsibility to care for God's creation. God knew that His creation was not complete without a caretaker (Gen. 2:5,15). The animals could not fill this role, since they lacked those traits that make for a morally responsible, rational, creative, and personal being. We have those traits, thus enabling us to function as God's stewards. A caretaker or steward is one who looks after the property of another and who is morally responsible to the owner of the property. Stewardship, by its very definition, transcends individ-

ualism and self-interests and requires a morally responsible
agent. The principle of stewardship could not have been fulfilled
by any member of the animal kingdom, for animals not only lack
a moral constitution but instinctively function according to self-
interests.

Some infer from Genesis 2:8-9 that God created everything
purely for the sake of humanity and that people, therefore, have
a God-given right to exploit creation. Critics rightly condemn this
notion as pure anthropocentric arrogance, but they err in supposing that this is what the Scriptures teach. They fail to realize
that nature was not made primarily for our sake, but rather the
reverse. We were made for the sake of nature. Genesis 2:5
implies that nature was incomplete without a caretaker, and God
created Adam to share in the task of sustaining creation. This
places us over nature, but not in the role of a despot. Part of a
redeemed life-style is to learn to use our transcendent power in
cooperation with God for redemptive and healing purposes
rather than for destruction.

Many believe that our being created last and being endowed
with the image of God and special abilities suggest that we are
the crown of creation. Moltmann rightly argued that we may be
the apex of the created order but not the crown of creation or the
finale God had in mind in creation. God's aim was an entire cosmic community that functioned in perfect harmony, with
humans responsible to help maintain tranquility. Moltmann saw
the Sabbath as a symbol of the original and future conditions of
universal peace and harmony. The Sabbath reflects the consummation of God's purpose and is, in Moltmann's mind, the "crown
of creation."[29]

It is regrettable that Christian theology has emphasized our
being made in the image of God and our transcendence over
nature more than it has emphasized our immanence in nature.
It has focused on the dual relation of God and humanity rather
than the triad relation of God, humanity, and nature. The challenge of Christian theology today is to bring these themes into
balance and to see that true healing comes only when all relations are restored. We stand with nature as part of the earth's
ecological system and as such are to be included in the concept
of nature; conversely, we also stand with God as separate from
creation. We are both cocreatures with animals and plants, and
caretakers of them. We alone are able to cooperate with God in
the restoring of creation to its prelapsarian harmony. Our likeness to God in being both transcendent and immanent is a
wholesome idea. Nevertheless, there is resistance in accepting it.
Wilkinson remarked, "Perhaps another reason for the church's

reluctance to be, with Christ, the *logos* of nature is that, unlike God, we are unable to let our transcendence be the basis for a redemptive immanence; we have used our distance from nature as an occasion for the increase of our own comfort."[30]

The Human-Human Relation. The ecological triangle could be construed as a triangular pyramid and include one more link. Just as we are morally bound by God to the rest of creation, we are also morally bound by God to the rest of humankind. The prelapsarian conditions of peace and harmony reveal God's intent for social relationships. A mark of redemption is the restoration of social harmony with acts of love, kindness, and mercy such as feeding the poor, helping the oppressed, and caring for the sick. Acts of love, however, must be expanded to reflect an ecological view of reality. There can be no real love for one another as long as we continue to rape and pollute the environment. Our exploitation and pollution deprive others of the joy of sharing in God's providence and endanger their physical health. This especially affects the poor, who not only suffer from deprivation but also from toxic contaminants, for they lack the political voice to keep toxic-producing industries and dump sites out of their neighborhoods. Our mistreatment of nature has serious sociological implications for the poor and needy and cannot be considered in keeping with the redemptive love of Christ.

In summary, the Scriptures set forth a credible holistic view of reality which does not obliterate ontological distinctions, as does pantheism. All reality constitutes a oneness in relationships, not a oneness in being.

Evaluation of the Ecological Problem

The biblical framework provides excellent guidelines to evaluate the present ecological crisis. A crisis may be defined as a crucial point in the progress of something where the situation must either turn for the worse or start improving. In medicine it denotes that the situation is extremely precarious with the patient wavering on the verge of death or possible recovery. The earth is at such a crisis point. If the environmental situation worsens, nature may no longer be able to fulfill the purposes that God had intended.

The Problem: Broken Relations

The ecological crisis is a crisis of broken relations. The triad of relations in the cosmic ecosystem has been shattered by humanity's arrogant, self-willed lust for independence from the Creator. This craving for autonomy from a transcendent authority has left the human race in a state of chaos. There is no longer any basis for constructing an impartial and sustainable system of values and ethics to help heal the ecological wasteland that God's wayward children are creating. Furthermore, without the healing power of God, humanity is doomed to further degradation and death.

Scriptures refer to this quest for autonomy as sin. For the most part, however, the church has neglected sin's influence on nature. Because of the integrity of creation, the effects of sin extend into areas one would not expect. John Passmore remarked,

> When men act on nature, they do not simply modify a particular quality of a particular substance. What they do, rather, is to interact with a system of interactions, setting in process new interactions. Just for that reason, there is always a risk that their actions will have consequences which they did not predict.[31]

Putting Passmore's statement in context of the broader view of cosmic ecology, we can say that our rebellion against God has resulted in consequences we did not predict, namely the sickness and death of ourselves and others and the ecocide of God's creation.

The fall narrative links human disobedience with disharmony in nature. The ground was cursed on account of Adam's sin and no longer produced the lush vegetation to sustain human life that it once did without his laboring by the sweat of his brow (Gen. 3:17-19). All three sides of the triangle were severed, even that between God and nature. God withheld part of His sustaining power and permitted the land to be overgrown with thorns and thistles. Since the cosmic triangle was shattered, one could say that there are cosmic consequences of human sin: "When man falls out with God, the whole world is thrown out of joint."[32]

The Genesis account of the human race immediately after the fall reflects the disharmony of nature. No longer was there peace in God's creation: an animal was slain for clothing (3:21), Adam and Eve were banished from the garden (3:23), Cain slew Abel (4:8), the ground did not yield for Cain, who became a homeless wanderer (4:10-12), Lamech became a murderer (4:23), and the whole earth was filled with wickedness (6:5). This all suggests a general state of disharmony among divinely established relations. Before the fall, Adam and Eve lived in harmony with others and with the environment. They were not even permitted to kill animals for food or clothing. The animals had no fear of human beings (2:19-20) until after the deluge. Only when God permitted humans to kill animals for food did the animals begin living in fear (9:1-3). This portrait of postlapsarian life is indicative of the violence and death that prevail in a disharmonious cosmos.

No idea is more basic to Christianity than the belief that harmony engenders life and separation engenders death. Traditional theology has always defined life and death in terms of the divine-human relationship. The only reason Adam and Eve were not subject to death before the fall was because their relation with God remained in good order. When Adam and Eve sinned, they were separated from the Sustainer of life and began to die physically. With an ecological reading of Scripture, life and death motifs take on much broader connotations. Simply stated, maintaining relations enhances the life of an ecosystem, and disruption of relations commences the death of an ecosystem. This applies to all creation, for created life cannot continue in isolation from other aspects of reality, and that reality includes the God of life. The ramifications of this principle must be cosmic in scope because of the integrity and interconnectedness of creation. Thus when Adam and Eve broke relations with God, not only did they begin to die, but nature began to die as well.

The church has always recognized that nature is under a curse as a result of human sin. Conventional understanding, however, has not viewed this curse as the death of nature not that this death is an ongoing process as long as an autonomous spirit reigns in the heart of humanity. Continued rebellion against God means continued alienation from and disruption of the natural order. As Lampe said, "Man is continually in a state of fallen-ness from his intended relationship to God, and that his constant rebellion against the Creator's will has a profound effect upon the world around him." Lamp went on to say that it results in nature failing to serve the purpose God had intended.[33]

The fall into disharmony with the cosmic order also leads to a fragmented, atomistic view of life and philosophical disorientation. Everything becomes isolated and dislocated from everything else. Secularized thinking has divorced society from the true unifying principle of the cosmos and from all hope of finding meaning and healing for humanity and nature. It is therefore understandable that when secular men and women attempt to save the planet they do so in piecemeal fashion, trying to justify saving each part on economic grounds.[34] This fragmented, non-relational, mechanistic worldview stands in the way of genuine ecological recovery. We must add that many Christians also fall into a similar mode of thought. They maintain that it is the soul that needs saving, not the animals, the earth, or even the human body. This dualistic thinking fragments reality into parts, assigns values to them, and then proceeds with what is perceived as most important. This way of thinking fails to understand that God's plan involves the restoration of paradise conditions and that this necessarily involves the physical realm.

Furthermore, alienation from God breeds an ecologically destructive, materialistic outlook on life. The security God once provided will inevitably be replaced with bank accounts and possessions. Elsdon noted that man without God "is insecure because he is in a totally wrong relationship with his physical world."[35] One must accumulate goods and investment securities as a safety hedge against the future (Luke 12:18-19) because there is no God to take care of him. Since material goods and wealth function in place of deity, materialism is tantamount to deifying the physical.

The Solution: Restoring Relations

Healing takes place only as an organism exists in harmony with its environment. With a broadened concept of ecology, one's environment must include the Creator. We could call this a cosmic ecosystem as long as we understand that it is an ecosystem characterized more by relationships than dependencies; that is, everything is related to everything else, and everything except God is dependent on everything else. Thinking theocentrically is to think holistically, but qualifications must be made to allow for the unique distinctions between Creator and creation.

Only as we find peace within this expanded environment of God, humanity, and nature will we find genuine healing for the community of creation. Only then will we find the joy of existence that God intended, the "abundant life" that Christ promised, and what it means to be authentically human. We, indeed, will find ourselves when we exist in proper relationship with the entire cosmic ecosystem, a relationship without stress, fightings, wars, hate, envy, greed, materialism, and exploitation. It will be a life reconciled with God, others, the environment, and self. In biblical terminology, the word for this state of complete reconciliation is *shalom*. The *shalom* promised in the Bible is the peace of restored relations, healed wounds, and renewed harmony. It suggests the wholeness of unbroken relationships that God had intended in creation.[36] This healing will not come until relations are restored. We must learn to coexist in harmony with the natural processes and cycles God has established and in harmony with God Himself. Our use of the land and its resources, as well as our attitudes toward population growth, economics, and lifestyle, must all reflect environmental harmony within the natural limits God created.

The Scriptures seem to set forth a cosmic law of harmony: everything works when it works together. That is, the parts work properly only when they work in harmony with all the other parts. Disharmony leads to decay and death, and harmony leads to healing and life. This is just as true on the physical plane as it is on the spiritual. The church has long recognized that one's spiritual life is contingent on being in harmony with God. This, however, is only the tip of the iceberg, for the Scriptures depict everything following the cosmic law of harmony, such as society, ecology, spirituality, and psychology. This law was set in motion by the triune Creator who fashioned the cosmos to function by the same principles with which He is characterized. The triune God is depicted as the fountainhead of all life not only because He is the source of life but also because He is the exemplar of impeccable harmony. Although the cosmos cannot function properly without being in harmony with God, the reverse is not true. God can function without the rest of reality being in harmony with Him. The cosmic law, therefore, pertains only to the created realm.

With these considerations of a cosmic ecology, the popular phrase "No man is an island" takes on new and cosmic dimensions. We cannot live a healthy, satisfying life with broken relations on any level. How can we speak of a healthy economy or even a healthy body as long as the earth is sick? We must acknowledge our codependence on the natural order as well as our dependence on God and seek to live in harmony with the whole.

4

THE VALUE OF NATURE: SACRED, UTILITARIAN, OR INTRINSIC?

One of the major problems frustrating any attempt to heal the environment is misplaced values. The value placed on nature by our society is directly linked with economic interests. If a profit can be gained, the resource or commodity has value; if not, then it has no value. As long as society continues to view nature in this manner, as resources to plunder or commodities to trade, the degradation of nature will persist. What is needed is a restructuring of values, a restructuring that will find value in nature for its own sake. Many are beginning to realize that such a value system must be rooted in religious rather than humanistic ideals. The need for a radical shift away from a purely utilitarian value structure has been echoed by Lynn White, Thomas Berry, and many others.[1]

The utilitarian value of nature set forth by the church has been a major obstacle preventing many from recognizing the ecological wisdom in the Christian Scriptures. For example, Joseph Meeker states, "Both the Greek and the Judeo-Christian origins of our civilization agree that the world exists in order to be useful to mankind, and that we enjoy special privileges over nature but

75

bear almost no ethical responsibilities for maintaining natural processes."[2]

The Concept of Nature

What is nature? Most think of nature as animals and plants, and perhaps inanimate things such as lakes and mountains, but what about human beings? As Passmore noted, the English word *nature* is just as ambiguous as the Greek near-equivalent *physis*.[3] In common usage, the word *nature* refers to the nonhuman world including plants, animals, mountains, lakes, rivers, stars, and the like. This usage sets humanity apart from the rest of the natural realm and encourages the idea that nature is an object to exploit.

Properly speaking, nature should include human beings but exclude the supernatural. We participate in the interrelated processes of nature as any other organism. We do not exist on the earth as if we were alien intruders. A viable construct to understand the meaning of nature is the Judeo-Christian concept of creation which joins humans together with the rest of creation as fellow creatures, all fashioned by the hand of God.[4] From a biblical perspective, nature excludes God and the supernatural realm, such as angels, even though they were also created.

I will follow Passmore's lead and will use the word *nature* in its common parlance to refer to "everything except man and what obviously bears the mark of man's handiwork."[5] Although this usage might seem artificial and somewhat contradictory to our discussion, the distinction is needed to focus on the problem of our relation to the other parts of the natural world. We need a term for the other parts, and in common usage *nature* is that term.

Assigning Value to Nature

The three major worldviews, pantheism, humanism, and Christianity, offer different images of nature and different frameworks for assigning value to humanity and the subhuman world. The first views nature as divine, the second as a machine, and the third as creation.[6] Thus, some seek to find value in nature by assigning it the status of divinity and others by its usefulness to humanity. The biblical view sees nature as valuable because it comes from the hand of the Creator.

Value Based on Nature's Sacredness

There is a growing consensus that the emerging environmental awareness must be accompanied by a spiritual awakening.

There must be some religious or philosophical framework to give the awareness vitality, motivation, and sustainability and to provide science and technology with moral direction. In an attempt to provide the necessary paradigm required by the environmental challenge, many are turning to Eastern and primitive thought to reclaim the notion that nature is sacred. They believe that if nature is viewed as sacred, this view will put an end to its desecration.

A basic tenet of many ancient traditions is that nature is either divine and therefore of highest value, or that nature is the domicile of guardian spirits and deities and therefore to be respected and placated. In either case, the words *Nature* and *Mother Earth* represent divinity and are spelled with capital letters. The first reflects pantheistic beliefs such as those found in Hinduism, Buddhism, and Taoism. Pantheism is the belief that there is only one substance in the universe, and that one substance is God. Since everything is part of the divine substance, everything has supreme value.

The second reflects panentheistic beliefs such as those in ancient pagan religions, animism, nature religions, and shamanism. Although there is some revival of the primitive polytheistic belief that deities inhabit objects of nature, most modern panentheists are saying that the universe is *in* God. For the universe to be in God does not exhaust the concept of God, for God is greater than the universe. That is, the concept of God includes the universe but yet goes beyond it. Panentheism is presently witnessing a resurgence as an attempt to account for both God's transcendence and immanence. Being immanent in the world suggests that God is concerned with it and, therefore, it must be of value. Catholic theologians Thomas Berry and Matthew Fox both hold a form of panentheism, as do process theologians. Fox is trying to revive the mystical traditions in medieval Catholicism, where Christ is in all, and all is in Christ. This truth is realized as one has a mystical encounter with the Cosmic Christ. Thomas Berry verges on a form of panentheism by saying, "The ecological age fosters the deep awareness of the sacred presence within each reality of the universe."[7]

In biblical tradition, the earth is not sacred in the sense of being deity. There is only one God, and that one God is not to be identified with nature but rather as its Creator. Through primitive paganism, however, moderns are rediscovering the sacred in dance, nature, esoteric ritual, and mystical experiences. Neopaganism is essentially nature worship in which nature is identified as God. If nature is divine, then it unquestionably has supreme value. There are, however, several objections that could be raised against such a basis for values.

The observation that the world is contingent and not self-sustaining defeats any thought that nature is divine. The contingency of the universe was argued for in chapter 3 from the first two laws of thermodynamics. Moreover, the very notion that humans and nature could be destroyed by a nuclear holocaust (a common ploy in New Age writings) or by environmental degradation suggests that neither can be divine. The pantheistic plea for environmental action based on the sacredness of nature is therefore somewhat self-defeating.

Nature worship and animism engender fear of the unknown and tend to place more value on nature than people.[8] Primitive peoples did not fear human enemies they could see as much as they feared natural forces they could not see. These unseen forces became associated with demonic entities or deities that controlled the movements of nature and had to be placated before they granted food, health, and safety. This fear led to a higher regard for the subhuman world than for humans. Cobb remarked, "In overcoming our alienation from nature, a return to the primitive consciousness would involve also the loss of our hard won sense of human dignity and worth."[9] The devaluation of humankind has serious consequences for social and ecological justice.

Holding nature as sacred, either because of its being divinity or containing divinity, has not prevented environmental abuse and destruction. Regardless of religious beliefs, human beings still have an inward tendency to value nature by its utility and to manipulate it for their own benefit. Even in primitive peoples, there was a tension between nature being divine and nature being something to control.

It must be admitted, however, that peoples of Eastern cultures have for the most part displayed better attitudes toward nature than those in Western cultures. Montefiore questioned whether this is due to religious beliefs or whether it is indicative of any preindustrialized society that lives close to the land.[10] That is, one's attitude toward nature may be more cultural than religious. The Amish are a prime example of a Christian subculture that is somewhat skeptical of technological advances. Their attitudes toward nature are just as admirable as those of the Native Americans. The converse is also true. Modern Japan, with its high technology is guilty of extensive ecological abuse despite its traditional religious beliefs. Their attitudes toward nature are just as deplorable as those of Europe and America. The question whether pantheism or Christianity (properly understood) offers a more plausible environmental alternative cannot be discerned solely on a pragmatic basis. Simply having better working relations with the land does not necessarily point to a better belief system regarding the human-nature relationship. Our quest must run deeper than such superficial observations.

Pantheism does not provide any basis for assigning value and worth to the physical realm. If the physical will eventually fade away into nothingness as it merges with the cosmic soul, then of what value is it? Only the eternal spirit has value since alone it is deity, and only it will remain. In the Christian tradition, the physical realm will continue with the new heavens and earth, thus ascribing it value. In absolute pantheism the natural realm is merely a projection of the Cosmic Mind. In trying to affirm value in nature by saying it is in some way part of a nonphysical deity, pantheistic-minded ecologists have destroyed a necessary concept for any ecological discussion, the inherent value of the physical universe.

Most would generally agree with White's contention that Christians do not value nature as much as the animist does and that the environmental attitudes of Western Christianity are wanting. This is not due to the Bible not having the answer but rather to an unconscious synergism of biblical teaching and secular thought. To abandon the biblical construct for values because of the deviant practices of its adherents in favor of a pantheist construct may end up causing more problems than it solves.

Yet there is a sense in which we could view nature as sacred. Something is sacred if it is consecrated or belongs to God or if it elevates one's consciousness toward the divine, such as a sacred song. The latter is clearly one intent of creation (Ps. 148). Also, the ideas of ownership and sacredness are closely linked in biblical thought. Just as the firstfruits of the harvest (Ex. 34:26), the firstborn (Num. 3:13), the artifacts in the tabernacle (Ex. 40:9; Num. 16:37-38), or the first conquest in war (Josh. 6:18-19; 7:11) belonged to God and were thereby considered holy or corban, so the entire creation belongs to God and may be considered holy. We are to respect what belongs to another, especially if it belongs to God. The sacredness of creation, rightly understood, is not a totally alien idea for biblical faith. It is in these two senses that we can speak of the damage being done to the earth as the desecration of nature.

Some, such as Philip Sherrard, speak of a "sacramental idea of nature" in which creation is an "incarnation of divine power and life."[11] Creation is then a sacramental means of divine grace in which God is totally present and active. This also suggests a sacred character of creation without absorption of one into the other. As Eliade said, "Rediscovering the sacredness of Life and Nature does not necessarily imply a return to 'paganism' or 'idolatry.' Although in the eyes of a Puritan the cosmic religion of the southeastern European peasants could have been considered a form of paganism, it was still a 'cosmic, Christian liturgy.'"[12]

Value Based on Human Utility

With the rise of our modern technocratic society, nature has increasingly become an object for manipulation and control. The goal is to harness nature and direct its resources and energy to satisfy human needs and wants. Western society is interested in nature primarily on the level of human benefit. If something can benefit humanity, then it has value and is to be exploited; otherwise, it has no value and is expendable. The growth of science and technology during the past several centuries, coupled with the economic structure of our society, has obliterated any notion of intrinsic value in the subhuman world. It has turned nature into a secularized object to be observed, analyzed, controlled, exploited, and used apart from any reference to God.

Perceiving nature as an object is not wrong in itself. Christianity rightly maintains that there are ontological distinctions between individual objects, the primary distinction being between Creator and creation. In biblical thought, nature is an object created by and belonging to God and thus to be respected and cared for. The problem is not the objectification of nature as much as it is the secularization of nature. Maltreatment is not a necessary corollary of perceiving something with the senses, but it is when God is lost sight of. An object may be either viewed apart from the unifying and valuing principle of the cosmos or with respect to it. Biblical thought rejects the first and affirms the second. When an object is viewed apart from the unifying and valuing principle, it loses its intrinsic value and becomes a detached object, fit for manipulation. It is thus the secularization of nature, not its objectification, that destroys a healthy relation between observer and object. This is true when the object is part of the subhuman realm or when the object is humanity itself. The belief in a transcendent God can protect all life from being turned into mere objects for manipulation and control.

What secular society has done is to sever the entire creation from any thought of a Creator and assign it value by society's own standards. Just as humans have sought their own autonomy from God, they also have sought it for nature. Nature does not have value because of its relation and worth to a Creator but because of its relation and worth to humanity. This has a significant effect on a secular environmental agenda, an agenda that becomes nothing more than efforts to maintain the welfare, safety, and affluence of the human race. The environmental dilemma of anthropocentric utilitarianism is that it is not concerned with nature for nature's sake.

David Ehrenfeld, in *The Arrogance of Humanism*, argues that if something does not have economic value, then it is very difficult for the secular mind to justify preserving it. He listed nine ways contrived by our humanistic society to rationalize conservation of various elements in nature that seemingly do not have a direct economic value: (1) value for recreational and esthetic purposes; (2) potential value in undiscovered or undeveloped aspects of nature; (3) value in species diversity to stabilize ecosystems and preserve life-support systems; (4) value as examples of survival to help our quest for survival; (5) value in present life forms to determine effect of our alteration on nature; (6) value in animals for scientific research; (7) value for teaching purposes; (8) value for habitat reconstruction; and (9) value for conservative purposes to avoid possibility of irreversible change.[13] The nine reasons are all anthropocentric. The inadequacy of secular environmentalism is accentuated by its piecemeal approach of requiring utilitarian justification for each action. Dollar-based priorities determine what portions of the environment receive conservation attention.[14] Ehrenfeld added that "there is no true protection for Nature within the humanist system—the very idea is a contradiction in terms."[15]

Unquestionably, our secular society places more value on those aspects of nature that can return short-term economic benefits. The value system of secular society, driven as it is by the "tyranny of the urgent,"[16] is hopelessly at odds with nature. Schumacher observed that, "an activity can be economic although it plays hell with the environment, and that a competing activity, if at some cost it protects and conserves the environment, will be uneconomic."[17] Secular society will always have trouble enacting long-term environmental policies because of the restrictions of its economically based value system that has difficulty seeing beyond itself and because the results would not be realized within one's lifetime.

Consumers are also a vital part of this "cash value syndrome."[18] They are not really concerned with how something comes to be placed on the shelves of their favorite discount store. It is there, they want it, and they buy it. Of course, the demand has been artificially created with a mass-advertising campaign by profit-hungry manufacturers. The producer-advertisement-consumer-landfill syndrome is a self-contained, self-perpetuating system. It is impermeable to influences outside the system that call for caution, restraint, and a simpler life-style. There is no real concern with depletion of nonrenewable resources or the overflowing of landfills. Both consumer and producer live in happy harmony, each helping the other acquire as much as possible, and each rather resistant to anything that might extinguish their bliss. The whole process is fueled by the fire of human greed. This mind-set glorifies the GNP rather than the God of creation, respects human interests rather than nature, and seeks human fulfillment in things rather than peace, harmony, and security from God. The world, as one writer put it, is looked upon "as a giant cookie jar."[19] People are hungry for something. They think they need cookies so they are grabbing all they can get.

This anthropocentric way of thinking can be found in all traditions at all ages, although not with the force and vigor of modern Western society. No one questions that materialism and affluence are closely connected with environmental degradation, but it is a rare person who would be willing to sacrifice the luxuries of life for the sake of the environment. The roots of the whole problem reach down into the very essence of our economic system and perhaps into the very essence of the human race. Peter Drucker noted that solving the ecological dilemma "will require a major change in the way we think about the economy."[20] It will require, at the very least, a complete restructuring of values. More basic yet is the question of human greed that dominates our value system and thus lies at the foundation of our secular economic structure.

Ironically, as Robert Runcie said, the conviction that nature does not exist solely for the benefit of humankind "finds its source deep within the human spirit. . . . It is not a conviction unique to any one religion, and it is shared by some who would profess no religion at all."[21] We will elaborate on this dissonance in the human psyche in chapter 9.

Value Based on God's Considering Nature Valuable

From a biblical perspective, the Creator of the universe alone is Deity and, therefore, the ultimate Source and Sustainer of values. The value of nature does not come from its being deity but from its being valued by deity. Nature has intrinsic value by virtue of its being planned, created, owned, and sustained by God. The value of nature, therefore, belongs to its fundamental essence, having been so fashioned by its Creator to be of value to Him. The value that is intrinsic to nature's very existence is then derived from the preeminent value-giver Himself. Fackre wrote:

> The Judeo-Christian tradition affirms, in the case of both man and nature, a *derived* dignity, and accords each a respect commensurate with its source in God. It is the *relationship* in which creation stands to its Creator that confers upon it value, not any presumed virtues or vitalities whose claims outrun the facts.[22]

Thus nature's value is not contingent on human need or economic profit.

God alone has the right to assign value to His creation. Just because we fail to find human utility for something does not give us the right to devalue it. To take this right upon ourselves and declare that something is "not necessary" or "not important" is a "usurpation of authority."[23] This attitude is derived from the autonomous spirit that led to humanity's fall and has no place in the life of the church or society. If something has value to God, then we have no right to say otherwise. It would be utterly inconsistent with the Christian faith to devalue what God values. We should value, love, and care for our cocreatures as God values, loves, and cares for His creatures. With a theocentric framework, all creation, whether animals, plants, or minerals, has derived value and should be protected from ruthless exploitation and possible extinction or depletion.

The intrinsic value of nature obligates us to respect creation the way God made it. This suggests that we should work within the ecological structure God established as we invoke change and that we should permit living organisms to live the life God intended for them. This does not negate the need for certain population controls, but it does help define animal abuse. Animals have a right to live the life that God had intended rather than being cooped up in some animal factory. As Schaeffer said, "We should treat each thing with integrity because it is the way God has made it."[24] We can honor and respect the ant, fly, or even the mosquito since each one was created by God to fulfill a particular niche in the earth's ecosystem. This way of honoring plants and animals has more substance than romanticism, which transfers human feelings to the subhuman kingdom, or pantheism, which deifies everything.

Thus nature is not an object that we may use or destroy as we wish, nor is it something to be worshiped. It is the property of God and, therefore, is to be valued, cherished, and protected. In other words, Christianity presents a middle ground between the two extremes; nature is neither divine nor godless. It is to be understood within the framework of a theocentric cosmology which affirms that nature is to be respected and cared for rather than worshiped or abused. The question posed by the Christian paradigm is: How can we hate and abuse what God loves and cares for? Geisler remarked, "Of all the great religious and philosophical systems, none gives greater dignity to the material creation than does the Judeo-Christian tradition."[25] The Christian perspective liberates us from the constraints of nature worship yet does not give us freedom to mistreat the environment.

Biblical Basis for the Intrinsic Value of Nature

Nature has intrinsic valve because (1) God created it, (2) God owns it, (3) God designed it for a purpose, and (4) God recognized it as good.

God's Creation of the Earth

The ecological implications of nature as creation have been ignored by both our secular society and the church.[26] By eliminating the idea of a Creator, secular society has lost all notion of a transcendent unifying and valuing agent, along with any hope for a sustainable environment. Also, with much of the attention of conservative Christianity devoted to the creation-evolution controversy, the deeper theological and philosophical ramifications of creation have been overlooked. The ecological perspective of creation passed over in the debate over origins needs to be reclaimed.

Berkhof defined creation as *"that free act of God whereby He, according to His sovereign will and for His own glory, in the beginning brought forth the whole visible and invisible universe, without the use of preexistent material, and thus gave it an existence, distinct from His own and yet always dependent on Him."*[27] Genesis begins with the ecological affirmation, "In the beginning God created the heavens and the earth" (see Neh. 9:6; Isa. 45:18). God created out of His free will (Isa. 46:10), for His own glory (Ps. 8:1; Rev. 4:11), and out of nothing or *ex nihilo* (Gen. 1:1; Job 26:7; Rom. 4:17; and Heb. 11:3).

The first ecological implication of creation is the dichotomy between Creator and creation that places the source of values outside of that which is being valued. For builders to step back and observe what they made suggests an ontological distinction between builders and their work. There is a relation, but that relation does not imply identity of essence; the thing built is not part of the builder. The same holds true of God. God and the universe are not the same. The valuing and unifying principle is then transcendent to nature. This avoids the impasse encountered when humans attempt to construct a basis for values or when nature is viewed as self-valuing.

The second implication is that creation has value to God by virtue of His creating it. When we make something, whether woodwork, ceramics, or clothing, it is special to us. Part of ourselves went into our creation. Artists do not only view their creations with delight but also as extensions of their own person, "a kind of 'emanation.'"[28] Although artists transcend their creations, they still impart something of themselves into their work and are in a sense, immanent with what they made. Their creations become extensions or expressions of their life and thoughts. When a painting is destroyed, we have not only offended the artist but we have, in a sense, defaced his or her character.

The cosmos could also be considered as an artistic expression of a creative mind. We can see the hand of God in creation, just as we see the hand of Rembrandt in his paintings. By analogy, we know that God's creation is special to Him, because He poured Himself into what He created. Whatever is special to God is of supreme value and should be cared for with the same respect one gives to God Himself. You might even say that when creation is destroyed, we have destroyed God, but, of course, this is not to be understood in a pantheistic sense, for only the expression of God is destroyed.[29] To pollute the environment, therefore, not only defaces the beauty of creation but also insults the Creator and should be reckoned as a sin against God. If God created the world, then the world and everything in it must have value. This would include all forms of animate and inanimate matter.

The third implication is that the created order provides the model for relational tranquility and harmony between humans and their environment, others, and God. Our roots are planted in this aura of peace, and we will not rest until we once again discover it. Our very longings affirm that we recognize value in the peaceful relationships God established at creation.

Creation did not arise out of conflict. The Babylonian creation epic *Enuma elish* depicts creation as resulting from a conflict between Marduk and Tiamat, in which Tiamat's body was hewn into pieces to form the present creation. Other polytheistic creation motifs, especially those of Sumerian and Egyptian cosmogonies, envision creation to have occurred by the regenerative processes of the gods. In some pantheistic traditions creation is due to an imbalance in the cosmic spirit. Modern secular thought suggests that our existence sprang from the "survival of the fittest" conflict. In contrast to the violent beginning motifs of pagan cosmogonies, the Bible depicts creation as the tender loving act of a gracious God. Our roots are grounded in peace and love, not conflict. To recapture our roots, we need to find that peace we have long lost. Although Christians have not always lived out the implications of this model (for example, Crusades, Inquisition), it alone can provide the basis for harmonious relations in the created realm.

The fourth implication is that nothing is coeternal with God to claim the right to sovereignty and the right to legislate values. The biblical teachings of *ex nihilo* preserves God's absolute sovereignty and confirms the dependency of the entire universe on the self-existent God (see John 1:3; Col. 1:16; Heb. 11:3). God alone is ultimate reality and reigns supreme over the entire creation—not humanity, nature, nor anything else. If something were coeternal with God, then God's sovereignty and right to assign values would be challenged. The biblical concept of creation negates any such thought.

God's Ownership of the Earth

The natural corollary of God's creating the world is that He owns what He created. This is analogous to the right of ownership artists or writers have to the works they create. It is a cultural norm in most societies to value and respect property belonging to others. If this is true on a human level, how much more so when considering God's property? Since the world and everything in it has been made by God, it belongs to Him and has supreme value. Not only is God's ownership the basis for value, it is also foundational for environmental ethics and our stewardship of creation. God has entrusted His property to the human creature to help maintain and manage. Management must be done in accord with the wishes of the owner. Furthermore, a person cannot rightfully own what belongs to another. One may obtain permission to borrow it for a time, to manage it, to care for it, even to lease and make use of it, but whatever is done must be approved by the owner.

The Old Testament contains many references to God's ownership of the earth. Moses lifted up his hands to stop the plague of hail so that the Egyptians might "know that the earth is the Lord's" (Ex. 9:29; see 19:5). The laws regarding the Year of Jubilee also confirm the idea that the land belongs to God and not to the people. Every fifty years the land was to be returned to the family that was responsible for it. If a person sold the land, the sale price was based on the number of harvest years left until the Year of Jubilee, "because what he is really selling you is the number of crops," not the land (Lev. 25:16). The land was never actually sold, it was only leased for the purpose of raising crops. "The land must not be sold permanently, because the land is mine and you are but aliens and my tenants" (Lev. 25:23). God promises that the land will yield bountifully as long as His laws of land use are followed (Lev. 25:18-19). These regulations prevented individuals or families from accumulating vast holdings of land and ensured an equitable use of God's resources. This should hold in check one's preoccupation with accumulating wealth and neglecting its benevolent use (Luke 12:16-21).

The sabbatic regulations involving land and animals also remind us that nature belongs to God. Even though creation has been entrusted to us for safekeeping, God still exercises His right of ownership by forbidding people and animals from working the land on the Sabbath. It is to be a day of rest to reflect upon the Creator and His creation. The Sabbath, as Brueggemann noted, "is a theological affirmation of Yahweh's ownership of the land."[30] When Christianity replaced sabbatic observances for Sunday worship, this aspect of Jewish creation wisdom was lost, being supplanted by the weekly commemoration of the resurrection.[31] For most, the first day of the week observances emphasize personal implications of the resurrection rather than cosmic implications of divine ownership. We must reclaim the full significance of the Sabbath typology by uniting the Jewish and Christian themes. The Sabbath should be seen as marking the beginning of the new creation and anticipating the future redemption of the earth.[32]

When Moses brought down the second set of stone tablets, he reminded the people that God owns everything, "To the Lord your God belong the heavens, even the highest heavens, the earth and everything in it" (Deut. 10:14; see 1 Chron. 29:11; Job 41:11). David restated this theme in Psalm 24:1-2,

> The earth is the Lord's, and everything in it,
>> the world, and all who live in it;
>> for he founded it upon the seas
>> and established it upon the waters.

This passage clearly links creation with ownership. Since God created all things, He owns all things (see Ps. 89:11-12; 95:5). In 1979 Vincent Rossi, the director of the Holy Order of MANS, established what he called the "Eleventh Commandment Fellowship." Rossi's eleventh commandment is partially based on this passage. It states, "The earth is the Lord's and the fullness thereof: thou shalt not despoil the earth, nor destroy the life thereon."[33]

The psalmist Asaph said,

> For every animal of the forest is mine,
>> and the cattle on a thousand hills.

> I know every bird in the mountains,
> and the creatures of the field are mine (50:10-11).

The observation that even the animals belong to God suggests that they do have certain rights, but those rights are actually God's rights regarding His property. God has the right to demand that humans respect and care for His animals. He desires that animals be allowed to live the life He intended for them. Like the rest of creation, animals have intrinsic value derived from being created and owned by God.

In Jeremiah 2:7, God rebukes the people for defiling His land:

> I brought you into a fertile land
> to eat its fruit and rich produce.
> But you came and defiled my land
> and made my inheritance detestable.

The reason for the degradation is given in verse 8: the people turned away from God and ignored His laws for the care of His land. Having left God's laws, they began to covet the land and accumulate unto themselves wealth at the expense of others. God condemns all coveting because the land and everything else belongs to Him (Isa. 5:8-9; Mic. 2:1-2).

The New Testament affirms the Old Testament view of God's ownership. Paul, in justifying the freedom to partake of all foods, quoted from Psalm 24:1, "The earth is the Lord's, and everything in it" (1 Cor. 10:26). The ultimate custody of the earth belongs to the Lord. We must, therefore, reject both Thomas Berry's biocentric statement that "the ultimate custody of the earth belongs to the earth"[34] and the accepted anthropocentric notion that the ultimate custody of the earth belongs to humanity.

It is rather difficult to interpret Genesis 1:28 as giving people license to exploit nature when God's ownership is taken into consideration. The idea of divine ownership also prevents the opposite extreme, that of worshiping the earth, for ownership presupposes a dichotomy between the owner and owned, between the Creator and creation. If we understand that the earth belongs to God, it cannot possibly become either an object to exploit or an object of worship. As the hymnist says, "This is my Father's World, O let me ne'er forget."

God's ownership raises the question of private ownership. From a biblical perspective, we do not have the right to absolute ownership or to do anything we wish with what we think belongs to us. In the Old Testament, the land belonged to God; the Jews were not allowed to buy or sell property. They could only lease it until the Year of Jubilee. Humans are considered tenants holding the land in trust (Lev. 25:23; see 1 Kings 21:2-3). Therefore, we cannot be thought of as true owners nor do anything we please with the land. As Aldo Leopold said, "We abuse land because we regard it as a commodity belonging to us."[35] Mining and timber companies, developers, and farmers are pushing for antienvironmental legislation based on the right of private ownership. They claim that environmental regulations have restricted their right to use their own property. The biblical view quickly repudiates such arguments.

Aquinas viewed the right to private ownership as the best way to preserve property in a postlapsarian state. He taught that the common possession of all things was part of the natural law of the created order.[36] In the state of innocence, there would have been no danger of strife because individuals would have used the community possessions in accord with each one's needs.[37] After the fall, however, this would have engendered strife. Private ownership, on the other hand, may foster care of one's own possessions, but it does not lead to true stewardship where one is concerned with both preservation and benevolent use of the land. Since individuals are now primarily concerned with promoting their own interests, a system of absolute ownership can easily degenerate into power grabbing in which the poor are oppressed and the land is exploited. There is little regard for what effects such actions might have on the land, animals, or other persons. Private ownership may be regarded as a somewhat risky accommodation to humanity's fallen state and not part of the redeemed state.[38] It does not readily lend itself to managing God's property for the benefit of all God's creation.

God's Purpose in Creation

God did not create out of necessity or deficiency but out of His freedom and goodness. It would be contrary to the biblical concept of God to suppose that God created to fulfill a need, for this would imply that God is primarily concerned with Himself, that He is in some way limited or incomplete, and that He acted under necessity. Such notions have a tendency to devalue nature. Nature would not be a freely loved, independent entity as much as it would be a needed crutch for a dependent God. It would become, as modern society has made it, an object fit only for utilitarian purposes.

Nor can we say that God arbitrarily created the universe, for then what happens to it would be of little concern. It would not really matter to God if we rape the environment and destroy ourselves. God would be a detached and insensitive observer. The only plausible reason for creation and the only one in accord with Scripture is that God created to let others share in His bountiful goodness and in the joy of existence. The philosophical question "Why is there something rather than nothing?" finds a satisfactory answer in the biblical tradition: there is a God, and He is infinitely good.

Such a concept of creation has far-reaching ecological implications. If God created to share the joy of existence with others and if He is, therefore, preeminently concerned with others, then one of the foundational laws of the cosmos must be selfless love in which we share our existence with the rest of God's creatures. Serving God then becomes cooperating with His creative purpose and seeing that all creation shares in His goodness. Another way of expressing it would be that since nothing had to be, everything that exists is an act of free will and love. This includes the pests and varmints that some would like to exterminate.

Scripture does state that all things were made for God. This not only gives supreme value to nature, but it also negates the idea that nature was made for human benefit. Paul wrote in Colossians 1:16, "For by him all things were created: things in heaven and on earth, visible and invisible, whether thrones or powers or rulers or authorities; all things were created by Him and for him" (see Rom. 11:36). This should not lead one to think of a selfish God. In view of God's character, the phrase "for Him" could easily mean "for the purpose He intended." Thus, when Paul said that all things were made for Him, it could be interpreted in view of God's overarching purpose of sharing the goodness, happiness, and joy of existence with others.

Recognizing that all things exist for God in this wholesome sense will inhibit our natural tendency to pervert the concept of dominion into irresponsible devastation of the planet. Everything was designed and made by God and for God, to fulfill a variety of purposes, all of which affirm the value of nature.

God Intended Nature to Testify of Him. There are many reasons for the existence of nature other than meeting human needs, one of which is to testify of the glory and power of God and proclaim His loving kindness. God reveals Himself through nature, disclosing not only that He is the Creator but also that He is the Source of the peace and harmony that people desire. As we look at our own lives we often see a dysfunctioning array of fragments, but as we ponder nature we find a concord of beauty, evidently designed to function together as one harmonious whole. To defile nature is to block one of the channels God had intended to share His message of peace.

A common theme of the nature Psalms (such as Pss. 8:19a; 104; 148) is to testify of the Creator. David wrote,

> The heavens declare the glory of God;
> the skies proclaim the work of his hands.
> Day after day they pour forth speech;
> night after night they display knowledge
> (19:1-2; see 97:6-7).

Nature reflects the infinite wisdom and creative power of God. Everywhere one looks the hand of God is seen. When addressing the people of Lystra, Paul said that God has not left Himself without a witness. The very rain that enables a bountiful harvest testifies of God's goodness (Acts 14:17). In Romans 1:20 Paul wrote, "Since the creation of the world God's invisible qualities—his eternal power and divine nature—have been clearly seen, being understood from what has been made, so that men are without excuse." Fitzmyer commented, "Contemplating the created world and reflecting on it, a human being perceives through its multicolored façade the great 'Unseen' behind it—the omnipotence and divine character of its Maker. Though essentially invisible, these qualities are mirrored in the 'great works' (*poiēmata*) produced by Him."[39] Nature's testimony indeed "has gone out into all the earth" (Rom. 10:18).

"To contemplate nature is an invitation to wonder."[40] Plato imagined that if people who had always lived in caves were suddenly brought out into the open to view nature, they would assume that a universal author of all things must exist who caused all the realities of the world of light.[41] According to Aristotle, "It is owing to their wonder that men both now begin and at first began to philosophize."[42] Immanuel Kant remarked, "Two things fill the mind with ever new and increasing admiration and awe, the oftener and the more steadily we reflect on them: the starry heavens above and the moral law within."[43]

Most religions of the world associate the wonder and mystery of nature with the concept of deity. For some the numinous quality of nature suggests that nature itself is divine, for others it suggests a pantheon of gods that gave birth to nature, and for others a monotheistic Creator of nature. Nature does raise the awareness of the divine, but the clarity of nature's witness does not seem sufficient to prevent diverse religious expressions. Christians affirm that God is aware of this potential dilemma and has revealed Himself in such a manner as to give guidance to the human quest, that is, through the Scriptures and incarnation. God would not be a loving God if He left us to wander aimlessly amid the smorgasbord of religious options. It is reasonable to assume, then, that God has revealed Himself and has provided knowledge of Himself far superior to that which could ever be obtained from nature.

Nevertheless, nature is the only source of revelation many have to inspire them to seek God. The divine witness is especially needed in our secular society to bring a shattered and torn world to a sense of harmony and peace. We could say with Thomas Berry that "to wantonly destroy a living species is to silence forever a divine voice"[44] as long as we understand it as a voice that testifies of God rather than the voice of God Himself.

God Intended Nature to Sustain All Life. Part of the purpose of creation is to be mutually supportive of other parts of creation. In Psalm 104, God made the springs of water to quench the thirst of the beasts of the field (vv. 10-11), birds (v. 12), and trees (v. 16). He makes grass grow for the cattle (v. 14), provides trees for the birds to nest (v. 17), and makes the mountains for the wild goats and rock badgers (v. 18). The psalm also mentions that the created order functions to sustain human beings (vv. 14-15, 23). We can value plant life because it is food for both animals and ourselves, the worm because it is food for birds, and the water, air, and soil because they support all life on the planet. There is value in creation because each part, according to the divine plan, serves the needs of other parts.

In saying this, however, we must not slip into an anthropocentric mind-set. There is a big difference between saying that everything was made for the created community and everything was made for human utility.[45] The Scriptures affirm that there is a utilitarian or instrumental value to nature because of God's design of interrelated dependence, but this utility is for all forms of life.[46] An anthropocentric valuing of nature, which asserts that nature was created only for human utility, is not only unbiblical, it also depreciates the intrinsic worth of nature as nature. It implies that only the cow's meat and milk are of value, not the cow as a cow. This notion of value has devastating effects on the treatment of cattle, as witnessed in the veal-producing factories. What is true of our treatment of cattle applies equally to the rest of creation.

The biblical model challenges this narrow utilitarian view of nature. God, for example, waters the land where no one lives (Job 38:26). Obviously, not everything was made for the sake of humanity. Also, God's command to take two of each kind of animal into the ark was irrespective of their worth to Noah (Gen. 6:19-20). Many of the animals were classified as unclean and thus had absolutely no utilitarian value for Noah or his family. Nevertheless, all had to be saved from extinction; no animal was insignificant, worthless, or expendable in the eyes of God. If Noah were a modern, he would probably balk at the expense of building an ark to save swine. Noah, however, was not concerned with the utility of the animals, with the economics of building an ark that size, or even, as Calvin DeWitt said, with the "price of gopher wood."[47] It would have been much cheaper to build an ark just big enough for his family and the animals they needed, but this did not enter Noah's mind. He valued all the animals because God did. The cost factor did not enter into their preservation.

We cannot ignore that one of the reasons for the natural order is to serve human needs, but as we make use of nature we must acknowledge that other creatures have a right to partake of it also. This requires that our stewardship be faithful to God's intent in creation. "We have to *tend* the creation, use it for our own sustenance and flourishing, but we also have to respect it in itself as a manifestation of God's creative energy and cooperate with God in bringing out the full splendor of the created order as reflecting the glory of the Creator."[48]

God Intended Nature to Praise Him. Another purpose for creation is to praise the Creator. Whether this expression of exuberant praise is the natural consequence of a joyful existence or a designed purpose in the mind of God could be questioned. The Scriptures do depict nature praising God, and God honors this praise; therefore, nature must be of value to Him. Nature's praise of God is intended to stir people to recognize and worship the Creator (Isa. 43:20-22). This suggests that some of the praise reflects a designed purpose for nature apart from serving human utility. To destroy nature is again to thwart God's intent.

Nature's praise of the Creator is especially prevalent in the Psalms.

> Let the heavens rejoice, let the earth be glad;
> let the sea resound, and all that is in it;
> let the fields be jubilant, and everything in them.
> Then all the trees of the forest will sing for joy;
> they will sing before the Lord
> (96:11-13a; see 69:34; 89:5; 89:12; and 98:7-9).

The reason for nature's singing in Psalms 96 and 98 is that God is coming to judge the world in righteousness. For nature this means that God will put an end to environmental misuse and bring peace and harmony. In Psalm 148 praise is given by the sun, moon, stars, ocean creatures, lightening, hail, snow, clouds, winds, mountains, hills, fruit trees, cedars, wild animals, cattle, small creatures, and birds, as well as humans. The Psalter closes with, "Let everything that has breath praise the Lord" (150:6; see 145:10,21).

The beauty and majesty of nature also elevate awe and reverence within the human soul, inviting us to join nature in the praise and worship of the Creator and of His power and wisdom in creation (Prov. 3:19-20; Jer. 10:12-13). Schaeffer remarked:

> If I let the wonder go from the thing, soon the wonder will go from mankind and me. And this is where people live today. The wonder is all gone. Man sits in his autonomous, "decreated" world, where there are no universals and no wonder in nature. Indeed, in an arrogant and egoistic way, nature has been reduced to a "thing" for man to use or exploit.[49]

One of the adverse effects of modern technology is a loss of the wonder and beauty of the earth. We are more enamored with human creations than those of God.

We are expected to join in with the rest of our fellow creatures in joyful praise to God for His grace in sharing the wonder of existence with us. Existence is indeed a mystery that not even modern science can explain. It above all invokes our praise to an infinitely powerful and wise Creator. As we join in with the cosmic symphony of praise, we are brought to the realization that the praise ceases when choked by pollution, disease, and extinction. Each part of nature can only lift joyous praise as it exists in joyous harmony with the rest of nature as God intended. This praise and appreciation for the wonder of existence and for God's faithfully sustaining His creation is valued by God and should not be frustrated. To destroy life or any part of the created order unnecessarily shows disrespect to the Creator and stifles a channel of praise.

God Intended Nature to Be Enjoyed. A final purpose for creation and another reason for valuing it arise from God's delighting in the beauty of creation, enjoying what He made, and wanting to share His joy with others. Again, whether this is a premeditated intent of creation or a natural consequence could be debated. Nevertheless, the mere fact that God rejoices in the beauty of His creation gives it supreme value.

We tend to value and consider worth saving those things in which we find joy and consider beautiful even if created by someone else. Although we do enjoy nature, what is more important is that God also enjoys it. We do not seek to preserve it merely because we find it beautiful, but because God does. This gives nature the highest value possible and the strongest inhibition against defiling it.

The observation that God delights in His creation is well attested in Scripture. In replying to Job, God mentioned that He delights in the mountain goat (39:1-4), the wild donkey (39:5-8), the ox (39:9-12), the ostrich (39:13-18), the horse (39:19-25), the hawk and eagle (39:26-30), the behemoth (40:15-24), and the leviathan (41:1-34). The point of God's reply to Job is to show "that man's whole attitude to what goes on in the created order is wrong, because it is totally egoistic, totally anthropocentric."[50] God is attempting to get Job to consider the workings and purposes of His creation and to realize that much of it has no relevance to human beings. The behemoth and leviathan were created for God's delight and for them to enjoy life themselves; they were not made for human utility. Solomon depicted Wisdom at the side of God during creation,

> Then I was the craftsman at his side.
> I was filled with delight day after day,
> rejoicing always in his presence,
> rejoicing in his whole world
> and delighting in mankind (Prov. 8:30-31).

God's joy and enthusiasm over His creation suggest that the natural realm is important, valuable, and meaningful without any reference to its satisfying human needs.

Enjoying nature is part of a spiritual life. Although contrary to common thinking, spirituality cannot be divorced from the need to appreciate, value, and even enjoy the beauty of nature. To love God is to love what God loves. We cannot be in spiritual communion with God if we destroy and mistreat what He cherishes. To reduce nature to an object for manipulation or even theologically to a mere witness of God's existence and character is to miss an important purpose of nature. One of the reasons God designed nature the way He did was so that His creatures, both human and nonhuman, could enjoy it. God even made the seas for the leviathan to frolic in and enjoy (Ps. 104:26; compare 1 Cor. 15:39-41). Enjoying the beauty of creation is a mark of spirituality, not carnality, for it reflects the mind of the Creator.

John Black noted that since God placed the trees in the garden of Eden first to be pleasant to the sight and then to be good for food, He obviously did not design it to serve only the physical needs of humanity. God intended nature to have an aesthetic value as well.[51] Unless we recapture the biblical theme that nature is valuable for the sake of its beauty, then the whole ecology movement could erode into an anthropocentric plea to save the human race from extinction. Joseph Wood Krutch once remarked, "But without some realization that 'this curious world' is at least beautiful as well as useful, 'conservation' is doomed. We must live for something besides making a living. If we do not permit the earth to produce beauty and joy, it will in the end not produce food either."[52]

God's Recognition that His Creation Is Good

The final argument for the intrinsic value of nature is God's recognition that His creation is good. Six times in the first creation narrative, God expressed pleasure in the goodness of creation (Gen. 1:4,10,12,18,21,25). After everything was complete, "God saw all that he had made, and it was very good" (Gen. 1:31). God did not declare or pronounce creation to be good, rather He saw that it was good. If all creation, both animate and inanimate, are seen as good, then no part of the natural world could possibly be considered evil. The biblical affirmation stands in contradiction to world-denying Gnostic and Manichaean dualisms, the extreme asceticism of medieval monasticism, the Eastern philosophies that hold the world to be an illusion or *maya*, and even the dualism in some segments of conservative Christianity. These all in one way or another reject the material realm as insignificant or evil. In the biblical tradition, the world is not to be shunned and withdrawn from, but affirmed and loved in all its goodness, reality, and splendor as reflecting the hand of the Creator who fashioned it.

Whatever the precise meaning of "good," it must be deemed good apart from its human utility, for God pronounced creation good six times before creating Adam. The Hebrew word for "good" *tôwb* has various meanings, such as joyous, pleasing, desirable, usable, suitable, lovely, friendly, kind, or good. There are several interpretations of "good" in Genesis 1.

Divine Purpose View. Westermann argued that the "good" in Genesis 1:31 "can only mean that Creation is good for that which God intends it."[53] He wrote, "'Good' in this context does not mean some sort of objective judgement, a judgement given according to already fixed and objective standards. It is rather this: it is good or suited for the purpose for which it is being prepared; it corresponds to its goal."[54] Koehler and Baumgartner suggest that in Genesis 1 it means "efficient," which implies that creation was suited for God's purpose.[55] God celebrates and rejoices in creation, for it is well suited to fulfill the role He intended. Nature, therefore, has value because it is an integral part of the divine purpose. The outworking of God's plan of peace and harmony is hindered as humans seek their own glory and destroy and pollute the environment in the process. The divine purpose view does, in a sense, reflect a utilitarian purpose. Creation is good like a hammer is good: it serves the purpose of the carpenter. For the creation to be of instrumental value to God, however, is far different than its being of instrumental value to humanity.

This view does not rule out the possibility that death was part of the original creative order.[56] Theistic evolutionists adopt this view, saying that creation was good in that it suited God's plan, and this plan called for death of living organisms and entire species as life evolved. Many Christian ecologists also consider death to be an essential part of the ecological processes and therefore part of the divine plan. They refer to the complex food chains and the decaying of organic matter to keep the soil naturally fertile as examples of an intricate design that was seemingly fashioned by God. The food chains and decaying of organic matter presuppose the death of plants and animals. Theistic evolutionists reject the perfect or absolute view of *good*, which calls for a perfect state without death. However, one may rightly question whether the "harmony" in nature that we now observe is the ideal situation or whether humanity's fall had more of an impact than merely bringing out the worst in human behavior toward the environment. In Genesis 1:29-30 both humans and animals survived on a vegetarian diet, not a carnivorous diet. This implies that the present food chains are different than what God intended in the beginning and that animals perhaps did not die before the fall. Support also comes from the images in Isaiah of the redeemed state where the lion and calf will lie down together (11:6-9). It seems as if God did not intend death as part of the creative order. However, the divine purpose view can be maintained without postulating death before the fall. These thoughts will be developed further in chapter 7.

Divine Character View. Others say that *good* means that creation is an appropriate reflection of God's love, goodness, glory, and benevolence. That nature testifies of God's goodness is well attested in the Psalms. It is obvious that God's creation is a reflection of His goodness and cannot be called evil without accusing God of evil. Just as God is good, so is His creation (Ps. 25:8; 34:8; 106:1; Nah. 1:7; and Matt. 19:17).

Ecological View. Others argue that *good* refers to the harmony, interdependence, and interrelatedness of the created realm. This harmony existed until it was corrupted by the fall. Delwin Brown wrote, "God's affirmation of the goodness of creation is an ecological statement; it indicates the importance of an interrelationship in which each aspect of creation makes its essential contribution to the whole."[57] Santmire agreed with von Rad that the "very good" of Genesis 1:31 means that creation displays a "wonderful properness and harmony."[58] Thus, creation is good in that it is a well-ordered whole that exists in harmony with itself.

Aesthetic View. Bernhard Anderson, with a slight variation on the ecological view, says the "very good" of Genesis 1:31 "is an esthetic judgment in the sense that in the view of the Cosmic Artist all creatures function perfectly in a marvelous whole which is without fault or blemish."[59] Just as a skilled craftsman or painter is pleased with the production of a masterpiece, so was God as He proclaimed His creation good. Since He deemed His creation good in an aesthetic sense, He would consider it of high value. This not only provides intrinsic value in the created order but also suggests that it is something to be desired rather than shunned.

Absolute View. Others believe that *good* implies that creation is good in an absolute or perfect sense. In this view, there is no evil, death, or corruption in the original creation. God's created order reflected perfect ecological harmony, not the relative or defective one that we observe in wilderness areas today. John Klotz wrote, "The world that He established was perfectly balanced. It was not red in tooth and claw. Only with the coming of sin into the world was there suffering and death."[60] One problem with this view is that every ecosystem we know of continues to function as a result of the death of its members, whether it be the complex food chains or building the soil through decaying organic matter. Something is always dying, and death enables other life to continue. Life as we know it would stop if there were no death.

Whatever the exact meaning, one aspect remains, the entire created realm has value due to God's recognizing it as good. If creation is good in any of the above senses, then we cannot condone withdrawal from the created world, indifference toward it, or an exploitative attitude that allows humans to rape it for selfish gain. If God has deemed His creation "good," then how can we say that something is not good and fit for destruction? We, like Jesus, should be concerned with the sparrow as a sparrow, not as something that could possibly benefit us.

From a theocentric perspective, nature has intrinsic value because God made it, owns it, designed it for a purpose, and recognized it to be good. This perspective invites us to look upon nature as precious without the need to dissolve nature into the divine or subjugate it to human utility. Since the basis for nature's value rests in God Himself, there is a solid foundation for a sustainable environmental ethic. Furthermore, since God's character never changes, His values will never change. It will never be right to wantonly destroy what God has created. This cannot be said of a secular value system. Biblical Christianity sets forth a dependable and sustainable ground for valuing nature and therefore a more viable ecological option than any alternative.

5

The God of Creation: Transcendent or Immanent?

Those contending for a biocentric or pantheistic approach to environmental problems often condemn Christianity's belief in a transcendent God as being detrimental to the environment. They claim that God's other-worldly image gives the impression He is not concerned with this world. If God is not concerned, then why should we be? Since we are made in the image of God, we should echo God's transcendence in our lives by also living apart from nature. The belief in a transcendent God, it is argued, has removed God from nature and thereby removed all basis of reverence and restraint, allowing people to dominate and exploit nature at will.

Wendell Berry argued that God's transcendence spawns a very unhealthy attitude toward nature:

> The great disaster of human history is one that happened to or within religion: that is the conceptual division between the holy and the world, the excerpting of the Creator from the Creation. . . . If God was not in the world, then obviously the world was a thing of inferior importance, or of no importance at all. Those who were disposed to exploit it were thus free to do so.[1]

Thomas Berry concurred, saying:

99

> When we inquire into the reasons for this inefficacy in our spiritual traditions, we might observe that our identification of the divine as transcendent to the natural world makes a direct human-divine covenant relationship possible, but also we negate the natural world as the locus for the meeting of the divine and the human. . . . This makes possible the conception of the natural world as merely external object.[2]

According to Joseph Campbell, "The idea of the supernatural as being something over and above the natural is a killing idea."[3] Process theologians are equally critical of traditional Christianity's emphasis on a transcendent God. Jerry Robbins remarked:

> How can humans be expected to care for the earth if God is an absentee landlord? Will they obey a God who seems to show little personal concern for the material world? If God does not care, why should we? A stewardship theology that builds on a transcendent, deistic God undermines its own well-meaning program.[4]

There might be some within Christendom who would be guilty of this charge. For the most part, however, the accusation is ill-founded. It actually amounts to a charge against deism, not Christianity. The position is almost untenable when one considers the emphasis placed on prayer in many churches.

Why pray if God is not concerned with this realm and does not intervene? There would be more substance in the charge if it were directed to the overemphasis of the transcendence motif found in some sectors of Christianity, rather than to the supposed denial of the immanence motif.

Differing Viewpoints

Scriptures avoid both extremes of total immanence where God is identified with the world, as in pantheism, or total transcendence where God is completely removed from the world, as in deism. Both pantheism and deism, however, have detected elements of truth.

Pantheistic Identification

God is immanent in creation but not in the sense pantheists would have us believe. Pantheists do not actually identify God with the physical world, but what they teach is tantamount to the same thing. To unequivocally equate God with the physical realm would be to limit the infinity and perfection of the absolute. It would also mean that the absolute is knowable, something pantheists reject. By immanence they usually mean that the indefinable divine substance pervades the entire universe, but is not limited by it. The basic fabric and essence of the universe is the divine substance, which alone has being, nothing else has. Thus the physical world is ontologically non-existent. When we speak of pantheistic identification, therefore, we are referring to the underlying substance of the physical, not the physical.

Rather than being one with creation, the God of the Bible acts upon it and through it. God sustains the entire created realm, providing sustenance, guidance, and help for His creatures. Thus He is immanent within creation in the sense of involvement rather than identification. To identify God's working in and through nature with nature itself is a confusion of basic categories. But since people can only see the results, they tend to confuse creation with the Creator. It is God who provides and blesses through nature. Nature itself does not provide, for it is rather indifferent to whether or not anything survives.

To worship Mother Earth as the giver and sustainer of life is, in biblical terminology, to commit idolatry (Isa. 44:9-20; Rom. 1:21-23). God is not in nature. Elijah did not find God in the wind, earthquake, or fire but in a "gentle whisper" (1 Kings 19:11-12). Despite the efforts of New Age thinkers to assign a governing mind to Mother Earth, she remains as Paul described in 1 Corinthians 12:2, a dumb idol. A dumb idol cannot feel, sympathize, help, or conscientiously care for its creatures. The earth produces fruit only because God commanded it to be fertile and bring forth life (Gen. 1:11-12,20-21,24-25); Mother Earth does not and could not produce on her own accord. The psalmist noted that "the earth is satisfied by the fruit of his [the Creator's] work" (104:13). The pagan symbolism of the female fertility cults in which Mother Earth is the provider is conspicuously absent in the Scriptures. The earth is not a female deity, neither is it referred to with sexual connotations. This thought is refuted in Job 38:28-29 where the rain does not have a father; nor does ice come from a womb. It all comes from Yahweh. Furthermore, Mother Earth is not as benevolent as many would suppose. She indiscriminately kills and destroys her children. If nature were deity, that deity would be capricious and wicked. In contrast, the Scriptures depict nature (before being knocked out of balance by humans) in terms of paradise, with no natural evils or disasters.

Deistic Isolation

God is also transcendent, but not in a deistic sense. Deism teaches that God is an absentee landlord, a distant, inapproachable God, who is not concerned with the affairs of this life. With the rise of modern science in the sixteenth and seventeenth centuries, with Copernicus, Galileo, Kepler, Descartes, and Newton, people became enamored with the precision working of the universe and likened it to one large machine, governed by natural laws. Descartes and Newton both believed that God had created the universe and set in motion the laws by which it operates. God simply wound up the earth as if it were a clock and then let it run on its own accord by natural laws. According to deism, God does not intervene in the affairs of this world; thus, He did not work miracles among His people, did not reveal His Word through the prophets, did not come to earth to redeem humanity from sin, and will not return to conquer the forces of evil. Although God does not act in this world, He is still necessary to account for its existence and order. Deists see the world as a complex clock that could not be explained without a clockmaker. The shift from an intervening God to an absentee God constitutes a significant worldview change and a major step toward the secularization of nature and the present ecological dilemma.

Deists correctly infer from the concept of creation that God is external or transcendent to what He made. God's externality or transcendence, however, is perceived by biblical writers as one of being rather than lack of involvement. God and creation are different entities, differing in their basic essence. The being of God is neither dependent on the earth nor part of it in any way. This, however, does not imply that God must remain aloof. A husband and wife are different entities and come from different backgrounds, but this does not mean they must remain detached or distant from one another. The Christian concept of transcendence, therefore, does not mean that God exists apart from creation in the sense that He does not interact with it, but God exists apart from creation in the sense that His substance and that of creation belong to completely different spheres of existence.

Deists run into problems when they view the universe as an autonomous, self-sustaining entity, a sort of perpetual-motion machine. First, perpetual-motion machines will forever remain fantasies of the imagination because of the laws of thermodynamics. Second, by definition only God is self-sustaining and eternally existent. This puts deists in a dilemma with three possible options, all of which are contradictory to their system: (1) the universe is another god, (2) the universe is not another god and will die of entropy, or (3) the universe is not another god but depends on the one God. To argue for the absolute inviolability of natural laws suggests that God created another god who can exist independently of the Creator. From a Christian perspective, the natural laws are not self-perpetuating but rather are upheld by the power of God. Just as all machines eventually run out of energy and need repair, so will the universe, unless it is sustained by an external force. This implies that the universe is contingent and that it is dependent for its continuation on the Agent that brought it into existence.

With an ecological view of reality that includes both the natural and supernatural, divine intervention and even "miracles" are to be expected and are just as normal to the cosmos as the laws of nature. To define miracles as acts of God contrary to natural laws is somewhat ambiguous. We live in a supernatural world with every operation ultimately sustained by supernatural intervention.[5] "Nature itself is one vast miracle."[6] Loren Eiseley reminded us "that each one of us in his personal life repeats that miracle."[7] Deists and most moderns following in their train have tended to make nature natural, reducing it to a commonplace object explainable by the ordinary laws of nature and fit for manipulation and exploitation. However, in so doing, they are left without any basis to contend for a sustainable environment.

Christian Balance

The belief in creation presupposes a God who exists apart from His creation. This might lead one to envision a transcendent, otherworldly deity. The Scriptures, however, balance God's transcendence with His immanence. In the creation narrative, God walked in the garden in the cool of the day, enjoying communion with creation (Gen. 3:8). God is transcendent in that He is neither part of the created realm nor dependent on it in any way. He is immanent in that He is concerned for His creation, sustains it, and intervenes in this realm, either through the working of His Spirit or through the person of Christ.[8] Theologians from differing Christian traditions, however, have emphasized either one or the other. The Eastern church has emphasized more of God's immanence in the world, whereas the Western church has focused more on God's transcendence over the world. For the most part, theologians from either persuasion have not completely ignored the opposite view, for this would have resulted in either pantheism or deism.

Some, such as Harvey Cox, understand the Judeo-Christian tradition as completely separating God from creation, allowing people to manipulate nature. Cox maintained that the roots of secularization are found in the Scriptures and must be nourished rather than shunned.[9] Although few would go this far, it seems as if Cox was grappling with a fundamental motif of Western theology. The transcendent theme has been so pervasive that nature has been all but neglected. Theologically, nature is merely a peripheral addendum to the redemptive history of humanity.

Many theologians recognize that the dominant tradition of the Western church lends itself to ecological indifference and are offering alternate models to correct this oversight.[10] Christianity must maintain a balance between the two extremes as Pelikan has reminded us, "The distinction as well as the link between the Creator and his creation had to be maintained: immanence without pantheistic identification, transcendence without deistic isolation."[11]

Biblical Evidence of God's Immanence

The Scriptures give ample evidence that God is actively involved in the affairs and operations of the created world. Most importantly, God is directly involved in sustaining the life-support systems of the earth's ecosystem and in restoring the peace and harmony of the original creation. The involvement of God in this realm provides additional grounds for the intrinsic value of nature and for our cooperating with God in its renewal. It also provides us with the moral categories and moral imperative to be involved in environmental issues. If God were identified with nature in a pantheistic sense, there would be a lack of "ethical compulsion" for ecological action.[12] When all distinctions are eclipsed in the cosmic fog, the concepts of good and evil and, consequently, all ethical imperatives become rather nebulous. From a biblical perspective, God motivates His children to proper moral behavior by His injunctions as a transcendent and sovereign God and by His examples as an immanent and caring God. The following discussions give ample support for God's immanence in creation.

God Is Omnipresent

Scriptures teach that God is everywhere present. David said,

> Where can I go from your Spirit?
> Where can I flee from your presence?
> If I go up to the heavens, you are there;
> if I make my bed in the depths, you are there.
> If I rise on the wings of the dawn,
> if I settle on the far side of the sea,
> even there your hand will guide me
> (Ps. 139:7-10; see Jer. 23:23-24).

Paul told the Athenians that God is not far from each of us (Acts 17:27). The constant testimony of Scriptures is to a God near in time of need, who offers encouragement, help, and comfort when troubles come.

God Is Concerned About His Creation

The Scriptures depict God as intimately concerned with life on this planet and with our proper management of creation. God's concern for the plight of creation is suggested by the covenant He made in Genesis 9:8-17 with Noah and with "every living creature on earth" (Gen. 9:10). The Noahic Covenant is sometimes misunderstood. First, it did not bring humanity and nature into an ecological relationship that had not existed before. The ecological relationship of interconnectedness was part of the created order. Neither did it establish a covenant relationship between them. Humanity and nature were merely corecipients of a unilateral promise of God to His entire creation (animate and inanimate) that He would never destroy it again by flood (Gen. 9:11-12). Second, God's promise does not imply that He would never again upset the regularity of nature to judge humanity, for a contrary thesis runs throughout the Old Testament and the apocalyptic visions of Peter and John (2 Pet. 3:3-13; Rev. 6-19). On the positive side, it shows that God is concerned for creation, that humans and nature are perceived together as a community of creation, and that God is in absolute control of the created order. When we mistreat the land, we break the land-use regulations of the Mosaic legislation, not the Noahic Covenant (see Lev. 25).

God's concern for creation is seen throughout the Scriptures. The Book of Jonah concludes with the question, "But Nineveh has more than a hundred and twenty thousand people . . . and many cattle as well. Should I not be concerned about that great city?" (Jonah 4:11). God's concern with non-human life is explicit in Mosaic legislation. One reason for the weekly Sabbath rest was that the animals could rest: "Six days do your work, but on the seventh day do not work, so that your ox and your donkey may rest" (Ex. 23:12). The focus in this text appears to be more on providing rest for animals than people. The statements in the Decalogue, however, suggest that the Sabbath was established equally for the sake of *all* living creatures (Ex. 20:10; Deut. 5:14). God's concern for animals is seen also in the command not to muzzle an ox when it is threshing the grain (Deut. 25:4).

Divine ecological concern extends to maintaining biodiversity and protecting species from extinction. Human intervention tends to reduce the variety of species in an ecosystem, especially in modern agribusiness techniques. It is a well-known ecological principle that the greater the diversity within an ecosystem, the more stable it is. This ecological principle is actually a divine principle for proper management of creation. God commanded Noah to bring two of every living species, one male and one female, into the ark "to keep them alive" (Gen. 6:19). As noted before, this included both clean and unclean animals, many of which were of no utilitarian value to Noah or his family. In Deuteronomy 22:6-7, God forbids taking a mother bird along with the young. The young birds may be taken, but the mother is to be released so she can continue to propagate and maintain the species.

In regard to nonrational creatures, Aquinas argued that God cares more for the maintaining of species than for individuals.[13] Since God is not overly concerned with individual animals and plants, people are permitted to do anything they wish with them short of exterminating the species. God, however, is just as concerned for the welfare of individuals as He is for species (Matt. 10:29; Luke 12:6).

A few openly argue against biodiversity. Teilhard maintains that "the multitude of beings is a terrible affliction."[14] For Teilhard, the highest state is pure Being. This occurs when everything merges into the Omega Point and when all distinctions and dualities fade away as Christ becomes all in all. This shows similarity to pantheistic visions of everything merging back into the cosmic spirit. Hinduism teaches that when an individual reaches nirvana, his or her illusory existence is literally "blown-out"; the individual becomes extinct and is absorbed into pure nothingness or Brahman. What Teilhard has done is to apply the logical implication of pure Being to the notion of biodiversity. His conclusion is obviously detrimental to ecological interests. Those who look to monistic solutions to the present crisis should realize that unity at the sake of diversity is ruinous to their agenda. With disastrous implications like this, pantheistic approaches to environmental problems are rather dubious. Christianity affirms both individual identity and concern for species' preservation without losing an infinite reference point or unifying principle for all life.

God also shows ecological concern toward the land, stipulating that the land is to lie fallow every seventh year (Ex. 23:10-12; Lev. 25:1-7). The people were permitted to sow the land for six years, but in the seventh the land was to have a year of rest, "a sabbath to the Lord" (Lev. 25:4). The land was also to have rest on the fiftieth year or Year of Jubilee (Lev. 25:11). The text implies that the rest is for the sake of the land, not for the laborers in the field. Letting the ground lie fallow improves fertility and subsequent yields, thereby indirectly benefiting the people, but the focus still seems to be on giving the land rest for its own sake. The Jews, however, plundered the land for all they could get, not letting it rest as prescribed. Their continued disobedience finally resulted in God's deporting them to Babylon. The length of their captivity in Babylon (70 years) was determined by the number of years of rest due the land according to Leviticus 26:34-35: "Then the land will enjoy its sabbath years all the time that it lies desolate and you are in the country of your enemies; then the land will rest and enjoy its sabbaths. All the time that it lies desolate, the land will have the rest it did not have during the sabbaths you lived in it" (see 2 Chron. 36:21).

God's desire that the land not be ruthlessly exploited is seen again in Ezekiel 36:1-12. God denounces the nations and especially Edom for greedily making His land their own possession and plundering its resources. God promises that those who ravage the land will inevitably suffer the consequences (Ezek. 36:7). He also promises to restore the fertility and fruitfulness of the land from the ruin left in the wake of human greed (Ezek. 36:8-12). It would be somewhat presumptuous to construct an ecological agenda without considering the promises of God.

God is also concerned with the proper care of plant life. In Leviticus 19:23-25 He stipulates that the fruit of a newly planted tree not be taken for three years. The fourth year's fruit is to be given to the Lord. The fifth year's fruit may be eaten by the people. Proper care of the orchard will increase its yield, "In this way your harvest will be increased" (Lev. 19:25). Also, God commanded the Israelites not to cut down fruit trees as they laid siege to a city (Deut. 20:19-20).

Although references are not as abundant, the New Testament also shows God's concern for nature. God will not permit one sparrow to fall to the ground without its being divinely permitted (Matt. 10:29); not one sparrow is forgotten by God (Luke 12:6). This shows that He is concerned with individuals as well as whole species. However, in 1 Corinthians 9:9 God appears to be not really concerned with animals at all. Paul appealed to Deuteronomy 25:4 to show that he and Barnabas had the right to financial support, "For it is written in the Law of Moses: 'Do not muzzle an ox while it is treading out the grain.'" He then asks the rhetorical question, "Is it about the oxen that God is concerned?"

One way to interpret the Greek construction in the rhetorical question is to view the initial negative as a question tag that elicits a negative response, "God is not concerned with the ox, is He?" The implied answer would be, "No, God is not really concerned about the ox." Paul then commented on the implicit response by saying, "Surely He says this for us, doesn't He?" (1

Cor. 9:10). This interpretation implies that the command to permit oxen to eat was not given for the sake of the ox at all. God was concerned that preachers be paid, not that oxen have enough to eat. Therefore, many interpreters insert the word *only* in the rhetorical question, "God is not only concerned with the ox, is He?" The implied response would then be, "No, He is also concerned about His preachers." Another option for interpreting the Greek construction is to view verses 9b and 10a as a single question with the initial negative raising an element of doubt rather than expecting a negative answer. "Is God really concerned only for the ox, or is He saying this for us as well?"[15] Paul then answered, "Indeed, for us it was also written." The point we should emphasize is that Paul was referring to a divine principle to avoid being accused of arguing from a self-centered point of view. Thus to interpret the passage anthropocentrically is contradictory to Paul's intent. Just as a shepherd has the right to drink of the milk of the flock, a husbandman has the right to eat of the fruit of the vine, and an ox has the right to eat of the grain it threshes, so Paul and Barnabas had the right to be sustained by the churches.

Two other passages critics refer to in support of their contention that the Bible sets forth an apathetical attitude toward the environment are Jesus' curse on the fig tree (Mark 11:13-14,20-24) and His treatment of the swine (Mark 5:1-20). Both could be considered from the viewpoint of an object lesson, the strength of the lesson being contingent on the tree and the swine having value. If they were of no value, then a major element in the messages would be lost. The stories are somewhat analogous to a Buddhist monk pouring gasoline on himself and then setting himself afire. The monk's protest, designed to horrify the onlookers and incite them to action, is based on their recognition that life has value. The cursing of the fig tree is an enacted parable representing the spiritual bankruptcy of religious hypocrites and the need for faith in God. Because both the fig tree and the persons represented have value, the disciples stood aghast both at the action and the message. It is not that Jesus lacked concern for the tree (see Luke 13:6-9), but His overriding concern was for the need to impel people to believe in God. Because of the interconnectedness of creation and the dependency of creation on God, any human departure from God will invariably result in the unproductivity and devastation of the land (illustrated by the withered fig tree). Jesus was, therefore, very concerned about nature, for it is only as people return to God that the land will be healed.

The treatment of the swine could be handled in similar fashion, although the message differs. Again, the observation that the swine were a matter of concern and that they had value was crucial to the message. The astonishment was precipitated because of their having value, not because they lacked it. The message, of course, was directed to a Gentile audience. The entire event graphically represents the power of the demonic in one's life and the power of God in deliverance. The demonic within has the power to destroy not only an individual but nature as well, a thought much needed in our age of rampant materialism and exploitation. The message of this parable points to the future conquest of all demonic influences and the restoration of peace to the entire natural realm.

This survey of biblical data reveals that God is not only concerned with human life but also with the entire animate and inanimate creation. He cares for everything He made, including the animals we regard as pests, the trees and weeds that are in our way, and the rich topsoil that is smothered by urban expansion or washed into the sea by poor farming practices. If God is concerned for nonhuman creation, surely we as His appointed stewards must also be concerned and eliminate environmental harm and destruction. Our concern cannot stop with those parts of the nonhuman creation that are of value to us. In order to reflect God's glory and character, we must be concerned about what He is concerned about. How can one who claims to be born again (that is, re-created in God's image) ignore something of such significance to God?

God Sustains His Creation

Scriptures present a God who is active in upholding His creation, controlling natural processes, and sustaining life. There is no thought of a deistic First Cause who merely set in motion the laws of nature and then departed. It is God who ultimately controls the rains, storms, winds, darkness—not the laws of nature. God is the energizing agent who upholds natural laws and the ecological relationships that support life. From a biblical perspective, nature is not an autonomous, self-contained, and self-sustaining entity, governed by natural laws, but is entirely dependent on the sustaining hand of God. God continues to be very much involved in creation, directing it toward the goal of restored peace and harmony.

The sustaining influence of God demands that He is both external to creation and immanent with it. Because of the law of entropy, one cannot expect the universe to be sustained indefinitely from the energies found within the universe itself. The only hope for a sustainable environment is to be found in a transcendent God who is self-sustaining and willing to impart His energy to uphold the cosmic order. The whole discussion of a sustainable environment is nonsense without a transcendent God who can give it stability by His providential governance. Without God's influence all hope of a stable, ordered, and peaceful existence vanishes (see Job 34:14-15; Ps. 96:10-13; 104:29; and Acts 17:25,28). A helpful analogy would be a military squadron marching in unison. They can only keep in step if there is a drill sergeant to count off the pace. Without a transcendent voice, order in the cosmos would collapse. Moreover, the transcendent voice, like the drill sergeant, must be alongside the troops.

The deist's predicament is essentially the same as the pantheist's. Pantheists say there is nothing outside this realm to which one can look for sustaining power. The universe is all there is, but the haunting truth is that the only universe science knows is a universe subject to the law of entropy. It cannot sustain itself. The deists, on the other hand, might allow for an external power who could sustain the universe but who refrains from doing so. Again, the universe is left on its own, but this time with a transcendent God who refuses to act within His creation.

The mutual dependence of everything on the earth implies that the earth is itself dependent, or at least not self-sustaining. The earth's dependency is obvious from its relation to the sun, a transcendent source of energy that is not part of the earth's interdependency network. Although not fully accepted by the scientific community, there seems to be a hierarchy of dependency in the universe with each rung depending on a source higher up the ladder. The movement of the sun is dependent on the solar system, the movement of the solar system on the galaxy, the galaxy on local groups, local groups on clusters, clusters on super clusters, super clusters on strings, as each higher rung drags the lower ones through space. The implication is that the entire universe is dependent on a transcendent Source or prime mover for its continuance.

God's sustaining activity is both direct and indirect. He indirectly sustains the universe by working through established laws of nature and through His appointed caretakers. God directly sustains the universe by actively upholding the natural forces He established. This assures that a reasonable order continues so as to give stability to the earth's ecosystem.

God maintains His creation by exercising His creative rule over the forces of disintegration. The danger is not that the universe might slip back into chaos from which it came (the so-called chaos theory, in which there was a hint of order in chaos).

The Scriptures affirm that God created *ex nihilo*, not out of chaos. The disorderliness of Genesis 1:2 merely reflects a step in the process from nothingness to orderliness or to the state of being a *kosmos* (an orderly arrangement). The order envisioned in the original state slipped into partial chaos with human sin and continues to reflect a partially chaotic state as sin persists. Genesis differs from pagan mythologies in that it depicts a movement from creation to chaos, not from chaos to creation. The only movement from chaos to creation known in Scripture is God's redeeming conquest over the death principle by which He restores creation to its original harmony.

The Book of Job abounds with references to God's sustaining His creation. Most notable examples are found in Elihu's speech,

> If it were his intention
> and he withdrew his spirit and breath,
> all mankind would perish together
> and man would return to the dust (34:14-15).

Elihu also reminded Job that God's greatness could be seen in His acts in nature. God called down the rain and snow (37:6), controlled the temperature (vv. 9-10), caused the lightning (v. 11), and moved the winds (v. 12).

The psalms likewise abound with thoughts of God's preservation of creation. God preserves both man and beast (36:6), waters and cares for the land so it will bring forth bountifully (65:9-13), and controls the clouds, thunder, lightning, and earthquakes (17-18). In Psalm 89 the psalmist praised God for His faithfulness in upholding His covenant promises with His people, comparing it with God's faithfulness in sustaining the created order. Psalm 104 is so replete with references to God's upholding His creation that Joseph Sittler calls the psalm an "ecological doxology."[16] It categorically states that when God removes His sustaining hand, life perishes:

> When you hide your face, they are terrified;
> when you take away their breath,
> they die and return to the dust (v. 29).

Because of this, the psalmist declared,

> The eyes of all look to you,
> and you give them their food at the proper time.
> You open your hand
> and satisfy the desires of every
> living thing (145:15-16; see 147:8-9,16-17).

The prophets also state that the Creator controls His creation, sending thunder, clouds, lightning, rain, and wind at His will

(Jer. 10:11-13; see 51:15-16). God also "appoints the sun to shine by day" and "decrees the moon and stars to shine by night" (Jer. 31:35). Nahum focused on God's manipulating the forces of nature as agents of punishment,

> The Lord is slow to anger and great in power;
> the Lord will not leave the guilty unpunished.
> His way is in the whirlwind and the storm,
> and clouds are the dust of his feet.
>
> (1:3; see vv. 4-6).

The New Testament likewise testifies to God's sustaining creation. Jesus taught that we should not have to worry about the necessities of life, for God even feeds the birds of the air (Matt. 6:26) and gives nourishment to the lilies of the field so that they might grow (Matt. 6:28). If God sustains the birds and lilies, surely He will sustain us. Paul explained to the Athenians that God "is not served by human hands, as if he needed anything, because he himself gives all men life and breath and everything else. . . . 'For in Him we live and move and have our being'" (Acts 17:25,28). Apart from God, nothing would live, for only God is self-sustaining and nondependent. Everything else is dependent on Him. In Colossians 1:16-17 Paul wrote, "For by him all things were created: things in heaven and on earth, visible and invisible, whether thrones or powers or rulers or authorities; all things were created by him and for him. He is before all things, and in him all things hold together." The Agent behind creation is also the Agent behind preservation. The Son's sustaining agency is also expressed in Hebrews 1:3, "The Son is the radiance of God's glory and the exact representation of His being, sustaining all things by his powerful word." We are to pattern our lives after the Christ, the One who upholds creation, not after Adam, the one who destroys creation.[17]

Far from being an absentee Landlord, God is actively involved in sustaining life on the planet. Since God is the primary sustainer of creation, our efforts to provide an environmentally sound habitat for life cannot interfere with His efforts. We are called on to cooperate with God in the managing and sustaining of creation, and our efforts must be complementary with God's program. This casts doubt on some proposed "solutions," such as using genetic engineering to alleviate environmental problems. We cannot set ourselves up as gods or masters of creation, but we must submit to the Creator and work within the structure and principles He established.

God Acts Within His Creation

The history of the Hebrew people is a story of God's working among them. The Jews, however, did not construe this notion in a theanthropocentric fashion. They regarded the earth as an integral part of God's dealing with them; it was not some autonomous realm that existed or operated apart from the Creator, nor was it merely a stage for human redemption. The judgment and blessing motifs illustrate that the people and the land cannot be separated (see Deut. 28:15-68). God would bless or judge His people by altering relations. Sometimes it was their relations with foreign powers, other times it was their relations with the land. When the people rebelled, God sent Assyrians, Philistines, Babylonians, and Egyptians to harass them. Other times He caused the land to languish and not produce its crops. The land is often said to have mourned when the Jews wandered from God.

The Scriptures depict God working many miracles in the course of leading His people to wholeness and peace. God could stop the sun from moving (Josh. 10:13), dry up the Red Sea (Ex. 14:21), float axheads (2 Kings 6:6), and cause a plague of locusts (Ex. 10:13). Moule, however, raised the question, "But have we not outgrown such a naïve idea? The answer, I would urge, is that, in principle, it is not naïve nor alien to Christian thought today." Moule suggested that it would be reasonable to believe that "the infinitesimally tiny pieces on the cosmic chessboard," such as meteorological changes, could be controlled by the Creator. "No one who believes in a Creator who is both transcendent and immanent should find this idea impossible."[18]

The New Testament's doctrine of the incarnation continues the Old Testament theme of God's acting within the created realm. The incarnation is the supreme statement that the physical realm is not inherently evil but rather is of utmost value. If Christ assumed a physical body and willingly suffered for the healing of creation, then God must be intimately concerned with the physical and value it highly. Since the natural order can neither be sustained nor brought into harmony without His intervention, there is a sense in which one may consider the life of the planet to be organically united with God.[19] As mentioned in chapter 3, all reality could be considered as a cosmic ecosystem, which, with qualifications, includes God. When relations within an ecosystem are severed, the death process begins. Christ has come to mend broken relations and to bring life, peace, and harmony to creation. Just as Christ was an active agent in the original creation, He is an active agent in the re-creation (see John 1:1-3). There can never be full healing until relations with the

Creator are fully restored, for it is only through proper relations with the Fountainhead of life that life can be sustained.

It is in the sense of renewal that we can speak of a continuing creation. We could infer from God's recognizing the goodness of creation and His resting on the seventh day that no new life forms or elements need to be created *ex nihilo*. His creative activity, however, must continue in order to sustain and renew that which He created in the beginning. His renewing power is especially needed to heal the relations shattered by the fall and to reverse the death process (Ps. 51:10; Isa. 48:6-7; Jer. 31:22; 2 Cor. 5:17; and Eph. 2:15). This process of upholding and healing might be thought of as mediate creation, in which God creates out of preexisting materials and brings new life out of old forms (see 2 Cor. 5:17). If God continues to uphold and renew life and harmony on earth, then re-creation and salvation must be ongoing processes that pertain to all creation.[20]

The idea of God's continuing creation takes on fresh connotations with the creative activity of the Spirit. Through His Spirit, God is restoring relations and making lives anew. This creative energy is manifest most prominently through Christ, the eternal *logos* and "master workman" of the universe.[21] God through Christ is actively involved in the process of re-creation, in which creation will be brought into conformity with its original design. The Great Physician mends all broken relations, not simply those between humans and Himself.

In summary, the Judeo-Christian God is both transcendent and immanent: transcendent in that His being is not part of this realm, immanent in that He acts within His creation. The contingency of the present order demands exactly such a being. There is hope for the present crisis, but only because God is both transcendent and immanent. His transcendence removes Him from the natural processes of decay, and His immanence assures us that He is willing to impart His life-sustaining power to redeem the earth. Thus the transcendent/immanent theme of biblical thought is an ecological necessity. He is not at all a deistic God unconcerned with what is happening on earth, as many critics suppose.

6

THE BIBLICAL PERSPECTIVE: ANTHROPOCENTRIC, BIOCENTRIC, OR THEOCENTRIC?

It is commonly agreed that humans with their anthropocentric view of life have brought upon themselves the environmental problems that are threatening their very existence. To perceive humanity as the pinnacle of existence with everything else as raw material for exploitation is becoming recognized not only as pure human arrogance but also as a malignancy that can destroy all life as we know it. Many trace this arrogant view of humanity to Christianity and the Christian Scriptures. Part of the impetus to find a new religion is due to the supposed anthropocentrism in Christianity.

What is being advocated to replace Western anthropocentrism is a biocentric view of life. That is, the entire biosphere with all its varied relationships is the center of all meaning, value, and guidance; humans are simply part of the complex whole. The science of ecology seems to predicate such a view. There are, however, several questions we must interact with regarding how the whole is to be viewed. Do the Christian Scriptures teach anthro-

115

pocentrism? If not, what perspective do they set forth? Is biocentrism a workable alternative to anthropocentrism? Also, is there any validity to an enlightened anthropcentrism? Many Christian thinkers question any form of anthropocentrism and suggest theocentrism, or a God-centered view of existence, as the only viable alternative to meet the environmental crises.

In his book *Crisis in Eden*, Frederick Elder called attention to the importance of different perspectives regarding humanity and nature. He distinguished between the inclusionists who include humans in a holistic view of the environment from the exclusionists who remove them from the study of ecology and the environment. Elder listed Loren Eiseley, Rachel Carson, Ian McHarg, Aldo Leopold, and Barry Commoner as inclusionists and Pierre Teilhard de Chardin, Herbert Richardson, and Harvey Cox as exclusionists.[1]

Anthropocentrism

Anthropocentrism is a way of viewing reality that places humanity at the center. Everything in the universe is seen in terms of human values and human interests. It perceives humanity as the final authority and arbitrator of values, meaning, ethics, rights, and the direction society should take. In other words, anthropocentrism in its secular form deifies humankind. There is no higher authority to restrict human manipulation and exploitation of nature. The human goal is the total conquest of nature for the betterment of their own kind and the continuation of their sovereign claim to be absolute potentates of the earth.

The Predicament of Modern Western Society

Anthropocentrism is so much part of our way of life that it seems sacrilegious even to question it. The ever-expanding economy, industrialization, progress, and affluence are the hallmarks of modern society and are accepted as proper and right. It is as if humans, being intoxicated with power, autonomy, and hubris, are unable to sober up to see where this reasoning is leading them. There are no limits, boundaries, or inhibitions imposed on secular, autonomous society. If God is dead, as Dostoyevsky wrote in *The Brothers Karamazov*, then "All things are lawful";[2] humans are free, absolutely free, to do anything they wish. This mind-set, however, is beginning to backfire.

Ian McHarg commented,

> Show me a man-oriented society in which it is believed that reality exists only because man can perceive it, that the cosmos is a structure erected to support man on its pinnacle,

> that man exclusively is divine and given dominion over all things, indeed that God is made in the image of man, and I will predict the nature of its cities and their landscapes. I need not look far for we have seen them—the hot-dog stands, the neon shill, the ticky-tacky houses, dysgenic city and mined landscapes. This is the image of the anthropomorphic, anthropocentric man; he seeks not unity with nature but conquest. Yet unity he finally finds, but only when his arrogance and ignorance are stilled and he lies dead under the greensward. We need this unity to survive.[3]

The anthropocentric predicament is somewhat paradoxical on two accounts. First, concern for personal well-being and survival has raised ecological awareness to the level that many now question the anthropocentric basis for modern society. The motivating factor for change (self-preservation) and the source of the problem (self-centeredness) both stem from self-interest. Appealing to self-preservation, therefore, only accentuates self-centeredness, and the root of the problem does not go away. Second, humanistic society still approaches environmental problems from an anthropocentric perspective despite knowing that this attitude is ultimately self-destructive. To preserve wilderness areas for recreation purposes, to convert to compact fluorescents for economical purposes, or to save the rain forest because of the pharmaceutical products it can yield is to act out of anthropocentric interests. There has been much environmental activity recently, but most of it is, in one way or another, still anthropocentric. Anthropocentrism seems to be so entrenched in society that there is an ingrained resistance against accepting the observation that humanity's priority on self is self-destructive.

The Charge Against Christianity

The quest to find solutions impels us to find causes, for "solutions" will be only superficial until the causes are rectified. For example, if we clean up a polluted reservoir but fail to find the source of the pollutants, it will soon become fouled again. The growing recognition that anthropocentrism is polluting our environment has prompted many to investigate the root source of this destructive mind-set. Owing to the influence of Christianity on Western society for the past thousand years, many assume that modern anthropocentrism is derived from Christianity. The Scriptures seemingly yield ample support for this hypothesis with the dominion passage in Genesis, our being made in the image of God, and the emphasis on human salvation. These elements prompted Lynn White to assert, "Especially in its Western form, Christianity is the most anthropocentric religion the world has seen."[4] White reasoned that Christian anthropocentrism, with its notion that nature has no value except to serve humanity, has permeated Western society and has engendered the destructive attitude toward nature that plagues us today.

The Presence of Anthropocentrism in the Church

Although it would be historically precarious to assign direct causes, it must be recognized that the church is partially guilty of propagating a type of anthropocentrism. The paradigm through which the church views reality is more properly theanthropocentric; that is, everything revolves around God and humanity. The anthropocentric drift in Christian theology is partially due to the Reformers' concentration on justification by faith, where humanity's relation to God became the primary locus of theological endeavor. Everything, including nature, was subsumed under the grand design of God to redeem the fallen human race. Nature became the backdrop to salvation history, a mere stage in which God worked out His redemptive plan with humanity. This theanthropocentric view permeates most of the modern church, from liberalism to fundamentalism.

Perhaps the most characteristic application of mainstream twentieth-century theology to environmental issues is Thomas Derr's *Ecology and Human Need*, a work which incidentally represents the environmental position of the World Council of Churches. Derr maintained the need for responsible stewardship, but this is understood as management of the earth's resources for the benefit of humankind, especially the poor and needy. This echoes Luther and Calvin where humans are to be responsible stewards, but at the same time everything was made for their sake.

Evangelical pleas for environmental involvement are often theanthropocentric as well. For example, in *Project Earth* William Badke argued that we are to care for creation because it will enhance creation's witness to the glory and nurturing power of God and consequently lead others to Christ. Justification for environmental involvement is therefore found by subordinating it to the Great Commission.[5] Furthermore, as with Barth and Brunner, nature is peripheral to the primary focus of theology, but instead of nature being the stage for human redemption, it is merely the mirror of human morality before a holy God.[6]

It cannot be denied that some Reformers held that nature was intended only for human benefit. However, it was never allowed to be pursued to its logical and destructive end because of being held in check by responsible stewardship to God and other tidbits of ecological wisdom. About this same time, Renaissance humanism was coming into full bloom, attaching foremost importance to the faculties, capabilities, ambitions, and well-being of the human race. Renaissance humanists protested against Medieval Christianity's belittling of human value before death. Humanists claimed that humans possessed intrinsic value in this life as well as great potential to advance in knowledge and well-being. As the influence of the church waned during the Enlightenment, the humanistic tendency ascended to a societal norm, and humanity became the measure of all things.

The church's notion that humans were the crown of creation and that everything was made for them coincided with the rising consensus of humanistic thought. As the church capitulated to the emergent social order regarding the role of nature, she was left without any basis for a sustained protest against the ideals and goals of modern society and the way it was treating nature. The faint glimmers of ecological wisdom in reformational theology were quenched by the church's secularization of nature. Thus the confluence of the anthropocentrism of humanistic society and the deviant anthropocentrism in Western theology (imported from Greek philosophy) issued into a pervasive motif that continues to this present day. Because of its widespread acceptance, anthropocentrism is presumed to be a universal truth by modern Western society.

The Absence of Anthropocentrism in the Bible

Some within the Christian community, such as Thomas Derr, contend that the Bible teaches anthropocentrism. Derr stated, "The Biblical view of man's relation to nature is, then, definitely anthropocentric, but devoid of false confidence in the results of man's mastery."[7] As with many writers in mainline denominations, Derr's major environmental concern is justice for the poor and oppressed. Scriptures, in his view, pertain to God's dealings with humanity, not nature. He argued that although nature has value, it is not "equivalent to the value placed on man."[8] Therefore, whenever there is any conflict between the needs of people and the needs of nature, the needs of people will be served. The concern that the poor and oppressed be treated fairly and receive their share of God's grace is commendable and cannot be neglected. But if our interest in environmental causes stems only from humanitarian concerns, we fall into the anthropocentric dilemma of finding adequate basis for caring for nature for nature's sake.

Although the primary focus of Scripture is on the divine-human relation, there is still considerable ecological material, especially in the Old Testament. Since nature is an integral part of the whole, God cannot meaningfully discuss humanity without also discussing nature. Some New Testament books, such as John and Hebrews, however, are almost devoid of nature themes. Theological terms, such as *salvation, reconciliation, sin, forgiveness, faith, grace, mercy,* and *repentance,* seem to refer only to humans in New Testament literature (especially when interpreted from a theanthropocentric viewpoint). It is quite understandable then that theology has become concerned with expounding the character of God, the human predicament, and one's relation with God and others.

The New Testament emphasis, however, does not negate the previous revelation. It is the nature of divine revelation to develop themes progressively. The revelation regarding humanity's relation to nature and nature's purpose found relatively full expression in the Old Testament. It only needed some finishing touches in the New Testament, especially regarding the relation between humanity's redemption and that of nature (see Rom. 8:19-21). What did not find full expression in the Old Testament were the details of human redemption. This accounts for the unbalanced weight each testament devotes to nature themes.[9]

The divine-human focus in the New Testament is to be expected, since God is talking to humans about the human predicament (that is, their estrangement from Him and their need to be reconciled). It would be rather inappropriate for a young man to write a letter to his girlfriend and then talk at length about some other girl. He would be concerned with his girlfriend and most of the letter would be taken up with the various aspects of their relationship. In the same way, as God spoke to humans, He was primarily concerned about their relationship with Him.

Perhaps the crux of the problem in Western theology is the confusion between the subject matter the Scriptures discuss and the worldview perspective it sets forth. For example, just because doctors and psychologists often talk about human beings does not mean they endorse an anthropocentric worldview. In the same way, just because the Scriptures discuss at length the divine-human relation does not mean it sets forth a theanthropocentric worldview. The Bible unequivocally focuses on the divine-human relationship, yet it does so from an underlying theistic perspective.

Furthermore, the focus on the divine-human relation should not be scorned since the redemption of nonrational creation revolves around that of humanity. It is because God is concerned with nature that He is talking with the culprit who shattered the peace of the original creation. God's purpose is to restore all the relations broken at the fall, including the human-nature relation, and that restoration has to begin with humanity's relation to God. To criticize the human emphasis in Scripture is to misapprehend the true cause of the environmental crisis. This led Santmire to remark, "The Divine purpose is profoundly cosmocentric, as well as anthropocentric."[10]

Nor can we avoid the biblical teaching that humanity is, in some way, in a position of responsibility over nature. God endowed humans with the ability to be caretakers of the earth, and as such they can be considered as the highest creatures, but it does not follow that Scripture teaches anthropocentrism or even enlightened anthropocentrism.[11] The idea of being God's delegated caretaker is the antithesis of anthropocentrism. It is God who is the center of all meaning and purpose. Humans are called to serve God's interests, not their own interests. The biblical worldview and anthropocentrism in any form are therefore worlds apart.

On closer examination we will find that the biblical writers did not conceive of nature as simply a stage for human redemption. Santmire points out:

> Although man is surely the central actor, as Barth and Brunner have rightly emphasized, nature itself has its own distinct role to play in the Divine drama. The God witnessed to in the Bible plays out a *history with nature*, as well as a history with man.
>
> Together these two histories, inseparable yet distinct, comprise the Universal Divine Story of creation, redemption, and consummation.[12]

The biblical emphasis on the divine-human relationship is therefore quite understandable and in no way negates the broader theological framework of God's concern for the entire cosmos.

The Different Forms of Anthropocentrism

Not all forms of anthropocentrism are the same. Christian anthropocentrism (or more properly theanthropocentrism) differs from secular anthropocentrism in that it still recognizes God as the sovereign Lord of the universe. Although Christian anthropocentrism would agree that everything exists for the service of humankind and that humanity is the crown of creation, people are still accountable to a higher authority for their conduct. Humans are given a prominent place, but they are not autonomous masters of creation and are not completely free to do anything they wish. Nevertheless, with Christian anthropocentrism everything does revolve around God and humanity;

nature is simply not in the picture. Most of the preaching we hear concerns human salvation or moral behavior toward one another. The exclusive attention on maintaining proper divine-human and human-human relationships must be classified as anthropocentric. The implication of this thinking appears to be that God is not interested in anything but humanity.

All forms of anthropocentrism, including theanthropocentrism and secular anthropocentrism, have as their common denominator the centrality of the human race. What is meant by this will differ, yet the outcome will be the same. In either form, the value of nature is diminished in the rising ascendancy of the human species. This valuing of humanity and devaluing of nature encourage the notion that the world is a huge grab bag of goodies, an attitude that must be rejected as utterly destructive to God's intent for creation. Both secular and Christian forms of anthropocentrism suffer from this same malady; both contain an element of egotistical hubris that must be condemned as sin. In addition, Christian anthropocentrism fails to appreciate the wider theological context of God's concern for all creation and its future redemption. Theology from an anthropocentric orientation is incomplete and distorted. As Schwarz said, "An anthropocentric view of nature or of life is in the long run no viable option. It must, by necessity, lead to exploitation and eventual destruction of both man and nature."[13]

The Perversion of All Anthropocentrisms

All forms of anthropocentric thought are ultimately derived from humanity's rebellion in the garden. When Adam asserted his independence from God, the seeds of secular thought were born, and the human race became autonomous. The theocentrism that controlled the thinking of the prelapsarian race was exchanged for anthropocentrism. Humans were now the central figure on the stage, and everything revolved around them. One prominent theme in Scripture is to revive a theocentric mind-set in the conscious life of God's people (see Rom. 12:2; 2 Cor. 10:5; Phil. 2:5).

Seen in this light, the anthropocentric focus in the church is actually a perversion of what the Scriptures teach. Vincent Rossi asserted,

> The modern western paradigm is related to Christianity only as a *heresy*—a subtle counterfeit, a demonic caricature of authentic Christian values. . . . The anthropocentric paradigm is not Christian, not even close. It is a *new faith entirely.* And if some Christian denominations have tended to capitulate before the new faith, they do so not as biblical

and traditional Christians but as moderns who are nominally Christian but who are as lost and rootless as the rest of the moderns.[14]

Hans Schwarz added that the anthropocentrism which White labeled as a Christian axiom

> stands contrary to fundamental Judeo-Christian beliefs. It is the result of a process through which the theocentric world view of Judeo-Christian faith was turned into the anthropocentric world view of our present secular age. God was replaced by man and thus not only did the source and direction of history become obscured, but he "for the glory of God" was replaced by the glorification and deification of man.[15]

H. Richard Niebuhr considered Christian anthropocentrism an inversion of true biblical faith.[16] We concur that anthropocentrism is an alien philosophy derived from extra-biblical sources and has no place in Christian thought.

The Need to Abandon Anthropocentrism

Not all ecologically concerned thinkers would agree with the need to abandon anthropocentrism. René Dubos, for example, championed the idea of enlightened anthropocentrism, which means that we are to manage the earth with wisdom and concern for all life forms:

> Environmental health implies that the environment remains in a desirable ecological state for a long period of time. The very use of the adjective desirable points to the anthropomorphic attitude inherent in the human approach to environmental problems. Ecologic purists notwithstanding, all ecology is anthropomorphic in the final analysis.[17]

Thomas Derr, like Dubos, argued that anthropocentrism properly understood is healthy for both humanity and the environment. He reasoned that when properly managed and cared for, the earth can supply all our needs without undo harm to the environment.

The underlying attitude of anthropocentrism, however, will ultimately foil such noble intentions and inevitably lead to despotism and destruction, not only of the environment but also of fellow humans. Whenever a conflict arises between humanity and nature, humans are going to triumph. Carmody remarked, "Anthropocentrism therefore can seem a gigantic self-indulgence. Perhaps it made sense when *homo sapiens* was in its adolescence, but if we are to come of age it will have to go."[18]

To save the environment, Western society must undergo a massive paradigm shift away from anthropocentrism. Such drastic changes never come easy; they always tend to take place over several generations with some segments of society always clinging to the old school. The real question, however, is whether fallen humanity is willing and able to abandon the anthropocentric paradigm. There seems to be a deep-seated quirk in human nature that locks people into this way of thinking. Even though we may make some progress correcting environmental problems, anthropocentrism will always be present to plague every effort we attempt. This will continue as long as our attitude is controlled by our egocentric bent.

John Cobb recognized that even the transformation of Christian thought may be difficult because the dominant view has so entrenched itself in the life and practice of the church. "The Christian tradition cannot transform itself by the extension of concern to man's fellow creatures without first overcoming the extreme man-centeredness of the dominant philosophy."[19] Most writers are in agreement that anthropocentrism is a blight on the human race and must be repudiated. Vincent Rossi stated, "Modern humanity needs to be humbled, and anthropocentrism needs to be denounced as a pernicious cancer upon the earth."[20] Jürgen Moltmann concurred saying, "We have to overcome the old anthropocentric world picture by a new theocentric interpretation of the world of nature and human beings, and by an eschatological understanding of the history of this natural and human world."[21]

Biocentrism

Biocentrism teaches that the entire natural realm, with its interlocking chain of dependencies, is the nucleus of all existence on earth and the ultimate reference point for all meaning, purpose, values, and ethics. The earth's ecosystem is to be valued for its own sake, since it is the fountainhead and sustainer of all life. Biocentrism emphatically denies that everything on earth is for human benefit; instead, everything exists for the sake of the whole. This gives ultimate value to everything in nature because when working in harmony with everything else, the whole supposedly has the potential to sustain the life and structure of the entire biosphere.

A New Ecological Paradigm

With Christianity perceived as anthropocentric and therefore part of the environmental problem, many are turning to biocentrism. Catholic theologian Thomas Berry, for example, states that the "move to a biocentric norm is essential."[22] Biocentrism is often depicted as an emerging ecological worldview "that has arisen in answer to the human need for a unifying sense of order."[23] It is being set forth as the only hope to save humanity from the evils of anthropocentrism, especially its greed and materialism. This new holistic paradigm is the **product** of the rising ecological awareness in society, the influence of Eastern philosophies, systems theory, quantum mechanics, and a renewal of interest in primitive paganism and Native American cultures.

Environmentalists tend to emprace this new paradigm, for it coincides not only with what the science of ecology is teaching but also with the pop philosophy of Eastern mysticism. Biocentrism's focus on the web of life precludes human ascendancy. No one organism can claim supremacy over anything else, for all are needed to support the ecosystem. As a result, humans are simply part of the complex whole, no higher or lower than any other part of nature. And people are listening with open ears. This sounds like the ideal corrective for despotic anthropocentrism.

Biocentrism and Pantheism

Although there are many forms of pantheism, its unifying theme, as discussed before, is that there is only one substance in the universe and that one substance is the inexplicable deity. Pantheism is commonly depicted as teaching that God is all and all is God. Divinity pervades all things as the spiritual fabric behind everything we see. This monistic model patches up a glaring weakness in the secular model and, on the surface, seems to provide a workable framework for environmental healing. The earth is no longer to be ravaged, instead it is to be revered. What was formally natural and fragmented is now sacred and whole. As such, pantheism offers a very appealing framework for many environmentalists who trumpet its virtues as the panacea for all environmental woes.[24]

There is a striking similarity between biocentrism and pantheism. Both advocate that all existence is part of one undivided entity (monism), that humans are on the same level as everything else, that all things are interconnected and interdependent, and that the source of value and meaning is somehow to be identified with the cosmos itself. It is no surprise that a large number of ecoactivists embrace some form of pantheism.

A common presupposition of both biocentrism and pantheism is the rejection of a transcendent deity. In finding values in the structure of the natural order, biocentrism is, by default, at odds with Christian theism. Both pantheism and biocentrism look to nature as their teacher rather than to the God behind nature. It is very appealing to look to nature for guidance because there is a mystic wonder and awe in the pristine beauty of the cosmos, as if it were deity itself. Primitive peoples have long sought counsel from nature. It is even becoming quite fashionable for moderns to seek nature's wisdom. Thomas Berry asserted,

> Our best procedure might be to consider that we need not a human answer to an earth problem, but an earth answer to an earth problem. The earth will solve its problems, and possibly our own, if we will let the earth function in its own ways. We need only listen to what the earth is telling us.[25]

From a biblical perspective, one could agree that all creation is one interrelated system and that the human race is one with nature in the sense of being codependent and a cocreature with the rest of God's creation. However, to say that this interconnected oneness is all there is would be to encounter severe philosophical problems and court ecological disaster.

The Dilemma of Biocentrism

Any system that rejects a transcendent God and includes humanity with the rest of nature on the same hierarchical level may be as detrimental to the cause of environmentalism in the long run as secular anthropocentrism. Most ecophilosophers in their zeal against anthropocentrism want to eliminate any hierarchy that places humanity over nature. This includes jettisoning the Scriptures because of their hierarchical structure of reality, but categorically rejecting the biblical testimony instead of interacting with its wisdom will lead to serious problems.

First, as mentioned in chapter 3, when value structures are flattened, there is no way to adjudicate conflicts of interest. Monism's rejection of all distinctions and dualities tends to obliterate value structure. Logically, humans have no more intrinsic value than a rock since both are emanations from the same cosmic force, and both will eventually merge back into that force. This leveling of values is also characteristic of biocentrism. Bill Devall and George Sessions in their book *Deep Ecology* argue for biocentric equality in which "all organisms and entities in the ecosphere, as parts of the interrelated whole, are equal in intrinsic worth."[26] They do recognize mutual predation and that it is not wrong to take an animal's life to sustain oneself. This leveling of hierarchical value structure may sound appealing, but it is fraught with difficulties. What is to prevent mutual predation within the human race, or why not allow the rats to eat the grain shipments destined to feed the hungry in distant lands? After all, the rats have rights and needs the same as people do.

To dethrone anthropocentrism without shifting to theocentrism leaves ecologists with the moral dilemma of resolving conflicts of interests without an objective basis for doing so. How far do we take animal rights or the rights of nature? When humans have a legitimate need, how can one decide what and how much of nature can be appropriated? What constitutes a legitimate need? When all hierarchical structure has been flattened and the transcendent God has been pronounced dead, there is an ethical deadlock that shatters the entire enterprise.

The logical end of bioequality is that ultimately humans are back making decisions, and those decisions are invariably linked with human survival and human welfare. Biocentrism, by its very nature, cannot transcend the natural and as a result lacks a metaphysical dimension to govern ethics. The physical realm is all that there is. Hence we are back at the starting point of secular thought and have jumped once again into the morass of naturalism that got us into trouble in the first place.

Second, when we are reduced to the same level as the rest of nature, it tends to depersonalize us and to ignore our special endowments. We have certain qualities that transcend normal functioning of ecosystems and enable us to act as responsible caretakers of God's creation. We have the intellect and freedom to alter, modify, or manage our ecosystem according to our will or according to the divine will. When biocentrism is adopted, humanity's potential position over nature as a steward and compassionate overseer of the planet must be discarded, for biocentrism lacks the basis for humans to assert such supremacy. With the natural workings of the ecosystem dictating what should be done or not done, we no longer have a voice in the management of the earth and become reduced to the level of brute beasts. Nature becomes the ultimate law giver and its own governing agent, and a "red-in-tooth-and-claw" ethic becomes the norm. Some may object that we can still engage in caring for the earth, but as Vincent Rossi said, "One simply cannot claim that humankind is just another species and in the same breath talk of 'holistic' or 'righteous management.'"[27] It is somewhat of a myth therefore to appeal to "absolute biological egalitarianism"[28] as the solution to environmental problems.

We cannot exist as animals. We are rational and moral beings who possess extremely powerful tools for either destruction or healing. Deep within the human psyche there is a moral awareness that the destruction of the planet would be wrong. Animals lack the potential for taking care of God's creation, the potential for massive destruction, and the moral pangs when wrong is committed. To rob us of our uniqueness is to destroy our humanness. We will never be able to find our true self and place in the cosmos as long as a biocentric view is maintained.

Third, biocentrism lacks an existential imperative; that is, nature does not in itself contain the reason for its own existence or for its continuation. Nature does not tell us that we ought to preserve ourselves and other life forms. Although it indirectly tells us *how* to live for maximum pleasure (that is, harmoniously), it does not tell us that we *ought* to live or live in a particular way. Who says that our existence must continue? Who says that the rain forests must continue? Nature is silent. It is not saying a word. If we want to kill ourselves, then it is our business. The problem is that one cannot logically jump from an *is* to an *ought*. Just because the rain forests *are* does not mean that they *ought* to continue. The problem of biocentrism is the same as for anthropocentrism. There is no impartial and reliable ought-giver. Justification for this argument will be given in chapter 10.

Theocentrism

Theocentrism teaches that God is the center of the universe and that He alone is the Source and Upholder of meaning, purpose, values, and ethics, as well as the unifying principle of the cosmos. Everything finds existence, value, purpose, and meaning in the infinite and transcendent God. As one writer put it, "Where God is the center of value, *all* things have value in relationship to him."[29] Without this infinite reference point, there would be no stable basis for values nor any compelling reason for the continuation of life. All human endeavors would be doomed to futility and absurdity. Theocentrism teaches that everything exists for the sake of God and to serve His purposes. There is meaning to human existence, but only as we find our place in the overarching divine purpose of the universe.

A Viable Alternative to Anthropocentrism

The only plausible alternative to anthropocentrism is theocentrism, where everything revolves around a transcendent God. Whatever governs one's perception of reality in a sense becomes for that person his or her god: whether humanity, nature, or the God of the Bible. To maintain that the correct view of the universe is biocentric, then we have for all practical purposes deified nature. The same holds true for anthropocentrism. If these gods cannot provide a model for a sustainable environment, then they must be false gods.

As Vincent Rossi says, the true Christian "answer to anthropocentrism is not biocentrism but *theocentrism.*"[30] "Theocen-

trism condemns the tragic distortions of anthropocentrism,"
says Rossi, "while affirming mankind's priestly role at the center
of creation. Theocentrism turns stewardship away from management, wise or unwise, and toward *servanthood.*"[31] Paul Santmire
also saw theocentrism as the only viable option:

> To avoid setting the human creature over against nature on
> the one hand (the tendency of anthropocentrism), and to
> avoid submerging the human creature and humanity's cries
> for justice on the other hand (the tendency of cosmocen-
> trism), I am suggesting that we see both humanity and
> nature as being grounded, unified, and authenticated in the
> Transcendent, in God. This is the theocentric framework.[32]

Implications of Theocentrism

The ecological implications of theocentrism far surpass those
of anthropocentrism or biocentrism. First, it resolves the ethical
dilemma without giving humanity absolute rights to legislate values and without dissipating value structure altogether. Since all
values and ethics are grounded in a transcendent God, it avoids
the problems inherent in any system that tries to derive imperatives from mere existence.

Second, theocentrism preserves the uniqueness of humanity
without yielding to anthropocentric arrogance. Humans have
been gifted and commissioned to serve God in the household of
creation as humble caretakers. There can be no arrogance in the
heart of a true servant. Theocentrism views humanity as an integral part of the "community of creation" rather than the crown of
creation.[33]

Third, theocentrism alone provides the basis for true stewardship. A steward is one who has been delegated the responsibility
to manage the estate or affairs of another. To advocate stewardship of the earth without positing a transcendent God will soon
degenerate into management for one's own benefit, for responsibility inevitably fails without accountability. The effectiveness of
the stewardship would be contingent on the moral sensitivity of
each person to the needs of others and the environment, something that is unlikely to take place in view of the track record of
the human race.

Fourth, theocentrism provides direction in resolving environmental problems. That direction or model is indicated by the
divine intent in creation, that is, for every relation in the cosmos
to be ruled by peace and harmony. What we find today is the
opposite: greed, exploitation, mistreatment of the poor, and
abuse of nature. We have been called to work together with God
to help the creation community function as God intended.

Fifth, theocentrism provides hope of an ecological utopia or future kingdom where peace and harmony will be restored, something that will always elude the biocentric or anthropocentric quest in which the death principle is an integral part of the earth's processes.

Sixth, theocentrism encourages us to place faith and trust in God for the ultimate solution to our problems rather than trusting in ourselves and our technology.

Seventh, theocentrism provides a reason for the existence of every creature. The divine reason for creation provides rights to all God's creatures to live the life that God intended for them. God designed this planet to be their home as well as ours. Theocentrism says that God's intent is paramount and that we are to be subordinate to this intent. To hold to a theocentric position and to rape the environment are contradictory, for exploitation of God's creation is to disrespect His purpose for nature and ultimately to disrespect God Himself.

Eighth, theocentrism provides the only plausible rationale for a sustainable environment. In all other systems the source for sustainability must be found in the contingent and degenerating universe.

Ninth, theocentrism is large enough to encompass the concerns of both anthropocentrism and biocentrism without doing injustice to either one and without acquiescing to their shortcomings. The one who serves humanity tends to neglect the earth; the one who serves the earth tends to neglect humanity; but the one who serves God is sensitive to the needs of both humanity and the earth, for that person will think as God does, and God is concerned for His entire creation.

Tenth, theocentrism produces a holistic view of life. Not only is everything interpreted by our concept of God, but everything is related by virtue of its being created by God. There simply cannot be divergent and incompatible elements in the original creation, for it would be incongruous with the unity of God. Thus theocentrism corresponds to the ecological concept of interrelatedness, since the one Creator made the universe as a single harmonious whole that can only function properly when it functions together and in harmony with the Fountainhead and Sustainer of all life. That is, the cosmic community functions best when it reflects the unity of its Designer.

Theocentrism is truly revolutionary in that it completely undermines the framework for modern values. Humanity is not the center of the universe; God did not create the earth merely for human utility, and humans do not have the authority to legislate values, to take life, or to rape the environment. There is a

Higher Power to whom we all must bow. God alone is the Determiner of values, purpose, meaning, rights, and ethics. God is the Source and Sustainer of all life, the sovereign Ruler of creation, and the One who by His Spirit will bring harmony to His creation. Only when God is recognized as supreme can we find our true place in the cosmic order, and in finding our true place we find ourselves and the meaning of the whole. If we seek a center that does not transcend ourselves or the natural order, then life on this planet is bound to degenerate at the hands of a confused and floundering species. Theocentrism provides a creation wisdom that not only answers the basic questions of existence but also gives hope for the environment and offers a realistic framework to analyze the environmental crisis.

Biblical Support for Theocentrism

It is a common misconception to assume that the Bible teaches anthropocentrism, that nature was created for the sake of humanity and the human race is the zenith of creation. True biblical Christianity is anything but anthropocentric. The Christian Scriptures emphatically declare that God created the heavens and earth for His glory and that the pinnacle of creation is paradise where the entire created realm exists in perfect peace and harmony.

Perhaps the most forceful statement for theocentrism over against anthropocentrism is found in God's response to Job. Job's confronting God with the evidence of his case implied that Job had rights that God must acquiesce to, as if humans are really the center of the universe and can make claims against God. After lengthy discussions between Job and his friends, God arrived on the scene as a voice out of the whirlwind. He talked about nature and about creating and controlling all things by His sovereign power. He talked about the wonders of nature and delighting in all that He had made, even the rain that waters the "land where no man lives" (38:26). He caused Job to ponder His position in the cosmic order by asking, "Where were you when I laid the earth's foundation?" (38:4). Job finally realized the narrowness of his own thinking, submitted to God's authority, and abandoned his anthropocentric outlook (40:1-3). There is hope for the environment, and that hope partially rests on us. We all need to be broken and humbled as Job was and to recognize the centrality of God in everything we do.

David acknowledged the centrality of God as he praised his Lord:

> Yours, O Lord, is the greatness and the power

> and the glory and the majesty and the splendor,
> for everything in heaven and earth is yours.
> Yours, O Lord, is the kingdom;
> you are exalted as head over all (1 Chron. 29:11).

Even Nebuchadnezzar recognized the centrality of God, saying:

> All the peoples of the earth
> are regarded as nothing.
> He does as he pleases
> with the powers of heaven
> and the peoples of the earth.
> No one can hold back his hand
> or say to him: "What have you
> done?" (Dan. 4:35).

Jesus encouraged us to depend on God rather than on self for our sustenance and for solutions to our problems. "Seek first his kingdom and his righteousness, and all these things will be given to you as well" (Matt. 6:33). John the Baptist recognized the proper role of humanity in God's order of things, "The one who comes from above is above all; the one who is from the earth belongs to the earth, and speaks as one from the earth" (John 3:31).

Paul set forth a theocentric perspective in his doxology closing the first section of the Epistle to the Romans: "For from him and through him and to him are all things. To him be the glory forever! Amen!" (11:36). This thought is reiterated in 1 Corinthians 8:6, "Yet for us there is but one God, the Father, from whom all things came and for whom we live; and there is but one Lord, Jesus Christ, through whom all things came and through whom we live." For Paul the exaltation of humanity was tantamount to blasphemy, "May I never boast except in the cross of our Lord Jesus Christ" (Gal. 6:14). Paul returned to his theocentric theme in Colossians 1:16, "All things were created by him and for him." In 1 Timothy 6:15 Paul called God the "only Ruler." God was at the center of Paul's thought, not humanity, not nature.

Thinking Theocentrically

It is inevitable that we as human beings perceive the world as human beings. Yet the child of God, who is bringing every thought captive to Christ (2 Cor. 10:5) and who strives to have the mind of Christ (Phil. 2:5), is not to be governed by the anthropocentric inclination within to go his or her own selfish way. The renewed mind no longer values things by their human utility but rather by God's perception of their value. Even though we see through human eyes, those eyes must see with the mind of

Christ, recognizing God's value and purpose in all things. Because our vision is clouded by our selfish disposition, we often fail to comprehend the cosmic whole as seen by God. Our problem is that the regeneration of the heart does not automatically bring with it the necessary transformation of our minds to view creation as God does. Converts are often plagued by hangovers from previous modes of thinking.

As we let the mind of Christ dwell in us, we will no longer think anthropocentrically and therefore have no need to turn to biocentrism or seek to merge biocentrism into Christianity. The evils of a human-centered worldview can only be disposed of as we are transformed by the renewing of our minds (Rom. 12:2). The idea of renewing suggests that humanity's thinking once had God at the center. Paul's plea is that we reclaim the prelapsarian theocentric vision that saw everything through God's eyes. A Christian who thinks theocentrically will be concerned about what God is concerned about, and God is very concerned about the environment. When God looks down from heaven, He sees more than humanity. This line of reasoning led Vincent Rossi to end one of his essays with the thought-provoking statement: "To be Christian is to be ecologist."[34]

7

THE COURSE AND DESTINY OF ECOHISTORY: DOOMSDAY, UTOPIA, OR KINGDOM?

From a biblical perspective, the present ecological state is abnormal, the abnormality being due to human sin. It is significant that a theocentric position does not burden us with the entire task of rectifying our mistakes. We are not alone in the universe but assisted by a loving, gracious God. It is ultimately by God's power that the conditions of Eden will be restored, rather than by the dubious wisdom, scientific achievements, or technology of the human race. The cosmos is not headed toward an ecological doomsday, nor toward an ecological utopia brought about by human ingenuity, but toward a divinely restored kingdom with the triune God reigning in peace and righteousness.

The Garden of Eden

The garden of Eden depicts conditions of perfect peace and harmony in the cosmos. It exemplifies harmony of relationships between humanity, nature, God, and the luxuriant vegetation that is possible when all relations are in proper order (Gen. 2:9;

3:7). The unmarred ecological conditions depicted by the garden naturally preclude death. This is implied from the vegetarian diet prescribed for both humans and animals (Gen. 1:29-30; see Gen. 9:3) and from descriptions of the restored state where "there will be no more death" (Rev. 21:4). Whether or not the garden of Eden is taken literally, one must admit that it represents harmonious conditions that are beyond the present knowledge of ecological science and that the hope of a restored Eden far exceeds the ecological expectations of the most optimistic environmentalist. Within a theocentric framework, such conditions are entirely feasible.

If the garden is taken literally, the question arises whether it occupied a specific locale or whether it pervaded the entire earth. Genesis 2:8 seems to imply that it was a specially created paradise of peace and harmony and that outside of the garden conditions may have been different: "God had planted a garden in the east, in Eden; and there he put the man he had formed." When Adam fell, he was expelled from the garden "to work the ground from which he had been taken" (Gen. 3:23). It is obvious that the garden and the earth were not coextensive. We should note that the garden and Eden were not coextensive either. God planted a garden in the east, in Eden (2:8). Eden could be interpreted as the proper name of a region in which God planted the garden. Some suggest that the name is derived from a similar sounding root, meaning "delight." Others interpret Eden as a common noun derived from a Sumerian word meaning "plain" or "steppe." Whether God planted the garden in the region known as Eden or in the eastern plains, the fact remains that Eden and the garden were not coextensive, thus supporting the thesis that the garden did not cover the entire earth. This might allow for death prior to the fall outside the garden, a topic we will return to shortly.

Some, such as Gerhard von Rad, question the idea of a perfect paradise. In commenting on Genesis 2:15 von Rad remarked that the task to work the garden "and preserve it from all damage" suggests "a destiny that contrasts decidedly with the commonly accepted fantastic ideas of 'Paradise.'"[1] It is questionable whether the idea of protecting against danger is intended in the context. The word *shamar*, translated "keep" in the *King James Version*, often takes the meaning of "safekeeping what belongs to another." Yet this does not fully settle a potential problem. If the garden had to be looked after, then in what sense is it to be considered perfect? Some suggest that the earth was created in partial completeness and was dependent on us to continue its creation and to bring it to perfection. A better alternative is to view creation in a state of relative perfection, meaning that it still needed to be sustained. God did not create something that was self-sustaining, but something that was dependent on Him. That is, God did not create another God. Creation is perfect in every regard except that it is contingent or not self-sustaining. This would imply that a perpetual state of ecological harmony cannot exist in a contingent world without a sustaining influence external to it. Genesis records God's enlisting the services of humanity to join Him in the process of sustaining harmony in creation.

The Fall

The fall of the human race as recorded in Genesis 3 paints a grim picture of a crisis in Eden. The harmonious relations that existed on earth were shattered by human disobedience. Behind that willful act of disobedience lay the disruptive qualities of greed, pride, arrogance, and selfishness. Whenever these negative forces emerge, they shatter any peace and tranquility present. As a result the lush and tranquil garden turned into an unyielding and harsh desert. The consequences of the fall involve every aspect of life, whether religious, social, ecological, or economic. The following expounds on some of these consequences.

The Multiplicity of Alienations

Sin shattered the peace and tranquility of the garden as humanity and nature alike became estranged from the multiplicity of relationships that made life the joy it should be. Humans became alienated from God by their disobedience (theological alienation); alienated from one another, as shown by the hatred and bloodshed that followed (sociological alienation); alienated from nature, as depicted by the curse on the ground (ecological alienation); and finally alienated from themselves (psychological alienation). As Bruce Birch said, "Sin is not a matter internal to human life. It breaks the *shalom* intended by God in creation."[2]

One reason all relationships that relate to us are broken when we disobey God is that the same attitude that severs the divine-human relationship severs all others. Arrogance, self-centeredness, and greed tend to fracture any relation. Harmony cannot coexist with such negative dispositions. This attitude eventually destroys everything it touches, including ourselves, since it turns every relation into an arena of hostility. This is especially true of the human-nature relation; as peace is shattered, nature becomes an enemy, an object fit only for aggression and conquest. There are elements of truth in the Japanese Zen philosopher D. T. Suzuki's comment regarding the biblical state after the fall: "Man is against God, Nature is against God, and Man and Nature are against each other. God's own likeness (Man), God's own creation (Nature) and God Himself—all three are at war."[3] It would be better to say that humanity is at war with the other two, not God.

The irony of our grasping is that we end up losers. What is becoming painfully evident on the ecological scene is also true on the theological, sociological, and psychological scenes. Psychologically, we lost our true humanness and identity when we attempted to become something of our own making, for we cannot be what God intended us to be without all relationships in proper order. The search for self-actualization or the true self will never be fruitful without perceiving the holistic structure of a theocentric cosmos. We find ourselves at the end of our rope, having a deep-seated awareness of an ideal state of perfect harmony, yet torn by our self-grasping Adamic nature that defeats any attempt to repair our estrangements.

The Perversion of the Dominion Mandate

God intended that we rule over creation as His vice-gerent and govern in love and justice just as He would. Before the fall, this intent was being carried out, as all relations were in proper order. When Adam asserted his autonomy, he abandoned all responsibilities to God, including the charge to care for the earth. The human race began to look upon nature from its perspective rather than God's; that is, the race had undergone a paradigm shift from theocentrism to anthropocentrism. This primeval worldview shift twisted the dominion mandate from responsible stewardship to irresponsible exploitation, so that what was dominion now became domination. People disregarded their accountability to God and began to exploit the earth for self-interests and selfish gain. One need look no further for the cause of the environmental crisis.

In Psalm 8 we see where all creation was placed under our rule, to be cared for by us in a responsible manner. It is in this sense that we should also understand Psalm 115:16, "but the earth He has given to man." The rebellion against God twisted the commission to be caretaker into a license for exploitation. This is why in Hebrews 2:8 the author comments, "Yet at present we do not see everything subject to him." We are not fulfilling the assignment God delegated to us. It is Christ, as the next verse makes clear, who has conquered the death principle, thus enabling us to live out our intended role.

The Ramifications of Autonomy

The story of the fall is the story of our dethroning God as the supreme authority of values and ethics and enthroning ourselves. By rebelling against God's order, we have set ourselves up as the final authority regarding right and wrong. This could be what is meant by the tree of the knowledge of good and evil (Gen. 2:17; 3:3,5). By eating its fruit, Adam would become like God in that he now decides what is morally proper.[4]

Ironically, the quest for autonomy has plummeted humans into a twofold ethical dilemma. They not only lose contact with the universal reference point for ethics and meaning but also become depraved creatures who cannot rise above their own egoism and self-centeredness to construct a workable ethics for themselves and the environment. They have chosen to go their own way, and that choice plagues every effort they make to correct their problems. Humans have taken responsibility for the moral governance of the world upon their shoulders and are teetering under the weight of a burden they were not expected to carry. By disposing of God, they not only lose all sense of meaning of the whole but also plunge into a sea of moral relativity, in which they make up the rules as they go along.

What happens, as Paul graphically portrays in Romans 1:18-32, is a deepening moral degradation of society. Value structure and ethical standards both become subject to the whim of the fallen human race. This loss of ethical mooring naturally leads to the destruction of the environment and mistreatment of fellow humans. Nature and humanity alike become devalued and subject to the caprice of a secular ethic. Just as Adam and Eve decided for themselves that it was proper to eat of the fruit of the tree, so people today are deciding for themselves that it is proper to place their own values on nature and others and turn both into objects for exploitation. It is obvious that our autonomous society treats creation as if it were also autonomous and liberated from the value assigned by God. As people cut themselves and nature off from God, everything loses its frame of reference and becomes meaningless. The human race is suddenly up to its neck in the quicksand of freedom. Without an infinite reference point, everything becomes absurd. The environmental misery that confronts us is not the result of theism but a departure from theism.

The Curse on the Ground

God told Adam,

> "Because you listened to your wife and ate
> from the tree about which I commanded you,

> 'You must not eat of it,'
> Cursed is the ground because of you;
> through painful toil you will eat of it
> all the days of your life.
> It will produce thorns and thistles for you,
> and you will eat the plants of the field.
> By the sweat of your brow
> you will eat your food
> until you return to the ground" (Gen. 3:17-19).

It is clear from Scripture that nature was affected by the fall and that the curse on the ground marks a relational skewing between humanity and the earth. The problem is to comprehend the precise cause-effect relation. Is the curse on the ground to be understood as a direct pronouncement of God or the natural consequence of humanity's deviant behavior? That is, did God directly cause a change in the ground and vegetation so that they would not yield as before, or did God indirectly allow a change in productivity by letting humanity's chosen path take its natural course?

In the first segment of Genesis 3:17, God said, "Cursed is the ground because of you." The wording is ambiguous. It could mean that the ground will produce poorly because of divine action or human abuse. In either case the notion of a curse as judgment is upheld, either direct or indirect. Yet one cannot ignore the potency of a divine pronouncement nor the Hebrew notion that a curse carried with it the power to make it happen. Behind the utterance in Genesis 3 stands the omnipotent God, the God who spoke things into existence (Heb. 11:3), who healed with the spoken word (Matt. 8:8), and who pronounced a curse on a barren fig tree and it withered to the ground (Mark 11:14,20-21). This suggests that the curse is more than merely the natural consequences of human abuse of nature.

It is very appealing today with crimes against the environment making headlines to interpret God's curse on the ground as indirectly resulting from human wrongdoing. The authors of *Earthkeeping in the Nineties* contend that "the ground is cursed because we are set against it. . . . In short, the curse describes not a quality in the earth itself, but human misuse of dominion."[5] Granberg-Michaelson agreed, saying, "Adam's disobedience does not intrinsically change the character of God's good creation. Instead, the picture presented is that human rebellion will infect and mar the creation; yet God's grace acts to restore the proper fellowship between God, humanity, and all creation."[6] If the curse represents the natural consequences of our abuse of the environment, then Paul's statement in Romans 8:20, "the one who subjected it," must refer to us (represented by Adam) rather than God. That is, God did not subject the earth to futility, we did.[7] The intrinsic goodness of creation, however, can be maintained without having to dissipate the curse into "human misuse."

Traditionally, the curse on the ground has been understood as a direct action of God in which He holds back the natural productivity of the land. Genesis 5:28-29 reads, "When Lamech had lived 182 years, he had a son. He named him Noah and said, 'He will comfort us in the labor and painful toil of our hands caused by the ground the Lord has cursed.'" The unproductiveness of the ground was not only attributed to God but also characteristic of the antediluvian era. The antediluvian unproductiveness could not be the result of pollution from modern technology or centuries of harmful agricultural practices.

The history of the Hebrew people and their land also supports the notion that God directly administers curses. When Israel sinned, the land mourned and did not yield its fruit. When Israel obeyed Yahweh, the land rejoiced and produced a bountiful supply. The Hebrew writers attributed these variations to the working of Yahweh. Isaiah, for example, sets forth the Hebrew concept of divine environmental retribution in chapter 24. "The Lord is going to lay waste the earth and devastate it; he will ruin its face and scatter its inhabitants" (v.1). The reason for this environmental retribution is:

> The earth is defiled by its people;
> they have disobeyed the laws,
> violated the statues
> and broken the everlasting covenant.
> Therefore a curse consumes the earth;
> its people must bear their guilt
> (vv. 5-6).

Romans 8:20-21 also tends to support the traditional view: "For the creation was subjected to frustration, not by its own choice, but by the will of the one who subjected it, in hope that the creation itself will be liberated from its bondage to decay and brought into the glorious freedom of the children of God." The agent that caused creation to be subjected is not stated, which leads some to contend that humans, by their irresponsible environmental behavior, have subjected creation to bondage. Against this is the parallelism of the two passive verbs. The same One who subjected creation to bondage will be the One who liberates it from that bondage. Traditional understanding recognizes God alone as the Liberator and Savior of humankind and all creation.

The biblical evidence supports the idea that God directly cursed non-human aspects of creation as part of the judgment upon the human race. The curse did not change the inherent quality of nature, only its relational status. With the fractured harmony of the original ecosystem, the death process began for all creation, and the present ecological structure emerged. Because of the integrity of the created order, God could not have pronounced death upon humans and not include the rest of creation. Paul says in Romans 8:22 that all creation groans, being under the curse.

The most common interpretation of the thorns and thistles according to the direct-curse view is that they did not exist before the fall, but God created them as a form of judgment to plague human efforts at cultivating the land. Other alternatives congruous with the direct-curse view include: (1) the prior existence of thorns and thistles in a less bothersome condition, (2) a divine modification of existing species that produced thorns and thistles, (3) the symbol of weeds in general that God introduced to hinder agriculture, or (4) the symbol of the difficulty of reaping a harvest from the ground. Whatever the exact meaning, it is clear that it depicts the unyieldingness of the new condition. Adam could no longer sit in the shade of the garden and pick fruit off the trees. He must now labor under the hot sun (by the sweat of his brow) to eke out a living. God's curse should be understood as His easing up on His sustaining influence on the natural order so that it begins the process of disease and decay. As such, the curse affects relations within the creation order, not the quality of creation. God's creation remains intrinsically good.

Genesis 6 describes the impact of human sin on the earth: "The earth also was corrupt before God, and the earth was filled with violence. And God looked upon the earth, and, behold, it was corrupt; for all flesh had corrupted his way upon the earth" (vv. 11-12, KJV). Bernhard Anderson argued that all flesh "refers to all that is fleshly, including birds, animals, humans."[8] He draws on the meaning of the identical expression in the same context where God resolved "to destroy all flesh, wherein is the breath of life, from under heaven; and every thing that is in the earth shall die" (6:17, KJV). Violence, death, and corruption, whether speaking socially or ecologically, is like a cancerous disease that cannot be contained. Once it starts, it spreads throughout creation as a killing blight. And as Anderson remarked, "The biblical story makes the reader face one uncomfortable truth: the violence that corrupted 'all flesh' is traced to the noblest creatures of God's creation, those whom God elevated to the highest position of honor and responsibility."[9]

If all creation is suffering under a divine curse, then it might be inferred that nature is also in a fallen state and that there was a cosmic fall; but if so, nature's fall cannot be analogous to the fall of humanity. Nature is not morally responsible and could not fall on account of its own crime. It might be better to say that humanity morally fell, and nature was implicated in that fall, not that nature fell. It is only in this sense that we can speak of a cosmic fall and the need for a cosmic salvation. The solidarity of humanity and the environment necessitates the idea of a cosmic disordering as the result of Adam's sin and a cosmic reordering through the work of Christ (Col. 1:20).

This perspective retains the inherent value and goodness of nature. There is no evil in nature that precipitated its fall, nor did the curse render the physical realm evil and something to be shunned. Joseph Campbell remarked that the "story of the Fall in the Garden sees nature as corrupt; and that myth corrupts the whole world for us. . . . You get a totally different civilization and a totally different way of living according to whether your myth presents nature as fallen or whether nature is in itself a manifestation of divinity."[10] This is a monstrous misconception of the biblical narrative. Nature lost neither its value nor its inherent goodness; God still values it, and we are still responsible for taking care of it.

The Pronouncement of Death

In Genesis 2:17, God told Adam and Eve that in the day they ate of the tree of the knowledge of good and evil they would surely die. Paul says in Romans 5:12, "Therefore, just as sin entered the world through one man, and death through sin, and in this way death came to all men, because all sinned." He went on to speak of death reigning through Adam and life reigning through Christ (5:17). It is obvious that death is a result of the fall. But what did Paul mean by death? Also, does the death pronounced on humankind, however one perceives it, imply that the rest of creation died also?

The Kind of Death. Death could be understood literally as biological death, metaphorically as the severing of relations with God, or both. Theistic evolutionists argue for metaphorical death. What resulted from Adam's sin was separation from God, not biological death, for biological death had previously existed, being part of the created order. It is noted that Adam did not physically die the day he ate the fruit; he was, however, driven from the garden. Thus what came upon humanity as a result of Adam's sin was separation from God and the consequential severing of other relations, not physical death. This relational death will be the last enemy conquered as Christ restores all things back to peace and harmony (1 Cor. 15:26).[11]

The metaphorical aspect was hardly in view when God told Adam that "dust you are and to dust you will return" (Gen. 3:19). It seems as if the curse included physical death on humanity and by extension to the rest of creation. Also, Paul's argument in 1 Corinthians 15, which parallels that of Romans 5, suggests physical death: "For as in Adam all die, so in Christ all will be made alive" (v. 22). The context of the Corinthian passage clearly pertains to physical death and a physical resurrection. Paul's being in danger of death every day due to the enemies of the cross cannot be construed metaphorically as broken relations (1 Cor. 15:30-32). Nor can the transition from the physical body of flesh to a resurrected body be taken any other way except as a physical death (1 Cor. 15:35-44). The last enemy to be conquered must mean biological death.

The death God speaks of as the consequence of eating the forbidden fruit (Gen. 2:17) therefore includes both literal and metaphorical death, both the death of the body and the death of relationships. The two cannot be separated. Cutting vital relations with one's life-support system commences the degeneration processes that culminate in physical death. This ecological concept permeates the entire Bible. It is obvious that Adam did not physically die immediately upon eating the forbidden fruit. What happened was that Adam severed his relations with the Creator, the Fountainhead of the earth's life-support system, and the death process commenced. Life cannot be sustained apart from maintaining proper relations with the rest of the cosmic ecosystem, which, as mentioned before, must include the Giver and Sustainer of all life, God Himself. Life can only be sustained as one is in continual communion with the living God. This implies that Adam never possessed immortality as part of his essence; he was always a contingent being, dependent on maintaining proper relations with God for his prelapsarian "immortality."

The Extent of Death. Some argue that since the garden was confined to a specific locale rather than being worldwide, its conditions of immortality likewise were not pervasive over the earth.[12] This implies that physical death did prevail outside the garden and allows the possibility of God's employing evolution as the means of bringing life to its present state. Death, then, would be part of the original created order and included in God's recognition that creation was good (Gen. 1:31).

Several observations militate against this position. First, Genesis 1:29-30 suggests that animals were not carnivorous anywhere before the fall. God told Adam, "I give you every seed-bearing plant on the face of the whole earth and every tree that has fruit with seed in it. They will be yours for food." The next verse specifies that every green plant was also given to animals for food. The implication is that every animal on the earth was herbivorous, not simply in the garden.

Second, the garden was indeed unique. The context of Genesis 2 implies that this uniqueness should apply to the vegetation and climatological features rather than to the presence or absence of death. Absence of death is a function of relationship, not of locality.

Third, the original creation is the archetype of the new creation where there will be no death of any kind (1 Cor. 15:26,54-56). John wrote, "There will be no more death or mourning or crying or pain, for the old order of things has passed away" (Rev. 21:4). If the new creation has no death, neither did its archetype.[13] What constitutes the new order is not total destruction of the old but the conquest of the death principle. It is plausible to assume that although the garden did not extend over the entire earth, God's perfect ecological conditions did. The garden was a special place with unusually pleasant and lush conditions in which God placed Adam.

Fourth, Genesis 2:19-20 says that God brought every beast of the field and bird of the air into the garden for Adam to name. Evidently these animals freely came in and out of the garden. It would be rather fanciful to suggest that lions were carnivorous outside the garden and herbivorous inside, or at least refrained from eating other animals when in the garden.

Fifth, the contrasts between Genesis 1:29-30; 2:19-20 and Genesis 3:21; 9:2-3 strongly suggest that an abnormal state had developed on the earth, a state characterized by death and violence. Even the violence that characterizes nature as "red in tooth and claw"[14] is abnormal. Perhaps this is why we recoil at the thought of death, any death. There is something deep within that says death is wrong and should not be. Biblically speaking, sin disrupted the normal state, severed vital relationships, and threw the entire cosmic ecosystem into disorder, decay, and death (see Rom. 6:23). Since death was now part of the postlapsarian order, God allowed animals to be killed for food and clothing, whereas before it was forbidden (Gen. 3:21; 9:2-3).

Most ecologists would contend that the absence of death is impossible because all life forms we know depend on the death of other life forms. Most notable are the complex food chains for both plants and animals, chains which are maintained by death and decay. The decaying animal and plant life provides nutrients for the soil to produce more growth. Insects feed upon other insects as well as plant life. Birds feed upon worms and insects. Fish feed upon plankton. Larger animals on smaller ones, and so on. It seems to be a universal law of ecology that life comes from death, meaning that life is sustained by the death of something else. This law, however, does not need to be absolute in a theistic universe. Scriptures teach that all life ultimately comes from and is sustained by the God of life. Death is the enemy of life, not its friend. It is true that life as we know it is partially sustained by the death of something else, but this certainly does not represent the ideal state. Just because the prelapsarian ecological harmony spoken of in Genesis is unknown in a postlapsarian world, and thus unknown to science, does not preclude the possibility of its being true.

Another objection to the absence of death before the fall is that the earth would quickly become overpopulated with life forms, especially those with short life cycles such as insects. This criticism neglects God's ability to sustain perfect order and harmony before the fall and to keep the numbers within balance. When the death process began, God no longer needed to control population growth in order to have a relatively stable ecosystem. Death would take care of it naturally. God's sustaining power could also answer the question of entropy before the fall. Most scientifically minded critics point to the consistency of the natural laws and presume that entropy must have been part of the original creation. If the universe were truly a closed system, this might be plausible. From a theistic point of view one must conclude that the universe is not a closed system and that the transcendent God does exert a sustaining influence on the created realm (Col. 1:17; Heb. 1:3). This influence most likely was greater before the fall. God's curse upon the ground is best explained by God's relaxing this controlling influence, allowing entropy to commence and thereby causing the earth to become unyielding apart from human toil.

One cannot presume that the processes observed in our ecosystem are the only ones possible. The portrait of Eden gives us a glimpse of a far grander ecosystem, one that depicts perfect cosmic harmony. To argue that the present ecosystem is the only one possible is to ignore the breakdown of relationships and the ensuing death that occur when one part of the cosmic community asserts complete autonomy from the rest. Since the continuity from the original creation to the present has been broken, uniformitarian arguments cannot be maintained.[15] We conclude that Adam plunged himself as well as the entire creation into mortality as he fell.

The Problem of Natural Evils

Natural calamities present somewhat of a problem for a theist. Because they are events in the natural realm, it would seem strange to regard them as consequences of a moral choice. If natural evils were not somehow linked with humanity's disobedience in the garden, then they must be part of the original creation, which would then implicate God as being unjust. Paul, however, inferred that natural calamities are abnormal and not part of the original creation, for the whole creation is now groaning and travailing in pain (Rom. 8:22). Although God has in the past directly caused natural calamities as judgment against humanity (Gen. 6:7; Isa. 45:7), it would be unwarranted to regard all natural catastrophes in this way.

One way to interpret natural evils by the integrity model is to view the universe as a unit that can only function properly when it functions in harmony. Any disruption of this harmony would ripple throughout the cosmos, causing other relations to be impaired. Thus, when Adam sinned, a chain reaction of disruptions was started that eventually reached the workings of the physical universe. Human sin would be analogous to throwing a wrench into a smoothly running engine. It may still run, but not like it did before. Along the same lines, C. F. D. Moule suggested that natural calamities might be due to the cumulative effect of sin in the world. Since the whole system is one interlocking whole, human disobedience caused "strains and distortions in the world's fabric by manipulating the ecology of the world." Thus collectively we are indirectly responsible for upsetting "the whole system of interlocking movements in all the world." Moule maintained that natural disasters and disease existed before humans appeared and therefore cannot be due entirely to the fall. It is only those that affect people that we are collectively responsible for.[16]

Another explanation of natural evils could be found by linking the curse with the concept of the integrity of creation. It is entirely feasible to view today's disasters as the natural consequence of God's relaxing His sustaining influence over the processes of nature. This was done as a judgment against humanity to make cultivation difficult. Because of the interrelatedness of nature, the natural forces were also implicated, causing earthquakes, floods, hurricanes, and volcanoes.

The network of relations broken at the fall therefore includes not only the human-nature relation but also the nature-nature relation. Nature pollutes and destroys the environment as much as people, with hurricanes and tornadoes devastating the landscape, toxic gasses pouring from volcanoes, and even millions of tons of the greenhouse-producing gas methane coming from ingestion activity of grazing animals, such as cattle and sheep, and from termites. Millions of innocent animals and people are killed annually as a result of natural disasters. The entire creation has been thrown into a state of disorder as a result of the fall.[17] If natural disasters arose as a corollary to God's agricultural curse on the ground, then they will vanish when the curse is lifted and God rejuvenates the earth.

Redemption

Redemption pertains to persons or things that are in bondage and need to be set free. The whole creation, as Paul says, is in bondage to the curse and subject to decay (Rom. 8:20-21). The victory of the cross is the victory over the death principle (1 Cor. 15:54-57). The broken relations of the cosmic ecosystem that bring about decay and death have been mended by the Great Physician. The work of Christ has reversed the degenerating process initiated with the act of Adam and has commenced the healing process. When death is totally destroyed through the power of Christ, paradise will be restored, and perfect harmony, peace, and immortality will return to creation. There is no return to Eden unless the death principle is conquered, and the only way the death principle can be conquered is along the path that leads through Calvary.

A Cosmic Salvation

The heart of the Christian message is salvation. Although traditionally this has been understood in terms of human salvation, the Scriptures present a much broader concept. It is obligatory on the Christian community, especially considering today's growing environmental problems, to articulate the concept of a cosmic salvation. In the Old Testament, *salvation* basically meant deliverance from bondage, disease, trouble, or enemies. The idea of deliverance carries over into the New Testament but with spiritual and moral connotations. A cosmic understanding views both humanity and nature as being overpowered by the forces of decay and death and in need of divine healing. This does not remove the idea of human sin from soteriological discussion; instead it moves it into the forefront, for it is sin that fractures relations and leads to the dying of the planet.

Salvation can no longer be limited to humanity.[18] Because humans are bound together with the rest of creation, what happens to one happens to the other. Just as nature was implicated in the fall, so will it be included in the restoration. The destiny of nature is therefore inseparably linked with the destiny of the human race. Christ's work on the cross was intended to restore every consequence of Adam's sin and heal every broken relationship, including those that affect nature. This means that "the gospel has implications of good news for nature as well as for man."[19] Christ's victory over the death principle is the promise of a new life for all creation. Salvation then cannot be complete without the salvation of nature.

Paul often referred to the cosmic significance of Christ's sacrifice (Rom. 8:18-21; Col. 1:20; Eph. 1:10). In Colossians 1:20 Paul wrote, "And through him to reconcile to himself all things, whether things on earth or things in heaven." Implicit in this passage is that the entire created order is estranged from God and needs to be reconciled. Ephesians likewise speaks of bringing "all things in heaven and on earth together under one head, even Christ" (1:10). A similar expression is found in Philippians 2:10, "At the name of Jesus every knee should bow, in heaven and on earth and under the earth."

The notable addition in the Philippians passage is "under the earth," a metaphorical reference to the realm of the infernal. This was omitted in the Colossians and Ephesians passages. It might be inferred from this that the phrase "all things" has reference to the entire animate and inanimate creation excepting those conscious creatures that refuse to be part of the cosmic order. The Scriptures clearly teach that those who reject God's invitation to participate harmoniously in the community of creation will be displaced. The term *cosmic salvation* therefore does not imply the Teilhardian notion of cosmic universalism.

A cosmic salvation is not as alien as it might seem. Peter remarked that God sent Christ into the world on a two-phase mission, to redeem the world and to usher in the times of refreshing (Acts 3:19-21). Christ is to remain in heaven until the second phase, in which He will return and "restore everything." God's objective for the incarnation was to restore all relationships in creation, not simply to save humanity from damnation. When relationships are restored, healing will occur, and a new creation will emerge, one that reflects the wholeness, balance, and harmony it once enjoyed. Just as Christ was the active agent in the original creation (John 1:1-3), so is He the active agent in the new creation.

The Redemption of the Physical

The redemption of the physical world can be understood by analogy to human redemption. When we are redeemed, our whole being is restored. This includes both our physical bodies and our souls, as implied by the doctrine of the resurrection (1

Cor. 15). The resurrection affirms God's value on the material creation and implies that it is part of His redemptive plan. For Christians to shun the physical because of some preconceived association with evil and to view salvation as pertaining only to the soul is to court Gnostic and Neoplatonic dualism that equates matter with evil.

Throughout the Old Testament, redemption was seen in light of physical deliverance and a physical restoration of land, animals, and plant life to its prelapsarian conditions. A passage that points to restored peace among the animal kingdom is Hosea 2:18:

> In that day I will make a covenant for them
> with the beasts of the field and the birds of the air
> and the creatures that move along the ground.
> Bow and sword and battle
> I will abolish from the land,
> so that all may lie down in safety.

This return-to-Eden motif reflects a strong creation theology in Jewish thought that values the peace of the original creation and rejects as abnormal the violence and destruction in the present order. Jewish messianic expectations were not for a redeemer of the soul but for a redeemer of the earth. The new creation had primarily cosmic and physical dimensions rather than personal and spiritual ones.

The Ministry of Reconciliation

The word *reconciliation* refers to the breaking down of barriers and the restoring of harmony between two parties. It is obvious that one of our greatest needs is to be reconciled with the environment. What is not so obvious to many is the greater need to be reconciled with the Creator. True reconciliation with the environment cannot be realized without a prior reconciliation with God through Christ (Col. 1:20). Paul mentioned that God has entrusted to believers the ministry of reconciliation, to do our part in healing the broken relations that are making shambles of life (2 Cor. 5:18).

The empowering agent in the ministry of reconciliation is the Holy Spirit.[20] The Spirit enables believers to live out a redeemed life-style and manifest a prelapsarian harmony in every relation. Through the efficacy of the divine Spirit, the redeemed will be helping to heal a broken world and to realize the divine intent in creation. For a professing child of God to claim the indwelling Spirit and show a lack of concern for others and for nature is an utter contradiction. How can the Spirit mend one's broken relation with God without affecting other broken relations? All relations are interconnected and are all healed by the working of the Spirit in and through our lives. This is true reconciliation.

Basic to healing of any relationship is the victory over the sin principle, for it is sin that breaks bonds and engenders death. This is something we cannot accomplish by our own strength. As Paul cried out in desperation for God to deliver him (Rom. 7:24), we must seek God's help to deliver us from that deep-seated disposition that is feeding the flames of death. Paul argued that this victory can only come through the efficacy of the Holy Spirit (Rom. 8:1-4). Total harmony in creation, however, will not occur until all submit to Christ and receive His Spirit, something that cannot realistically be expected in the present age. Nevertheless, the Spirit is willing to help us fulfill our God-given task of caretakers of the earth and mend whatever relations we touch, thus leading to partial healing and reconciliation of current dislocations.

The New Creation

The new creation must be seen in light of the original creation, the archetype of ecological harmony and destiny. The tranquillity of the garden, with an absence of war, hate, hostility, and death, exemplifies the new creation. The new creation has partially come into existence now as the redeemed manifest the harmony of the new creation by the Spirit of Christ (Rom. 8:1-4; 2 Cor. 5:17). As a peaceful disposition is realized in our lives, it will inevitably spill over to nature as well. Expressed another way, when Christians become truly Christlike, everything they touch will be influenced with the peace of Christ. It is this new humanity that will help usher in a new creation.

The new creation commences when the wounds about us begin to be healed. It would be unbiblical to suggest that the new creation begins only after Christ returns. As Schaeffer said, "Christians who believe the Bible are not simply called to say that 'one day' there will be healing, but that by God's grace, upon the basis of the work of Christ, substantial healing can be a reality here and now."[21] Schaeffer commented on his choice of "substantial" saying that "it conveys the idea of a healing that is not *perfect*, but that is real, evident, and substantial."[22] Although the regeneration process Christ initiated will be fulfilled at the end of the age, to live in defiance of this process and claim the name of Christ is contradictory. Christians are morally obligated to live a redeemed life-style that displays harmony with God, fellow humans, and with nature. Schaeffer remarked, "When the church puts belief into practice, in man *and in nature*, there is substantial healing."[23]

This substantial healing could be inferred from the wording in Romans 8:21-22: "The creation itself will be liberated from its bondage to decay and brought into the glorious freedom of the children of God. We know that the whole creation has been groaning as in the pains of childbirth right up to the present time." What is clear about this passage is that humanity and nature share a common history. Both originated in a state of harmony and life, are presently in a state of disharmony and death, but will return together, by the grace of God, to their former state. Traditional understanding of this text points to a future time when the curse will be lifted and the children of God manifested in glory. This liberating of nature could begin once people are freed from their bondage to sin. This can be deduced from Paul's statement that nature has been in travail up to the present. Now that people are being set free, so is nature. It stands to reason that as we are regenerated, our redeemed conduct toward nature will further its healing as well. Nature is reborn as we are reborn. This interpretation does not negate the future aspect when the curse will be entirely lifted. Substantial healing and the beginnings of the new creation are possible now for both humans and nature.

Restoration

The Scriptures depict a future restoration of the earth in which Eden-like conditions once again flourish (Rev. 22:1-5; see Gen. 2:9-10). The return to Eden is the return to a perfect ecological state, without any disease, decay, or death. This conquest over death can only be achieved by the Creator of life (Isa. 25:8; 1 Cor. 15:25-26), a thought that precludes any notion that we can be the savior of nature. It is human arrogance to believe that our fallen race, especially in view of its blemished track record, can heal the earth and usher in an ecological utopia.

Restore or Replace?

The term *restoration* (see Acts 3:21) implies that the world will be transformed rather than completely annihilated and remade. Many ecologically minded writers have noted that the idea of annihilation tends to devalue the present creation and detract from environmental involvement. Granberg-Michaelson, for example, argued that the old order is completely transformed and restored so that Edenic conditions once again prevail: "In one sense, creation is totally new, unlike anything in our experience. Yet, it is the stuff of this creation that is so radically transformed; the physical material and creatures of this creation, of which we are a part, are made into a new creation, which is beyond our ability to describe rationally."[24]

Several Scriptures, such as 2 Peter 3:10-13 and Revelation 21:1, suggest a total annihilation of the old creation followed by an entirely new creation. This would mark a radical break in the continuity between the old and the new, with even the elements dissolving with fervent heat:

> The heavens will disappear with a roar; the elements will be destroyed by fire, and the earth and everything in it will be laid bare. . . . That day will bring about the destruction of the heavens by fire, and the elements will melt in the heat. But in keeping with his promise we are looking forward to a new heaven and a new earth, the home of righteousness (2 Pet. 3:10-13).

In Isaiah 51:6 the present state is depicted as a worn-out garment, no longer able to fulfill its intended use. The earth, like a worn-out garment, will be rolled up and exchanged (or changed) with the old being discarded (Ps. 102:26; Heb. 1:11-12). The image of exchanging an old garment for a new one tends to support the idea of a totally new earth. Some passages speak of this present order being in the process of passing away (1 Cor. 7:31; 1 John 2:17).

Passages that teach the earth is everlasting suggest that there will be a renewal rather than a replacement. The Psalms mention that the Lord established the earth forever (78:69), that the earth "can never be moved" (104:5), and that the heavenly bodies "will never pass away" (148:3-6). Quoheleth said, "Generations come and generations go, but the earth remains forever" (Eccl. 1:4). If the earth is going to be restored rather than replaced, then the phrase "pass away" in Matthew 24:35 would refer to the passing away or purging of worldliness rather than the physical creation. This seems to be supported by Paul's statement that it is only this world in its present form that is passing away (1 Cor. 7:31). John even defined what he meant by the world that is passing away: the cravings of sinful man, the lust of his eyes and the boasting of what he has and does" (1 John 2:16). The reference to earth's being laid bare (2 Pet. 3:10) also suggests that it continues.

It seems somewhat inconsistent for God to place such a high value on the created order and then utterly destroy it. What God desires to abolish are the effects of the fall on all life. This would include human sin, the curse, disease, entropy, physical death, and all alienations and estrangements within the creation community and between that community and God.

There is nothing that precludes the notion of a transformation of the existing earth once the metonymy of *world* is recognized. The term often represents the "worldly mind-set" that characterizes this age. With the purging of the worldly mind-set and other evil influences, the death principle that governs the present ecosystem will be destroyed, and the earth will once again experience the peace and harmony of the prelapsarian state. There will indeed be a cosmic reconciliation or, as the Scriptures phrase it, a new heaven and a new earth. Thus, it is not the earth itself that will be annihilated but those aspects that sever relations and cause death.

The analogy of the resurrection seems to suggest that there will be both a change and a continuity between the former existence and the new existence. The disciples on the road to Emmaus had difficulty recognizing the Lord after the resurrection, but later did (Luke 24:13-32). John, however, had no difficulty recognizing him from a fishing boat off shore (21:7-8). Paul argued that the resurrected body bears some marks of continuity with the former, just as a seed contains the pattern for the plant; yet it will be different (1 Cor. 15:35-49). The resurrection of the Lord is the promise of a new creation, not only for us, but also for all creation (Acts 3:18-21). The power that raised Jesus from the grave now enables us to walk in newness of life and will fully restore us and the rest of creation as well at the end of the age. It is reasonable then to suppose that there will also be a continuity between the old and new earth; nevertheless, the new earth will be noticeably different.

What is annihilated therefore is the reign of sin and evil that mars God's creation, not the earth itself. By purging these, God can completely restore the heavens and earth, fashioning them after His original creation. Figuratively, this purging is expressed by the common metaphor of fire (see 2 Pet. 3:10; 1 Cor. 3:12-15). As Granberg-Michaelson said,

> Thus, the Bible can speak of the world, existing under the mad rule of humanity, as being annihilated. But in the same way, the creation, originally fashioned to be God's, is brought into perfection at the end of time through the creative, saving work of Jesus Christ.[25]

The Stages of Renewal

The Scriptures clearly depict God as redeeming the land, lifting the curse, and bringing renewal. Restoration seemingly passes through two stages. The first or millennial stage will have conditions similar to Eden, though not exact (Isa. 5:13; Ezek. 36:35). Isaiah 51:3 says that the Lord "will make her deserts like

Eden, her wastelands like the garden of the Lord." Ezekiel utters the same idea, "This land that was laid waste has become like the garden of Eden" (36:35). God will send rains, and the deserts will blossom with flowers (Isa. 35:1-2) and trees (Isa. 41:18-19). The lifting of the curse is signified by the absence of thorns and briars (Isa. 55:13). The Scriptures are replete with allusions to the bountifulness of the restored land (for example, Isa. 30:23-26; Jer. 31:12-14; Joel 2:19-26). There will also be a return to a vegetarian diet among animals (Isa. 11:6-9; 65:25; Hos. 2:18) but perhaps not fully by people (Ezek. 43:22-27; 47:10).

There seems to be a difference between the millennial stage in which there will be aging and death (Isa. 65:20; Zech. 8:4) and the final stage that follows it in which there will be no death.[26] In addition, there will be sin during the millennial stage, for Christ will have to rule with a rod of iron. There will also be disease and drought (Zech. 14:12-17). Thus, the millennial stage cannot be considered to be restored Eden but an approximation of it and a foretaste of its full restoration. Much of the harmony of Eden will be restored, but it will not be perfect until the last enemy, death, is conquered (1 Cor. 15:26). The full restoration will come with the eternal state. It is then that the vision of *shalom* will be fully realized, and all relations restored.

The Dilemma of Millennial Expectations

The expectation of a literal return of Christ and a literal millennium often encourages neglect of nature rather than concern. Many Christians are more concerned with looking for God's intervention than working out Christ's redemption in all aspects of life. They are so consumed with aspirations with the next life that they often see no reason to be concerned with improving this life. Eschatological anticipation, in essence, becomes an avenue for escapism rather than involvement. This view is heightened when humanity is perceived to be saved apart from the rest of creation. The redeemed are headed toward heaven, leaving the corrupt earth behind for God's judgment. The earth becomes nothing more than a temporary place for testing one's loyalty. Once this physical level has served its purpose and the saints ascend to higher ground, it is no longer needed. After all, "This world is not my home, I'm just a passing thru."

For many Christians, sympathy for ecological concerns seems inconsistent with their belief in the imminent return of the Lord. If the world is going to be destroyed anyway, why should Christians worry about pollution and overflowing landfills? Eschatological expectations may even engender an exploitative attitude. Why conserve resources when this world is passing away and there is no certainty of future generations? For some, millennial expectations have even degenerated into a form of sadism in which the rise of evil and environmental destruction are joyful signs of the coming of the end.

The Bible depicts things getting progressively worse both in the moral and physical realms until the Lord returns to destroy all evil (see Matt. 24:4-14). Working to reverse this trend appears to be acting contrary to biblical prophecy and the divine plan. But if this reasoning were valid, then why try to combat pornography, abortion, social injustices, drug abuse, and the other evils of society, or why offer help to flood victims, refugees, the hungry, and the poor? Yet Jesus clearly taught His followers to be concerned and involved with social issues (for example, Matt. 25:34-40). To reject this is to cease being a true follower of Jesus. The same holds true for ecological concerns.

God expects His people to take care of the earth; yet at the same time the Bible predicts that the heavens and earth will be remade. Properly understood, this does not pose a tension between the present and future. God still loves His creation and is not going to destroy it. It is the evil principle that God hates and will purge as He remakes heaven and earth. God's eschatological intervention to purge the corrupting elements does not nullify our present responsibility for taking care of His creation. It should rather encourage the opposite. We are to assist in the purging of evil and the reclamation of the earth. The earth is still of value to God, and we are still to be faithful stewards, helping nature be all that God intended in face of the ever-present evil.

Even if God were to destroy the physical earth, it still should not induce neglect. Lack of concern for temporal things is contrary to the way we normally conduct our lives. We know that our buildings will not last forever; yet we spend considerable amounts of money to maintain them. We know that our bodies will end in the grave; yet we go to great effort to exercise and eat the proper diet. We know that our cars will one day join the ranks in the local auto graveyard, yet we do all we can to preserve them. Much of our preserving of temporary things is motivated by economic reasons or self-interest. As we think theocentrically regarding the preservation of the earth, a much grander motivation looms forward, that of honoring God's interests. Among the many reasons for God's wanting us to maintain the created order would be to allow nature to fulfill its intended purposes. Moreover, as we fulfill our ecological responsibility we emulate Christlikeness by showing compassion for all God's creatures, human and nonhuman alike.

Also, dispensationalism need not be contradictory to environmental concern and action. Dispensationalists should acknowledge what dispensation they are living in and live accordingly, rather than becoming so other-worldly minded that they disregard everything God intends for them to do except winning souls. Care for the environment, feeding the hungry, helping the poor, and showing compassion on the afflicted are still part of God's plan for this age. The next age has not arrived, and until it does the Christian is to be faithful fulfilling duties of the present age. Dispensationalists must also recognize that since the ecological mandate (Gen. 1:26-28) was given to all humanity before the fall, it is part of the created order and has universal validity for all dispensations.

The Biblical View of the Kingdom

A related problem for dispensationalists is that working in any way to enhance kingdom conditions on earth conflicts with their notion of kingdom. For most dispensationalists, the kingdom is entirely future and is ushered in only by an act of God.

The concept of kingdom could be understood as the geographical territory ruled by a monarch, or as the sovereign rule over the subjects of the kingdom, or both. The idea that the kingdom is entirely the spiritual rule of God in the hearts of believers has had its advocates since the early days of the church. There are many passages that speak of a spiritual dimension of a present kingdom (Luke 17:20-21; John 18:36; Rom. 14:17; Col. 1:13; and Rev. 1:5-6). There are also many references implying a physical dimension of an eschatological kingdom (Ps. 22:27-28; Isa. 2:4; 11:9; 35:1-10; Jer. 31:34; Mal. 1:11; and Rev. 20:4). When Peter spoke of the restitution of all things, he intended the physical to be included: "He must remain in heaven until the time comes for God to restore everything, as he promised long ago through his holy prophets" (Acts 3:21). The NRSV translates "restore everything" as "universal restoration." Other references that speak of all things being restored include Romans 8:21; 1 Corinthians 15:28; Ephesians 1:10; and Colossians 1:20. Thus it is highly reasonable to extend the kingdom concept "to comprehend the whole natural world."[27]

If we understand the image of the kingdom as the restoration of the harmony of the created order, then the kingdom must include both.[28] The kingdom of God reflects God's objective for creation history. His plan is to restore creation from the adverse effects of the fall, to purge it from all evil, disharmony, and death, to depose those who are illegally usurping authority, and to regain dominion over His creation.[29] The kingdom is both a present reality and a future expectation. It is, as commonly said, both now and not yet. The kingdom was inaugurated during the first advent of Christ but will not be consummated until His second advent.

George Ladd combined both the spiritual and physical to formulate a definition of the kingdom of God: "The sovereign rule of God, manifested in the person and work of Christ, creating a people over whom he reigns, and issuing in a realm or realms in which the power of his reign is realized."[30] Ladd limited the physical to the future aspect of the kingdom. God, however, expects the subjects of the present kingdom to submit to His rule and cooperate in restoring creation from the adverse effects of the fall in their own lives, in society, and in nature. The future state of restored Edenic conditions should be, as much as possible, a present reality as a semblance of the eschaton is realized in the thoughts and conduct of the church. Any other course of action for the redeemed amounts to a contradiction of terms; the only life worth living for the redeemed is a redeeming life. The present aspect of the kingdom, therefore, should not be limited to the spiritual dimension.

If any of the various aspects of the kingdom (spiritual, physical, present, and future) are denied, the idea of a kingdom becomes detrimental to a biblical theology of ecology. For example, if the kingdom is perceived as totally future, as many dispensationalists do, it will eventually lead to a dualism between the present and future with the present age being devalued. This in effect destroys all incentives for believers to instill kingdom principles into the present order. If the kingdom is perceived only as a present spiritual kingdom, as many amillennialists do, then the ecological implications of a theology of creation would collapse, and the idea of a restored Eden would lose all meaning. Furthermore, there would be no physical realm over which the King is to rule.[31]

The kingdom, as Moltmann said, is a "symbol of cosmic hope."[32] The hope of a restored paradise is not mere ecological idealism. It is based on the resurrection victory of Christ over the forces of death. Since Christ demonstrated He can conquer the death principle, there is a real hope that everything contributing to disharmony, disorder, decay, and death will be annihilated. The hope of the Christian and the hope of creation (Rom. 8:20-21) is therefore the same: that the entire created order will be restored to its prelapsarian peace and harmony by the same divine power that raised Christ from the grave. This brings our role into proper focus, for with limited knowledge and powers we cannot possibly hope to achieve an ideal ecological state. Any hope placed in human invention or philosophical wisdom will only lead to despair. The Christian hope rests in God, not humanity.

In summary, a proper view of the kingdom nurtures rather than hinders ecological responsibility. The kingdom advances as relations are restored and the new creation emerges. We need to realize "that a new creation is a distinct possibility"[33] in the present life (2 Cor. 5:17) and that this new creation pertains to more than the individual. Schwarz said, "The promise of the new creation, foreshadowed in the resurrection of Jesus Christ, can serve as a powerful stimulus."[34] Also, knowing that God will restore nature should heighten our appreciation and valuing of nature rather than the opposite.

Linear Versus Cyclical Concept of Time

In biblical thought, creation exists on a linear time scale. Both humanity and nature share a history and destiny that will not be repeated. Their beginning is marked by God's initial act of creation, and their destiny is determined by the new creation. Because this linear teleology is energized by a divine decree, it provides an optimistic outlook and a sense of direction and purpose. It also encourages active participation rather than passive acceptance of the circumstances and a defeatist attitude, dispositions which often surface when cyclical views are adopted. Since the consummation is a morally perfect state, absent of any death-causing elements, such as hatred, anger, and war, a linear teleology instills a moral obligation to live accordingly.

Eastern religions that promote a cyclical concept of time often convey a pessimistic and passive vision of life that generates ecological indifference. Everything is involved in a perpetually repeating cycle. If the whole cycle is going to repeat itself, why bother? All aspects of reality are as molecules of water being swept along by the river into the ocean, only to evaporate and repeat the cycle. Existence may be advancing by the natural law of cause and effect toward some unifying point, but that unifying point will only break down and start the long tedious process all over again. Such a notion of endless repetitions cannot be regarded as beneficial for the environment, since any effort one makes toward improvement is self-defeating. A world process that is destined only to repeat its agonizing history logically leads to indifference and despair. The very thought of trying to improve the environment becomes an absurdity. Christianity and its concept of linear time liberates us from the imprisonment of this mode of thinking and generates a sensitivity for all life.

This charge against cyclical time is often countered by referring to the Dharma in Hindu tradition in which good deeds are praiseworthy. Still it cannot be denied that the prevailing attitude of societies influenced by pantheistic thought is that of social and cultural apathy. The world is the way it is because of bad karma, and we must passively endure the pollution and injustice as a way of paying off the karmic debt. With a cyclic view of time and the law of karma, there are no ethical imperatives and no hope for the environment. The only hope is escape. True hope for the environment can exist with a linear view of time that looks toward a consummation of peace and harmony on earth.

Nevertheless, Christianity with its linear concept of time has often been blamed for fostering the modern attachment to progress. "Our daily habits of action," said Lynn White, "are dominated by an implicit faith in perpetual progress which was unknown either to Greco-Roman antiquity or to the Orient. It is rooted in, and is indefensible apart from, Judeo-Christian teleology." [35] Another writer remarks, "The linear, noncyclical character of Judeo-Christian millenarianism ensured the birth in Western (i.e., historical) man of a faith in infinite progress through myriads of years to come."[36]

The biblical notion of progress, however, differs radically from the secular notion. Biblical thought recognizes our finiteness and dependence on God for direction in healing. It defines progress as advancing toward the goal God intended. Secular progress, on the other hand, is propelled by such destructive elements as human greed, egocentrism, and materialism. These elements lead to a distorted view of progress that has for its underlying assumptions the unlimited consumption of raw materials and a continuously expanding economy. It defines progress as the increase of luxury and affluence for as many as possible. Secular progress is blind, always going somewhere, but not always knowing the consequences. Thus it can be very destructive.

What is needed is a new model of progress that does not play havoc with the environment and that offers a solution for the destructive demon of self-interest. The biblical model can provide exactly what is needed as it totally rejects the arrogance and destructive tendencies embedded in the secular notion of progress. In biblical thought, desirable direction focuses on the qualitative measure of health, peace, and harmony, rather than the quantitative measure of economic growth (see Rom. 14:17).[37] This direction honors the divine plan for creation and serves as a guideline for every aspect of life. The biblical model also recognizes human limitations, encourages humble dependence upon the Almighty, and affirms that God's grace is greater than our sins.

8

THE DOMINION MANDATE: EXPLOITATION OR STEWARDSHIP?

Ecological critics invariably refer to the dominion mandate in Genesis as a major cause of the environmental crisis. It is commonly understood as giving humans absolute rights and freedom to do as they wish with nature. God, however, never intended His injunction to be taken as a divine license to exploit and mistreat creation. Any such notion is a distortion of the biblical text.

Meaning of Dominion

In Genesis 1:28 God told Adam, "Be fruitful and increase in number; fill the earth and subdue it. Rule over the fish of the sea and the birds of the air and over every living creature that moves on the ground." Because these are the first words God spoke to humanity, they must be of paramount importance. The passage has often been labeled the cultural mandate, especially when viewed in conjunction with its restatement in Genesis 9:1-7 that seemingly expands it to social concerns (death penalty for murderers). However, as Schultz observed, this is an anthropocentric reading of the mandate, since it views nature as the raw material to construct human culture: "It fails to perceive that human vicegerency also has the purpose of promoting the welfare of nature."[1]

The mandate has nothing to do with the artifacts of human culture and should be considered as the ecological mandate, not the cultural mandate. God's concern when He finished creation was not our impacting society with theistic values, but taking care of what He had just finished making. This was preeminent on God's mind. The passage is erroneously used as a proof text to support a Christian cultural agenda in response to the rising influence of non-Christian ideologies in society. To interpret Genesis 1:28 as a cultural mandate is reactionary eisegesis in response to a present situation, not exegesis of the biblical text.[2] Ruling over or at least impacting society with Christian principles and ruling over nature in the sense of responsible stewardship are totally different ideas.

The restatement of the mandate in Genesis 9:1-7 reiterates the command to multiply and fill the earth. The injunction to care for God's creation, however, is now modified to permit killing of animals for food. This extension is understandable since animals are also subject to mortality as a result of the fall. God added two qualifications on the permission to kill: the blood of animals is not to be eaten; neither are humans to be killed. This passage does not extend Genesis 1:28 to include a cultural dimension; rather, it readdresses the ecological mandate in light of a fallen creation governed by the death principle.

Subduing and Having Dominion over the Earth (Gen. 1:28)

Genesis 1:28 unquestionably gives humanity some type of charge over the rest of creation. There are two words in the passage that express this idea: *subdue* and *dominion*. The first word (*kabash*), translated "subdue" (KJV), is the stronger of the two and occurs fifteen times in the Old Testament. Its root meaning is to tread down, with resultant meanings to conquer an enemy (Num. 32:22,29; 2 Sam. 8:11; Zech. 9:15), to bring conquered people under military control (Josh. 18:1), to bring people into subjection (1 Chron. 22:18; 2 Chron. 28:10), to bring into slavery (Neh. 5:5; Jer. 34:11,16), to tread our sins under foot (Mic. 7:19), or to molest the queen (Esther 7:8). The image often depicted in *kabash* is that of a conqueror putting his foot on the neck of a conquered enemy (see Josh. 10:24). Dumbrell suggested that "the word indicates the exertion of force against some resistant object which requires coercive effort to bring it under control."[3] When used of the earth it denotes exercising "some form of control or power over nature."[4] The object of *kabash* is the earth, which must be understood as all creation, not simply the physical earth, for the following thought expands it to include living creatures.

The other word, (*radah*), translated "have dominion" (KJV) or "rule" (NIV) occurs twenty-four times in the Old Testament. It comes from a root meaning to trample and usually means to rule over a nation or over a group of people. *Radah* does not necessarily imply force as *kabash* often does. It may refer to divine rule over the earth (Pss. 72:8; 110:2), Israel ruling over her oppressors (Isa. 41:2), nations ruling over Israel (Lev. 26:17; Neh. 9:28), one nation ruling another (Ezek. 29:15), or leaders ruling the people (2 Chron. 8:10). God instructs His people not to rule ruthlessly over the poor, treating them as slaves, but rather as hired workers (Lev. 25:43,46,53). In Ezekiel 34:1-6 God rebukes the shepherds of Israel for ruling harshly and brutally. In 1 Kings 4:24 it is used of Solomon's peaceful rule over His kingdom. When used in reference to creation, it would convey the idea of ruling or governing the natural order. The idea conveyed by *radah* is simply to exercise one's right of rule or authority over another. There is no connotation in the word itself of being harsh or ruthless. These ideas must be supplied by modifying phrases. In the Leviticus and Ezekiel passages, the word *perek* (cruelty) is used to modify *radah*. *Radah* and *kabash* alone do not tell how the ruling is to take place.

Regarding *kabash*, Barr doubted "whether more is intended here than the basic needs of settlement and agriculture: man is to fill up the earth, take possession of it, and take control of it." Barr associated it with the working or tilling of the ground mentioned in Genesis 2:5 and 15.[5] Moltmann argued that the command to "subdue the earth" (*kabash*) pertains to extracting a vegetarian diet (1:29) from the land. Seeing that animals are also to exist on a vegetarian diet, the rule over the animals (*radah*) "can mean no more than that human beings have the function of a 'justice of the peace.'"[6] Humans are to keep animals from killing one another and to maintain a peaceful coexistence among God's creatures. If Moltmann is correct, then what remains of the passage after the modification in Genesis 9:1-7 is the general principle to maintain harmony (as much as possible) in the postdiluvian era.

It is clear that humanity is to exercise control over the created realm (*kabash*) and this control is to be a type of governance of rule (*radah*). This rule must extend beyond the needs of settlement and agriculture, because care is to be given to every living creature, not only domestic animals. The commands to exercise control and to rule were given before sin entered the world. What we see in the creation narrative is rule without corruption, or what Calvin DeWitt called "sinless dominion."[7] Sinless dominion would be analogous to God's rule. The dominion that Adam exercised in the garden then is an appropriate model for our dominion. The solution to our environmental problems is not found in abandoning the dominion mandate, but in recapturing its original intent and purging the sinful tendencies of greed and materialism so that we may rule as God rules.

Tilling and Keeping the Earth (Gen. 2:5,15).

Closely associated with the commands to subdue and rule are the ideas of tilling and keeping found in the second creation narrative: "When the Lord God made the earth and the heavens . . . there was no man to work the ground" (Gen. 2:4-5). "The Lord God took the man and put him in the Garden of Eden to work it and take care of it" (Gen. 2:15). According to the second narrative, the reason God made Adam and placed him in the garden was to take care of what He created. This divine purpose clarifies what is meant by the general statements to subdue and have dominion in Genesis 1:28.

The word translated "work" (NIV) or "till" and "dress" (KJV) in Genesis 2:5 and 15 is *abad*, the common Hebrew verb for *serve*. The most common meanings are (1) to work, used especially when there is no object (Ex. 5:18); (2) to cultivate, when the object is the ground, vineyard, or the like (Gen. 3:23; 4:2; 4:12; Deut. 28:39; Prov. 12:11; 28:19; Ezek. 36:34); (3) to work for someone either as a servant (2 Sam. 16:19) or slave (Ex. 21:2-6); and (4) to serve or worship a deity (Ex. 3:12; Judg. 2:11; Ps. 100:2); or to serve in a place of worship (Num. 4:37,41).[8]

Normally when *ground* is the object, *abad* means to till or cultivate, implying cultivation for one's own sustenance. The context of Genesis 2:5, however, suggests a different focus. God's concern is not with people managing the garden for their own sustenance, for they had not been created yet, but with the need for a manager to help keep order and harmony in creation. The service is to be rendered to God, not to ourselves.

The word rendered "care" (NIV) or "keep" (KJV) in Genesis 2:15 is *shamar*, another common Hebrew verb. Its nuances include (1) to watch or guard something, such as sheep (1 Sam. 17:20), an entrance (1 Kings 14:27), or a captive (1 Kings 20:39); (2) to protect from danger (Ps. 121:7; Prov. 6:24); (3) to save or retain something, such as food (Gen. 41:35); and (4) to do something carefully or attentively, such as observe God's laws (Ex. 15:26) or covenant (Ex. 19:5). The third meaning sometimes conveys the idea of safekeeping something for someone else, such as silver, goods, and oxen (Ex. 22:7,10). The probable meaning of *shamar* in Genesis 2:15 is to preserve the order of creation so that it can fulfill the purposes God had intended for it.

Thus our service is to God and involves both preserving and managing in agreement with His intent. Attfield noted that God placed Adam in the garden "to preserve the garden's beauty and protect it from harm, as well as derive his food from it."[9] One aspect of the ecological mandate, then, is God's delegating to us part of the work of sustaining or preserving creation. The need to keep the garden implies that it cannot exist on its own in perfect ecological equilibrium. The order and harmony of the garden had to be sustained, perhaps to prevent overgrowth of certain plants that would choke out others. As the garden is preserved it will produce enough for all God's creatures as well as fulfill the other purposes God intended. The second aspect of the ecological mandate is that of managing creation. One reason behind God's placing Adam and Eve in the garden is for them to maintain the productivity of the garden and see that all animals and people receive a fair share of fruits, nuts, grains, and vegetables.

Reflecting the Image of God (Gen. 1:26-27)

The dominion mandate is contextually interwoven with references to our being made in the image of God and cannot be interpreted apart from it. The implications are that we can neither reflect the image of God without exercising proper dominion nor exercise proper dominion without cultivating the image of God. Although the textual proximity of image and dominion does not justify equating the two, neither does it justify dissociating them completely. "Then God said, 'Let us make man in our image, in our likeness, and let them rule over the fish of the sea and the birds of the air, over the livestock, over all the earth, and over all the creatures that move along the ground'" (Gen. 1:26). Various interpretations have arisen regarding what constitutes the image of God.[10]

Substantial View. The traditional view of the *imago Dei* is that it consists of certain divine qualities that we possess which enable us to exercise dominion. Since God is a spirit, the *imago Dei* must consist of spiritual characteristics, such as a highly developed reasoning ability, moral constitution, and volition, aspects which distinguish us from the rest of creation. However, it does not follow that other creatures are denigrated by our possessing certain godlike qualities that they lack. All creatures are still valued by God.

These godlike qualities have been marred (but not totally destroyed) by the acquisition of the sin nature. The goal of redemption and sanctification is to restore our original nature by the grace of God. Thus the *imago Dei* becomes the standard that defines the direction of the Christian life and, by extrapolation, the basis for defining moral behavior. Paul follows this reasoning in Romans 3:23 by equating sin with falling short of the glory of God. The ethical obligation for Christians is to put on the new self and be restored in the image of the One who created them. Part of what is to be restored includes knowledge, righteousness, and holiness (Eph. 4:23-24; Col. 3:10). It is reasonable to assume that these spiritual characteristics were part of the original image. The image of Christ in the believer is the re-creation of the image of God present at creation.

Substantial Plus Dominion View. Some say the *imago Dei* consists of having both spiritual qualities and dominion over nature. Francis Schaeffer said, "Dominion itself is an aspect of the image of God in the sense that man, being created in the image of God, stands between God and all which God chose to put under man."[11]

Dominion View. Some say that the *imago Dei* is the dominion; that is, the image refers to function rather than substance. Our dominion over the earth corresponds to God's dominion over the universe, and as such we resemble God by acting as His representative on earth. This, however, does not fit the context of Genesis 5:3 and 9:6. Barr commented, "Homicide was to be punished not because man had dominion over the animals, but because man was like God."[12]

Whole Person View. Some say the *imago Dei* consists of our whole being, both spiritual and physical. Gerhard von Rad rejects those interpretations that limit the *imago Dei* to the spiritual nature, arguing that "the whole man is created in God's image."[13] Regarding the relation of the *imago Dei* to the dominion mandate, von Rad states, "This commission to rule is not considered as belonging to the definition of God's image; but it is its consequence, i.e., that for which man is capable because of it."[14] He then gave the analogy of powerful kings who erect statues of themselves in distant conquered lands to reflect their dominion over them. In the same way, "man is placed upon earth in God's image as God's sovereign emblem. He is really only God's representative, summoned to maintain and enforce God's claim to dominion over the earth."[15] Our physical presence, like a statue of an earthly king, represents the dominion of the Creator. Von Rad was not saying that God is a physical being, but that our physical presence is part of the imaging concept.

Relational View. Others say the *imago Dei* consists of our relational or social nature. Just as the triune God is a relational being, so are we. Claus Westermann argues that the *imago Dei* is not so much a matter of imparting qualities as it is a matter of creating a being with whom God can interact and maintain a relationship. The *imago Dei* means that we have been created as God's counterpart "'to correspond to him,' that is so that something can happen between creator and creature." He comments that "humans are created in such a way that their very existence is intended to be their relationship to God."[16] Joseph Sittler concurred, saying, "The fundamental term *imago Dei* is not a term that points to a substance, an attribute, or a specifiable quality, but one which specifies a relation."[17]

This tends to ignore the observation that certain qualities are needed before a meaningful relationship can be established. Yandell noted, "Since what relational properties an item can and does have is a function of its non-relational properties, the latter theological tendency seems to me incoherent."[18] To say that the essence of the *imago Dei* consists only of our relationship or function is a logical impossibility.

In summary, what exactly the *image Dei* consists of is not explicitly stated in the text. However, it is implicit by virtue of the role we are expected to exercise and the relationship we are expected to maintain with God. There is, as James Barr has noted, a "consequential relation" between being made in the image of God and having dominion, "since man is in the image of God, let him have dominion."[19] In order to function in the role and relationships God intended, certain qualities were needed, such as those that make humans personal beings. The focus of the text, however, is not on the qualities, but on the role. "What is clear," Bauckham observed, "is that it enables human beings to be God's representatives on earth. . . . Creation in the image of God seems to refer, not to the dominion itself, but to whatever characteristics of human nature make human beings capable of this dominion."[20] Dominion is a delegated responsibility, not inherent in the *imago Dei* but made possible by it.

Since everyone possesses the image of God, there is an innate consensus regarding proper values in the social and environmental arenas. It is true that many of our attitudes and behavior traits are shaped by our heredity and environment, but there still appears to be a silent voice of conscience deep within the fabric of humanity that beckons us to wholeness and harmony with our surroundings. It seems as if there is a faint recollection of primordial peace which calls us to reevaluate our present path and to return to love and harmony. Perhaps this is similar to what Thomas Berry called "genetic coding."[21] Yet our attempts to follow this inner light often end in failure.

If, as Barr noted, proper dominion is a consequence of being made in the image of God, then restoring the *imago Dei* becomes an ecological necessity. The image will be restored only as we humble ourselves before God and submit to His Spirit, thereby receiving strength to overcome the sin principle. Then and only then will true dominion and healing be realized.

Filling the Earth (Gen. 1:28)

The injunctions to have dominion and to multiply and fill the earth are contextually related and cannot be construed as being in opposition. God told Adam, "Be fruitful and increase in number; fill the earth and subdue it" (Gen. 1:28). This charge is repeated after the deluge (Gen. 9:1,7). The command to be fruitful and multiply and fill the earth was given to other creatures as well, specifically fish and birds (Gen. 1:22), and then to all living creatures after the deluge (Gen. 8:17). Several observations regarding filling the earth need to be made.

(1) *The charge should not be construed to mean that we are to indulge in unrestrained population growth.* God could not have meant for us to overpopulate the earth, but only to populate it. Overpopulation would be contradictory to God's desire that we take care of creation, for countless habitats and species would have to be destroyed to make room for the ever-expanding human race. Uncontrolled expansion would cause a colossal ecological imbalance and would threaten the existence of God's creation. Unrestrained population growth therefore is the antithesis of proper dominion.

(2) *The posdiluvian command was necessary due to the small numbers kept alive through the deluge.* By analogy, one may infer that God did not create vast numbers of any animal species in the beginning and that the prelapsarian command meant for them to fill their respective niches around the earth, not to overflow and endanger other species. The same would hold true for humans.

(3) *The charge is given to entire species, not to individuals.* The Bible does not condemn those who choose not to propagate (Matt. 19:11-12; 1 Cor. 7:7-8).

(4) *The injunction is fulfilled when the "full" level is reached.* Yet what is meant by the "full" level for humans is directly related to one's standard of living. The more things people want, the fewer people the earth can support; the less people want, the more it can support without undo environmental stress. This leads to the next point.

(5) *Responsible stewardship will limit human expansion in accord with the earth's carrying capacity.* As Cross said, "Fidelity

to the biblical text gives a new reading: do not multiply in excess, be fruitful within limits appropriate to the ecology of the earth's flora and fauna, of which we are one species; do not overfill the earth."[22] There is a limit to what the earth will support.

(6) *Excessive human population endangers the quality of life for all creatures.* Regarding humans, Derr said, "A certain population level is obviously needed to diversify and enrich life, making man's mastery a fact. But beyond a certain point the numbers of people have a reverse effect, so diminishing the quality of life that man's mastery over the earth is actually weakened. Overpopulation is the enemy of dominion, not its partner."[23] Overpopulation tends to destroy life, not preserve it.

The need to limit population has not been recognized by many in the church. This is especially true among Roman Catholics who use Genesis 38:9-10 as a proof text against contraceptive practices. It also poses a dilemma for many conservatives concerned with the environment and yet are pro-life on the abortion issue. Many national environmental organizations are increasingly promoting pro-choice policies. However, the murder of unborn infants is contradictory to the quest for ecological peace and harmony. There can be no peace as long as murder is sanctioned. The proper avenue for environmentalists to take is not abortion or infanticide, but family planning.

Naming the Animals (Gen. 2:19-20)

After God formed all the beasts of the field and birds of the air, "He brought them to the man to see what he would name them; and whatever the man called each living creature, that was its name. So the man gave names to all the livestock, the birds of the air and all the beasts of the field" (Gen. 2:19-20).

In allowing Adam to name the animals, God was permitting him to begin exercising his ruling responsibilities of keeping and maintaining creation order. In the ancient world, the idea of a name expressed the nature of the thing named. In order for Adam to be able to name the animals, he had to live with the animals and get to know them. Naming "involves a deep knowledge of the creature and a sympathetic relationship with it."[24] This suggests that by divine necessity we are immanent with what is being named.[25] Rather than emphasizing our transcendence, the naming allows us to be part of the community of creation, yet a part that involves responsible care.

Many emphasize the negative connotations of naming, such as control and domination. Lynn White, for example, remarked, "Man named all the animals, thus establishing his dominance over them. God planned all of this explicitly for man's benefit and rule: no item in the physical creation had any purpose save man's purposes."[26] In modern usage, the act of naming implies having both knowledge of the thing being named and a certain authority or power over it. Knowledge of something and how it operates gives a person insight to manipulate it for personal advantage. This is something the postlapsarian race would be prone to do, provided there were no constraints. Again, we must refrain from interpreting something that occurred before the fall in light of human tendencies after the fall. Naming the animals could not have had any negative connotations for Adam, since he recognized God's sovereignty and authority over all creation. Furthermore, Adam's authority cannot be divorced from the responsibility to care for the earth. Since all authority invokes responsibility, "the person who names them will be responsible for their welfare within the garden."[27] Naming of the animals was a positive and creative exercise of responsible rule.

Conclusion: The Meaning of the Dominion Mandate

The words *subdue* (*kabash*) and *have dominion* (*radah*) in Genesis 1:28 cannot be interpreted properly without considering the immediate context and the context of the second creation narrative. The two creation narratives represent different perspectives of the same event and are thus complementary rather than contradictory. The first narrative lays out a general outline of creation. The second amplifies and explains the general terminology of the first narrative, especially regarding humanity's role in creation and what was meant by having dominion.

The focus of the words *work* (*abad*) and *care* (*shamar*) in the second narrative is on actions done for the sake of God and creation. We have been called to serve in a garden owned by another, not to ransack it for our own profit. Our commission is to preserve the harmonious relations that God established and manage the earth for the sake of the entire creation community. In addition, our rule is to be compassionate and beneficial to all forms of life and not to be tainted by human greed. Human greed did not enter into the picture until after the fall. With this understanding, the words *subdue* and *have dominion* do not suggest environmentally destructive behavior. Scripture as a whole, with its focus on divine ownership, human stewardship, imaging Christ, value of all creation, and condemnation of greed and materialism cannot possibly be construed into giving a mandate for brutal exploitation.

Models for Dominion

The Model of God's Dominion

The primary model for our dominion over the earth is God's dominion. God's exercise of dominion is marked by loving care (1 Pet. 5:7), sustaining life (Heb. 1:3), helping creatures in need (Heb. 4:16), and always doing what is morally right (Ps. 45:7; Isa. 9:7; Hos. 14:9; Heb. 1:8; and Rev. 15:3). Since God delegated to us the responsibility of dominion, it is reasonable to assume that our dominion should be modeled after God's dominion. Thus, it is to be a loving and caring dominion, concerned with justice and the well-being of the whole. Christians should express compassion for the earth, not because it is a living organism that has feelings or because human feelings are transferred to it as in romanticism but because this is how God rules.

The biblical focus on love is traditionally understood as our love to God and one another. We are commanded to love our neighbors (Lev. 19:18), but who exactly are our neighbors? Should we include animals and plants? This thought is not really as preposterous as it might first appear. To have a genuine love for others, one must have a genuine love for the environment. For if one destroys the environment, that person has for all practical purposes destroyed the quality of human life. That is, to destroy the environment is to hate fellow human beings. Since everything belongs to one interconnected community, to love God and other people demands that we also love the environment. Love is the bond that knits a community together. Our neighbors in this ecological community must include everything God created, and our love must extend to all our cocreatures.

God exhorts His people to exercise the same loving care toward creation that He does. For example, we are commanded to respect the life of birds (Deut. 22:6), to have regard for the well-being of domesticated animals (Ex. 23:5; Deut. 5:14; 22:4; 25:4; and Prov. 12:10), to care for the land (Lev. 25:1-5), and not destroy the trees (Deut. 20:19). From this latter passage comes the Jewish environmental principle of *bal tashhit* (do not destroy), which has been applied to a wide range of environmental crimes.[28] We are to oversee God's creation in love and justice, making sure that all God's creatures are cared for just as God would. To think only of ourselves and our well-being would not be dominion patterned after the divine example where love and justice for others is paramount.

The Servanthood Model

The notion that "dominion is servitude"[29] or that "lordship is servanthood"[30] is a biblically based principle that utterly reverses the common understanding of what is meant by exercising dominion. In biblical thought, the calling to have dominion is the calling to be a servant. As we serve the Creator all the needs of creation will be accommodated, both human and non-human.

Although the idea of dominion as servanthood is implicit in the creation narratives, it is made explicit in the incarnation and crucifixion of Christ.[31] Our rulership or dominion is to be modeled after Jesus Christ, who did not come to exercise lordship over creation but to give His life in service for others. Christian Scriptures depict the Lord and Master of creation as the Good Shepherd, the One who willingly lays down His life for the flock (John 10:11). The charge to follow Christ leads us in paths of service to all God's creatures, not in paths of arrogant domination to fill our lusts. Jesus taught His disciples, "You know that the rulers of the Gentiles lord it over them, and their high officials exercise authority over them. Not so with you. Instead, whoever wants to become great among you must be your servant, and whoever wants to be first must be your slave—just as the Son of Man did not come to be served, but to serve, and to give his life as a ransom for many" (Matt. 20:25-28).

The connection between dominion and service is illustrated by Christ's willingness to humble Himself even unto death (Phil. 2:6-11). Christ did not consider His exalted position something to be held onto at all costs but willingly left it behind so that He could give His life to help others (Phil. 2:6). Paul exhorts the Philippians to have this same attitude (Phil. 2:5) and to give themselves totally in service to others, just as Christ did. The Philippian church seemed to be suffering from divisions, disharmony, and self-seeking attitudes, for Paul constantly made appeals to be one in spirit and purpose (for example, Phil. 2:1-4; 4:1-3). The same attitudes plague society today. We, like Christ, also have authority over creation, but that power must be used as Christ's was, to help restore it to its prelapsarian harmony.

Thus the incarnation and crucifixion provide a model of authority exercised in service. Christ left His majesty to die as a servant. We, too, are to use our dominion in a "radical kind of servitude,"[32] one that forgoes material affluence and security for the sake of serving God and caring for all creation. This notion of dominion is contrary to common usage where it is linked with domination and opportunism. As Linzey reminded us, "Lordship without service is indeed tyranny."[33]

The Kingship Model

Our rule over the earth is to follow the intended role of a Hebrew king who was to be responsible to God for how he managed the nation. Hebrew kings were not to take advantage of their position for exploitation and personal gain (Deut. 17:16-17); rather, they were to read from the Law every day so that they might learn to revere God and obey His laws (Deut. 17:18-19). The biblical notion of rulership therefore condemns the abuse of an office for self-advantage. Thus the proper notion of rulership recognizes a higher ruling authority. The Mosaic legislation lays down three qualifications for rulers: they must fear God, be trustworthy, and hate dishonest gain (Ex. 18:21).

David's attitude of kingship is vastly different from the attitude of our modern society regarding their position over nature. Among David's last words is the thought,

> When one rules over men in righteousness,
> when he rules in the fear of God,
> he is like the light of morning at sunrise
> on a cloudless morning,
> like the brightness after rain
> that brings the grass from the earth (2 Sam. 23:3).

Solomon also conveys the proper role of a Hebrew king before God:

> Endow the king with your justice, O God,
> the royal son with your righteousness.
> He will judge your people in righteousness,
> your afflicted ones with justice
> (Ps. 72:1-2; see 1 Kings 3:5-12).

However, most of the kings of Judah and Israel failed to live up to the expected standards. They abused their office and turned their authority into occasions for self-indulgence, sin, and violence. Both the people and the land suffered as a result of corrupt exercise of leadership.

The Stewardship Model

The word *steward* is the usual New Testament translation of the Greek *oikonomos*, which means "the manager of someone's estate or household" (*oikos* meaning house, household, or estate, and *nomos* meaning law).

Some prefer not to use the term *stewardship* because present usage associates it with *management*.[34] Management is normally viewed anthropocentrically; we manage the earth so that we can continue to reap as much of its resources as possible.

Stewardship, properly understood, refers to taking care of another's property (see Matt. 25:14-30); it does not refer to taking care of one's own possessions, as in the stewardship of our finances. The duties of a steward include managing, but never for one's own benefit or in such a way as to be contrary to the desires of the owner.

The notion of stewardship is closely linked to one's cosmology. If stewardship is reduced to management for the sake of humanity or even the sake of future generations, then humanity becomes not only the trustee but the truster; that is, humanity becomes the owner of the earth and the arbitrator of all value regarding its use. If we "serve as our own administrators, our existence must gain meaning from ourselves, and our actions are done to glorify ourselves."[35] If stewardship is reduced to preservation of wilderness areas for the sake of nature, then nature becomes the *terminus a quo* for all philosophical endeavors and the center of meaning. Our actions would be done to bring glory to nature. The deification of nature, however, is an absurdity if we have to take care of it, for such a deity would not be able to care for itself. If, however, "we serve God as His administrators, our existence gains meaning from God and our actions are done to glorify God."[36]

Stewardship Implies Delegated Authority. Only God has absolute authority and dominion. "Dominion and awe belong to God" (Job 25:2).

> Dominion belongs to the Lord
> and He rules over the nations (Ps. 22:28).

Since all dominion belongs to God, human dominion over nature must be regarded as delegated dominion. That is, our authority to care for creation must be thought of as a function, extension, or derivative of God's dominion. This automatically excludes any notion of self-assertive, autonomous tyranny over nature. God delegated responsibility to us, and we are responsible to the delegating authority for how we handle the charge. This is the essence of biblical stewardship.

Stewardship Involves a Trust. God entrusted the earth to the human race for its safekeeping. Paul says in 1 Corinthians 4:2, "Now it is required that those who have been given a trust must prove faithful." We are obligated to be faithful to the One who had enough confidence in us to entrust us with something of extreme value. The trust encompasses everything that has been placed under our care, including children, animals, personal possessions, and the earth itself. The biblical ideas of divine ownership and human tenancy underlie the idea of trust, "The land is mine and you are but aliens and my tenants" (Lev. 25:23). Since everything still belongs to God, anything we receive should be looked upon more as a trust than a gift.

Stewardship is analogous to being permitted to stay in someone's house for awhile. By allowing us to stay in their home, the owners have implicitly charged us with the responsibility to take care of it as they would. In the same way, because we have been permitted to live in God's creation, we have an obligation to take care of God's property. A trust has been committed in virtue of God's grace in sharing existence with us and in providing a place to live.

Stewardship Is Inconsistent with Autonomy. Our role in creation is neither autonomous nor sovereign. Only God is the sovereign Lord of creation; we are simply stewards or vicegerents who are to remain subject to the authority over us. This automatically limits our freedom. Nowhere in Scripture are humans granted unlimited freedom or unlimited rights. We do not have freedom to use nature in such a way that it needlessly destroys God's creatures, mars the beauty of His creation, robs its resources, or causes others to be in need. Santmire commented that our freedom is limited both vertically by our accountability to God and horizontally by our responsibilities to nature.[37] These responsibilities include preserving the integrity and fruitfulness of creation for future generations and for nonhuman life. The initial limitation on our dominion was God's restricting our diet to plant life (Gen. 1:29). Dominion under God cannot be autonomous dominion.

The responsibility of stewardship therefore limits freedom. The basic nature of the postlapsarian race rebels against any effort to limit its freedom. When the pressures from the media, society, and government slacken off on environmental items, secular men and women will inevitably seek to regain their freedom, live as they please, and resume their wanton attack on nature.

Stewardship Implies Moral Responsibility. We are responsible to God for how we use and manage nature. Our responsibility must be clarified in two important points. First, we are not totally responsible for sustaining the earth, for this is beyond our capabilities. We merely cooperate with God in the task of maintaining creation. Second, we are responsible to the delegating authority. To focus attention upon our responsibility to human beings or to other parts of the natural order without including our primary responsibility to God plummets us into a moral dilemma: Why should we be our brother's keeper? The only way the *why* can be answered in an environmentally constructive way is to seek a reason that transcends this realm. There would be no compelling reason to be accountable to others, if we were not ultimately accountable to God.[38] Our responsibility to God circumscribes our responsibility to others, to future generations, to animals, and to the rest of nature. "Ultimately the principle of public accountability is grounded in our answerability to God. Love of the neighbor is love of God. Creator and Lord, he is the real owner and proprietor, the only One whose right in the world is absolute."[39]

The moral obligation attached to the office of a steward is illustrated by the unfaithful steward (see Luke 16:8):

> The unethical steward is the person who violates that trust (1) by neglecting to care for that which has been entrusted; (2) by destroying without adequate reason the substance of that which has been entrusted; or (3) by appropriating or assigning to oneself the exclusive use of that which has been entrusted, and doing so in a way which denies the legitimate claims of others.[40]

The unfaithful steward is calloused to the need of others and is only concerned with advancing self at the expense of the estate. That person "is characterized by insensitivity, pride, avarice and greed."[41] Being unfaithful stewards of God's estate must be viewed as a moral offense and a sin against God.

Faithful stewards, on the other hand, display compassion toward all in their master's household, humility in not taking advantage of their position, dependability in carrying out their master's instructions, and thankfulness that their master has provided for their needs. They are those who know their lord's will and do it (Luke 12:42-48). Faithful stewards realize that something of great value has been committed to them and are responsible to the owner for its safekeeping. Since the characteristics of the unethical steward arise from sinful tendencies within, the virtues of the ethical steward can only be achieved through "the healing power of the grace of Christ."[42] Titus 1:7 gives the qualifications for those who are to be entrusted with God's work. They are to be "blameless—not overbearing, not quick-tempered, not given to drunkenness, not violent, not pursuing dishonest gain." Although the specific reference is to the office of an elder, the principles are apropos to any commission of trust.

Stewardship Implies Proper Use and Management. One of the reasons for nature's existence is to sustain human life. No one would deny the utility of nature, but it should not be viewed anthropocentrically. Rather than saying that the reason for nature's existence is to serve humanity, we should say that one of its many reasons is to serve each member of the community of creation in a mutually supportive manner. Every creature makes use of nature to survive, and we are no different. Stewardship helps assure that this and other divine purposes for creation are met.

The dominant view of the church, as previously noted, has been that everything has been made for human use. But as Montefiore said, "To imagine that God has created the whole universe solely for man's use and pleasure is a mark of folly."[43] An unbalanced view of the purpose of nature will inevitably result in a twisted stewardship. For most of the church, stewardship is management for the sake of humanity. The biblical view of stewardship, however, is not anthropocentric or even theanthropocentric, it is theocentric.

It is not the use of nature but the abuse that is the problem. It is not wrong to eat meat, to make clothing of animal skins, to chop down trees for fuel and shelter, or to transform areas for human habitation. Whatever use we make of nature, we must not destroy its ability to replenish itself and to continue fulfilling the design for which God intended. "Our manipulation of creation must be in conformity with God's own moral design for the cosmos."[44] Anything less constitutes abuse. Stewardship then involves both use and management in keeping with God's design.

Some argue that we should focus on preserving nature. The parable of the talents strongly argues against such an ecopurest or preservationist mentality (Matt. 25:14-30). The master commended the servants who did something with the talents and reprimanded the servant who merely preserved the talent by hiding it in the ground. Stewardship cannot be reduced to preserving wilderness areas. It is a creative endeavor involving both wise use of the parts for the benefit of the whole and preservation of the whole for the sake of the parts. The biblical perspective avoids both extremes, that of preserving nature solely for humanity's sake and that of preserving nature solely for nature's sake.

Stewardship Involves Creativity. It is impossible for ecosystems not to change. Living organisms alter their ecosystem by extracting nutrients from it and contributing by-products that can be reused by other organisms. Maintaining a uniform state or trying to preserve the way a wilderness area was is somewhat of a misconception. Just as it is natural for nature to change, so it is perfectly natural for us to change our environment. Christians must see their place as cooperating with God not only in a sustaining capacity but also in a healing capacity. This implies change, but a change for the better, a change in which we use our God-given powers of wisdom, intellect, and creativity to manage the earth and solve ecological problems.

> Proper stewardship of the earth, then, is a matter of recovering the creative rule that God intended people to exercise toward the natural order. This is a rule that involves a proper husbanding of resources so that they will produce enough to care for the needs of all, and a respect for the order as accomplishing purposes that transcend even our understanding.[45]

As people are re-created in God's image, they will use their creativity for positive ends rather than for destruction. There are many examples of creating a beautiful landscape in harmony with nature while at the same time gleaning from it the necessities of life. It takes creative skill to maintain the fertility of the soil and a bountiful crop without adding synthetic fertilizers, pesticides, fungicides, or herbicides. It also takes creative skill to use science and technology to rectify the destruction already done without introducing more adverse effects. In addition, it takes creative skill to reap the necessities of life without devastating the lives and livelihood of our fellow creatures.

When we are transformed by the power of Christ, we become new creatures with new desires and potentials. With the stranglehold of sin broken by the divine Spirit, we are liberated to fulfill our responsibility as loving caretakers of God's creation. The new person in Christ will release creative power in a positive way to help heal the ailments of the environment, society, and human lives. The redeemed individual forms part of a redemptive community that works in concord with the Divine Healer to bring healing to an ailing world.

In conclusion, the stewardship model will work only when viewed in a theistic context with all nature being valued and treated as God would. If theism is absent from a stewardship model, then there would be no effective restraint on human exploitation, and stewardship would eventually degenerate into management for human concerns. We are not stewards merely for the sake of humanity, or even for nature, but for God, the One who commissioned us as stewards. This is true Christian stewardship. Yet as Hans Schwarz reminded us, "Our Christian appeal toward stewardship can only be persuasive if it is not just a verbal appeal but illustrated by our own actions."[46]

A Twisted Mandate

Because Christianity was the dominant religion in Western culture during the rise of the modern technocratic society, it was natural to seek its justification for societal trends.[47] If society's direction was at odds with the prevailing religious mood, then its headway would be severely hampered. The dominion passage in Genesis, when interpreted in light of the social context of the day, provided just what was needed, a quasi-religious sanction or divine license for human conquest and exploitation of the environment. Little attention was given to the context of Genesis or the rest of Scripture, as is typical of those who use proof texts to support their position. Cultural assumptions and predispositions are read into the text rather than letting the text express itself. The distortions of the dominion passage are nothing more than rationalizations to justify humanity's sinful tendencies.

The only way the words of Genesis 1:26-28 could be taken in a negative sense is to ignore the context, the moral injunctions in Scripture, the purposes in creation, and the character of the Creator. The Hebrew words for *subdue* and *rule* could be taken as raping the environment and trampling it underfoot. The Jews, however, never interpreted their own Scriptures in this way. Ehrenfeld and Bentley stated no evidence exists "that we are aware of, that these verses of *Genesis* were ever interpreted by the rabbis as a license for environmental exploitation. Indeed, such an interpretation runs contrary to their teaching and to the whole spirit of the oral law."[48]

Nevertheless, we have adopted just such a distorted view of dominion and have gone forth to conquer nature for our own glory. The Bible often depicts humans as not ruling as they should (see Heb. 2:8). The notion of wrong dominion is illustrated by the rebuke of the shepherds of Israel who feed themselves instead of the flock (Ezek. 34:1-6). Rather than looking after the welfare of the sheep, the shepherds "ruled them harshly and brutally." The Hebrew word for "rule" in Ezekiel 34:4 is *radah*, the same word used in Genesis 1:26 and 28 for our dominion or rule over nature. "The lesson about dominion is clear: unless such dominion is used for the benefit of the dominated, it is misused."[49] Dominion must be concerned with the welfare of that which is under the dominion. Any dominion that takes advantage of the office for individual greed is a distortion of true biblical dominion (see Ezek. 34:18-19).

The ecological mandate does give us authority over nature, but this authority has been twisted by our disposition toward selfishness and autonomy. As Montefiore observed, "The arbitrary and reckless misuse of power by man proceeds not from the divine purpose but from human sin."[50] Ehrenfeld and Bentley added that this autonomous spirit has serious effects on the environment:

> When stewardship is corrupted by power in the absence of restraint, it becomes ecological tyranny and exploitation. This is the central problem of stewardship, a problem that has always existed but has become critical only with the rise of modern technology and its side effects, including over-population.[51]

This is not to imply that a false concept of dominion has not been present in the church. Indeed it has. The Puritans helped to prepare the modern "ethic of exploitation" with their doctrine of humanity's dominion over nature.[52] They found in the dominion passage a divinely given right to conquer nature and bring order out of the chaos of the newly settled American wilderness. They believed that they were called to exercise dominion to evidence their election and to glorify God. Santmire noted that this "is what Max Weber referred to as the Protestant Ethic. Generations of Americans were instructed by their churches that nature is man's proper sphere of lordship, given by God to use, by the sweat of his brow, in order to bring honor to the name of God."[53]

Peter Steinhart correctly observed that "many fundamentalists believe it is man's duty to develop and exploit nature, citing the Biblical injunction to subdue the Earth and have dominion over all living things." He quoted former Interior Secretary James Watt, who once said, "'America's resources were put here for the enjoyment and use of people, now and in the future, and should not be denied to the people by elitist groups.'"[54]

C. F. D. Moule began his essay *Man and Nature in the New Testament* with an apt illustration of the common misconception within the church:

> Gavin Maxwell, the well-known writer of books about otters, described, in an article on the *Observer* for October 13, 1963, how he lost two lovely otter cubs brought back from Nigeria: "A minister of the Church of Scotland, walking along the foreshore with a shotgun, found them at play by the tide's edge and shot them. One was killed outright, the other died of her wounds in the water. The minister," added Maxwell bitterly, "expressed regret, but reminded a journalist: 'The Lord gave man control over the beasts of the field.'"[55]

Modern society fashions itself as the conqueror of nature to exploit its bounty and transform it into artifacts of elegance and opulence for the royal courts of human affluence. Just as the Babylonians were feasting in pomp while the enemy was sneaking into the city, so modern society continues to feast off nature, holding to a false sense of security that all is safe. "The conqueror role," as Leopold once said, "is eventually self-defeating."[56] Our continued domination of nature, increasing affluence, and rising population are on a collision course that can only spell doom for life as God intended.

Bryce-Smith noted,

> These beautiful verses of Genesis undoubtedly have encouraged the narcissistic belief that man is set apart from all other animals in a qualitative sense as a sort of steward administering and ruling the estate for an unseen landlord. And with the passage of time and the growth of knowledge of the estate the steward has found it increasingly attractive and "rational" to doubt the existence of the landlord and to appoint himself to the honor, as in the ultimate absurdity of Humanism where man the usurper worships himself as a quasi God.[57]

The irony of the situation is that when society departs from God, it will never find peace and fulfillment, but rather its waywardness will lead to its own disintegration, first in values, then morals, social order, and then physically, implicating nature in its own descent. There is, as John Black noted, a direct correlation between the destruction of nature and the destruction of society.[58] The further society travels on its autonomous journey, the further away it becomes from the peace and harmony it desperately longs for. True peace for an individual or society will never come until the entire cosmic ecosystem is at rest, something an autonomous spirit prevents from taking place.

9

A Realistic Portrait of Humanity: Depraved or Capable?

In Dostoyevsky's *The Brothers Karamazov*, Father Zossima remarks, "Man, do not pride yourself on superiority to the animals; they are without sin, and you, with greatness, defile the earth by your appearance on it, and leave the traces of your foulness after you—alas, it is true of almost every one of us!"[1] There is no question that the human race is the cause of the environmental crisis. Who else can we blame? Casting blame on anything else, whether religion or technology, is nothing more than scapegoating to avoid the guilt. As the cartoon character Pogo says, "We have met the enemy, and he is us." The solution is to be found neither in technological innovations nor mystical enlightenment but in restructuring the values, attitudes, and ethics of individuals at the deepest level. Since we are the culprits behind the ecological crisis, no cohesive and comprehensive environmental strategy can avoid the problem of the selfish tendency embedded in human nature.

In his book *Imaging God*, Douglas John Hall comments, "If, as one who attempts to reflect on the human situation through the medium of the Christian story, I ask myself 'What is wrong?' I

181

invariably find myself answering, 'We ourselves are wrong.'"[2] There are universal tendencies in humanity that cannot be explained away, ignored, or circumvented. Calvin DeWitt once conducted a student survey that identified three underlying problems of the environmental crisis: arrogance, ignorance, and greed.[3] All three point back at us and our unethical attitudes and behavior. To view the problem solely in physical terms with physical remedies rather than in moral terms with moral remedies would be to invoke disaster.

Somewhere along our journey, we have made a wrong turn. Saying that something has gone wrong is, in itself, a value judgment. Any value judgment presupposes some basis for values, some criteria by which one can judge whether something is right or wrong.[4] Most pantheists, humanists, and Christians agree that human abuse of the environment is wrong. This tends to support the contention that there is an underlying awareness of right and wrong present in everyone, although expressed through different channels. From a biblical perspective, the underlying awareness that things should exist in peace and harmony reflects the image of God in each person.

Humanity's Dual Coding

In Psalm 8:4, David raised the question, "What is man?" The answer we give to this question has far-reaching implications on how we live and view our relation with the environment. There seems to be a never-ending quest in humans to be something that they presently are not, to ascribe to values they consistently violate, to enjoy the harmony and peace they say should exist but never can achieve, and to find, as it is commonly phrased, their true self. Humans appear to be torn between what they are and that level of existence to which their inner aspirations beckon. There seems to be another aspect of human nature hidden behind the appearances, an aspect that embraces morality without bondage to rules, perfectionism without fear of failure, and community without fear of rejection. It is evident that humanity suffers from acute schizophrenia. There appear to be two conflicting natures, one that encompasses the realm of present experiences and one that encompasses the realm of the ideal or, as some say, an "earthly bent" and a "heavenly bent." As long as we dwell in our present state there will be a hunger within for meaning, purpose, values, peace, and joy. We are hungry creatures, but is this our natural state? Were we created hungry?

Some would discount the upper realm entirely. According to secular humanists (or naturalists), Homo sapiens is merely a freak accident of nature, the end result of the random process of evolution. We are nothing more than the sum total of the elements that compose our body. The idea of an inner nature (the soul, spirit, sin nature, and image of God) is regarded as a holdover from primitive superstitions. The abolition of the inner nature, says B. F. Skinner, is long overdue.[5] But what happens when one's inner longings are discarded as myth and wishful thinking? C. S. Lewis argued that this abolishes what makes human beings human.[6] Humans are reduced to mere machines, operating in accord with the dictates of the environment, with no possibility of meaning, purpose, or values. Their freedom, dignity, and sense of self-worth are destroyed. Humanity becomes a zero with nothing to look forward to but death to end a miserable existence. This, however, does not correspond to what we know about ourselves. Whether we want to admit it or not, we are very much aware of another dimension of our being, something that beckons us beyond the present state.

Others would discount the lower realm altogether. According to many New Age pantheists, humans are impersonal spirits, part of the cosmic life force of the universe. Nothing exists except this universal soul or life force. The physical aspect is simply an illusion or projection of the ultimate. In order to satisfy their spiritual hunger and to find their true selves, devotees must become enlightened through a mystical experience of oneness with the cosmos. They must cultivate occult techniques to wipe out their rational mind (which is part of the lower realm of illusion) and to achieve an altered state of consciousness. Only then, it is claimed, can they experience awareness of their true divinity and oneness with the universe. This view also fails to correspond to what we know about ourselves. The physical realm is real. We cannot live as though everything around us is an illusion. We must eat food, avoid being run over by the traffic, have our medical problems taken care of, and put a shelter over our heads.

The only view of humanity that corresponds to reality is the Judeo-Christian alternative that affirms the reality of both realms. We were made in the image of God and, therefore, have an affinity with a transcendent system of morals, a desire for perfect harmony and peace, and an innate knowledge that there must be ultimate meaning and purpose. We were not created hungry. When the urge to feed self captivated our soul, not only did the pristine beauty and harmony of the original creation become marred, but we acquired a selfish blight in our character. Ironically, we are now hungry creatures, desperately longing to regain what we lost. The original image still exists, impaired by the ascendancy of the demonic nature, but just vibrant enough for us to recognize that the way we are now is not the way we should be and that we live in an abnormal state. We are faintly aware of the harmony, values, peace, tranquillity, meaning, and purpose that were part of our original constitution, a state to which we long to return.

Humanity's Problem

One's view of human nature determines the character of humanity's problem. That there is a problem scarcely needs to be commented on. The apostle Paul observed,

> Ruin and misery mark their ways,
> and the way of peace they do not know (Rom. 3:16-17).

One quick glimpse at the morning newspaper reveals the horrors and devastation that lay in the wake of the human path. Everywhere we go, we leave behind a trail of death, bloodshed, ruin, hatred, disharmony, suffering, misery, and destruction. We are bent on contaminating the earth with our own corruption. Although something inside condones this wanton life-style, it seems as if we suffer from a crippling and incurable flaw in our character, an addiction to wickedness that no amount of education or religiosity has yet been able to cure.

Secular humanists would say that our problem is superstition and ignorance. Our adherence to religious myths has given us a distorted view of human nature, in particular, that we possess an immaterial nature enabling us to act autonomously from environmental stimuli. Skinner maintained that before we can make any headway in solving the problems that plague humanity, we must dispose of this prescientific view of humanity. Only then can we turn to real causes of behavior and offer solutions. Skinner contends that the solution to our problem is a technology of behavior in which behavior is controlled by the environment and genetic makeup.[7] "A scientific view of man offers exciting possibilities. We have not yet seen what man can make of man."[8] In his novel *Walden Two*, Skinner projected a utopian society resulting from his technology of behavior.

New Age pantheists would say that our problem is also ignorance of our true nature, but with a much different twist. We have forgotten that we are part of God, they say. Shirley MacLaine remarked, "The tragedy of the human race was that we had forgotten that we are all divine."[9] If God is all and all is God, then everything is part of this cosmic one, including humans. Most people, however, live in a state of ignorance, a state controlled by a lower level of consciousness that prevents them from realizing that they are part of God. As long as they continue in this state of ignorance, they will never be able to tap into the unlimited divine potentials within and will never be able to solve the problems of life and society. The introduction for the "New Dimensions" radio program begins, "It is only through a change in human consciousness that the world will be transformed. The personal and the planetary are connected. As we expand our awareness of body, mind, psyche, and spirit so will the world be changed." The change of consciousness is usually achieved through mind-altering techniques such as yoga, hypnosis, biofeedback, meditation, or chanting mantras. In this heightened awareness one supposedly attains God consciousness and the realization of unlimited psychic abilities. For those of a pantheistic persuasion, our problem is ignorance, and the solution is mystical enlightenment.

Christians would say that our problem is a sinful disposition, not ignorance. Something has happened to alter our original nature and to destroy the peace, harmony, love, virtue, and tranquillity that we inwardly know should be the laws of the universe. The Bible depicts a primeval rebellion against God that plunged the human race into a state of chaos and disharmony. In biblical terminology, this rebellious, autonomous spirit is called *sin* (1 Sam. 15:23). It is sin that has alienated us from God, one another, nature, and ourselves, thereby causing the void in our lives. No biblical doctrine is supported with more empirical evidence than the persistent sinful disposition of the human race. The race is now abnormal, intoxicated with going its own way. We live in an abnormal world, a world full of hatred, war, crime, fear, and death. Our problem is a moral problem, and the only solution is through the person and work of Jesus Christ.

Humanity's Corrupt Nature

The Bible presents a realistic portrait of our fallen race. It does not deny human ability to do good (Luke 6:32-34; Rom. 5:7), but it does assert that all have an overriding disposition toward evil (Rom. 7:14-25). There is, as Eric Rust said, "A demonic twist in his make-up, a tendency to reject absolute claim and to turn his back on unconditional obligation."[10] Scripture therefore denies the ability to live completely without sin and thus to restore broken relations with the Creator. The demonic is still present to thwart any such attempt.

The Definition of Sin

According to the *Westminster Larger Catechism*, Question 24, "Sin is any want of conformity unto, or transgression of, any law of God, given as a rule to the reasonable creature."[11] The law could be thought of as a contextualized expression of God's character. Sin could then be defined by the nature of God and the commands of God. First, those acts and thoughts at variance with God's character are considered sin. Paul made this clear when he said, "For all have sinned and fall short of the glory of God" (Rom. 3:23). The word *glory* refers to God's moral character, His goodness, love, mercy, kindness, and faithfulness. Coming short of this standard is sin. This suggests an objective, absolute standard that is grounded in the character of the unchangeable God. Second, those acts and thoughts at variance with God's laws are considered sin. John focused on the second aspect of sin by saying "sin is lawlessness" (1 John 3:4). The two are connected. As we conform our lives to the law of God, we become that much more like God.

The moral laws of God should be thought of as universal principles that guide creation to function in peace and harmony as God intended, not as a club that God uses to harass people. The laws reflect the perfect harmony that exists in the triune God, a God who cannot create anything contrary to His character. Thus creation itself was so ordered to function by the same principles that characterize the Creator. Things work when they follow the physical and moral laws of the universe.

But when God is forsaken, society is left without a stable and unbiased foundation for determining direction, values, and ethics. Without such a base, it is doomed to moral deterioration. In Romans 1:18-32, Paul depicts the downward path of degradation that follows once God has been abandoned. This passage is unparalleled for its analysis of our present situation, whether social, psychological, or ecological. The inevitable has happened. As Bryce-Smith says, "A man, or a nation, without the guidance of a moral sense is like a ship without a compass. We do not see so much these days of the sad-faced chaps who used to parade in sandwich boards bearing 'the wages of sin is death,' but they seem to have had the truth of the matter."[12] Without a compass, there cannot be much hope for finding our way through the environmental maze.

The Demonic Twist

In addition to using the term *sin* to refer to an act or thought that is out of conformity with God's character or injunctions, the

> The time has come for judging the dead,
> and for rewarding your servants the prophets . . .
> and for destroying those who destroy the earth (Rev. 11:18).

Because of greed and avarice, humans no longer treat the land in a responsible, loving way.

Second, as previously noted, the implication of Genesis 6:5-13 is that human sin somehow disrupted the harmonious working of the entire cosmos. This is perhaps due to the interrelatedness of everything in the community of creation. It is analogous to an organism that is healthy only when disease is totally absent. When we are smitten with flu, our whole body slows down to a snail's pace. In the same way, when something in the cosmos is dysfunctional, the whole cosmos is affected.

The organic unity of creation is substantiated by Hosea's remarkable statement:

> There is no faithfulness, no love,
> no acknowledgment of God in the land.
> There is only cursing, lying and murder,
> stealing and adultery;
> they break all bounds,
> and bloodshed follows bloodshed.
> Because of this the land mourns,
> and all who live in it waste away;
> the beasts of the field and the birds of the air
> and the fish of the sea are dying (4:1-3).

When people lie, fish die. When someone throws a wrench in an engine, the engine dies. This brings us back to the interrelatedness of the entire cosmos and the cosmic law of harmony: things work only when they work together. Although very few in today's scientific age would accept the connection, it seems as if ecological disharmony can result from moral wrongs on the sociological level as suggested in the Hosea passage.[14] Even if the language is taken metaphorically, one cannot escape the connection between unfaithfulness to Yahweh and environmental degradation. The Scriptures have done nothing more than take the implications of ecology to their logical end. They present a cosmic ecosystem that includes all reality, physical and metaphysical.

Perhaps Numbers 35:33-34 could be taken the same way. Apparently, murdering humans causes environmental degradation. "Do not pollute the land where you are. Bloodshed pollutes the land." Jeremiah spoke of the land being defiled by the sin of prostitution (Jer. 3:2-3). When people sin, everything is thrown out of harmony with the divine intent. Even the land is defiled or polluted and thrown onto the path leading to death. There is the possibility, however, that some references to the land being polluted could be taken metaphorically as referring to the people who occupy the land (see Amos 7:10). Thus when people sin, the nation is defiled (see Josh. 7:11,20). Yet the distinct possibility remains that the Jews perceived the land and the people as a single entity, extending the corporate identity to all creation. When something happens to break the harmony of the cosmic community, its effect ripples throughout the natural order.

In Leviticus 18 God warns His people against defiling themselves by illicit sexual activity, "Because this is how the nations that I am going to drive out before you became defiled. Even the land was defiled; so I punished it for its sin, and the land vomited out its inhabitants" (vv. 24-25). Here the Canaanites committed sexual sins, yet the land is said to have sinned. It would appear that *land* means "people," and it was the people whom God judged by driving them out of the land. But perhaps we should not try to distinguish too closely between the literal and metaphorical uses of "land." Jewish thought evidently saw a closer relation between moral acts and the state of the environment than we do. We tend to look at Scripture through a modern worldview that likes to compartmentalize everything rather than see wholes. For the Jew, however, the land and its inhabitants were inseparably linked together, an idea that Christianity has lost.

Third, God often judges humans through nature, either by withholding part of His sustaining influence, causing the land not to yield freely, or by manipulating the elements and forces of nature, causing catastrophic disruptions of the environment (such as the deluge). The notion that sin causes the land to strike back at the disobedient is a common Old Testament theme (see Deut. 11:13-17). This was almost always attributed in some way to a divine decree or divine permission, since Yahweh was perceived as in control of the forces of nature. The biblical framework therefore suggests that we should understand the ecological problem in terms of a triangular relationship between God, humans, and nature, not in terms of a linear view consisting only of humans and nature.

Isaiah often spoke of this divine retribution,

> See, the Lord is going to lay
> waste the earth
> and devastate it;
> he will ruin its face
> and scatter its inhabitants (24:1).

The reason given is human sin:

> The earth is defiled by its people;
> they have disobeyed the laws,
> violated the statutes and broken the everlasting covenant.
> Therefore a curse consumes the earth;
> its people must bear their guilt (24:5-6).

The curse cannot be thought of as human abuse of nature, but the acts of God in punishing His people. Perhaps God's repaying "them double for their wickedness and their sin" (Jer. 16:18) refers to God's directly acting upon nature and indirectly allowing the people to suffer the natural consequence of broken harmony. God's judgments are actually acts of love, for He sends these adverse conditions on nature to cause people to turn to Him for healing (Amos 4:6-13). The judgment is a mild form of rebuke. One can still live off the land, but it takes much more effort (for other references of God's judging the land because of human sin, see Gen. 4:10-12; Ps. 107:33-34; Jer. 4:17-28; 9:9-11; 49:20; and Hos. 2:3).

Just as God can impose the curse, He can also lift it, allowing the rivers to flow through parched lands and the vegetation to blossom (see Isa. 41:18-20; Hos. 2:21-22). God will bless people with the earth's bounty as they walk in obedience (Gen. 26:12; 27:27-28; Deut. 28:1-6; and Jer. 32:42-44). This fruitfulness is figuratively depicted in terms of the land's rejoicing (Ps. 96:11-13; Isa. 44:22-23; 49:13; and 55:12-13). Since everything is under divine control, the only way the environment can be fully healed is for people to return to their Maker:

> "When I shut up the heavens so that there is no rain, or command locusts to devour the land or send a plague among my people, if my people, who are called by my name, will humble themselves and pray and seek my face and turn from their wicked ways, then will I hear from heaven and will forgive their sin and will heal their land" (2 Chron. 7:13-14).

When people return to God and keep His covenant (meaning the underlying principles behind all God's moral injunctions), then God will heal the land. As Lampe said, "When God's covenant is renewed with his disobedient people, and men come to be restored, through forgiveness, to a right relationship towards God, there is to be a renewal of all creation."[15]

Our continued sin therefore is preventing healing of the land. There can never be harmony and healing as long as self asserts its own way. Human vices stemming from self-centeredness such as greed, arrogance, self-glory, affluence, and covetousness are contrary to God's moral laws of ecological harmony. Greed for materialistic gain is depleting our natural resources, depriving others, and robbing future generations, as well as devastating the environment, turning rivers into sewers, and our land into waste dumps. In the process, millions of animals are killed, and the beauty of pristine landscapes is being vandalized. Greed also causes people to have difficulty seeing past themselves. What results is a myopic vision of the ecological problem that sees everything in bits and pieces at short range. Being primarily concerned with what could benefit them within their lifetime, humans lack the long-term commitment needed for most environmental remedies.[16]

The Scriptures imply that there will always be polluters until Christ returns to conquer the death principle, evidenced by greed, selfishness, autonomy, and separation (1 Cor. 15:26). Although this is somewhat pessimistic, it presents a realistic view of humanity that we all must face. As long as there is pollution within, there will be pollution without. This malady plagues every approach to rectify the ecological crisis, whether or not the system acknowledges human frailty. It is not a weakness unique to the biblical approach. Everyone recognizes that there are going to be some who will refuse to sort their trash for recycling, continue to toss cans out of car windows, and live their lives as usual. No approach can guarantee perfect cooperation by everyone.

Since the cause of human abuse of the environment is the demonic twist in human nature, there is no need to continue the search for the roots of the problem. Biologist Richard Wright said,

> We have come to the wellspring of the ecological crisis. I suggest that there is no need to search the past to find the basis—the common denominator—for man's exploitation and misuse of nature. The explanation reveals itself every day, if we care to look for it, because it is present in each of us—human greed, carelessness and ignorance. To solve the ecological crisis, we must come to grips with these very evident and very basic aspects of human nature.[17]

It is obvious that if sin is responsible for the present crisis, Christianity cannot be. This does not excuse individual Christians, who along with the rest of humanity share in the burden of guilt. It seems as if "Christianity has become the scapegoat for human failure. It is not religious belief, but human greed and ignorance which have allowed our culture to come to the point of ecological crisis."[18] Because of human sin, "the whole creation has been groaning as in the pains of childbirth" (Rom. 8:22).

The Myth of Materialism

Philosophically, materialism is the belief that the physical realm is ultimate reality. Matter is all there is, and everything, including thoughts and feelings, can be explained in terms of matter. This atheistic cosmology is closely tied with the popular understanding of materialism, which holds that the pursuit of wealth, affluence, luxury, and pleasure constitutes the highest good. If nothing exists beyond the physical, then the physical becomes divinity, and the pursuit of it becomes the goal of one's life. Money, not God, is all powerful and is even able to manipulate values and purchase peace and health. All meaning, purpose, and security are derived from the material rather from a personal God. This notion of materialism is the prevailing cosmology or myth of contemporary society. Although the myth of materialism is being challenged by the environmental crisis, it will continue to be a powerful ideology in society until its energizing catalysts are destroyed.

Materialistic thinking pits us against one another and against nature in the never-ending contest to have the newest, best, fastest, or most of whatever the current fad happens to be. Although there is some awakening to the impact such thinking has on the environment, most remain unmoved. Why should I bother when I only live a short time anyway? If this life is all there is, then why not grab as much as I can get and enjoy the short time I have? It seems as if unrestrained economic progress, the human inclination toward selfish accumulation of goods, and a secular cosmology are inseparably linked in a polygamous marriage that our modern society is pronouncing a blessing on.

Having an affluent, luxurious life-style has become the expected norm for society and the benchmark of success. Even young married couples starting out want a large suburban home with all the conveniences. The spirit of conformity overpowers any notion of a simpler life-style and justifies the rat race for more. The pursuit of things and pleasure is not only the consuming preoccupation of our society, it is the consuming blight on our environment. Americans literally sacrifice their lives in slavery to their jobs to obtain things they could easily do without. It is unfortunate that the American way is becoming the model of success for developing nations. The raging quest to satisfy the lust for quantity overrides and kills the quieter quest for tranquillity and quality of life.

We are apparently held captive by the structure, values, and mores of our society. To denounce materialism is to denounce the American way and the very thing that has made this country great. Besides being almost unpatriotic, it seems impossible to break the stranglehold that the myth of materialism has on the structural fabric of our technological society. Society is stuck in the quicksand of greed and materialism and cannot pull itself out. Schumacher remarked,

> The modern economy is propelled by a frenzy of greed and indulges in an orgy of envy, and these are not accidental features but the very causes of its expansionist success. The question is whether such causes can be effective for long or whether they carry within themselves the seeds of destruction.[19]

The quantitative standard for self-fulfillment is a killing idea; it is not only environmentally destructive, it is personally self-destructive. Jesus recognized the truth of this principle by saying, "Whoever wants to save his life will lose it, but whoever loses his life for Me will find it" (Matt. 16:25). This is a general axiom that cannot be limited to the human soul and its salvation. When people try to conquer the world for themselves, they will end up destroying everything. Jesus consistently taught that life is to be measured qualitatively rather than quantitatively. In the parable of the rich fool, He said, "Be on your guard against all kinds of greed; a man's life does not consist in the abundance of his possessions" (Luke 12:15; see Rom. 14:17). Jesus also exhorted us to lay up treasures in heaven, not on earth (Matt. 6:19-21). Attachment to self and power twists whatever it comes in contact with, whether love, friendships, relations, business, ethics, as well as our commission to care for God's creation. Whatever becomes twisted by egocentrism finally withers and dies.

This attachment to self and power is symptomatic of a much larger disease, one that pertains to the modern cosmology. The problem is that our society has lost all perspective of a supernatural metaphysics that will give a sense of security and eliminate the endless striving for things. Accordingly it defines a fulfilled life quantitatively rather than qualitatively. A life that is measured qualitatively lives in peaceful coexistence with the rest of reality, including God. If God were not included, the striving would continue.

The values of greed and materialism that propel the modern economic enterprise are the very values that Christianity denounces. Yet it is sad to see the church caught up in the materialistic norm of society. It is the church above all that should recognize the myth of materialism and denounce it for the destruction it is causing God's creation. The general tendency of Christians to refrain from tithing suggests how far the myth of materialism has stretched its influence. C. S. Lewis observed that "in every age the human mind is deeply influenced by the accepted Model of the universe."[20] This applies equally with those professing to be Christian. As long as self-interests prevail in the church, so will materialism, thus effectively silencing a needed voice against the wrongs humankind is inflicting on the environment.

The Bible condemns the accumulation of wealth that neglects the need of others. Money and possessions in themselves are not evil, but the love of money is (1 Tim. 6:10). When one loves money more than others, money becomes a cancerous disease that eventually kills the person. The rich young ruler who was unwilling to part with his riches to help the poor went away grieved because he had missed the healing Jesus had to offer (Matt. 19:21-22). He was unable to keep the Tenth Commandment that forbids coveting a neighbor's possessions (Ex. 20:17; Deut. 5:21).

Materialism is not only antithetical to genuine love but also symptomatic of a spiritual malady that seeks security in things rather than God. Jesus encouraged His followers not to have a fixation on material wealth, seeing that God had promised to provide their needs (Matt. 6:19-21; 6:24-34; see Phil. 4:19). Paul instructs Timothy to "command those who are rich in the present world not to be arrogant nor to put their hope in wealth, which is so uncertain, but to put their hope in God" (1 Tim. 6:17; see Jas. 5:1). Jesus also taught that the love of the things of this world stifles the working of God's Word in a person and is poison to the soul (Matt. 13:22; Mark 4:19; Luke 8:14; see 1 John 2:15). Attachment to one's money and possessions hinders one from attaining the kingdom of God (Matt. 19:16-24; Mark 10:17-25; Luke 18:18-25).

Jesus reminds us that we cannot serve God and mammon (Matt. 6:24). We cannot serve God and be a steward of His creation if we are caught up in the materialistic spirit of our age. Stewardship of God's creation requires a modest view of material possessions and a benevolent use of what passes through our hands. Since all things belong to God, we cannot use them as if they belonged to us; we must use God's possessions as He would—to help those in need.

In his article "No More Business as Usual," Douglas Daetz presented the ecological problems as being "due to our trying to have too much for too many. Either the 'too much' or the 'too many,' or both, must be reduced." "If we are to successfully head off impending ecocatastrophe, we must keep reminding ourselves of the 'no more business as usual' basis of our faith, and our actions must accord with the urgency implied by such a basis."[21]

Human Depravity

Scriptures teach that the human race is totally depraved. Some have felt this means that we cannot do anything good without divine grace, such as working toward environmental improvement. This misconception has raised doubts about what possible contribution Christianity could make in helping correct environmental degradation. Theologically speaking, humans are totally depraved in that they are totally unable to come to God by their own strength. It has nothing to do with the capacity to do good, only with the capacity to be perfectly good.

There are several ways total depravity could be misunderstood. (1) Total depravity does not mean that people are totally wicked or totally ungodly. Nor does it mean that they indulge in or are prone to indulge in every kind of sin. (2) Total depravity does not mean that people are totally unable to do good. There is still a glimmer of moral fiber in every person. People can still display goodness, kindness, love, and many other virtues. (3) Total depravity does not mean that people are totally devoid of an inner conscience to discern good from evil. Everyone still possesses the image of God and can recognize and appreciate good.

What total depravity does mean can also be summarized under three points. (1) Total depravity means that every human faculty, such as the mind and conscience, has been corrupted. This does not mean that the image of God has been destroyed, only overpowered or marred by the demonic nature. (2) Total depravity means that people are devoid of genuine love for the true God. The natural corollary of a preference for self is an aversion to God. Any expression of love for God is a mixed, imperfect love. (3) Total depravity means that people are utterly unable to come to God on their own. They cannot change their character or conduct in order to be pleasing to God. To be in harmony with the perfectly righteous God, people must be morally perfect themselves. Thus humans are totally unable to reach up to God and save themselves; God must reach down to them. In summary, total depravity means that there is absolutely nothing in humans that would commend them to God for salvific purposes.

They have been estranged from God, and they lack the capacity to rectify the situation.

One point often overlooked is that total depravity does not mean that people cannot do good. Fallen humanity has accomplished much good throughout history, and there is no reason for this not to continue. This would even apply to rectifying some of the wrongs inflicted on the environment; but this need not imply Pelagianism, as Passmore suggested.[22] Pelagianism teaches that we inherited neither a sin nature nor imputed sin from Adam. We are able to live a perfect life of righteousness and can by our works achieve acceptance before God. Traditional Christianity has rightly condemned this as heresy.

There are passages that seem to imply that the unregenerate cannot do any good. Isaiah, for example, said that "all our righteous acts are like filthy rags" (64:6), but this is in the context of our stance before God, where one sin renders us totally unclean (Jas. 2:10). When a person saves another from drowning, the act itself is good, but the accumulation of all the person's acts and thoughts invariably includes evil, which in the eyes of God renders the person unrighteous. Therefore, it is just as if all the person's righteous deeds were as filthy rags. What Isaiah is saying is that a person cannot possibly merit salvation by good works because of the presence of the sin nature. People can to a certain extent do right without regeneration, but the good is neither persistent nor pure all the time. Often acts of benevolence are done because of a reciprocal benefit. Since people cannot be totally free from sin, they cannot be restored to God apart from divine grace. The Christian belief in total depravity does not stand in the way of ecological progress. But it does negate the possibility of a human-made ecological utopia.

Human Finiteness

Scripture tells us much about humans, our nature, the reason we are as we are, and the remedy for our predicament. One of the things it teaches is human finiteness. Although we would rather not be reminded of it, we are finite creatures. We cannot know all there is to be known, especially about the complex relationships that exist within the earth's ecosystem (Job 8:9; Eccl. 11:5; 1 Cor. 13:12). Yet with partial and often erroneous information, we proceed as if we knew, falsely trusting in science and technology to make decisions regarding the direction of the planet.

Society indeed exults in the vast array of knowledge it has accumulated, but this is nothing more than deceptive boasting.

The assumption humans often have that they think they have the answer and know what is best in a certain situation is pure egocentric arrogance (see Isa. 13:11). We know very little in relation to the whole. Yet our knowledge, as imperfect as it is, constitutes the primary basis for policy decisions, some of which have had devastating effects on the environment. To accept our limitations is a sign of humility, something we are not naturally prone to do (see Matt. 23:12). Regardless of the amount of research we will still make mistakes, mistakes that should alert us to the fact of our finiteness. They should also caution us to investigate consequences of new technology more thoroughly before proceeding. Our whole attitude and approach to knowledge should be rethought (see Job 28:28; Prov. 28:26; Jas. 3:17).

The present approach to knowledge is atomistic or particularistic, governed by a Newtonian piecemeal worldview. Knowledge is gained when something is reduced to its lowest divisible form and isolated from all other influences. Only then can it be categorized and understood. This reductionist procedure loses touch with the whole and the relationships that bind individual entities together. True perception and knowledge cannot be attained apart from viewing the object as an interconnected part of the whole, and the whole cannot be discerned by our finite minds. We must be dependent on the omniscient Creator for a true vision of the whole.

Our limited knowledge of ecological relationships dampens the hope in finding solutions through technology. Because of the complexity and magnitude of such relationships it is impossible for finite minds to know perfectly in advance the full consequences of a certain act. As one writer put it, "The ecosphere is not only more complex than we think but more complex than we can ever think."[23] Simply stated, we are not gods; we are neither omnipotent nor omniscient. Many environmental problems are partially attributable to human ignorance. Even attempts to improve the environment often lead to further complications, such as the Aswan Dam affecting agriculture along the lower Nile and sardine populations in the Mediterranean.

If we retain our present attitude toward knowledge and continue our present course of action, it will be disastrous for the environment. The attitude of former Secretary of the Interior James Watt must be condemned as utterly damaging to the environment, "We're gonna make lots of action happen. . . . I'm out to make decisions and I will make them quickly and that is so that I can make the corrections to all the mistakes I make. I make lots of mistakes, 'cause I make a lot of decisions. But we're in a hurry and we're willing to take risks."[24] Such attitudes could cause mistakes that no one can correct.

Environmental Implications

Considering the demonic disposition of the human race, a disposition well attested to by our frightful track record, many have wondered where the incentive for remaking humanity might come and if any significant change is possible at all. Ward and Dubos comment, "With war as mankind's oldest habit and divided sovereignty as his most treasured inheritance, where are the energies, the psychic force, the profound commitment needed for a wider loyalty?"[25] E. F. Schumacher raised the same question:

> It will need many ounces, however, to lay the economic foundations of peace. Where can one find the strength to go on working against such obviously appalling odds? What is more: where can one find the strength to overcome the violence of greed, envy, hate and lust within oneself?[26]

Some of the ways suggested to control or change human disposition and behavior include (1) coercion, (2) appealing to the human instinct of preservation, or (3) changing the way people think, either through mass media saturation, education, religious beliefs, or by changing their underlying worldview. All are plagued with difficulties that hamper their being entirely satisfactory or successful. The first invokes the danger of a totalitarian state, the second would result in a temporary fad that would fade once the "threat" is lessened, and the third is incapable of handling the persistent problem of human nature.

Will Coercion and Legislation Have Any Success?

Because of human nature, many feel that coercion is the only way to change human behavior and attain a safe environment. James Gustafson reasoned, "Since the resources of the earth are finite but the wants and desires of humans apparently almost insatiable, it is self-deceptive to think that restraints upon human action are not going to have to be developed and probably be enforced coercively."[27] It is reasonable to suppose that if pollution is ever going to stop, then the government will have to make it a legal offense and penalize the offenders. Coercion, however, has serious shortcomings. First, if the penalty becomes out of proportion to the crime and enforced with a ruthless power, it could very easily lead to a totalitarian state. Second, some types of legislation impinge on the natural God-given freedom and rights of individuals, such as a potential policy to forbid births, requiring sterilization, or compulsory abortion. Such restrictions would be very difficult to enforce unless accompanied by a police state. Third, coercion will ultimately fail because of the human disposition to do as one pleases anyway.

Alternatives to coercive tactics for curbing population growth might be government incentives or tax deductions to small families or submitting to voluntary sterilization. There could also be subsidies for free public transportation, organic farming, and industrial cleanup operations. The present tax structure encourages large families and continued population growth. The best approach in some areas may be for legislation to encourage compliance by a reward system rather than demand it. Yet this is still coercion, albeit indirect coercion, and it still may, in certain areas, impinge on God-given freedoms. Perhaps a way to circumvent coercion altogether is for government to encourage environmentally appropriate technology so that it will become economically beneficial to implement; that is, to press for economical motivation where economic priorities match environmental priorities. Yet this does not really solve the problem, for it appeals to the same greed that caused the problem in the first place.

Nevertheless, we can sympathize with those who advocate coercion, especially in view of human nature. There seems little else to turn to short of a mass conversion to God, something not likely to happen. If coercion is used, it should only be a temporary stopgap measure for emergencies, not a long-term policy. We should also recognize that it will never be the final answer. The success of legislation will depend on the relative importance the individual places on freedom versus the penalty and environmental problem being addressed. This brings us back to the tyranny of self and the high value humans place on freedom. People may grant the government right to pass laws that help protect them, such as making murder a crime, but they would object to laws that limit their speeding on the highways if they are prone to do so. It will be especially difficult to enforce legislation that either violates one's notion of freedom or will not reap benefits until future generations.

Even when compliance is demanded, some will continue to live their lives as usual. Why do some persist in tossing trash out car windows, even where there is a sign saying that litterers will be prosecuted? Or why do some evade paying taxes? Similarly, it would come as no surprise if some industries continue to dodge the law for proper disposal of toxic wastes. There is an aberration in human nature that no amount of legislation can correct.

Therefore, legislation cannot bring about all the necessary changes. It will not change humanity's inner disposition and attitudes. All that can be achieved is changing outward behavior. Paul argued that outward legalistic constraints will never bring a true change in the individual, but rather will lead to death (Rom. 7:7-13). Humans are still humans; they still have the demon within, and they will always resent being forced to do something they would rather not do.

Both unlimited freedom and unrestrained coercion are ultimately destructive to the quality of life that makes life worth living and contrary to biblical teaching. Those who advocate coercion indirectly attest to the pervasiveness of human sin. Having acknowledged this, the next logical step in a godless society is some form of coercion. However, there is a much better alternative, and it is found in submission to Christ and His moral principles.

Will Appeals to Human Survival Succeed?

Much of the environmental concern today has been induced by appeals to human preservation. We often hear that if we fail to reverse our present trend, we will end up killing ourselves. This is a very effective ploy, for it speaks to the instinct of self-preservation and also to the egocentrism that pervades society. "Human beings are moved more by their belief about what is beneficial to themselves, by their sense of what is real and fitting, and by their sensibility, than by ethical appeals."[28] Threat of a nuclear holocaust helped to draw many into the New Age holistic movement. Efforts to save the planet were actually efforts to save themselves in disguise.

This type of appeal could be faulted on several grounds. First, it often fails. If people enjoy doing something, they will continue doing it even knowing that it will eventually lead to their death. For example, the Surgeon General's warning on cigarette packages that smoking is hazardous to the health does not faze the habitual smoker. Death is normally perceived in the remote future and as nothing to be concerned about. If one is relatively healthy and enjoys smoking, the warning on the package becomes meaningless. The same could be applied to appeals for environmental action.

Second, it appeals to the very thing that has led to destruction in the first place, attention on oneself. Hence the root problem is not being addressed but rather is being stimulated. Such procedure is ill-founded and will in the long run be self-defeating.

Third, there could very well be a temporary trend for environmental ethics based on pragmatic self-centered concerns. However, once the fad passes and the media lays off their campaign, people will forget about the "crisis" and return to their old ways that are more directly gratifying to self.

Fourth, it does not generate concern for nature for nature's sake. The only species worth saving is Homo sapiens. Saving endangered species, tropical rain forests, or future generations do not enter into this framework. Appeal to human survival is, therefore, inadequate as a motivational force for environmental change.

Can Education Liberate Humanity from Bondage to Self?

Many regard education as the only plausible course to change humanity's destructive behavior towards the environment. Change the way people think, and we can change the way they act. The education of society could be achieved through mass media blitz, literature crusades, propagating religious or metaphysical beliefs, and even promotional campaigns, such as Earth Day. The goal is all the same, to alter one's way of thinking (that is, one's belief system or underlying worldview) to accommodate respect and concern for nature.

The problem with appealing to education to change one's attitude and behavior is essentially the same as appealing to religiosity: the discrepancy between belief systems and behavior. There is ample historical evidence that altering one's worldview to include a pantheistic or Christian concept of God does not necessarily bring the corresponding ethical changes. The way in which the world is perceived may change, but the attitudes and behavior may not. For example, the pantheistic reverence for nature did not constrain the deforestation of China or India; neither did the Judeo-Christian belief in God's ownership of the earth prevent people from claiming everything was theirs to exploit as they please. The implication might be to shelve all such theological and philosophical idealism as hopelessly irrelevant to the present crisis.

Several answers could be given for this discrepancy. First, there is a widespread lack of understanding regarding the teachings of one's particular belief system. Second, there is the failure to reckon with the power of sin in a person's life. Even if a new vision of nature's value and our place in the cosmic order were to permeate society, we would still be plagued by the demon within. Knowledge of the interrelatedness of all things cannot save a person from enslavement to self. Various means to raise the level of environmental awareness are all good and have their place, but they still do not address the root problem. The propensity to put self first would still hamper any effort to put the beliefs into practice, unless those beliefs were egocentric in the first place (such as, the philosophy of Ayn Rand). Third, there exists in the minds of many an unconscious dualism between the truth of faith and the truth of logical fact; that is, religious truth and scientific truth pertain to different aspects of life. Fourth, most people's beliefs are a synergistic blend of traditional religions and the prevailing cultural mores, both being colored by the human inclination toward self. It is true, as Lynn White observed, that the way people perceive nature will influence their behavior toward it.[29] But that perception must be interpreted according to the composition of individual beliefs, beliefs in which self still plays a large role regardless of what any religion or ideology might say. Fifth, most ethical codes lack the essential ingredients of motivation and enablement. Even though moral codes say something should be done, they lack the stimuli to bring it to pass. Three of the above pertain in one way or another to the human tendency toward self-interests and indifference toward anything else.

As Lewis Moncrief said, "No culture has been able to completely screen out the egocentric tendencies of human beings."[30] Not even Christianity has been able to eradicate the problem of sin, as evidenced by the history of sin in the church. Christianity does teach self-sacrificial service modeled after Christ, yet no one has so completely conquered the sin problem that this model is perfected in everyday experience. The sin nature is still present to distort the image of Christ from being fully incarnated in the believer. Furthermore, most Christians have not fully thought out the implications of a theocentric worldview. Paul had to exhort the Romans to be transformed by the renewing of the mind (12:2), the Corinthians to bring every thought in captivity to Christ (2 Cor. 10:5), and the Philippians to have the mind of Christ (2:5). If Christians fail to think through the worldview implications of their faith system, it would be impossible to expect them to carry out their beliefs, especially as they touch social and environmental concerns. If Christians fail to implement their beliefs, then the relevancy of Christianity to the environmental crisis is a dead issue.

Although education cannot be counted on as the end solution to change human behavior, it does, nevertheless, have its place. Passmore noted, "It would be absurd to deny that moral and metaphysical principles ever have any effect on human conduct, if only to justify courses of action which might otherwise arouse qualms. But their effect is a great deal less than is sometimes suggested."[31] Any model of behavior proposed through changing the way people think will invariably fail on two accounts: the lack of an environmentally sound motivational strategy and the enablement to carry out the injunctions. Both the motivation and enablement pertain to overcoming our self-promoting tendency. Thus the discrepancy between what people know they should do and what they do will persist. Education will help to a degree but cannot be looked upon as the antidote to environmental abuse.

What Can We Expect from a Biblical Framework?

The biblical framework will help us evaluate the cause of the problem and offer direction toward resolution. It does not promise a quick or easy remedy, but it does teach us how to live in harmony with God and all that God has made. The Bible realistically cautions against placing too much confidence in human effort or too much hope for total resolution in this age. The environmental problem is a sin problem. People will continue to play havoc with the environment as long as they are controlled by their sin nature, and the sin nature will continue in the human race until an apocalyptic intervention by the Almighty to defeat the forces of evil. Scriptures repeatedly affirm that evil will wax greater as the end approaches, not get better (see 2 Tim. 3:1-5). Although the Christian message offers an answer to human sin, not all will embrace it. Progress will nevertheless be made, but since the root problem would not have been fully addressed, problems will persist. From a biblical point of view, there can be no real ecological peace on earth before the Lord returns.

Limited Progress from Human Effort. Although the Scriptures paint a grim picture of human sin, it does not entirely reject human capability. Humans still bear the *imago Dei*, albeit hampered by the demon tendency, and are still able to do good. The biblical condemnation of the race should not be construed as totally pessimistic in terms of environmental improvement. Human depravity, rightly understood, primarily refers to our inability to live perfect before God and thereby lay claim on His salvation.

Developing a sense of place, recognizing God's ownership, practicing responsible stewardship, or perceiving the cosmos as one interconnected whole (whether from a pantheistic or Christian outlook) will all help some, but without addressing the problem of human sin, no abstract conception of humanity's place in nature will be able to sustain an ongoing ecological agenda. The demon within would still be present to resist any change that would impinge on the human impulse to obtain things and pursue pleasure. For the same reason, any form of generic ecumenical religiosity, coercive tactics, or mass media brainwashing will have only limited success, for they all overlook sin's stranglehold on the human race.

Partial Acceptance of Potential Solution. The only potential answer to the problem is found in yielding to Christ and receiving the Holy Spirit. Christianity provides answers to the deficiencies that plague secular models of ethics and behaviorism. The motivating impulse in the Christian model is our accountability to the Creator, and the enabling power comes through the indwelling Spirit. From a Christian perspective, what is needed is a radical and comprehensive shift in belief systems and the corresponding change in attitudes and behavior, empowered by God's Spirit. A shift of this magnitude would paralyze human greed and materialism and cripple the destructive technocratic structure that has such a stranglehold on society.

Although Christianity offers a solution to the root problem, it would be rather presumptuous to assume that everyone will be converted. Furthermore, not everyone who is converted will fully endorse a theocentric outlook or submit to the rule of Christ in their lives to realize partial victory over the sin principle. That is, we can neither expect a massive paradigm shift or corresponding behavioral changes (Luke 18:8; 2 Tim. 3:13; 4:3). The sin nature will even be present in the Christian until Christ returns to "transform our lowly bodies so that they will be like his glorious body" (Phil. 3:21). To a degree this transformation is taking place now in the believer. "And we, who with unveiled faces all reflect the Lord's glory are being transformed into his likeness with ever increasing glory, which comes from the Lord, who is the Spirit" 2 Cor. 3:18). But as the history of the church can well attest, the inclination to serve self has never been eradicated. Any framework to interpret the environmental problem must reckon with the power and persistence of sin in the human race. One need not even turn to the Bible to realize the enormity of the problem. Sin will continue regardless of the efforts of Christianity or any other religion.

Future Hope of Divine Intervention. In place of a human-made ecological utopia (which at best would still be imperfect), Christianity offers the hope of a glorious kingdom patterned after the garden paradise. This will only come through the intervention of God Himself. Christianity therefore does offer a plausible framework to understand the present situation and to work toward substantial healing, as well as a hope of complete restored ecological harmony.

Because Christianity addresses the sin problem, it potentially has a better prospect for substantial healing in the present age than any other option. But again, we cannot expect total healing by any approach during this age. As one writer put it,

> This realism will not blunt our intention or capacity to respond. It will save us from the despair that perfectionism produces. Our aim will not be more perfection, but *faithfulness*. That faithfulness will prevent our deafness to the call to help the sister or brother trapped in poverty. It will keep us from rationalizing away the will to act.[32]

10

THE ETHICAL DILEMMA: HUMAN RIGHTS, NATURE'S RIGHTS, OR GOD'S RIGHTS?

Environmental ethics pertains to what people should or should not do in regard to the use and management of nature. It delves into such questions as human and animal rights, sustainability, conflict resolution, ecojustice, and future generations. Although the question of our ethical relation to nature is not new, it has become much more critical in view of our increased technological capabilities. We now have the power to cause irreversible damage to the environment. Is such action morally wrong? If so, then on what basis?

Traditional moral systems appear to be incapable of responding to the growing problem of environmental ethics. Albert Schweitzer noted, "The great fault of all ethics hitherto has been that they believed themselves to have to deal only with the relations of man to man."[1] Aldo Leopold was one of the early advocates of the need to establish a new ethic that included nature. He stated, "There is as yet no ethic dealing with man's relation to land and to the animals and plants that grow upon it. Land, like Odysseus' slave girls, is still property. The land-relation is still strictly economic, entailing privileges but not obligations."[2]

207

For most evangelical Christians, ethics pertains only to inter-personal relations. It would be morally wrong to mistreat another person, for persons are moral beings. Nature, on the other hand, lacks a soul and a moral constitution and therefore falls outside the realm of ethical obligations. Most would have difficulty declaring that it is immoral to mistreat a tree or a cockroach. Trees and cockroaches are part of the creation that we are to have dominion over; they are not moral beings. Because nature was made for human use, it simply cannot have a moral claim against us. This apparent lack of moral status is only one of several problematic areas in environmental ethics that confront the church and society.

The Quest for a Metaphysical Foundation

The first problem is that of finding a credible metaphysical base for environmental ethics. When we decry environmental pollution as a hideous crime, on what basis are we saying this? There seems to be some glimmer of moral fabric that tells people that pollution and environmental destruction are wrong. Mere feelings, however, cannot form an adequate base for moral actions—feelings are changeable and cannot be defended philo-sophically. We need a cosmology that corresponds with our deep-seated notion of morality and that can be rationally defended.

It is well attested that humans possess a general notion of moral duty. Paul argued in Romans 2:14-15 that the Gentiles who do not have the written law are nevertheless aware of the law because it is inscribed on their heart. Their consciences either accuse or justify their behavior. From a Christian perspec-tive, this moral sensitivity reflects the remnant of the *imago Dei*. But conscience is no longer an infallible guide because it can be programmed by various elements, such as societal norms, expe-diency of a given situation, traditions, peer pressure, and the human propensity to favor self. Nevertheless, there is a general consensus of the way things should be. A workable metaphysical base should not only correspond to that consensus but also be free from logical pitfalls that could prove detrimental to the envi-ronment.

Thus the present crisis is demanding a cosmology that can provide an ethical foundation for environmental behavior, a foundation which can also provide ethical motivation and enablement. As John Black said, "It is thus not too much to say that one of the most pressing tasks facing the western world today is to find an acceptable basis for responsible conduct in relation to the natural environment."[3]

The Bankruptcy of a Secular Ethic

It is obvious that the dominant cosmology in Western culture is entangling humanity deeper in environmental carnage and is no longer acceptable. Its ethic of expansion is simply not sustainable. The evolutionary model in which all players on the cosmic stage are competitors and humans are pitted against one another and nature for survival is obviously inadequate. The survival of the fittest mentality kills ethical responsibility. Why not let the poor starve to death? Or why not continue to rape the environment? It is almost a given in our society for one to advance at the expense of another. This destructive notion is the foundation and energizing principle of our entire economic system. Everything becomes objects for conquest and commodities for exploitation, whether humans or nature. It is virtually impossible to construct an environmentally satisfying code of ethics from evolutionary theory.[4]

Moreover, since existence arose by blind chance, or as some say by a cosmic accident, there can be no reason for its being or its continuation. That is, there cannot be imperatives in a happenstance cosmogony. Things simply are. To say that anything is wrong, such as murder, is pragmatically derived from a social contract model of ethics that quickly leads into philosophical quicksand. "I'd rather not be killed, so I'll make an agreement with the rest of society that we shouldn't go around killing each other." But why should I continue to exist?   In secular thought there is more reason for nothing existing than for something existing. It cannot offer any reason for the existence of things or why they should continue. All meaning, purpose, values, and ethics have to be injected into existence, for these elements are not intrinsic to existence itself. This will invariably result in a relative, unstable, nonsustainable ethic based on the changing spectrum of human life and needs. Bryce-Smith remarked, "By replacing the concept of a purposeful superhuman God with the doctrine of blind chance, they remove the ultimate basis of that morality which I hold to be an ecological necessity if human society is to survive."[5]

A self-promoting humanistic system can never hope to provide motivation to sustain long-term interest in environmental issues. Since an individual's existence is short-termed, so are that person's interests, a killing idea for environmental policy making. Ian Barbour said that "ecological concern will be short-lived and ineffectual unless it deals with the values and social institutions that have led to this ravaging of the environment."[6] Those destructive values that must be addressed involve placing supreme value on self and utilitarian value on everything else.

Any ethic based on a worldview that accepts these tenets as given cannot possibly contribute anything more than temporary and piecemeal solutions to environmental problems. Humanity's primary commitment is still to self, and self is temporally bound.

The Dubious Hope of a Biocentric Ethic

In attempting to correct the "us-verses-them" mentality of evolutionary thought, many favor the dissolution of all subject-object distinctions. For example, Po-keung Ip argued that Taoism is a viable metaphysical base for environmental ethics because it does not separate between subject and object, or between humans and nature. He contended that a feasible base cannot be found in any system that maintains such dualisms.[7] Absolving distinctions will encounter serious ethical problems of its own, such as the inability to resolve conflicts of interest, being guilty of the naturalistic fallacy, and ignoring human uniqueness.

Some pantheists argue that moral categories exist on the earth plane and even constitute paths to salvation, but they do not exist on the spiritual plane. On the spiritual plane there can be no dichotomies, such as right or wrong. The alarming observation with this view is that there is no congruity between the metaphysical and the physical. There is a schism between the way things are on the two levels, which means that the higher level of reality is not relevant to the lower level. Thus multileveled pantheism is actually a dualistic system. The illusory form of pantheism, which denies the reality of the lower level, may solve these dualistic tendencies but encounters severe problems of its own, especially its devaluation of the physical. This lack of congruity between the two realms is in marked contrast with Christianity where Jesus taught His disciples to pray, "Your will be done on earth as it is in heaven" (Matt. 6:10). Here we see a harmonious continuity between the metaphysical and physical and thus the relevancy of a theocentric cosmology.

Whatever we base our ethics on, in a sense, becomes our God, for there is nothing higher to appeal to for direction. The three primary worldview models for environmental ethics—biocentrism, anthropocentrism, and theocentrism—derive their ethics respectively from nature, humanity, and a transcendent personal Being. Two environmental trends of particular interest today are deep ecology, arising out of a biocentric worldview, and shallow ecology, arising out of an anthropocentric worldview.

Deep ecology is primarily concerned with maintaining the biosphere on a long-term basis, with animals and plants having equal rights with humans and environmental action being done for the good of nature. It draws from religious and philosophical themes of various traditions and emphasizes that we should view ecosystems as wholes and preserve their integrity. One weakness is its insensitivity to human need. Some would even say that the human race is a cancer that should be eliminated to save the planet. Shallow ecology, on the other hand, maintains that humans are the center of values and that we must manage nature for the good of humanity. A primary weakness is its focus on short-term human needs and wants at the expense of long-term environmental interests. Thus it encourages myopic technological fixes. Deep ecologists advocate an ideological transformation that recognizes inherent value in life; whereas shallow ecology seeks to retain the dominant worldview with minor repairs on the environment. Neither approach is broad enough to comprehend the strengths of the opposing view while eliminating the weaknesses in their own. This shortcoming is inherent in any biocentric or anthropocentric approach. Although each provides insights, only partial solutions are offered. The new cosmology at the very least must look behind the appearances of nature and humanity and discover a unifying and ordering principle of the universe.

The Credibility of a Theocentric Ethic

At the heart of the issue is the credibility of the philosophical base for environmental ethics. Because metaphysical discussions transcend the realm of the physical, their validity cannot be determined by appealing to the scientific method. As Schumacher observes:

> That does not mean that they are purely "subjective" or "relative" or mere arbitrary conventions. They must be true to reality, although they transcend the world of facts—an apparent paradox to our positivistic thinkers. If they are not true to reality, the adherence to such a set of ideas must inevitably lead to disaster.[8]

Furthermore, all approaches to reality are in the last resort faith systems, even scientific materialism. The paramount question is then not the requirement of faith, but the plausibility of what is believed.

A plausible worldview must be able to provide a conceptual framework in which everything can be adequately accounted for, that is, to be able to integrate everything into a unified whole. Second, a worldview must be internally consistent or coherent; that is, the worldview must be consistent in the logic of its teachings, not necessarily in the practice of its adherents. Any claim for truth that contradicts itself disqualifies itself as a claim for truth, for truth cannot contain error. Third, a plausible worldview must correspond to observed facts and to common human experience. Arthur Holmes observed that the credibility of a worldview depends on its ability to unify effectively "all aspects of life and thought in a meaning-giving way."[9]

Nature is one of those particulars that must not only be included but included in a meaning-giving way. Any worldview that leads to the destruction of nature and as a result threatens life itself should be questioned, as should any worldview that reduces individual identity to nothingness. Such reductionist tactics hardly correspond to reality and cannot be expected to generate sustained love and concern for other entities in the cosmic community. Love for nature is a commonly acknowledged aspect of the new life that must be adequately accounted for by a philosophical system.

Genuine self-giving love, where one individual sacrifices self-interests for the sake of others, is an impossibility if everything were one organism. The only kind of love possible in monistic systems is self-love, a thought that comes dangerously close to the very cause of the ecological crisis. Self-love is really nonlove. Some, such as Krishnamurti, are forced to redefine love to be the cessation of conflict, rather than one individual caring for another.[10]

The Christian concept of love is epitomized by God's giving His Son for the sins of humanity (Rom. 5:8). This selfless giving of oneself for the sake of others is the core of Christian ethical teaching and is based on the character of God (1 John 4:7-21). The object of our love is not only God and fellow humans, but everything God loves, that is, His entire creation. If one does not love nature, the love cannot be called divine love, for it would be selective and partial.[11] Jesus summed up the law by saying, "'Love the Lord your God with all your heart and with all your soul and with all your mind.' This is the first and greatest commandment. And the second is like it: 'Love your neighbor as yourself.' All the Law and the Prophets hang on these two commandments" (Matt. 22:37-40). In view of the community of creation, one's neighbor, as mentioned before, must extend beyond humankind to all creatures. Furthermore, biblical love is an action rather than a feeling. It is the exact opposite of selfishness and the antidote to greed and materialism (see Mark 8:34-37; Gal. 5:16-26). Love, as Paul said, "is not self-seeking" (1 Cor. 13:5). True Christian love becomes an absolute essential for environmental ethics and proper stewardship.

Therefore, the biblical ethic is immensely relevant to the contemporary scene. Genuine love curbs the human tendency to engage in greed and materialism, to exploit the environment for selfish gain, and to mistreat any aspect of God's creation, whether human or nonhuman. Yet, at the same time, the Christian ethic is not guilty of pragmatic adaptation to meet current needs. The concept of selfless love is inherent in the Christian system, being based on the character of the transcendent God. Christianity is relevant without being relative and thus appears more credible than its major rivals as the basis for a workable environmental ethic.

The Pitfall of the Naturalistic Fallacy

The problem with most ethical systems (especially utilitarian and hedonistic models) is the logical problem of attempting to derive an *ought* from an *is*. The question is whether an imperative can be deduced from mere existence. The English philosopher George Edward Moore argued that any such attempt would be guilty of the naturalistic fallacy.[12] To reason in such a way would be a confusion of basic categories. For example, does having an urge for sexual gratification (a condition that exists) justify all types of sexual behavior (an ought)? If this argument could be sustained, one could justify just about any deviant act and negate ethical discussions altogether. This is the way things are, so this is how I should behave. Just as hedonism appeals to nature or natural conditions for a system of behavior, so do most biocentric approaches to environmental ethics. To reason from the existence of the natural order to a code of conduct violates the categorical distinctions between existence and ethical imperatives. Reducing this idea to its simplest form, many ecologists seem to be saying, "Since the world is, it ought to continue."

Just because things exist does not necessarily mean that they must continue to exist. This can be applied to ourselves, life as we know it, or to pristine nature which McKibben argued has been lost anyway. Thus to argue for environmental ethics (an ought) from nature or even from its interrelationships and interdependence (a condition that exists) is rather dubious. Just because nature exists, even as marvelous as it is, does not constitute in itself grounds for its continued existence or for any imperative to preserve it. Furthermore, what is to prevent people from justifying damming up a river and flooding a wildlife refuge on the basis that flooding is a natural occurrence anyway? Or what is to prevent people from slaughtering animals for the fun of it based on watching the natural behavior of a cat playing with its latest catch? Can we really derive environmental ethics from nature? There appears to be the need for an authority beyond nature that gives cogency to a sane ethical imperative. Just as it is impossible for the universe to be the cause of its own existence, it is also impossible for it to be the justification for its own continuation.

Advocates of biocentrism normally construct an environmental ethic and assign moral standing to some or all of nature by arguing in various ways from existence or an existing condition. Some, such as Peter Singer, would limit moral standing to sentient beings (that is, animals that can suffer pain).[13] Others extend moral standing to all nature based on the interrelatedness and continuing process of all things (John B. Cobb, Charles Birch), on the reverence of life (Albert Schweitzer), on God's immanence in nature (Matthew Fox) or on the idea that everything constitutes a single biotic community that must be preserved (Aldo Leopold).

Aldo Leopold derived his land ethic from the continuity of the entire biosphere: "A thing is right when it tends to preserve the integrity, stability, and beauty of the biotic community. It is wrong when it tends otherwise."[14] In a similar vain, Harold Schilling wrote, "Those decisions and actions that bring about maximization of such interrelation and interdependence as make for wholeness should therefore be designated as morally responsible and right, and those that operate to break or destroy it should be regarded as wrong."[15] The natural workings of nature might be pleasing, peaceful, and restful, and therefore good in a functional or aesthetic sense, but altogether lacking the imperative to be good in a moral sense.[16] They fall into different categories. To base ethical imperatives solely on the relatedness of all things violates the naturalistic fallacy.

Some, such as Carolyn Merchant, believe that contemporary developments in the philosophy of language "have critically reassessed the earlier positivist distinction between the 'is' of science and the 'ought' of society."[17] She contended that "descriptions and norms are not opposed to one another . . . but are contained within each other. Descriptive statements about the world can presuppose the normative; they are then ethic-laden."[18] But it is not quite this simple, and the issue is far from settled. The later Wittgenstein challenged the analytic view of language where meaning is the referent and naming or describing is the extent of language. Wittgenstein argued that the meaning of a word is its usage and that language can function in more than one way at the same time. For example, if we say that a certain painting is good to look at, we are doing more than merely giving an aesthetic evaluation. We are giving a moral directive, do not deface it. The distinction between description and moral imperatives seemingly fuses together in actual usage.

But this raises several problems. First, not all utterances are necessarily forms of indirect speech acts. There are descriptive statements that are just that, descriptive statements. A portrait of a boxer in a particular stance could either be taken as how a new fighter should or should not take a stance or how a certain person in the past took a stance. Second, one could challenge the premise that the meaning of every word is totally dependent on usage. Even Wittgenstein did not hold this. Third, the use of language is a social activity. That is, humans are injecting their ethics into the speech act or language game. The resulting moral implicature is therefore derived from a social norm or at least from the presuppositions of the person making or hearing the utterance. The imperative is not derived from the abstract statement. Viewing all aesthetical evaluations as ethical injunctions leads to moral relativism. A projected building can be very beautiful, but so is the woodland that presently occupies the spot. If all descriptions are ethic-laden, then what is one to do? It becomes a contest between the presuppositions of the environmentalists and those of the entrepreneurs, and the language game breaks down as a basis for ethics. Fourth, most would agree that objective reality exists apart from the constraints of language. The question then remains whether we can derive *oughts* that also exist apart from the constraints of language from this objective reality. It is only through the workings of language, an imperfect representation of reality, that descriptions and imperatives become fused. Therefore, the naturalistic fallacy, perhaps with some qualifications, is still valid in its general formulation.

Reverence for life, selfless love, sentiency, and romanticism all fall prey to the same naturalistic fallacy. If the reverence or love is not based on a source outside of the person, then it must be derived from some feeling within, an existing condition. This brings us back to the fallacy of the hedonistic basis for ethics where an *ought* is derived from an *is*. This does not negate the need for reverence and love toward creation, but this reverence and love must be derived from a theocentric perspective. The same fault can be leveled against romanticism. Romanticism is the projection of human feelings into nature and then treating it accordingly, as pet owners often do. I have certain feelings and assume my pet does also; therefore, I ought to have regard for its feelings and treat it accordingly. Besides being guilty of deriving imperatives from existing conditions, romanticism is also guilty of the pathetic fallacy, or the illegitimate projection of human feelings on animals. Furthermore, such intense feelings for nature often block any rational adjudication when conflicts of interest arise. Romanticism tends to be pantheistic and falls prey to the naturalistic fallacy, as does any monistic ethical system.

The is/ought problem also plagues anthropocentric approaches. Humans have a desire for affluence, material possessions, and pleasure far beyond their needs. Does having this lust for things (an existing condition) justify ruthless exploitation of the environment to acquire them (the ought)? The whole economic structure of our society is based on the assumption that the answer to this question is affirmative. If we take this idea of wants justifying behavior, then we must condone robbery, embezzlement, shoplifting, and all sorts of similar crimes.

We all recognize that this way of thinking would throw society into utter chaos, so we begin drawing arbitrary lines. Private property is protected from others, but not from the owner. Even more important, the property of the commons (air, land, water) is not protected from anyone, for it belongs to all. This takes us back to Odysseus, who hung a dozen slave girls on a rope because he suspected them of misbehavior while he was away. After all, they were his property, and he could do as he wished with them. This way of thinking leaves nature at the mercy of the owner. Since we are the owner of a piece of property, we apparently have the right to do what we wish with it. But do we? Do human wants justify any sort of action even if we own the property? Most would say that it does, but logically it does not. Ownership does not negate the general principle that one cannot argue from an existing condition (is) to an ethical choice (ought) in order to justify behavior. There must be some other basis to argue that the world as we know it ought to continue and be cared for; that is, the imperatives for an environmental ethic must come from without.

The only solution to the is/ought impasse is to posit a transcendent voice that can provide moral categories for our relations with nature. That voice must exist apart from both humanity and nature. The Judeo-Christian tradition posits such a transcendent ought-giver who has allowed us the right to partake of the environment to fulfill our needs but who condemns exploitation to fulfill our lusts. From a theocentric perspective, it is morally wrong to upset the harmony of the universe because it would be contrary to the design of the Creator. Hall remarked that the gospel of Jesus as the Christ implies a rudimentary indicative concerning this world, namely, that it is greatly loved, and that its mending is an immediate and vital dimension of the whole work of God. Only such an indicative (is) could sustain imperatives (ought to be) such as the command to tend the earth as nature's stewards.[19]

The Dilemma of Hierarchical Systems

Assigning relative values to various members of the creation community is a very complex and touchy issue. For many it appears to be a necessary evil. To opt for an egalitarian model and say that everything in God's creation is of equal value would create an ethical nightmare. Unless there is some way of prioritizing, there would be no way of discerning moral obligations when conflicts arise.

The problem of relative values has been accentuated by our exponential growth and territorial expansion, conditions that create fierce competition for land and resources. For example, does our need of hydroelectric power justify damming up a river and destroying the habitats of thousands of animals? Or does filling in a marshland for a needed housing development for the poor justify the destruction of a unique ecosystem? Although there usually are alternatives to consider, the decisions are normally decided on pragmatic and economic grounds. That is, they are colored by our egocentric and myopic vision and lean heavily in our favor. This despotic monarchical model is just as unacceptable as the egalitarian model where all values are leveled. Even with biocentrism, there still must be some workable hierarchical organization so that we can determine our proper limitations and role as we use nature; otherwise, it would be hands off entirely.[20]

Sustentative Hierarchy

The first of two types of legitimate hierarchy involve the natural use of lower forms of life by higher forms, as observed in the food chain. This is all part of God's plan (Gen. 1:29-30; 9:1-3). Biblically sanctioned use even extends to killing animals for food and clothing (Gen. 3:21) but only in the postlapsarian age. Plants utilize the organic matter and mineral content in the soil, herbivorous animals feed upon the plants, carnivorous animals feed upon the herbivores, and omnivorous animals feed upon both. This natural hierarchical chain is a form of value structure that places more value on those aspects of nature needed by more organisms, that is, on the lower forms of life. This value structure also helps determine proper and improper use. If the sustentative hierarchy were flattened to one level, we would be free either to eat anything we wished, including other humans, or nothing at all.

This hierarchy of use functions fine until it gets to humanity. Plants and animals extract from their environment only what they need for survival. They take what is there and use it in that form. All their waste returns to the earth, is decomposed, and used again. Humans, however, have the ability to transform what they find in nature into something totally alien to satisfy some need or want.[21] For example, they can take corn and produce whiskey, take a swamp and turn it into a city, or take uranium ore and produce electric energy and along with it the deadly plutonium by-product that remains hazardous for a half million years. Human-made transformations are not wrong in themselves, as long as the transformations are environmentally benign.

From a theocentric perspective, we have the same God-given rights to sustain ourselves from the environment as do other members of the ecological community. There are divine limits imposed on us because of our special abilities. We have a moral obligation to use our unique gifts creatively in accordance with the desires of the One who gave them to us, that is, for the care and healing of creation, not for the selfish destruction of nature.

The value placed on nature by a hierarchy of usage does contribute, along with other facets of value, to the inherent worth of nature. Its utilitarian value extends beyond human use to that of the rest of creation. Those parts of nature which benefit more organisms actually are of more value for sustaining the biotic community than those which are not directly used by any other (that is, humans). Thus, in one sense, we find ourselves placed within creation as caretakers of something of greater value than ourselves.

Institutional Hierarchy

The second type of legitimate hierarchy is an institutional or organizational hierarchy that is necessary for the operation of a business, institution, or marriage. The head of the institution accepts the responsibility for the proper functioning of that entity. The same is true in the natural order. God has placed us in a position of responsibility to see that His creation is properly taken care of so that all His creatures will be able to live the life He intended. The links in this hierarchical chain must remain intact if the whole is to function properly. For example, if the divine-human link is broken, humanity becomes a despot over nature. The value structure inherent in an institutional hierarchy is the reverse of that in a sustentative hierarchy, for it gives humanity facets of value to God that nature does not have.

The organizational hierarchy of a corporation does tend to give more value to the leaders, but their value exists only in regard to their ability to ensure the success of the corporation. They are of value to the CEO and to the organization as a whole. Their special value does not negate the value of others in the corporation, whose value is based on other factors. A department head may have more responsibility than the workers in regard to the integrity and functioning of the department and thus more value in this regard, but it does not follow that the department head has more inherent value as a person than others in the department. The same holds true for the biblical hierarchy in the home. God appointed the husband as head of the marriage relationship for the proper functioning of the home. Someone ultimately must be responsible (and take the blame when things go wrong). This does not mean that the husband has more intrinsic value than the wife. It is human sin that twists this necessary hierarchy into an absolute structure of inherent worth. Thus the value derived from a hierarchy of usage, which places more value on that which is of more use to the biotic community, is balanced by the value derived from the institutional hierarchy, which places more value on the caretaker of creation. Consequently, we could almost say that everything has equal value, or at least balanced value.

Value and Hierarchy

What repels ecoactivists from recognizing the need of a hierarchical system is that it does seem to imply a differentiation of values. They are afraid that it will end up devaluing nature. Value is determined by its importance to a valuing agent. The basis may be price, quality, utility, service, relationship, enjoyment, aesthetics, or the like. In chapter 4, we saw where nature has intrinsic value based on its importance to God. Normally intrinsic value is contrasted with utilitarian value. But when something is so designed by a transcendent Creator to benefit the community of creation, it becomes part of its intrinsic value, for it is so fashioned by its designer. The same can be said for other aspects of value.

The institutional hierarchy gives humans a facet of value to God that nonhumans lack, a service value as caretaker of His domain and as fellow worker in the redemption of creation. We cannot deny that Scripture places special value on humans. This is evident from such teachings of Jesus as "you are worth more than many sparrows" (Matt. 10:31; see Matt. 6:26). "How much more valuable is a man than a sheep!" (Matt. 12:12). These passages should not present a problem once the different types of value are understood. Humans do have unique value to God in that they have been given responsibility to care for creation and to cooperate in its redemption, but this does not negate the equally unique value of other parts of creation that humans lack. Everything in creation has value to God, because everything fits into His design and fills the role He intended.

Our unique position does not give us any more right to abuse our office and exploit nature than the leaders of a corporation have the right to embezzle money from their company. The rationale for God's creating us as He did yields a rather sobering and humbling view of our position and awesome responsibility. We must use our higher position in service to all creation for the sake of the Creator, the One who values us for this very reason. This concept of value shifts the problem of conflict resolution from a hierarchy of reality to God's design for nature.

Abuse of Hierarchical Structure

Hierarchical structures are not wrong; they are very much needed for various reasons. Yet all hierarchical systems can be corrupted by human sin. This is not the fault of the hierarchical system, but of fallen human nature. Despots can take over nations, businesses, institutions, and even marriages, regarding what is under their domain as objects for manipulation and exploitation to fulfill their lust for power, things, and pleasure. Rejecting the God-given hierarchy of human responsibility is not the solution to the environmental crisis. The crisis is due to our corrupt nature that perverts the necessary sustentative and institutional hierarchies into an absolute value structure, a perversion that gives supreme authority and value to humanity and destroys the intrinsic value of everything else. The hierarchical structure that places us under God and over nature does not give us any special rights to abuse nature, rather it gives us a responsibility toward God.

The model of proper attitude toward hierarchical supremacy is Christ's servanthood (Mark 10:45; Phil. 2:5-11). The ideas of being master and servant become merged as the God of creation became the Servant of all.[22] As we reflect the *imago Dei*, this model becomes a reality in our lives and the potential threat of hierarchical systems is dissipated. Hence it is the sinful perversion of hierarchy that is the problem, not the hierarchical structure itself.

The Assigning of Rights to Nature

Does nature have rights? If nature has no rights, then we have no moral obligation toward nature, and the whole discussion of environmental ethics is a dead issue. Asserting that nature does have rights, however, opens a Pandora's box. Can nature actually have rights in a legal sense? If so, then what is the basis for those rights and how far should they be taken? The more rights assigned to nature, the less rights we would have. What happens when our rights conflict with nature's rights? A more basic question is whether we have the right to arbitrate morality at all, regardless of what basis we might employ. Does anything apart from God have rights?

Before engaging in the discussion, we must rethink what is meant by "rights." According to *Black's Law Dictionary*, "rights" when used in an abstract sense means "justice, ethical correctness, or consonance with the rules of law or the principles of morals." It "serves to indicate law in the abstract, considered as the foundation of all rights, or the complex of underlying moral principles which impart the character of justice to all positive law, or give it an ethical content." When used in a concrete sense, it means "a power, privilege, faculty, or demand, inherent in one person and incident upon another. Rights are defined generally as 'powers of free action.' And the primal rights pertaining to men are enjoyed by human beings purely as such, being grounded in personality, and existing antecedently to their recognition by positive law." It is "a legally enforceable claim of one person against another, that the other shall do a given act, or shall not do a given act."[23]

The conferment of rights is therefore a legal extension of morality. The person or group that deliberates the claims of two parties and then decides the rights of each is actually establishing what is morally right and wrong. The violation of those rights is a moral infringement, since it constitutes a deviation from an established principle of conduct and duty.

Assigning rights to nature would give it a moral status and would place a moral obligation on us to respect those rights. If nature had rights, it would constitute moral justification for environmental ethics and for limiting human behavior. We could then commit a crime against nature. If animals and the rest of nature had rights, then their supporters could speak in their behalf as trustees or guardians, represent their claims in court, and put a halt to animal injustices and abuses against nature. But if nature were devoid of rights, then human behavior toward nature would be amoral, or outside the realm of morality and ethics, except where it touched human life. We would be legally and morally free to do anything we wished, such as animal experimentation, sport hunting, animal factories, and imprisoning animals in zoo penitentiaries. There would be no objection to animal experiments if they could possibly cure a human disease or result in a cosmetic that does not irritate the eyes. The question of nature rights then is foundational to any environmental ethics and could be conceived as an ecological necessity. The following are seven commonly held views regarding the rights of nature.

Nature Has No Rights

Some argue that animals and the rest of nature do not have any moral claim against humans. Only humans have the right to life; everything else exists to serve them. These beliefs, however, are not scriptural and can only lead to environmental chaos. For example, Father Joseph Rickaby said, "Brute beasts, not having understanding and therefore not being persons, cannot have any rights."[24] Many Christians are of the same mind-set as Rickaby, arguing that since animals are not moral agents and lack an immortal soul, they are not subjects of moral obligation. Animals have no value except for human utility and thus become the means to whatever end humans desire.

This view is based on the differences between humans and animals. Humans are rational, self-conscious beings, made in the image of God; animals are not. Therefore, humans have rights, and animals do not. It was thought that to grant animals rights would lead to chaos since animals are so heavily used in human culture. Advocates of animal rights accuse the no-rights position of speciesism, the discrimination against animals because of some distinctions. Just as the Nazis murdered the Jews because of racial differences, so humanity has a free reign to slaughter animals because of species differences. However, since humans who lack rationality and self-consciousness are granted the right to life, it is questionable to use this as criteria to discriminate against animals. Otherwise, the retarded, senile, or severely debilitated would also be open to abuse and exploitation. There needs to be some balanced way of assessing the rights of all creation that avoids absolutism on either end of the spectrum.

Others argue that rights can only be developed through a social contract model where free agents work out a legal solution depicting the rights of each party. This presupposes that each party is a rational person, capable of filing a just and fair claim. Since nature cannot sit down with another party and hammer out the privileges of each, it cannot have rights. Another way of stating this view is that human rights are cultural artifacts conferred by a cultural institution; they are not inherent. In order for a person to have rights, there has to be an "overarching system of justice, fairness, or law in which the individual claiming the right participates. If some such universal scheme of justice is lacking in nature, then so are natural rights."[25] This view ignores that courts have granted rights to nonpersons, such as estates, corporations, and universities. Lawyers speak on their behalf, as they do for infants and incompetents. Animals of endangered species do not have to be able to file a just and legal claim to be considered as having rights granted them by the Endangered Species Act. The state will press for legal claims in behalf of the animals, just as it does for abused children.

Human Interest

The early conservation movement in this country was based on the proper use and management of resources for human use, not on the preservation or protection of nature for nature's sake. The movement's early spokesmen included Gifford Pinchot, the first chief of the U. S. Forest Service, and Theodore Roosevelt. The only rights nature could have are conferred on it from the standpoint of human interest. That is, those aspects of nature that served humans had the human-given right to be protected for humanity's sake. This view is obviously inadequate since those segments of nature that lack human utility will also lack rights. Joseph Wood Krutch remarked,

> What is commonly called "conservation" will not work in the long run because it is not really conservation at all but rather, disguised by its elaborate scheming, only a more knowledgeable variation of the old idea of a world for man's use only. That idea is unrealizable. But how can man be persuaded to cherish any other ideal unless he can learn to take some interest and some delight in the beauty and variety of the world for its own sake, unless he can see a "value" in a flower blooming or an animal at play, unless he can see some "use" in things not useful?[26]

Since the old conservation movement is highly anthropocentric and utilitarian it cannot possibly offer an adequate basis for nature rights, for nature would be nothing more than a commodity to be used.

Evolution

Some have defended animal rights on the basis of evolution. Since humans are nothing more than advanced animals, they cannot claim any right that animals should not have also. Ingred Newkirk, the codirector of People for the Ethical Treatment of Animals (PETA) asserted, "There is no rational basis for saying that a human being has special rights. A rat is a pig is a dog is a boy."[27] Feder and Park argue that evolutionary relationships make "untenable the attitudes that allow us to grant rights to ourselves while denying them to our fellow animal species."[28] It is only by random chance that we evolved further than the animals. To say that one's fortune gives a person rights that the less fortunate do not have is to invoke a form of elitism that would spark all sorts of discrimination, from Aryanism to sexism.

One problem with this view is that it leads to vegetarianism as a moral necessity. If killing humans is wrong, so is killing animals. Second, if animal killing were permitted for human utility (food, experiments), then there would be no reason not to kill elderly or infirm humans for the same reason.[29] Third, it is logically invalid. The syllogism needed to argue from evolution is guilty of the fallacy of the illicit minor.[30] The syllogism would be: "All humans have rights; all humans are animals; therefore animals have rights."[31] The subject of the conclusion (animals) is the minor term, and the predicate of the conclusion (rights) is the major term. For the minor term to be distributed in the conclusion of a valid syllogism, it also has to be distributed in one of the premises. Otherwise, one could come up with such absurdities as: "All birds have wings; all birds are animals; therefore all animals have wings." Fourth, the rights of human beings cannot possibly be transferred to animals, because animals lack the moral constitution to respect such rights. Humans claim the right to life, a right others are to respect. But how can this possibly be conferred on the animal kingdom? Denying humans the right to kill other humans but permitting animals the right to kill other animals is speciesism in reverse. Fifth, it is precarious to base one's ethics on a scientific hypothesis, even though that hypothesis may be imagined as fact.[32] Thus, we cannot argue for animal rights based on evolution.

Sentiency

Many have argued for animal rights on the basis of sentiency, such as Peter Singer in *Animal Liberation*. Sentiency is the capacity to experience feeling or sensation, such as pain. Some, however, question whether animals can suffer. Advocates of the sentiency position argue that animals can feel pain, and since they can, it is immoral to hurt them. There are several problems with this approach. First, how far down the chain of complexity does it apply? Do worms, insects, and microorganisms feel pain?

The problem concerns human ignorance regarding which animals suffer and the difficulty to ascertain pain in animals. Second, it ignores plant life, water, air, soil, and rocks. Third, if a person is insensitive to pain, does this mean that the person does not have the right to be protected against abuse? Fourth, it confuses pain with evil, saying that pain is inherently wrong.[33] Fifth , it is guilty of the naturalistic fallacy of attempting to derive an *ought* from an *is*. Just because some animals may suffer (is) does not constitute logical grounds to argue that they should be spared from it (ought).[34] Sixth, it does not protect animals against painless forms of killing.

There may be an inner disposition in the sensitive person that cruelty to animals is morally wrong, but one cannot argue philosophically from sentiency to support this inclination.

Organic Unity

Some argue for the rights of nature from the organic unity and interrelatedness of all nature, including humanity. Since we have claimed for ourselves certain rights, it only stands to reason that nature has rights also. C. D. Stone argued that the legal profession historically has followed humanity's expanding horizon of moral compassion. The legal extension of rights has not been without its battles; nevertheless, new laws finally emerge (such as women's rights, civil rights, and endangered species). He noted that since we are currently expanding our consciousness to regard the earth as one organism, our sympathy and moral development will likewise be extended, followed by the legal conferment of rights on nature. Thus Stone argued from the interrelatedness of nature apart from human advantage as a basis to confer rights on nature. All nature should have rights because it forms "one organism, of which Mankind is a functional part."[35]

This reasoning also violates the naturalistic fallacy in trying to derive an *ought* from an *is*. In addition, a syllogism based on humanity's being part of nature would be invalid, as it also results in the fallacy of the illicit minor: "All humans have rights; humans are part of nature; therefore all nature has rights." However, if the minor premise were changed to express strict monism, that humans and nature constitute the same entity, a valid argument would result. This would be using material equivalence, where one term could be interposed for the other. Yet one could still challenge the validity of the premises. What is the basis for saying that humans have rights and that monism is valid? If both premises were valid, there would be the additional problem of resolving conflicts of interests. If everything were part of the same monistic structure and thereby had equal rights, society would end up in chaos. There still must be some structure by which conflicts can be adjudicated.

Extension of Human Rights

Some argue that because humans have a right to live and pursue their interests, so should animals. Roderick Nash in *The Rights of Nature* argued that civil rights, as represented in the Declaration of Independence and the abolition of slavery, can be used by extension as the basis of rights for nature.[36] Nash reasoned, "Even the most radical fringe of the contemporary environmental movement can be understood not so much as a revolt against traditional American ideals as an extension and new application of them. The alleged subversiveness of environmental ethics should be tempered with the recognition that its goal is the implication of liberal values as old as the republic."[37] Nash is a historian of ideas who has traced the evolution of ethics in which the human moral horizon has expanded from self, to family, tribe, religion, nation, race, humans, and now partly to animals. This expansion is paralleled by legal acts, such as the Emancipation Proclamation (1863), Nineteenth Amendment giving rights to women (1920), Fair Labor Standards Act (1924), Civil Rights Act (1957), and the Endangered Species Act (1973). Thus the American spirit of liberty has progressively witnessed moral extension to various groups, and as Nash argued, its next logical extension is to animals and then all nature.

The problem with all these arguments for the rights of nature is that society is attempting to construct an ethic within a two-dimensional human/nature framework. The rejection of a transcendent law-giver has left humans the impossible task of validating or invalidating certain actions. There is no real basis to say that exploiting nature or slaughtering animals is wrong or that taking care of nature for the common good of the biosphere is right. As Richard Griffiths says, "The search for an adequate secular basis for animal rights is bound to fail because of the overriding difficulty of establishing any rights at all (even human rights) on a purely two-dimensional plane, without including some notion of God."[38] This is true with either an anthropocentric or biocentric basis for ethics. There is no "greater than" that lies outside the system to establish the legality of an act. Without a transcendent voice, any attempt to assign rights to nature would be guilty of the naturalistic fallacy.

Perhaps Gödel's theorem is applicable to the moral quandary of naturalistic philosophies. Gödel demonstrated in the language of mathematics the general principle that a statement within a system could not be proven by the system itself. One could find statements that worked and regard them as axioms which are true in relation to the system. It would be impossible, however, to derive a formal proof for that axiom from the system itself. For example, if I were teaching a class the Greek alphabet and stopped after the letter *upsilon*, the class would never know that there were four more letters. It requires a level of explanation transcendent to the level of the student to say, "That's all," or "There are four more letters in the Greek alphabet." In the same way, when the system is extended to the entire natural realm, there cannot be any demonstrable concept of values or moral principles to govern life unless a transcendent entity exists. The explanation or moral guidance cannot come from the system itself.

God's Rights

The Scriptures offer the most satisfying basis for the rights of nature. The Bible recognizes that we are not the final arbitrators of values of rights: God is. Rights must be redefined as what is just or fair as decreed by God. We do not have the right to lay a claim against the sovereign God for what we feel is just and fair (see Rom. 9:14-21). That is, no member of creation can have any rights apart from what God so designed. God has designed His creation in a certain way and has the right to see that it fulfills His intent. By virtue of this divine right, every creature in the community of creation is endowed with certain privileges. We may call these privileges "rights" in that they reflect a fair and just claim of an individual member of creation to be allowed to live the life God intended. Nature's rights then are derivative from God's rights. Arguing for rights and environmental ethics from a theocentric perspective provides a more sustainable foundation than any secular approach. Atkins wrote, "Philosophically, the only way to found or establish such a thing as a 'natural right' [such as the right to life for man or animal] is to presuppose a god who bestows and secures such rights."[39]

Andrew Linzey formerly advocated animal rights on the basis of sentiency but has abandoned that position in favor of what he calls "theos-rights."[40] Regarding animal factories, he now writes, "It seems to me that the only satisfactory basis on which we can oppose systems of close confinement is by recourse to the argument drawn from theos-rights. To put it at its most basic: animals have a God-given right to be animals."[41] Another way of expressing it would be: animals have rights because God has rights.[42]

We can no longer say that certain insect or animal species are pests and fit for annihilation if they get in the way of human interests. We do have the right to rid a field of Japanese beetles, for we have a God-given right to derive our sustenance from the land. However, we do not have the right to annihilate the entire species, for we must honor the Japanese beetle as having a right to fulfill the role God designed for it. Furthermore, we do not have the right to expand ourselves to such an extent that we endanger other species. They too have a right to live and flourish as God intended, to breathe fresh air, drink unpolluted water, and live in natural conditions. The earth is, as Linzey said, "a *common* gift to both humans and animals."[43] One could argue that unlimited human expansion is in direct violation of the God-given rights of animals and plants. This would apply equally to the expansion of other species, such as rabbits and insects, but their population growth is normally held in check by natural means.

One problem with theos-rights is determining what is and is not part of the divine intent. Linzey addressed how God's intent might be discerned, saying, "The theos-rights perspective does not locate the value of beings in any faculty or capacity, but in the will of God, which may be deduced from the givenness of Spirit-filled individuals."[44] Making necessary clothing from animals is within the divine intent (Gen. 3:21), as eating animals (Gen. 9:3), using skins for shelter (Ex. 26:14), and sacrificing in rites (Gen. 4:1-5). But what about using animals for medical research? Although the Bible neither confirms nor condemns such use, one could argue that it might be part of God's intent since He sanctions the use of animals to sustain life as food and shelter in the postlapsarian age. Every major breakthrough in medical research has been achieved through animal experimentation; for example, cures for rabies and smallpox, surgery techniques for transplanting organs and reattaching severed limbs, the cardiac pacemaker, open-heart surgery, and reduced threat of lymphocytic leukemia. Progress is now being made in the fight against AIDS and Alzheimer's disease. Animal experiments have even benefited the animal kingdom with heart and cataract surgery and immunization against feline leukemia, rabies, distemper, and tetanus.

If medical research, however, is not part of God's intent for animals, then we must abandon such practices. Linzey made a challenging comment in this regard:

> One *Christian* answer to these questions has yet to be heard. It is that, deeply conscious of our divinely given stewardship over creation and our special bond of covenant with animals in particular, we should elect to bear for ourselves whatever ills may flow from not experimenting on animals

rather than be supporting an institution which perpetuates tyranny. This may be a hard option for many, but it is as arguably a Christian response as many of the others which claim that appellation. If it is the *good* shepherd as opposed to the hireling who actually lays down His life for the sheep, perhaps the *good* steward is the one who desists from any path of injury in deference to the prior right of God in creation.[45]

The Search for Sustainability

Sustainability is perhaps the most important topic in environmental discussions. By its very definition, it presumes that we ought to conduct ourselves in such a way that the continuation of the natural order is assured and that we can pass on to our descendants an environment at least as good as what we received. Where this *ought* comes from is not our concern at the moment, but rather how the *ought* can be sustained. It is obvious that there cannot be a sustainable environment without a sustainable ethic propelled by a sustainable motivational factor.

The entry point into the ecological movement is often egocentric pragmatism; if pollution is going to kill me, then I had better do something about it. Self-interest, however, will never generate an adequate environmental imperative because there is no real concern for aspects of nature not directly related to the individual. Moreover, some will not be concerned whether pollution could shorten their lives (for example, warnings on cigarettes); they are alive now, and that is all that matters. Self-interest is perhaps the strongest sustainable motivating force, but it should not be mustered for environmental causes because it is contradictory to the selflessness required for genuine concern for nature and future generations.

The problem with all ethical systems is that they are abstractions that become fleshed out only through human beings, and human beings are, for the most part, obsessed with a preoccupation with self. The problem of a sustainable ethic cannot be resolved until this inborn obsession is dealt with.

It is not enough to change structures around people without changing their basic makeup. The environmental revolution taking place today simply is not revolutionary enough. The most superficial level is the technological fix; the second level is a brainwashing of new attitudes and values through mass media and education. The most revolutionary and sustainable level of restructuring involves changing humanity's basic nature. The strength of the biblical worldview is that it paints a realistic portrait of humanity, confronts the problem of the demonic within, and offers a solution through the death of Christ and efficacy of the Spirit. It also provides the needed ethical imperative through our accountability to God. As such, Christianity is the most revolutionary and potentially the most effective approach to environmental ethics.

Its potentiality, however, is contingent on the type of response individuals make. To adopt a theistic worldview as the most plausible option intellectually or even to be converted to Christianity by a confession of faith is not enough to eliminate the sin problem in the lives of individuals, as well testified by the history of sin in the church. Scriptures exhort believers to submit totally to the Holy Spirit for liberation from the power of sin.

Nevertheless, in the light of today's environmental problems, it is still Christianity that looms as the most credible and most promising worldview option. One problem with both anthropocentrism and biocentrism is that the finite is elevated to the level of the ultimate as the center and source of value, meaning, purpose, and ethics. Yet the finite is contingent, ever changing, dependent, and deteriorating. The values derived from a finite source will of necessity be relative, imperfect, and always changing as well. A system that is prone to changes cannot guarantee an ethic that will always be kind to the environment. Furthermore, in order to have a sustainable environmental ethic, there must be a voice external to this realm that provides the reason nature ought to be sustained. If one denies the possibility of such a transcendent voice, any hope for sound environmental imperatives is lost. Without the divine imperative, the environment is ultimately left in the hands of capricious humanity. The only sustainable base for environmental ethics is found in the faith that places at the center and source of all value and meaning a transcendent God who exists apart from the contingent universe.

The Challenge of Ecojustice

During the early seventies, the poor were concerned that the focus on environmental problems would divert attention and funds away from social programs for them. The poor not only showed disinterest but open antagonism against environmental causes. The environmental craze was looked upon as a middle-class movement. Recently, however, the poor have begun to realize that their quality of life is threatened more by environmental disasters, exploitation, and pollution than other segments of society and have started to become concerned with the justice of environmental programs.

For example, there are going to be costs incurred to correct environmental disasters and pollution, and, more than likely, the poor are going to be disproportionately affected. This is a genuine need for concern. To pay for the necessary corrections, the price of the product will have to be raised, the government will have to subsidize the cost, or the corporation will have to absorb it. The latter is the most unlikely. With either of the first two, the poor will be financially burdened. They will have to pay the higher price for the product or share in the tax burden.[46]

The poor are also plagued with having toxic waste dumps or incinerators located in their neighborhood. In Chattanooga, for example, a government housing project for the poor is located in the Alton Park area, a neighborhood that has several dozen toxic waste dumps and through which flows Chattanooga Creek, one of the major Superfund sites. The NIMBY (Not In My Back Yard) syndrome appears to be a middle and upper-class strategy to locate harmful plants in rural or poor areas. The poor feel the affects of toxic wastes long before the more affluent, with a higher rate of cancer, miscarriages, birth defects, and mysterious diseases.

Many in the church have begun to champion the cause of the poor and push for ecojustice. Their voice is needed. However, most discussions of ecojustice are heavily anthropocentric; that is, there is more concern for the welfare of people than for the environment. It is without question that Christianity affirms the need to care for the poor and oppressed. There is a God-given responsibility for Christians to minister to the whole person, showing loving care in providing medical help, education, food, and spiritual help. From a biblical perspective, ecojustice concerns are not wrong in themselves, but the overemphasis on anthropocentric aspects can lead to a distorted vision of the human task. God's agenda for us involves the dual concern to care for both nature and people, tasks that could be subsumed under one responsibility—to glorify God. The reason for engaging in either aspect is not for the sake of either one, but for the sake of God to whom we owe supreme allegiance and who alone can decree the rightness of an act. Since God is concerned for both the poor and the environment, both must be on the Christian agenda.

Concern for people cannot be divorced from concern for the environment, and vice versa. Exploitation in either arena stems from the same underlying attitude, and when rectified, they are rectified together. It is our self-seeking tendencies that cause both social injustice (exploitation of people) and environmental destruction (exploitation of nature). Since all life is interconnected, an ethical system must address the needs of both if it is to be acceptable. The Bible often links concern for fellow humans with a nonexploitative attitude toward the environment. The prime example is the gleaning law. Instead of gathering everything possible from the fields for one's own storehouse, the workers were to leave part of the harvest for the poor (Lev. 19:9-10; 23:22). Ecojustice, rightly understood, involves justice for both humans and nature; the two cannot be separated.

A proper view of ecojustice is not a question of the rich pitted against the poor, or wealth verses poverty, for many poor choose to be poor, and many rich do not become rich through a miserly and selfish attitude. Disparity is not wrong, as long as those whom God has blessed use their resources in a benevolent manner. Although the Bible encourages sharing, it does not promote egalitarianism. Imbalance is not necessarily injustice, does not necessarily lead to disharmony, and is not hated by God. It is the injustice that God hates, not the imbalance (Jas. 1:9-11). Paul pinpointed the heart of the problem by saying that the root of all kinds of evil is the love of money, not the money itself (1 Tim. 6:10). The Bible condemns unethical methods of acquiring wealth and selfish use of it (Isa. 3:14-15; 5:8; Amos 5:11-12; 8:4-10). In the greedy drive for wealth, the poor and the land invariably suffer together. Oppression of the poor is often denounced (Ex. 22:21-24; Jer. 5:26-29; Ezek. 16:49-50; Amos 2:7; and Matt. 25:35-36). We are reminded in Proverbs 14:31, "He who oppresses the poor shows contempt for their Maker." Ethics should direct its attention to righting wrongs, and inequality is not a wrong, but selfishness is.

James condemned the rich, not for being rich, but for withholding due wages from the workmen, hoarding wealth to themselves, oppressing the poor, and living in self-indulgence (Jas. 5:1-6). James exhorted the rich to be humble in their fortune and realize that earthly riches are transitory (Jas. 1:9-11). The life God calls us to is not one of poverty, but one of sharing. Oppression of the poor and abuse of the land are both part of the same greed syndrome, and both are condemned.

Paul laid down a principle that might well be the goal of environmental ethics in providing for the needs of all creation: "Our desire is not that others might be relieved while you are hard pressed, but that there might be equality. At the present time your plenty will supply what they need, so that in turn their plenty will supply what you need" (2 Cor. 8:13-14). Paul is not advocating egalitarianism but the benevolent sharing of God's gifts. John repeats the same theme: "If anyone has material possessions and sees his brother in need but has no pity on him, how can the love of God be in him?" (1 John 3:17). John also reminded us that love is manifested in acts of kindness, not mere words (v. 18). As the proverb says, "He who is kind to the poor lends to the Lord, and he will reward him for what he has done" (19:17).

Some fear that the slowdown of productivity and simpler life-styles that some recommend would "institutionalize poverty."[47] People, however, can live happy, simple lives with a standard of living well below the so-called "poverty level." Increase in material goods does not always lead to a fulfilled life. Paradoxically, the inverse is usually true. A satisfying life only comes by replacing selfishness with selfless caring for what God Himself cares for. Any other path leads to a dehumanized and decadent life.[48] Furthermore, as people turn back to God, God will bless the land to produce its fruit in bounty. It is when people disobey God and greedily misuse the land that it cannot yield enough to feed the poor. The solution is not a forced redistribution of wealth but a return to God and a purging of our egocentrism.

The advocates of ecojustice have alerted us to a possible imbalance in our service to God. Balance must be maintained between Christian evangelism, social involvement, and environmental activity. The fear the poor once had that environmental fervor would divert attention away from social concerns parallels the fear of Christian fundamentalists who are afraid that it would divert attention from soul-winning. As Christians, we must be faithful to a spectrum of duties.

The Question of Future Generations

People have very little, if any, sense of obligation to future generations, other than their immediate children and grandchildren. The sense of moral obligation weakens as the concentric circles of concern expand outward from self. One often suffers inconveniences for the sake of close friends, sometimes for others in the community, rarely for others in a distant land, but there has to be a moral revolution for modern society to have a compelling reason to sacrifice its affluence for generations not yet born. Self-centeredness can produce a sense of obligation but only when there is a mutual contract between two parties.[49] We feel a moral obligation to pay back a loan, to return a library book, or to return a favor. The benevolent act of the other party creates a moral obligation on our part. But what has the future generation ever done for us? Self-interest is by its very nature confined to short-term concerns and cannot be evoked for long-term environmental service.

Those who argue for the rights of future generations are confronted with several problems: (1) the uncertainty of future generations, (2) the uncertainty of their numbers if there are future generations, and (3) the uncertainty of their needs. How can we possibly provide for the future when it is uncertain if there is going to be a future or what its needs will be? If one can argue reasonably through this maze, there is still the problem of conflict resolution between present and future generations. How much should we deprive the present generation to provide for the future?

It should be noted, as Black pointed out, that the problem of a posterity is relevant only with a linear view of time. If time is perceived as cyclic, as in pantheistic models, there would be no need of concern for future generations. Since the distant future becomes a new beginning, why should we deprive ourselves of the luxuries of life?[50]

Some argue for an obligation to future generations on the basis of their dependence on us.[51] If we cause irreversible changes in nature, deplete its resources, and contaminate it with toxic pollutants, we would, in a sense, be the executioners of future generations. We could envision them casting the blame on this generation as a corporate entity. But what impact would this have on an individualistic race, whose natural tendency is to pass the buck?

The Scriptures envision God as being concerned for the well-being of future generations by virtue of the covenants He made with Noah, "I now establish my covenant with you and with your descendants after you" (Gen. 9:9), and with Abraham, "I will establish my covenant as an everlasting covenant between me and you and your descendants after you for the generations to come" (Gen. 17:7). God is faithful and will keep His "covenant of love to a thousand generations of those who love him and keep his commands" (Deut. 7:9; see Ex. 20:5).[52]

We must therefore proceed with the assumption that there will be future generations and that God is concerned for their welfare, for there is nothing in Scripture that definitely says otherwise. Future generations have a moral standing or rights based on God's overall design of the ages. They are not contingent in God's plan but subjects of His providential care. As caretakers of the resource base for God's providence, we are answerable to the Creator for its management. The rights of future generations impose on us a moral obligation to leave the world at least as sound as what we have inherited from our ancestors regarding the level of pollution and availability of resources. Our obligations are epitomized by the Amish proverb, "We didn't inherit the land from our fathers. We are borrowing it from our children."

Some argue that God knows when the end will be and has provided enough resources to carry history (and the evangelistic task) through to its completion. This ignores human responsibility and encourages the very thing the Scriptures condemn—greed and materialism. It is precisely because we are unaware of how many generations remain that we must restrict our consumption of nonrenewable resources and halt our pollution of the environment. Do we have the right to deprive future generations of the quality of life that makes life worth living? As Attfield said, "There is the same obligation to future people as to the present."[53] This obligation is to see that needs are met.

Conflicts will surely arise between the present generation and future generations, even with the proposed model. We cannot permit people to starve to death today for the welfare of people tomorrow. Even though we do not fully know the number and needs of future generations, we do know that they have the right to expect "good health, food, shelter and security; and there is much that we can do to facilitate these needs." [54] If everyone partook only of their needs, there would be plenty for the present generation without harming the resource base for the future. The same problem that hampers ecojustice in the present also hampers ecojustice in the future; that is, we are extracting from the environment much more than we need. Perhaps we should remind ourselves of what Paul said, the kingdom does not consist of "eating and drinking, but of righteousness, peace and joy" (Rom. 14:17).

Conclusion

A theocentric ethic is based on the purpose God has for creation and the value He places on it. The Scriptures suggest that we live in an abnormal world. Its abnormality is due to our forsaking the intent of the Creator. The healing that we yearn for in ourselves, nature, and society can only be realized when we rediscover the direction God intended, and that direction can only be found through a theocentric creation-redemption model. This means that Christian environmental ethics is not based on what is but on a divine intent. That is, an *ought* is derived from an imperative that transcends the natural order.

The biblical ethic summons humanity to a solidarity with other members of the community of creation, a community under God with any conflict of interests to be resolved in view of God's purpose for creation rather than on arbitration of sectarian interests. The Bible calls us to love God and everything God created. It sets forth an ethic which recognizes that commons (air, land, and water) are intended to benefit the entire ecological community and must not be polluted or damaged in any way. We are obligated before God to ensure a benevolent and just use of His earth and, at the same time, to preserve the harmony and integrity of creation. Abuse of the land or animals constitutes a sin against God because it harms God's creation, ignores God's injunction for proper stewardship, and deviates from God's purpose in creation.

The Scriptures present a balanced ethic that favors neither humanity (anthropocentrism) nor nature (biocentrism). This balanced ethic is not merely concerned with management for the sake of human social justice, but with caring for everything God has made. We must make sure that no part of creation gets out of hand (including ourselves) so that it endangers the quality of life of any other part. Our commitment to the total environment is in recognition of the authority of God as supreme sovereign of the universe. Our commitment is not derived from a sense of belonging to a biotic community, the interdependence of all life, an awareness of the vulnerability of spaceship earth and its limited resources, or from mystic romanticism. Our commitment comes from a transcendent God to whom we owe utmost allegiance and loyalty. It is only through a theocentric framework that we can escape the dilemma of partiality that ultimately besets either anthropocentric or biocentric derived ethics.

Ethics cannot stop with a code of conduct. For any ethical system to be truly effective it must have a sound metaphysical base, a code of conduct properly derived from that base, the motivation to comply, and the enablement to overcome the problem of self. Only Christianity offers a true ethical system that meets these criteria. The motivational appeal is our accountability to God. The enablement comes as we submit ourselves to the Holy Spirit to gain victory over our selfish tendencies. Until self is conquered, we will invariably continue our destructive ways regardless of the ethical model. Thus, the only hope for a workable and sustainable ethics and the only hope for true healing for ourselves and all creation is through a theocentric framework.

11

THE CHRISTIAN STANCE TOWARD THE WORLD: RENUNCIATION OR AFFIRMATION?

The church's attitude toward the environment is rather mixed. Because of its perplexity, there is neither a clear message nor a homogeneous force for environmental action from the Christian community. Should we affirm the world or renounce it? In most forms of Christianity, there is more focus on the spiritual than the physical, upon the soul than the body, and on the eternal rather than the temporal. Churches send their converts out to win souls, not persons, for it is the soul that will escape this evil world and ascend into heaven. The body stays behind to rot in the grave. Such is the plight with everything in the physical realm. The importance given to the spiritual in many churches leaves the distinct impression that the physical is of no importance at all. This dualism is causing many to discount Christianity and to embrace Eastern thought as the basis for environmental action.

Dualisms and Distinctions

Dualism is a broad term that refers to any system that perceives reality as composed of two contrasting and irreducible principles, such as mind and matter, God and the world, the spiritual and the physical, the phenomenal and noumenal, or good and evil. The dualism may be either relative or absolute. In relative dualism, one element is either derived from the other element, dependent on it, or subordinate to it. In absolute dualism, there is no dependency or derivational relation between the two. Each element exists in total independence of the other. In many dualisms reality is composed of antagonistic principles which challenge people to take sides, to select one over the other and assign corresponding values. I will be referring to contrasting principles which are nonantagonistic as distinctions and to those which are antagonistic as dualisms.

All religions have some form of dualism that separates the sacred from the profane.[1] This even applies to monistic religions. New Age mystics have their sacred spots or power centers, the Buddhists have their sacred temples and shrines, and the Hindus have their sacred Ganges. On a more philosophical level, Chinese thought revolves around the interplay of the *yin* and *yang* principles, and the Upanishad and other Hindu traditions focus on transcending the physical body and reaching the higher or true self. The teachings of Zoroaster postulate two coeternal gods, one good and one evil. This type of absolute dualism influenced Gnosticism and Manichaeism. Mani taught an absolute and eternal dualism between the principles of good and evil. The evil principle (matter) invaded the realm of good (light), resulting in the present mixture. Salvation is understood to be a return to the primeval state of separation. Early Christian apologists condemned this particular dualism as heresy.

Christendom has its dualisms also, such as between the sacred and secular, spiritual and physical, and the soul and the body. These distinctions have been viewed as opposing principles which challenge a person to choose one and abstain from the other. Whether this idea finds biblical support could be seriously questioned.

Environmentalists arguing from a monistic persuasion advocate the elimination of all types of dichotomies. They perceive any distinction as a harmful dualism that hinders one from attaining a cosmic vision of the unity of the universe. Christianity, with all its "dualisms," such as good and evil, God and creation, humanity and nature, spirit and matter, is looked upon as a hindrance to the transformation of the planet.

The Bible does make some very crucial separations, such as between God and creation, good and evil, and the spiritual and physical. To obliterate the separation between God and creation or between good and evil is to destroy Christianity. But what about the separation of the spiritual from the physical? It seems as if this in particular has been a contributing factor of the environmental crisis. Are all separations or dichotomies harmful dualisms? Could some be helpful distinctions? Is it possible to maintain distinctions and live in the tension between them without having to solve the dilemma by either reductionistic tactics or resorting to antagonistic dualisms?

Dualism in the Church

There is a prevailing contempt for the natural realm in much of Christianity. The spiritual and physical are perceived as antagonistic polarities that demand a choice to be made (see Gal. 5:16-18). This unbalanced view overemphasizes the spiritual at the expense of the physical, relegating it to a second-class realm of existence, something which must be avoided for spiritual progress to be achieved. It indirectly mirrors a Manichaean or Gnostic type of dualism that comprehends matter as evil.

This dualistic framework carries over into the realm of behavior and morals. We are to live in this world as citizens of the next. Since this world is passing away (1 John 2:17), every action must be weighed in terms of its eternal value. Anything we do that pertains only to this life will be burned as wood, hay, and straw (1 Cor. 3:12). There is a common jingle in some Christian circles that says, "Only one life, 'twill soon be past. Only what's done for Christ will last." The only things of importance are the things done for Christ, and what is meant by this is the saving of souls, building super churches with fleets of buses, separation from every appearance of evil, daily devotions, and going to church three times a week. Many Christians seem interested only in escaping the present evil world and corralling as many as possible with them on the gospel train to glory. Whole churches are bent on this single goal, which when emphasized to the exclusion of other duties leaves the rest of creation to be trampled underfoot. It is obvious that such dualism lacks the ability to respond adequately to social or environmental issues.

The environmental crisis has stimulated awareness in some segments of Christianity that we are to be responsible stewards of God's creation. Other Christian groups still cling to their dualistic traditions, denouncing those who advocate environmental action as falling to a satanic deception that furthers the cause of

New Age globalism. Others are caught in a dilemma between the two without adequate understanding to resolve the conflict.

The Reasons for Christian Dualism

The biblical distinction between the spiritual and material has been distorted into a destructive dualism. There have been several factors leading to this development.

The Uniqueness of Humanity. One reason for Christian dualism is our being made in the image of God. This image not only distinguishes us from nature but, in the minds of many, leads to an irreducible polarity. The traditional view of the *imago Dei* understands the image in spiritual terms (see John 4:24). It is therefore the nonmaterial aspect of our being that relates us to God; the material aspect links us with the lower realm that is destined to destruction. This precipitates a dualism between the spiritual and physical with the human body becoming somewhat of an anomaly.

Some believe that our spiritual affinity to God enables us to be the unique recipient of salvation and to participate in a destiny that precludes the physical. It is thought that only humans possess souls, and when souls are delivered, they are delivered out of the realm of matter into the realm of spirit. The physical realm, including the body, is thus regarded as inferior and something to be dominated, controlled, and manipulated for specific ends (1 Cor. 9:27).

These thoughts are unwarranted extensions of the traditional view of the *imago Dei* and ignore its ecological connection in Genesis 1:26-28 (that is, to enable us to serve creation). By limiting salvation to individual souls rather than to the whole person and then to all creation, the Western church has failed to grasp the fuller implications of Scripture (see Rom. 8:21; Eph. 1:10; Col. 1:20). Furthermore, most Christians have never realized that the soul was never intended to leave the body. Physical death is abnormal. The whole point of salvation is to conquer death and to unite the body and soul forever. The physical is as much a part of salvation as the spiritual. Humans may be unique in God's creation in one respect, but this does not imply a dualism between humanity and nature or the spiritual and physical, for we are still very much part of nature and have been from the beginning.

The Transcendence of God. The notion that God is totally removed from the natural order impels those who desire to be Godlike to detach themselves from the physical as well. This transcendence of both God and people over the physical has helped to spawn the contrary attitudes of asceticism and materialism.[2] Asceticism attempts to imitate God's separateness from the physical realm; materialism attempts to imitate God's lordship over it. In either one the seeker aspires to God who exists beyond the physical, and, consequently, nature becomes devalued. Wendell Berry commented that the separation of God from this world is "inevitably mirrored in the lives of individuals: a man could aspire to Heaven with his mind and his heart while destroying the earth, and his fellow men, with his hands."[3]

As argued in chapter 5, God is transcendent in that His being is not derived, contingent, or dependent on this realm of existence. This does not mean that God is not concerned about this realm or is not present to sustain and help His creation. The doctrine of the incarnation teaches that God became human to redeem fallen humanity and restore nature to its primordial harmony. Also, the doctrine of the person of Christ teaches that Christ remains forever fully God and fully human in one person. To be fully human, Christ must still have a physical body. The answer to Question 36 in the Larger Catechism reads, "The only Mediator of the covenant of grace is the Lord Jesus Christ, who, being the eternal Son of God, of one substance and equal with the Father, in the fullness of time became man, and so was and continues to be God and man, in two entire distinct natures, and one person, forever."[4] Traditional understanding of the Creator-Redeemer God leaves absolutely no room for dualism between the spiritual and physical.

The Dominion of Satan and the Second Coming of Christ. It is a common understanding in some segments of Christianity that the world is evil because it lies in the power of the evil one and will thus continue until the Lord returns (1 John 5:19). In dispensational thought, the course of this age is under the control of Satan. Satan has usurped the dominion of the world and will retain it until conquered by Christ. We cannot snatch the dominion away from Satan for we lack power to challenge the usurper. There is nothing positive we can do to alleviate Satan's control on society, human institutions, or the environment. The only mission of the church is to save souls and deliver them from this "present evil age" (Gal. 1:4). As this effort advances, there might be a slight change in society, but to devote energy directly toward this cause is futile. Satan is the "god of this world" (2 Cor. 4:4, KJV) and will continue to reign until Christ returns.

This leads to an irreducible polarity between the present and future, the present being ruled by evil and the future by the righteousness of Christ. Seeing that this present age is ruled by evil and going to be utterly destroyed, all intrinsic value in nature is obliterated. Why not exploit and pollute the environment, since it is going to be annihilated anyway? The exploitative spirit of the age is the unquestioned spirit in many evangelistic churches as they pursue unlimited growth and progress with little concern for its impact on the environment. The "bigger-is-better syndrome" with its materialistic tendencies is sanctioned as an effective means in the modern era of exploding population to fulfill the Great Commission.

To appeal to Satan's dominion and the prevailing evil as a reason for abstaining from social and environmental involvement is contrary to the character and mission of Christ. Christ was very much concerned with feeding the poor, healing the lame, and doing whatever He could to restore harmony in spite of the stranglehold Satan has over people and society.

The Dualism of Soul and Body. The soul-body dualism in much of Christian thought parallels the spiritual-physical dualism that has led to a depreciation of nature. With either trichotomy or dichotomy there is an aspect of human nature that looks Godward and an aspect that looks earthward. The higher aspect relates us with God, while the lower aspect relates us with the earth and brute beasts. The first is the seat of noble qualities and virtues, while the second represents all that is base and carnal and is often linked with the physical. Feeding the higher part and denying the lower part seem to be the essence of spiritual teaching in many churches. At the translation, the higher aspect will be taken to heaven, leaving the lower to rot in the grave. If the physical body, by which we are associated with nature, is deemed nonessential, then the rest of creation will follow suit.[5] One cannot affirm the value and goodness of God's creation if the value and goodness of one's own body is denied.

This dualism has resulted from a misconception of Paul's use of "flesh" (*sarx*), which he regularly used by way of metonymy to refer to our sinful disposition. Human sin arises from the disposition toward evil, not from the physical flesh. Although human flesh cannot be evil itself because it was made by God, it is the vehicle through which sin is expressed. This led Paul to adopt *sarx* to designate the sinful nature in the human race. He defined exactly what he meant by *sarx* in Galatians 5:19-21: "sexual immorality, impurity and debauchery; idolatry and witchcraft; hatred, discord, jealousy, fits of rage, self ambition, dissensions, factions and envy; drunkenness, orgies, and the like" (see Col. 3:5). In Romans 7:18, he carefully distinguished the sin nature from the physical body, "I know that nothing good lives in me, that is, in my sinful nature." Paul could not have said that nothing good dwells in him, meaning the physical body, for everything that God made is good.

The Scriptures view humans as whole beings. When we are redeemed, the whole person is redeemed, not just the soul. As we worship God, we are to worship with our whole person: heart, soul, mind, and strength (Mark 12:30). The whole person is destined to be renewed to the prelapsarian state. Just as Adam had a physical body in the original paradise, so will the redeemed in the future paradise. The body is not a prison house that confines the immortal soul, as in Platonic thought. The body is an essential element of the human person, without which we would not be human beings. When God made us, He made us complete. When God redeems us, we are redeemed as complete persons. The physical resurrection helps to affirm the value of the material and the unity of the whole person. The hope of the believer is for Christ to return and transform our bodies to be like His (Phil. 3:21; 1 John 3:2), not to be divested of a corrupt body or prison house of the soul. As mentioned before, the soul was never intended to be separated from the body. It is the alien sin nature that will be purged, not the body. For the soul to be translated to heaven without a body is abnormal and undesirable (2 Cor. 5:1-5). The true Christian expectation is to be like Christ, and Christ will possess a body for all eternity.

The Influence of Pietism. Another reason for dualism in the church is the influence of pietism. Pietism comes in various forms, from extreme mystical groups that even reject external rites of the church to more sedate forms in many modern evangelical and fundamental churches. There is an otherworldly emphasis in pietism that militates against a balanced view of all life. The modern expression prevalent in conservative churches focuses on personal introspection, individual salvation, individual revival, individual sanctification, personal morality, legalistic duties, and a higher life (which is not this life). It is reflected in such songs as, "I'm pressing on the upward way, new heights I'm gaining every day," leaving, of course, the world behind.

Personal salvation, personal sanctification, and future deliverance are all linked to the idea of destruction of the physical. For one to develop spiritually, the physical must be abandoned or crucified. Paul told us that he died daily (1 Cor. 15:31), had been crucified with Christ and no longer lived (Gal. 2:20), and had been crucified to the world (Gal. 6:14). A spiritual Christian is one who is dead to the flesh and the world, for "they that are Christ's have crucified the flesh" (Gal. 5:24, KJV). Paul exhorted the Colossians, "Put to death, therefore, whatever belongs to your earthly nature" (3:5). If one refuses to die to the physical, then that person will die spiritually, "if ye live after the flesh, ye shall die" (Rom. 8:13, KJV). In the minds of many Christians, both sanctification and salvation pertain to neglecting the physical. In sanctification we are to separate from it; in salvation we are delivered from it. Salvation is completed when we are totally removed from this "present evil world" (Gal. 1:4, KJV), allowing God to utterly destroy it (2 Pet. 3:10-13). The aim of a spiritual Christian is to escape the contamination of the physical world with its sin and corruption.

The notion of a fallen, evil world is not biblical. It finds expression in the mythology of Zoroastrianism and Manichaeism. The curse does not mean that the earth is evil, but that it is impaired from its normal functions. The dualism that says the physical is evil and spiritual is good has not only engendered pietism but also various forms of Christian asceticism. Asceticism refers to self-denial or self-mortification, the renunciation of possessions, marriage, and pleasure. During the Middle Ages, processions of flagellants would parade through the streets scourging their bodies with a lash. The movement was a protest against the defilement of the material and a quest for true penitence. To the flagellants, the body was corrupt, something to be beaten so that sin could be conquered. The same attitude is seen today in some quarters of Christianity where the physical realm is perceived as an obstacle to spiritual growth, to be abstained from as much as possible. Although asceticism and monasticism have for the most part passed off the scene, the devaluation of the physical lingers on in the church. To renounce what God has declared good, however, is a theological inconsistency that cannot be permitted to continue.

A pietistic framework effectually blinds the reader to what the Bible actually teaches regarding the environment. Christians have a tendency to read their Bibles with the framework or presuppositions of their particular tradition. The focus on pietism has prevented the church from seeing beyond its narrow horizon to the horizon of God's concern for all life.

The Misunderstanding of "World." One of the basic causes for unwarranted dualisms in the church stems from a misconception of the biblical usage of *world*. The word seems to stimulate in one's thinking something evil and sinful that we are to separate from. There are several verses that might support such a negative view. John said, "Do not love the world or anything in the world. If anyone loves the world, the love of the Father is not in him" (1 John 2:15). Paul told us, "Set your minds on things above, not on earthly things" (Col. 3:2). James said, "You adulterous people, don't you know that friendship with the world is hatred toward God? Anyone who chooses to be a friend of the world becomes an enemy of God" (4:4). Other passages that could be used to support an antiworld mentality include Matthew 6:33; John 15:18; 1 Corinthians 7:29-34; Galatians 6:14; and 2 Peter 1:4. This notion of "world" along with the church's emphasis on pietism, human salvation, and apocalyptic destruction of the physical finds expression "in aggressive forms of world-negation."[6]

There are three Greek words rendered "world" in the New Testament: *kosmos, aiōn,* and *oikoumenē. Kosmos* has a wide range of meanings, such as literally referring to (1) the physical realm of the world or universe; metaphorically referring to (2) humankind, (3) the world system or philosophy opposed to God, and (4) the things of the world possessions. Other meanings are found in the New Testament, but these represent the four primary nuances. There is a reductionistic tendency to combine all these meanings so that the term refers to the physical world, its people and things, all of which are at enmity with God. This is no more valid than combining the different meanings of the word *run* and saying that a racehorse moves like the flowing of a liquid, the growing of a vine up a trellis, and the operation of an engine.

The basic meaning of *kosmos* is "order." The idea of order can be observed in 1 Peter 3:3 where *kosmos* is rendered "outward adornment." This basic meaning was then transferred to the physical world, which was perceived in Greek minds as an orderly arrangement. The Scriptures credit this orderly arrangement to God's creative wisdom. In 1 Corinthians 5:9-10, Paul used *kosmos* to refer to planet earth. He argued that in order for believers to cut off relations with sinners, they would have to leave this planet (*kosmos*) because all people on the earth are tainted by sin. Other passages in which *kosmos* refers to the earth include Matthew 4:8; 13:38; Mark 16:15; John 17:15; 21:25; Roman 1:8; and Colossians 1:6. None of these references have any evil connotations. *Kosmos* often refers to the place of human habitation, as when God sent Christ into the world (John 3:17; 1 John 4:9). It can even mean "universe." Paul said that believers are to shine in this crooked generation like stars shine in the universe (Phil. 2:15).

Very often *kosmos* refers, by metaphorical extension, to humankind rather than to the earth. In John 1:10 Jesus was unknown by the world, meaning people. When Jesus said that His followers are lights of the world (Matt. 5:14), He must have been referring to humanity rather than the earth. Also, when John the Baptist declared that Jesus is the Lamb of God who takes away the sin of the world (John 1:29), it is the sin of humanity that John had in mind. Paul said that the whole world, meaning humankind, is held accountable to God (Rom. 3:19).

In John 3:16, the "world" is the object of God's love: "For God so loved the world that he gave his one and only Son, that whoever believes in him shall not perish but have eternal life." But what is meant by *world*? Most assume that it refers only to human beings. Others say it refers to the earth and everything in it. For example, the authors of *Earthkeeping* write:

> When Christians affirm that God loved the world and that Christ died for the life of the world, they are speaking not just of humanity, but of the whole planet—indeed, the whole created universe. Thus, of all the people, Christians should be concerned for the future health of the planet—both for the narrow "world" of humankind and the broader "earth" of a complex and living ecosphere.[7]

Granberg-Michaelson agreed with this view. Commenting on John 3:16, he wrote:

> To our Western and largely evangelical ears, we have heard and read this passage as if "world" meant "people." And when people are saved, they are saved from the world. Our concept of salvation consists of God plucking people up and out of a world headed for destruction. The image is like a rescue helicopter sending down a line for passengers on a burning, sinking ship to grab onto and be hoisted to safety. But this is not what Jesus says in the third chapter of John. Rather, he has been sent by God to save the whole world— the entire creation. Salvation means saving our ship.[8]

However appealing this idea may be to ecologically minded Christians, it poses certain exegetical problems. The theme of John's Gospel is almost exclusively devoted to setting forth Christ as the divine Savior of humanity and the signs that attest to this truth (John 20:30-31). Conspicuously absent are references to nature as being included in God's redemptive plan. This is not to say that nature is not included but that John's concern was with the human element. To construe the meaning of *world* to refer to the entire created universe is to go beyond the meaning John intended. It is true that human salvation is associated with the salvation of nature (Rom. 8:21) and that the work of Christ was meant to redeem all creation, human and non-human, and to restore it to prelapsarian peace and harmony. But this idea should not be put into John's mouth if he did not intend to say it.

Santmire recognized two motifs in New Testament literature, a spiritual motif represented by the Gospel of John and the Epistle to the Hebrews and an ecological motif represented by Paul, especially in Colossians and Ephesians. He suggested that these two conflicting motifs have caused an ambiguity in Christian thought about nature.[9] These two motifs need not be conflicting if we understand each author's particular focus. John's focus on human salvation was not contradictory to Paul's focus on cosmic salvation. Paul offered the more comprehensive framework to interpret the doctrine of salvation. John simply chose to emphasize the human aspect. This interpretation of John 3:16 in no way lessens God's love for the rest of creation.

A third usage of *kosmos* is in reference to the world system that is hostile to God. The world hates Christ and His followers (John 7:7; 15:18-19; 1 John 3:13). One of the criteria James used to define pure religion was "to keep oneself from being polluted by the world" (1:27). It is the world system that James had in mind, not the physical earth. True spirituality includes honoring God through caring for His creation. Although we live in the world, we are not to partake of its philosophy (John 17:14-16; see 15:19). Friendship with any anti-God philosophy that happens to be in vogue amounts to "hatred toward God" (Jas. 4:4). When Paul said that "the world has been crucified to me," he was referring to the anti-God worldview of his day with all its self-centered interests (Gal. 6:14). When John said, "Do not love the world," he had in mind the world system that is hostile to God, not the physical world. John defined exactly what he meant by *world* in the following verse: "the cravings of sinful man, the lust of his eyes and the boasting of what he has and does" (1 John 2:15-17). God desires that we hate the world system opposed to Him, not His creation.

The fourth meaning of *kosmos*, that of pertaining to the activities and things of the world, may, depending on the context, carry evil connotations, since preoccupation with things of this world usually proceeds from a materialistic mind-set. For example, "What good will it be for a man if he gains the whole world, yet forfeits his soul?" (Matt. 16:26). The world here refers to material possessions and wealth.

The second word translated "world" in the New Testament (*aiōn*) also has various meanings. It can refer to (1) a period of time, (2) the anti-God philosophy of the age, or (3) the physical earth or universe. *Aiōn* usually refers to a long period of time, or age. The present age is contrasted to the future age in Matthew 12:32, Mark 10:30, and Ephesians 1:21. Every time the expression "end of the world" occurs in the *King James Version* New Testament, it is the word *aiōn*, meaning "age" (Matt. 13:39-40; 13:49; 24:3; 28:20; and Heb. 9:26). The word often refers to the anti-God philosophy of the age as in Romans 12:2, "Do not conform any longer to the pattern of this world." When Satan is called the "god of this world" (2 Cor. 4:4, KJV), it does not mean that he is the ruler of the physical world but rather of the present age characterized by his evil influence. Christ came to deliver us from the present evil age (*aiōn*), meaning the evil way of life that characterizes this age, not from the physical world (Gal. 1:4). Demas forsook Paul because he loved the present world (*aiōn*). Demas did not leave Paul because of his love for nature but his love for the ways of a godless society. On rare occasions it may refer to the created realm. In Hebrews 1:2 God made the universe (*aiōn*) through Christ.

The third word *oikoumenē* means the inhabited world. For example, the preaching of the gospel will go into all the world (Matt 24:14), all the world was taxed (Luke 2:1), famine spread throughout the world (Acts 11:28), and God will judge the world (Acts 17:31; Rev. 3:10). God is not going to judge the physical world, for it is morally neutral, but the evil human inhabitants of the world.

The misunderstanding of these words has contributed to a negative attitude toward the physical world. Nature has been stripped of its intrinsic value. It has also been stripped of any purpose in God's plan other than being the stage or scenery in God's redemptive plan. The world is something we must tolerate for the time being, since we are merely sojourners on the way to our real home in heaven. This idea is reinforced by our hymnology with such songs as "When We All Get to Heaven," "We're Marching to Zion," "When the Roll Is Called Up Yonder," "Higher Ground," "When the Saints Go Marching In," "I'll Fly Away," and a host of others. But contrary to the popular gospel song that says, "This world is not my home, I'm just a passing thru," this world is our home, for God so designed it in such a way to be habitable for humans as well as other forms of life. In his Athenian address Paul remarked, "From one man he made every nation of men, that they should inhabit the whole earth" (Acts 17:26). It is existential thought, not Christian thought, that affirms that we are aliens or misfits in this world. We do belong. God created humans and nature to complement each other in the ideal ecosystem. From this, one could conjecture that the future abode of the saints may not be as ethereal as many suppose. It could be the new earth rather than the new heavens.

Other reasons have also helped twist the necessary distinctions into harmful dualisms, such as misapplying the biblical warnings against nature worship and limiting the concept of salvation. Whether the dualisms in the church caused the dualisms in Western society is a complex issue that will perhaps never be resolved. If Christianity did contribute to the dualistic tendency in society, it would have come from a perverted Christianity rather than true biblical Christianity. Many trace secular dualism to the Cartesian dichotomy between mind and matter. The mind was of the highest level and consequently of the highest value. This notion subsequently evolved into the negative dualism of humanity's absolute supremacy over nature and right to dominate it, a dualism that found fertile ground and ample justification in Christian thought. It is understandable then why Western Christianity so easily capitulated to the dualistic tendencies of society and lent support to the whole fiasco.

Resolving the Dualism/Distinction Quandary

We cannot deny that the Bible makes distinctions between humans and nature and between the spiritual and the physical. Problems arise only when one makes these distinctions absolute, perceives antagonism between them, and then assigns values that differ from the theocentric value structure. The needed distinctions then become harmful dualisms. For example, the Bible affirms a distinction between humans and nature. Humans exist higher up in the hierarchical structure in that they have the ability and responsibility to care for creation. If this biblical distinction is not tempered by a theocentric perspective of the whole, then it may very well result in a destructive anthropocentric dualism, with a corresponding devaluation of nature.

The same may happen with the distinction between the spiritual and physical. God and angelic beings, for example, inhabit a different sphere of existence than humans. The distinction of two realms is absolutely necessary to Christian theology. If the dichotomy is not maintained, then God and angels must be understood in terms of this realm, as some sort of energy or vibration. The loss of this distinction would destroy Christianity, turn it into a pantheistic sect, and plummet it into the ethical dilemma of naturalism. It is pantheism that affirms one realm of reality; Christianity affirms two realms and sees value in both. The spiritual and physical realms cannot be antagonistic polarities, for they come together in God's providence, incarnation, and redemption. They are distinct, yes, but in no way an inimical dualism if viewed through a theocentric perspective. The necessary biblical distinction between the spiritual and physical promotes neither a negative attitude toward the physical nor a harmful dualism that plays havoc with the environment.

The distinctions between humanity and nature and between the spiritual and physical are not only necessary to Christianity, they are necessary for the health of the environment. These distinctions cannot be dissolved without plunging nature into chaos. There must be caretakers who have been endowed with abilities that set them apart from the rest of creation, who have been placed over nature in a hierarchical ladder, and who have been armed with an ethical imperative that transcends the physical in order for peace and harmony to be restored and maintained. All these observations presuppose that distinctions exist.

The ecologically necessary distinctions are easily distorted into dualisms when a theocentric perspective is lost sight of. The answer to the problem of dualisms is not to dispose of the distinctions or dichotomies that are inherent in biblical thought, but to reclaim a theocentric perspective. It is possible from a theocentric position to maintain the Bible's ecologically healthy distinctions without resorting to either reductionistic monism or destructive dualisms. Distinctions yes, dualisms no.

There are, however, exceptions to this. While the Bible does not present antagonistic polarities between God and nature, this world and the next, or between the spiritual and the physical, it does challenge us to choose good and reject evil, to choose God and reject idols, and to choose a theocentric way of thinking and reject all others. Here are true biblical dualisms in which we must make a choice between two opposing principles. Without the dualism between good and evil, there would be no basis for any moral agenda. Pantheism, with its dissolving of all dualities, including that between good and evil, offers a nonanswer to the moral perplexities of the environmental crisis. Christianity's dualism between good and evil is a healthy and needed dualism for the environment.

Biblical Affirmations and Renunciations

Proper affirmations and renunciations are in part derived from the distinctions and dualisms found in the Scriptures. Both sides of a nondualistic distinction may be affirmed, but only one side of a dualism. The Scriptures affirm both the physical world and the spiritual but renounce sin, self-centeredness, and the worldly mind-set that is hostile to God. The biblical affirmations and renunciations are all environmentally healthy and collectively cannot be found in any other system, especially not with the vigor of Christian theism. This vigor is due to the biblical affirmations and renunciations being grounded, not in contingencies, but in a necessary and transcendent being.

Biblical Affirmations

Biblical faith calls for several affirmations that Christians have not consistently made regarding the natural realm. Biblical faith is a world-affirming faith. As Bernhard Anderson said, "Israel's creation faith endorses a positive this-worldliness."[10]

The Unity of Creation. The Scriptures affirm the wholeness and interrelatedness of the entire created order. Many have observed the corporate identity or solidarity of the Israelite nation through Achan's sin. When Achan took the wedge of gold that was dedicated to God, the entire nation sinned (Josh. 7:11,20). The solidarity of the nation is also exemplified in Abraham's paying a tithe to Melchizedek. When Abraham paid the tithe, Levi also paid the tithe, for he was regarded as in the loins of Abraham (Heb. 7:9-10). The corporate identity of the church is expressed by the entire church suffering when one member suffers (1 Cor. 12:26). Paul built on the corporate identity of the human race in his argument in Romans 5:12-21. These examples of corporate identity are extended in biblical thought to the entire community of creation. When people curse, lie, murder, steal, and commit adultery, the land mourns, and the beasts of the field, the birds of the air, and the fish of the sea begin dying (Hos. 4:2-3). This depicts a solidarity of the entire creation where everything is perceived as one interconnected whole. Disruption of one part has repercussions on other parts. Lying, therefore, is not merely a social crime, it is a cosmic crime. The redeemed are called on to affirm the wholeness and unity of the original creation and then to reflect it in their thoughts and actions.

The Value of Nature. The Scriptures affirm the value of nature in various ways: (1) the doctrine of creation, (2) God's ownership, (3) God's purpose, (4) God's recognition of the goodness of creation, (5) God's providence, (6) God's concern for nature, (7) God's covenant with creation, (8) the incarnation, and (9) the bodily resurrection. As mentioned in chapter 4, nature has value because it is valued by God. This provides intrinsic value to nature, a value that is not contingent on human utility. Schaeffer remarked that to view nature as intrinsically low is "an insult to the God who made it."[11] Biblical faith affirms value in everything God made, the nonhuman and human, the material and spiritual.

Because God recognized the goodness of creation, the Christian cannot call it evil or even regard it as something to be avoided (Gen. 1:31). We cannot call matter evil without implicating God as the author of evil. Biblical faith requires the affirmation of the goodness of nature and rejection of any form of dualism that says the physical realm is in some way contemptible. Paul told Timothy, "Everything God created is good, and nothing is to be rejected if it is received with thanksgiving" (1 Tim. 4:4). Holding a low view of nature does not show proper reverence to the Creator, for as Linzey said, "Nothing that God has made can be in the last resort really alien to him."[12] This agrees with Paul who said that there is nothing unclean in itself (Rom. 14:14) and with Jesus who said, "Nothing outside a man can make him 'unclean' by going into him. Rather, it is what comes out of a man that makes him 'unclean'" (Mark 7:15).

The Purpose of Nature. Another area of biblical affirmation is the purposes God intended for creation. God's reasons for nature contradict the common understanding that nature's sole purpose is human utility. Some of the reasons include God's enjoying the creatures He made, admiring the beauty of creation, allowing nature to praise and testify of Him, inspiring awe and wonder in people, as well as being mutually beneficial for all God's creatures. Nature, for example, is to be enjoyed, just as God enjoys it (without having to use or consume it in order to enjoy it, as with materialism). Perhaps the ability to enjoy nature is part of what Jesus had in mind when He spoke of the abundant life (John 10:10). Dualism robs us of the joy God intended in this life and dissipates the awe and wonder of creation. Christians are called on to affirm the divine purposes of creation and protect them by faithful stewardship.

The Restoration of Nature. Another environmentally relevant affirmation the Scriptures make is that redemption extends to all nature (Rom. 8:20-21; Eph. 1:10; Col. 1:20). Salvation means making something whole or healing broken relations. In biblical thought it pertains to healing the wounds of the fall, bringing the entire creation back into the harmonious conditions of the original creation. The believer is called on to affirm that God's salvation extends to all creation and then to participate in its healing.

In summary, we must recognize that valid distinctions exist, that we are to affirm the value of both sides of a distinction, and that we should fulfill our obligations in both. Believers were never called to live in tension between the present and future or between their duty to nature and God's remaking it. Both aspects of a nonduality are always connected; for example, as believers fulfill their obligations to nature (physical), they are also fulfilling their obligations to God (spiritual). The necessary distinctions in some cases are not so far removed from each other as some think. The same applies to the distinctions between the present and future. Responsibilities in preparation for the future merge into present duties.

Biblical Renunciations

The renunciations of contemporary Christianity far exceed those of Scripture. Part of the problem, as mentioned earlier, is a misunderstanding of terms, such as *world* and *flesh.* For example, the common baptismal formula invokes new converts to renounce the world, the flesh, and the devil. This renunciation helps to liberate them from their past lives and to direct them toward proper relations with God. This is fine if the terms *world* and *flesh* are understood in Pauline usage as referring respectively to the world system that is hostile to God and to the sin nature. But more often than not, the terms are understood in modern parlance to refer to anything physical. Thus to be spiritual, one must renounce everything physical. After all, a spiritual person cannot be attached to this realm if God is a spirit being who exists in a spiritual realm. Contamination by the physical would only hamper the quest for the realization of God in one's life. This dualism, which parallels the God-quest of many Eastern and mystical sects, was never intended in Scripture.

Only in the case of an authentic biblical dualism can there be an authentic biblical renunciation. Biblical dualisms include those things the Bible affirms as good and renounces as evil, such as righteousness and sin or good and evil. Good and evil are two irreducible, contrasting, and antagonistic principles that demand a choice to be made. Evil, in all its expressions, must be renounced and purged from the life of the believer. Although we must repudiate evil and not allow it to influence our lives, we cannot totally isolate ourselves from the evil in society and withdraw to a monastic existence. The world is our mission field in which we must be involved. Just as Christ was involved in society yet not touched by its evil, so must be His disciples. It is our mission to combat evil by spreading the goodness of Christ's redemption throughout God's creation.

Proper renunciations include things the Bible condemns or calls us to choose against, all of which are subsumed in biblical language under the generic term *sin* (Job 28:28; Ps. 97:10; Prov. 14:16; Rom. 6:12; 12:9; 1 Cor. 10:6; 1 Thess. 5:22; and 1 Pet. 3:11). The following list suggests some evils that pertain to environmental issues which believers are called on to renounce.

Materialism. Partaking of the material or affirming its goodness should not be confused with materialism. God designed nature to be used by His creatures to meet their needs. Materialism, on the other hand, assumes that material possessions constitute the highest good, an assumption that underlies modern society. Since the only worthy objective in one's life is to pursue the highest good, materialists grasp after whatever material goods they can acquire. Scripture utterly condemns materialism, for it arises out of a godless, self-centered lust for possessions and power. Nature is not an object to be grasped but a trust to be cared for and enjoyed. The highest good is the pursuit of godliness. A theocentric view will produce proper stewardship and sharing with all forms of life; an anthropocentric view leads either to grasping for self (individual materialism) or grasping for the interests of the human community (corporate materialism).

Materialistic greed is condemned throughout the Bible. The Tenth Commandment forbids coveting a neighbor's house, wife, servant, livestock, or anything else that belongs to the neighbor (Ex. 20:17; see Rom. 7:7; 13:9). God condemned Israel's watchmen who took advantage of their office to accumulate wealth for themselves (Isa. 56:11-12). Scriptures warn that being consumed with the quest for riches causes one to become proud and forget the Lord (Deut. 8:12-14). The Scriptures also teach the futility of engaging in the endless quest for riches,

<blockquote>
Whoever loves money never has
money enough;
whoever loves wealth is never
satisfied with his income.
This too is meaningless (Eccl. 5:10).
</blockquote>

The New Testament is replete with condemnations against greed and materialism. Jesus taught that one cannot love both God and money (Matt. 6:24; Luke 16:13). The Lukan parallel adds, "What is highly valued among men is detestable in God's sight" (Luke 16:15). We are to lay up treasures in heaven rather than accumulate wealth upon earth (Matt. 6:19-21). In the parable of the sower, one episode represents the person who gladly received seed, but its effectiveness in that person's life was choked by the "deceitfulness of wealth" (Matt. 13:22; see 16:26; 19:16-30). In the parable of the rich fool, the Lord says, "Be on your guard against all kinds of greed; a man's life does not consist in the abundance of his possessions" (Luke 12:15). Officers in the church were not to be lovers of money or fond of dishonest gain (1 Tim. 3:3,8; see 6:10). The love of money is a characteristic of godlessness in the last days (2 Tim. 3:2). Paul exhorted Timothy to warn the rich not to be arrogant and put their hope in riches (1 Tim. 6:17), because strivings for riches "plunge men into ruin and destruction" (1 Tim. 6:9). The Scriptures encourage believers to renounce greed, materialism, and self-indulgence, the very things that propel our economy and have laid waste our environment.

Self-centeredness. The Bible condemns one's preoccupation with self and the corresponding neglect to serve others. Included in the rubric of egoism that the Bible condemns are: self-exaltation (Matt. 23:12), pride (Prov. 21:4), self-advancement (Luke 22:24-30), self-indulgence (Prov. 23:20-21), self-sufficiency (Prov. 28:26), selfishness (Prov. 11:26), and covetousness (Luke 12:15).

The crux of the entire environmental problem is the self-centered sufficiency that disavows any need for God. Humanity's self-proclaimed autonomy from God has precipitated an arrogant pride in human potentiality and a destructive spirit of egoism. Self-centered sufficiency can only lead to disaster, as well attested by both our present environmental distress and the biblical record:

> Pride goes before destruction,
> a haughty spirit before a fall (Prov. 16:18).

> He who trusts in himself is a fool,
> but he who walks in wisdom is kept safe (Prov. 28:26).

> Woe to those who are wise in their own eyes
> and clever in their own sight (Isa. 5:21).

> "Though you soar like the eagle
> and make your nest among the stars
> from there I will bring you down,"
> declares the Lord (Obad. 4).

Zephaniah's portrait of Assyria is an apt description of a modern Western society,

> This is the carefree city that lived in safety.
> She said to herself,
> I am, and there is none besides me.
> What a ruin she has become, a lair for wild beasts!
> All who pass by her scoff and shake their fists (Zeph. 2:15).

Many parts of this world have become ruins at the hands of arrogant humanity. The church in Laodicea also typifies the present generation: "You say, 'I am rich; I have acquired wealth and do not need a thing.' But you do not realize that you are wretched, pitiful, poor, blind and naked" (Rev. 3:17).

Paul reminded us that our confidence must be in God rather than in ourselves. Confidence in self is self-deception. "If anyone thinks he is something when he is nothing, he deceives himself" (Gal. 6:3). "So, if you think you are standing firm, be careful that you don't fall!" (1 Cor. 10:12). We are not to boast of our intellect, creativity, or powers, since everything we have is a gift from God (Eph. 2:10). If there is any boasting, let it be for what Christ has done for us (Gal. 6:14). The Scriptures call upon Christians to renounce the environmentally deadly sins of egocentrism and materialism, which together have devastated God's creation. The Scriptures that condemn the roots of the ecological crisis cannot possibly be the cause of the problem.

False Religions and Philosophies. Scriptures encourage people to embrace the true religion of Yahweh and renounce the false religions of the pagans (Ex. 32:26; Deut. 30:19; Josh. 24:15; and 1 Kings 18:21). Paul warned the Colossians to beware of philosophies based on ancient traditions and the basic principles of the world rather than on Christ (2:8). He reminded Timothy that there will be some who will turn from the truth to myths (1 Tim. 1:4; 4:7; 2 Tim. 4:4). The dualism between true biblical faith and pagan nature religions cannot be overlooked as Christian theologians seek to formulate a Christian response to the environmental crisis.

Idols. Idolatry is the veneration of an object that represents ultimate reality or some aspect of it. In the Judeo-Christian Scriptures, idolatry is not only the worship of false gods but also the making of any physical image of Yahweh (Ex. 20:4; Lev. 26:1; Deut. 7:25; and 1 John 5:21). Modern secular society also has its idols, such as money, position, affluence, possessions, pleasure, and fame. If the physical realm is ultimate reality, then all meaning and purpose must be derived from the material. The acquisition of physical artifacts becomes the consummation of one's quest for the significance of life. Yet as Hosea observed, the idols people make lead to their own destruction (8:4). We are seeing this destruction today as the idolatry of modern society has devastated the environment, threatening its own existence. Jesus' remark to His disciples in Matthew 16:25 is a very apt commentary on our present society, "For whoever wants to save his life will lose it." In seeking things and power to save ourselves, we are literally on the verge of self-annihilation.

While the idolatry of secular humanism worships the artifacts of human culture, the idolatry of pantheistic cults worships nature itself. We must distinguish between having a respect for nature because it is owned and valued by God and having a reverence for nature because it is God. For the Christian, nature can be an aid to worship that inspires thoughts toward God, but it cannot become the object of worship. To identify God with the universe, as done in pantheistic cults, is to make it an object of worship and source of divine power. In Romans 1:23 Paul condemned the worshipping of creation rather than the Creator, noting that it leads to the degradation of human society (vv. 24–32). When the personal, transcendent God is rejected, all basis for value and morals is lost, and society is plunged into chaos.

Neither the idols of secular humanism or pantheism can offer genuine help toward environmental solutions. Scriptures tell us that these idols cannot save us from the human predicament (Isa. 45:20) and, therefore, are not worthy of our worship (Acts 17:29; 1 Cor. 8:4). Humanity has lost a sense of relatedness to nature and to the entire cosmic order. The only way to regain harmony with the cosmic order is through a path that affirms the duality of good and evil, and to identify with the good, for it is the evil that fosters disharmony and eventually leads to the death of humanity and nature.

In conclusion, we should note that everything the Scripture affirms is good for the environment and everything it renounces is harmful to it. The dualism between good and evil is absolutely necessary to give positive direction to correcting environmental problems. The reductionistic approach of biocentrism certainly eliminates harmful dualisms that have contributed to the environmental crisis, but it also destroys distinctions that are necessary for nature's healing.

The Mission of the Church

For many the question of the mission of the church has become a perplexing problem, especially since there is a growing Christian concern for the environment. Involvement in environmental issues seems to pose more of a problem than participating in social concerns. At least with social concerns people are involved, and care shown to others may lead to their conversion. Environmental issues appear too far off base for many even to consider. Some feel that affirming the material realm would tend to distract people from the spiritual endeavors of evangelism and personal sanctification. What exactly is the mission of the church? Is the mission of the church evangelism, social issues, or environmental action?

For some the sole purpose of the church during this age is evangelism and missions. For anything else to be a legitimate concern of the church, it must be justified by its contribution to world evangelism. For example, giving food to the hungry is justified so long as a gospel message accompanies that bowl of soup, or giving medical aid is permissible as long as it is a front organization for a missionary outreach. If not, then the church is guilty of propagating a social gospel. Simply dropping food and medical supplies by parachute in a depressed area would not be acceptable, for there is no personal contact and no evangelistic witness. Any involvement in social or environmental concerns is looked upon as a diversion from the primary mission of the church.

Others see the mission of the church to be caring for the hungry, needy, and oppressed. The church is to imitate Christ, who went around healing the lame, restoring sight to the blind, and feeding the hungry. The idea of a wrathful God who judges people for their sins is viewed as a holdover from a primitive concept of God that lacks relevance for modern society. The gospel is a gospel of love displayed through social action. The love of God spread by acts of kindness is intended to soften the hearts of people and inspire them to change their godless ways. In order for environmental issues to be a legitimate endeavor, they must be subordinated to the church's mission of caring for the poor and oppressed. That is, the primary reason for engaging in ecological matters is to protect the rights of the poor.

The problem with both of these views is that they are not broad enough. God did not intend for the church to do only one thing. Just as each one of us has more than one function (such as fulfilling the roles of wife, mother, sister, employee, friend), so God intended the church to fulfill many tasks. The biblical writers show a widespread interest in various arenas of service: proclaiming the gospel (Acts 1:8), living a righteous life (Matt. 5:20), helping the poor and oppressed (Gal. 2:10), visiting the sick (Jas. 5:14), sending food relief to the hungry (Acts 11:29), caring for the widows and orphans (Jas. 1:27), and healing the sick (Luke 9:2). All these tasks have one thing in common: they presuppose that the present conditions have been distorted from the harmony of the original creation and lie under the influence of corrupt powers. Each of the biblical tasks of the church in its own way seeks to restore part of the created order.

Our primary allegiance is to God, not to the environment, evangelism, missions, the church, or one another. Said another way, the primary mission of the church is not evangelism or social action; it is pleasing God. When God occupies the primary place in our list of priorities, then everything else will fall into proper order with a proper balance between them. Otherwise, some important facets of God's will for His people during this age will be neglected. The mission of the church is to bring glory to God by being obedient to the broad spectrum of God's desires. Submission to God will encompass social concern, environmental action, and personal evangelism, for all play their part in the reclamation of the world for God. It is not a matter of choosing between evangelism or social activities as the primary mission of the church. The main focus is serving God. Thus, feeding the hungry, helping the poor, taking care of the environment, and winning the lost are all perfectly legitimate in their own right without having to be justified by their contribution to evangelism or social concern.

This is not to minimize spreading the gospel. This is still God's primary interest during this age. This does not mean that other activities are wrong or that they do not have a right by their own merits. It is not an either/or but a both/and. We all do more than one thing every day, such as get out of bed, wash ourselves, dress, eat breakfast, and go to work. Some things are more important than others, but there is an array of essential things that all need to be done. We do not question the dictum "make the main thing the main thing." There are other things Christians legitimately should do. To do nothing but the main thing actually defeats one in accomplishing the main thing, because it proclaims to all that Christianity is not relevant to everyday life. God does have other concerns to which we must be sensitive, all which lend credibility to the gospel message. The only way to make sure that all God desires will be attended to is to say that the primary mission of the church is to please God.

12

Epilogue: A Christian Environmental Agenda

The Christian Scriptures, when interpreted through a theocentric perspective, offer the most satisfying analysis and realistic solution of the environmental problem. They present not only the direction we should pursue toward what Schaeffer called a substantial healing but also the hope of complete healing through the work of God. They isolate the root cause of the problems we face as emanating from a demonic twist in human nature and offer a solution through Christ's redemption on the cross. The church has the responsibility to take this message of healing to the ends of the earth so that relations might be mended and peace might be restored.

The message of redemption and healing will fall on deaf ears unless accompanied by acts of love (1 John 3:18). If people today, in the spirit of our pragmatic age, do not observe Christianity at work, they will assume it cannot work and dismiss everything Christians say as nonrelevant abstractions. The Christian response to the environmental crisis should be twofold: first, a change in perspective; second, a change in activity. It must include reconsidering nature's role in God's plan as well as becoming involved. The rethinking process is critical for conservative Christianity, which stands in need of a radical shift in the

260

way nature is perceived. Changing the way people think is never easy, for it implies that former modes of thought were fallacious. People generally detest being told they are wrong, especially fundamentalists of any religion or group (this includes much of the modern scientific community). In such cases, beliefs, traditions, biases, theories, hypotheses, and prejudices become set in religious cement and, consequently, internalized within the individual. This effectively closes the mind to the possibility of being wrong. To challenge one's way of thinking then becomes tantamount to challenging the person and invariably encounters resistance.

Rethinking Nature's Role in God's Economy

The process of rethinking our presuppositions is a painful and humiliating experience. It encompasses listening to our critics, developing critical thinking in the arena of worldviews and religious beliefs, expanding our horizon to see the larger picture, redefining basic terminology, learning about God's creation from various sources, and developing a theology of nature. Critical thinking involves interaction with others of opposing viewpoints, open-mindedness, seeking justification for our assumptions, and a willingness to admit we could be mistaken in certain areas.

Interact with the Critics

There are several areas in which Christianity's critics are correct if we understand their accusations as being directed toward Christendom rather than the Scriptures. There have been unwarranted and unhealthy dualisms in the church, destructive attitudes of absolute dominion over nature, a focus on anthropocentrism and human salvation, failure to perceive God's interest in nature, and ignoring His injunctions to take care of creation.

The church has also uncritically agreed with the dualism of the modern scientific establishment and the utilitarian valuing of nature by our materialistic society, thereby lending theological sanction for the whole fiasco. Part of the problem is that the church has been infiltrated by materialistic, secular modes of thought, for which it needs to repent and return to biblical truth regarding proper attitude and responsibility toward the environment. Christians have, by and large, interpreted the dominion passage as giving them transcendence over nature and a license for unrestricted exploitation. Lynn White was partly right in saying it is a "Christian axiom that nature has no reason for existence save to serve man,"[1] but it would be a mistaken assumption to say it is a biblical axiom. As previously argued, this attitude results from misinterpreting Scripture, rather than Scripture itself. It is not God's Word that is at fault but the failure of Christians to understand and apply it properly.

Much of what the critics have said regarding the Scriptures has been in error. In the past twenty years Christian scholars have responded to many of the charges and have vindicated the Scriptures, but the greater part of the church has not been involved in the controversy, let alone even being aware of it. Most Christians have not heard what the critics have been saying that pertain to the beliefs and practices of the church. We need the critics. We need to interact with them so that we can see ourselves and our possible shortcomings more clearly and overcome our egocentrism which blinds us from seeing ourselves as we really are.

The critics indirectly have pointed out that the church as a whole needs to confess neglecting something very dear to God and beg for mercy and healing (see 2 Chron. 7:14). Ignoring God's design for nature, neglecting the ecological mandate in Genesis, and exploiting to fill one's greed are morally wrong. The Christian community not only has been an accomplice in the crime but is also guilty of failing to speak out against the atrocity. It has not been sensitive to God's desire to see His creation properly cared for and to campaign for justice for all God's creatures. Thus, the sin is one of both omission and commission. Santmire said that "if the Christian church is to make a positive contribution . . . many things within the sphere of the church's own life and thought must be corrected and reformed. The church must begin to set its own house in order if it is to begin to respond adequately to the monstrous environmental problems of our time."[2]

Think Critically

Critical worldview thinking will help keep the church theologically pure and honoring to God by helping purge materialism and secularism from its thinking. Worldviews within Christendom are actually blends of Scripture, anthropocentrism, tradition, stereotyped behavior, and cultural assumptions with gleanings from other religious and philosophical ideas. Even the most ardent defenders of the faith are unwittingly guilty of subconscious syncretism in the creation of their own personal view of the Christian message. We are all children of our age to a certain extent. We are born as little sponges, taking in pieces of whatever we encounter in the experience of life. Everything either consciously or unconsciously shapes our thinking. We have blinded ourselves by rigidly constricting ourselves in our narrow traditions and presuppositions. We must develop a critical mind to sort out our presuppositional baggage and bring every thought captive to Christ (2 Cor. 10:5; Rom. 12:2).

The return to a biblical base, however, is not without problems, such as overcoming interpretational and theological biases. How can the church isolate and purge alien ideas from its thinking when strains of secular thought have been so integrated into Christian thinking that a presuppositional framework has been formed that is difficult to see beyond? This is why critics are valuable and should be listened to. The church cannot step outside its presuppositional shell without interacting with the critics who help us see our belief systems a bit more objectively.

As other worldviews are studied, people soon discover that every system contains elements that resonate with their inner being; that is, certain aspects seem to be true in that they correspond to a universal perception of reality. A pantheist will look at nature and recognize that the cause of the present problem is due to imbalance, that healing comes when the present imbalances and alienations are restored, that all things are interconnected, and that healing concerns the entire natural order. These thoughts somehow resonate with our being. We all know that there is a sense of peace and fulfillment within when we live in harmony with others and with nature. Yet as soon as pantheists see it, they slip a presuppositional framework between them and what they observe and interpret everything in a monistic sense as being part of one cosmic entity.

Although we may not agree with the pantheistic interpretation, we still must recognize that pantheists are seeing something and that we might be able to learn from them. The reasoning is that all humans share a common world and common experiences of life and will observe the same truths, some seeing better than others. The interconnectedness of all things, for example, has been seen rather dimly in both secular and Christian circles because of their respective dualisms. Perhaps as we strip away the presuppositional framework of pantheism, we will see something there that can help us take the blinders off our eyes, in this case, that the theme of interconnectedness actually runs throughout the Bible.

Another aspect of developing critical worldview thinking is to rise above mere superficiality. For a Christian to have common interests with pantheistic environmentalists, to use the same vocabulary, or to cite favorable comments of their authors does not mean that the Christian is on the verge of apostasy. Whenever some people hear certain buzzwords, a red flag goes up, and everything is condemned as some demonic New Age heresy. No learning or interaction is possible under such conditions. The day we become so provincial in our ways of thinking that we turn a deaf ear to those of opposing positions is the day we cease to learn about life and what it means to be human.

Having said this, however, we must reaffirm that Christianity cannot be merged with any other philosophical system and remain Christian. Christianity and pantheism are irreconcilable opposites. The synthesis that results from a dialectical merger of the two conflicting positions is neither Christian nor pantheistic. This is not to say that we cannot listen and learn from pantheistic environmentalists. What we incorporate is not their interpretations, but what they are looking at, those bits of truth about reality that are common to all traditions but which have been dimly seen by most Christians.

Comprehend the Whole

Environmental problems, whether ecological disasters, pollution, or depletion of resources, are not local problems. This is especially true regarding the atmosphere, oceans, and waterways, all which pass freely over national boundaries. Most of us breathe air and drink water that has been polluted far from our own locality. For example, sulfur emissions from heavy industries of the Midwest are causing acid rain in Canadian forests. Swiss chemical plants that pour toxic chemicals into the Rhine contaminate the drinking water in Holland. Even if one nation cleaned up its emissions, it might still suffer from the pollution of neighboring nations. This observation requires environmental planners to work toward international policies and establish international bodies to enforce the policies. The ecological predicament demands global cooperation, a coming together of all peoples and religions to fight a common foe. This thought, however, poses serious problems for many fundamental Christians.

Some would contend that joining forces with pantheistic-minded environmentalists in fighting environmental abuse or even being involved in the same general issue constitutes religious compromise. Such compromise is thought to consist of either an endorsement, promotion of, or capitulation to pagan nature religions. But does being involved or working together on a common issue necessarily constitute religious compromise? To assume it does is a serious misconception. Being involved together in a common interest, such as fighting a fire or an epidemic, does not necessarily mean that religious scruples are being violated. In World War II the Americans joined forces with the Russians to combat Nazi Germany, but this did not lead to compromising ideologies of either Russia or America. Each country maintained its own political distinctive. Should Christians refrain from feeding the poor, caring for orphans and elderly, or building hospitals just because secular humanists are doing these things as well? Such thinking quickly leads to absurdities. What about our jobs where we often work side by side with those of differing beliefs? Separating our trash, campaigning for animal rights, or contributing to a worthwhile environmental organization does not compromise our Christian beliefs.

Another problem many fundamentalists fear is that worldwide cooperation to combat environmental problems will lead to a one-world government that would usher in the apocalyptic reign of the Anti-Christ. The obvious fallacy with this reasoning, even assuming the literalness of a future Anti-Christ to be correct, is the impossibility of establishing direct causal connections. Such thinking represents the fallacy of false cause. Coincidence or temporal succession is not logical grounds to establish causal connection. Just because it rained when the medicine man danced does not mean that the dancing caused the rain. International organizations have existed for decades without any move toward dissolving member nations into a single governmental body. Furthermore, there seems to be as much discussion in New Age writings on political decentralization as there is on political globalism.

Many fundamentalists who follow the teachings of sensational writers Constance Cumbey and Texe Marrs equate environmental involvement with New Age globalism. A March 1990 newsletter put out by Texe Marrs contained the following blurb advertising his audiotape message on Earth Day 1990:

> Some 2 billion people will view it on international satellite television. President George Bush and Communist party leader Mikhail Gorbachev have endorsed it. New Age occultist Jose Argulles, organizer of 1987's Worldwide Harmonic Convergence, is one of the masterminds behind it. Hollywood stars and politicians galore will participate in its activities. It's slated to become the event of the decade—the catalyst for a glorious coming One World Kingdom on our planet, led by a New Age Messiah. *It's Earth Day 1990!* [3]

In her books *Hidden Dangers of the Rainbow* and *A Planned Deception,* Constance Cumbey attacked the book *Earthkeeping,* put out by the Fellows of the Calvin Center for Christian Scholarship at Calvin College, as propagating New Age beliefs. [4] She was rather upset by a reference to Teilhard de Chardin that labeled him as a "Christian thinker." For Cumbey, Teilhard is the patron saint of the New Age movement. The authors of *Earth-*

keeping did not endorse Teilhard but used him as an extreme example of anthropocentrism, a view they totally rejected.[5] Cumbey entirely missed the intent of the authors, extracted a quotation out of context, and used it to implicate the authors as being influenced by Teilhardian thought.[6]

Cumbey represents a broad spectrum within the church who believe that Christian environmentalism is a sign of the end-time apostasy. The following criticisms of her books may be generally applied to the group at large, recognizing, of course, that there will be exceptions.

First, she falsely assumed a definite causal connection between the agenda of the New Age movement and the apocalyptic visions of Daniel and John regarding a future world leader. We simply cannot be that dogmatic in the interpretation of prophecy, much of which is given in the symbolism of apocalyptic genre. Many writers of a dispensational, premillennial bent are guilty of this sort of sensationalized eschatology.

Second, she assumed that all international agreements further New Age globalism and help usher in the apocalyptic world system. She claimed that the authors of *Earthkeeping* laid out the New Age political program "in its entirety—including a *duty* for Christians to support globalization of our structures."[7] She came to this conclusion by a reference that Christians should support international efforts to establish and enforce standards for proper use of air, water, and oceans, so all can benefit without dangers of pollution.[8] It is rather naive to assume that international agreements automatically further New Age globalism and deter the cause of Christianity. It would be preposterous for a Christian to oppose an international agreement that allowed missionaries free entrance into any country.

Third, she ignored the global scope of Christianity's redemptive mission and what exactly that mission involves. The redemptive mission of the church involves restoring all kinds of broken relations and combating the effects of sin in the entire world. Christians have always thought globally regarding spreading the redemptive love of God to others; we must now think globally in terms of manifesting the redemptive power of Christ to the environment. Just as God thinks globally and has given two global mandates, so must His followers think globally as they seek to please God. The Christian effort will not bring in a new world order, but it will testify of the peace and harmony available through Christ.

Fourth, she failed to recognize the interests that Christians, New Agers, and other peoples share in common, such as curing cancer. Having the same interests, using the same vocabulary, or even having some of the same symbols does not mean the underlying philosophical/religious base is the same.

Fifth, she followed an extreme dualism between the present world and the future which effectively blocked recognition of our divinely given responsibility to care for the present order. In all, Cumbey made hasty generalizations based on superficial similarities, misquoting and misunderstanding the intent of Christian authors, committing the fallacy of false cause, and assigning guilt by association. Her fallacious charges and those following the same suit are preventing a large segment of the Christian sector from being obedient to God.

Cumbey and Marrs are not alone by any means. An article appeared in *The New American* entitled "Six 'Crises' All Leading to World Government." The six crises that the author labels bogus are acid rain, the greenhouse effect, ozone depletion, deforestation, overpopulation, and auto emissions.[9] Another article entitled "Environmentalism: A Modern Idolatry" appeared in *Antithesis*, in which the author argued,

> The Environmentalist movement is founded on a false religious system. . . . Furthermore, this false religion stands in opposition to the Christian mandate to "subdue the earth" for the glory of God—to use the resources God has provided to improve the material circumstances of His creatures in service to His Kingdom. This is significant since it points out the differences between Environmentalism and Christianity.[10]

To condemn all environmentalism because much of it is infiltrated with pantheistic thought is to throw out the baby with the bath water. Christian environmentalism remains a valid category, even though much of what is termed environmentalism promotes a form of pagan nature worship, something Christianity cannot condone in any sense of the term. This, however, does not negate the legitimacy and need for Christian environmentalism. To label all who are involved in environmentalism as promoting paganism or nature worship is to commit the fallacy of guilt by association. Christians still have a duty before God to care for the environment. Refusing to take part would be disobedience.

The polarity lies between pantheism and Christianity, not between environmentalism and Christianity. Since there are metaphysical differences, some tension will exist as conservative Christians engage in environmental activities. This is nothing new. Tension should be expected whenever Christians engage in any venture with members of society. The Christian motivation and goals, for example will not coincide with that of a pantheist. Christians are not pressing for new world order but merely responding to God's desire to spread the redeeming love and power of Christ wherever possible in a fallen world controlled by the forces of evil. Christians know that they will not be able to eliminate evil in this world. The only ecological utopia possible from a Christian perspective is that which is ushered in by Christ Himself in the age to come.

Since the ecological mandate was given to everyone, Christians should rejoice to see God's desires being carried out and be willing to cooperate with those of differing faiths in the substantial healing of the planet. Whatever is done, regardless of who is doing it, would indirectly help to fulfill God's injunction to care for the earth. It is somewhat inconsistent for Christians to welcome the work of non-Christians in providing a more wholesome life for humanity and then turn around and condemn their activity because of differing religious beliefs. Jonas Salk, for example, who developed the polio vaccine, has definite New Age leanings. Christians are very thankful and dependent on his work and the work of thousands like him in making the earth a better place to live and should seek to work with them in such ventures.

However, since environmental issues have taken on religious overtones, Christians should express the basis for their involvement as they join forces to stop environmental deterioration. This is to avoid misrepresentation or confusion of the Christian message. Christian involvement would then provide opportunities to share the reasons for our concern and the hope the Scriptures present. Such involvement need not compromise the truth nor confuse the message. The Christian response must stem "from the realization that 'the earth is the Lord's,'" not from borrowing ideas from pantheistic or animistic thought.[11]

It appears, however, that if any measurable environmental improvement occurs, it must involve all faiths and nations, each addressing the problem from their own cosmology. Although this fragmentary and thus nonecological approach cannot be expected to be long lasting, improvement will be made. This improvement will advance the quality of life for all God's creatures, regain some of the pristine beauty of God's creation, and inspire some to seek the God who created it. Calvin DeWitt said, "All religions should rejuvenate and revitalize teachings which recognize the integrity of Earth and its life and support a respectful sustaining care and keeping of the Earth, its ecosystems, and its living beings."[12] There is no compromise or syncretism in this idea, only the sobering realization that no faith system (including

Christianity) will be able to bring about global environmental improvement by itself.

As Christians become aware that the environmental problem is a moral problem, they will begin to realize that the church must play a strategic role. Remaining silent or even attacking environmentalism would be an enormous mistake, for it would neglect perhaps the most open platform for spiritual discussion in Western society in the past several centuries. When agnostics, such as Carl Sagan, are asking for input from the religious sector, how can Christians sit back and do nothing? Sagan is indicative of much of the scientific community, who, although not embracing religion, are beginning to recognize its importance and to seek spiritual values to lead society through the maze of the environmental problem.

Environmental issues are indeed raising human awareness to the possibility of a spiritual dimension. Neither legislation nor technology can correct twisted behavior toward the environment. It seems as if many are bent on fulfilling their suicide mission, implicating the rest of the planet along with them. As the world is beginning to cave in on humanity, people are crying out for moral guidance and a restructuring of values to save them from disaster. To remain indifferent to this spiritual longing is tantamount to sending millions of searchers into the open arms of pantheism. What is needed is a moral and spiritual revolution. From a Christian perspective, the change necessary for sustainable planetary healing cannot be achieved apart from the gospel of Christ and the regenerating power of the Holy Spirit. This is because all immoral behavior, whether directed toward others or toward the environment, ultimately stems from ignorance of or disobedience to God's Word.[13]

Reconsider Stereotyped Terminology

Another aspect of changing our thinking about the environment involves redefining some of our vocabulary. Words are powerful entities. They can shape our modes of thinking, stir up the emotions, and motivate all sorts of behavior. For example the misconception of the word *world* has helped to confirm the false dualism between the spiritual and physical, thereby leading to indifference and abuse of the environment. There are numerous other terms that hinder an environmental response which we let our presuppositional framework define for us. One of the problems confronting the church is the lack of theological terms for the new paradigm. Old words, such as *salvation* and *love,* must be biblically redefined, and new words, such as *holistic,* must be baptized in Christian thought. When nonbiblical modes of thinking, such as false dualisms and anthropocentrism, are purged from our minds, these words come into a new light and help guide us into a fuller and more satisfying interpretation of Scripture. The following are some of the terms that need to be rethought.

First, *freedom* can no longer be understood as without bounds. Even those who reject the Christian God recognize that humans cannot continue living as they please but that the environment places restrictions on them if they wish their kind to continue. Humans can very easily exceed the carrying capacity of the earth and threaten their own existence or at least the quality of life that makes it worth living. Restriction of behavior becomes a necessity of life, or phrased another way, limiting behavior liberates one to experience life in its fullness. For a Christian, God has placed certain restrictions on life so that one might be free to experience an abundant life, restrictions such as those against greedily accumulating material wealth, exploiting nature for selfish gain, oppressing the poor for self-advancement, as well as those that encourage selfless giving of time and possessions to help care for the poor, hungry, sick, widows, orphans, or the environment, and helping the lost find their way in this confused world. These limitations are not only environmentally sound but they also liberate us to a life that is well worth living.

Second, the term *rights* needs to be stripped of self-asserting tendencies. We can have no rights that stand in contradiction with the sovereign rights of God. Since God is the ultimate legislator of rights, all claims for justice must appeal to His jurisdiction. We may claim that we have the right to do as we wish with our property, but it must pass before the divine tribunal before becoming a genuine right. Obviously, we do not have absolute rights, for the property is not really ours in the first place. A person does not even have the right to commit suicide. The only rights we or any other creature have are derivative rights, drawn from God's design for creation.

Third, the biblical concept of the *kingdom of God* must be redefined to include both the present reality and the future expectation of both humanity and nature. No longer acceptable are modes of thought that restrict the kingdom to either the present or the future, since this either leaves us without real hope of ecological peace or destroys all basis for present involvement. Both are contradictory to the biblical theme of redemption. The kingdom should be understood in cosmic terms of restoring the peace and harmony of the original creation. This is occurring now to a limited degree as more are brought into the kingdom and kingdom principles of redemption are lived out in the lives of its subjects. Yet considering the stranglehold that the forces of evil exert over the human race, we must conclude that true ecological hope can only be realized through an eschatological inbreaking of the kingdom in its fullness by divine intervention.

Fourth, *salvation* can no longer be understood solely in human terms. Individual human salvation is still the focal point of God's redemptive program. Until people are redeemed, nothing else can be. Yet to limit salvation to humanity fails to appreciate the extent of God's program. God's design is to liberate all creation from the bondage of the curse and restore it to wholeness. When Adam sinned against God, the harmony of creation was thrown into discord, all relations were shattered, and the present abnormal state came into existence. Salvation must be understood as the restoration of the original harmony through victory over the corrupting influence of sin. This can only be achieved through the substitutionary atonement of Christ on the cross and the empowering work of the Spirit in the lives of individuals. The death of Christ then has cosmic significance. When humans enter into the final phase of God's redemption, we will not be alone. All nature will likewise "be liberated from its bondage to decay" (Rom. 8:21).

Fifth, *love* has been traditionally defined by the church as giving of oneself to God and one another. This definition reflects the anthropocentric stance of much of Christendom. But once it is recognized that God loves His entire creation and gave Himself to redeem it from the effects of human sin, our understanding of love takes on a broader significance. We cannot manifest the love of God if we are indifferent to the things dear to Him, and this includes nonhuman creation. The scope of our love must be as extensive as the scope of God's love; anything less would not be considered godlike love. If we show partiality in our love, then our love is not genuine (Jas. 2:1-13). Love must be redefined as giving of oneself for the welfare of the entire creation.

Sixth, *wealth* can no longer be measured in economic terms as an abundance of money and possessions; rather, in subjective terms as qualities that make life worth living (emotional and spiritual well-being, inward joy, security, happiness, compassion for others, and a peaceful, harmonious relationship with God, others, and the earth). The two kinds of wealth are antithetical in that one nullifies the other. Peace with self, with one another, and with the environment will never come as long as people continue to grasp for more possessions (Matt. 19:13; Mark 4:19). The pursuit of true or qualitative wealth is not only ecologically healthy, it is spiritually, psychologically, and physically healthy. It leads to a much richer life for both people and nature. Poverty should be understood as a lack of these qualities in one's life (see Matt. 5:3-12).

Although this redefinition is somewhat idealistic in that it does not fit into our economic structure, it is already part of our lives. We do place value on such qualities as health, leisure, peace, safety, and enjoying a quiet walk through the woods. As Derr said, "A high quality of life obviously already means more to us than mere quantitative acquisitiveness."[14] Yet when people seek wealth, they normally are thinking in quantitative economic terms, rather than in qualitative biblical terms. If everyone were to seek qualitative wealth, there would be no problem of distributing enough material goods for everyone to have the necessities of life, and perhaps a little above that to make life comfortable for all.

Seventh, a high *standard of living* must represent an accumulation of qualitative wealth in a person's life, not an accumulation of quantitative wealth. Increase of material wealth does not bring a corresponding increase in personal peace and happiness as both life experiences and the Scriptures testify (Luke 12:15; 1 Tim. 6:17; Jas. 5:3).

It is rather disheartening to watch developing nations aspire to the standard of living in America as the goal to which they want to bring their nation. The very term *developing* carries a technological connotation. If all the nations of the world developed in a technological sense, it would spell ecological disaster. They see America's affluence and our "high" standard of living as the model of a successful nation, but what they do not see is the high crime rate, divorce rate, suicides, drug and alcohol consumption, and general unrest of a nation in pursuit of things. The quest for materialistic gain fosters an aggressive behavior that may very well be a contributing factor to the violence in our society. Societies that do not emphasize materialism are more peaceful, such as the Amish and Mennonites. Although a rise in material goods has increased the quality of life in some areas, overall this has tended to lower it with increased stress and anxiety. It is ironical that people experience more stress in the United States despite its abundance of labor-saving equipment than in a country like Burma.[15] Ideally America should lead the way in redefining what is meant by wealth and a high standard of living, but realistically we must confess that the prospects of this ever happening are rather dim. For a country that measures success quantitatively to shift toward a qualitative standard would be a social revolution of the first order.

Learn About Creation

Another aspect of rethinking nature's role in God's economy is simply to learn more about our environment. Modern people are woefully ignorant of nature. Once on a bus trip to Arizona, I overheard a comment by a teenage girl amazed to discover that cotton grows on plants rather than being sheared off sheep like wool. This may seem like an extreme example, but I am becoming convinced it is suggestive of the general ignorance of nature by our urbanized society. In removing ourselves from a rural setting where we adapt to the cycles of nature into an artificial life in the city where we have all the conveniences at our fingertips, we have lost touch with how God's creation works and in a sense have lost touch with part of life itself. Perhaps the church could play a role in this re-education process. "Each church," said Calvin DeWitt, "should become a creation awareness center."[16]

The science of ecology can teach us about the interrelatedness and interdependence of life, natural cycles and food chains, and what happens when pollutants are entered into the system or when the harmony is disrupted by human intervention. This knowledge will help us live more in harmony with the processes of nature rather than depending on goods and services that destroy nature.

Although we can learn from nature, nature is not a rational entity and cannot itself actively teach us. If it were, then it could instruct us about the consequences of new substances before they are released into the environment. We learn from nature only in the sense of learning how things function in relation to something else already present in the ecosystem; that is, we can only observe the results of past or present cause/effect relationships, not future ones. If the substance is not present, then nature will not teach us anything about its potential harm. Hopefully, we will learn from our past mistakes and exercise caution before introducing alien substances into the environment. It seems, however, as if Hegel's comment will still prevail, that the one thing we learn from history is that people do not learn from history.[17]

There is a certain ecological wisdom we can glean from nature, from science, from other religious traditions, and from our mistakes. But the most comprehensive guide is to be found in the Christian Scriptures. The Scriptures provide a holistic framework by which to understand all the parts of the cosmic ecosystem and how they relate to each other. Without a holistic framework, true ecological wisdom and understanding will never be achieved. The information gathered would only be piecemeal. We cannot really learn about humanity or the environment apart from a comprehensive worldview that acknowledges the interconnectedness of the physical and spiritual realms and the reality of human sin and guilt.

Develop a Theology of Nature

The church stands in need of a fresh reading of the Bible, a reading sensitive to God's concern and purposes for the environment and to humanity's relationship and responsibility toward it. It is not as easy as said. It requires a new paradigm for understanding life and doing theology, yet there seems to be an ingrained resistance against paradigm shifts in traditional Christianity. The shift must be away from the dominant theanthropocentrism of Western theology to some new framework. Several have been suggested, such as interpreting everything in light of the eschaton (Moltmann), creation (Anderson), or God (Rossi).

As argued in previous chapters, the only adequate construct for a theology of nature is a theocentric framework that includes the interrelatedness of all reality and the creation-fall-redemption theme of biblical theology. If a theology were based on nature or human interests, it would ultimately fail for the simple reason that neither one is large enough to explain or encompass the entire picture. Only a theocentric perspective can tie everything together and provide an answer to the root problem of human sin. As Santmire remarked, "Theocentrism, in the tradition of an Isaiah or a Jesus, will be the ultimate framework for defining human existence."[18]

Perhaps the slowness of the Christian community to become environmentally active is due to the slowness of theologians to formulate a theology of nature. Granted, there are scattered Christian voices rising from the grass roots level, but where is that unifying voice coming down from the theologians and seminaries? Where is the text in systematic theology that includes a section on the theology of nature? Why do the vast majority of seminaries not offer courses in ecological theology? As mentioned above, a relevant theology of nature requires a massive paradigm shift for doing all theology. This means that it would be highly inappropriate to append a section on ecological theology in a systematic theology text without rewriting the entire work to be consistent with the new paradigm. How can one chapter come from the holistic/theocentric paradigm and the rest come from a theanthropocentric paradigm? Only when this obstacle is overcome can we expect a theology of nature and a holistic paradigm for all life to start filtering down from the theologians to the seminaries to the clergy and then to the laity.

Living a Redeemed Life

As mentioned before, the Christian voice will not be heard unless it is accompanied by positive environmental action. "The Church," said Schaeffer, "ought to be a pilot plant concerning the healing of man and himself, of man and man, and man and nature. Indeed, unless something like this happens, I do not believe the world will listen to what we have to say."[19] This involvement, however, must be accompanied by sound biblical reasons; otherwise, it might appear as a pragmatic move of the church to make herself relevant in hopes of bolstering falling attendances.

Fulfill Our Duty

Our duty as Christians is to be totally submissive to God. This includes feeding the hungry, helping the poor, and caring for the environment, as well as evangelism of the lost and edification of the saints. Believers are called to become involved in the world, not to withdraw from it (John 17:15-18), and to manifest the love of Christ to all with deeds of kindness (Gal. 6:10).

Although we recognize that there cannot be a final solution apart from divine intervention, we can work to lessen the dissonance between humans and nature in keeping with the divine will. Our goal is not to try to solve the ecological crisis, but to please God by living an obedient life.[20] We are to obey God rather than worry about the outcome. The outcome is in His hands.[21] We are to be salt of the earth, the light of the world (Matt. 5:13-14), and a shining light in a crooked generation (Phil. 2:15).

Dave Hunt, a writer often linked with Cumbey's sensational brand of eschatology, recognized a broader spectrum of Christian duty, one that extends to society and the environment. He remarked,

> Christians have generally been and should continue to be in the forefront of relief work and charitable efforts, doing all we can to make this world a better place; safer, more moral, healthier, happier, more prosperous. We should be thrifty, hard-working, diligent, generous, and opposed to war, exploitation, and dishonesty—not just thinkers, but doers. At the same time, however, we must make it clear that these efforts are not the final answer. They are emergency first aid—but without radical surgery, the patient will die. We must boldly and lovingly proclaim that the real problem is that the human race at its very heart is morally sick unto death.[22]

Adopt a Simple Life-Style

In order to fulfill the Christian obligations to humanity, nature, and God, some suggest the need to practice ecological asceticism, meaning by this not a return to the dualistic practices of monastic orders but practicing a simple life-style that minimizes the number of material wants.[23] Ron Elsdon advocated a simple life-style with a renewed focus on the biblical principles of sharing and hospitality as an antidote to materialism. He said that Christians need to challenge the *status quo* of our affluent materialistic society. As we engage in simpler life-styles, we are "demonstrating an alternative to high-consumption materialism."[24] Such a life-style is not only ecologically and biblically sound, it marks a radical departure from the indulgent life-style that is being set forth as the norm for our society.

Paul said that he had "learned to be content whatever the circumstances" (Phil. 4:11). The present circumstance demands that we learn to live a simpler life and be content with what we really need, not with what we want in order to impress others or to bolster self-esteem. Extravagant living only brings misery on ourselves and others. The Lord did not have us pray for our daily wants but for our daily needs, "Give us today our daily bread" (Matt. 6:11). Reducing our consumption and using what we have more wisely will save our resources, cut back on pollution, and improve the quality of life for all members of the earth community. A wise consumer will eat lower on the food chain, replacing much of the meat in the diet with grains, fruits, nuts, and vegetables, and expend power lower on the energy chain, using solar, water, and wind energy rather than fossil fuels. Actually the energy chain and the food chain are part of the same process, converting the sun's power into usable energy.

The problem with our life-style is that we are taking out of the environment more than it can replenish in time for future demand. Our present life-styles are simply not sustainable. This predicament is analogous to living off one's savings account. There are two ways this could be done, one sustainable and one not. People could either live a modest life off the interest from the account and leave the principle intact, or they could lead a more extravagant life-style by drawing a portion of the principle along with the interest. The drawback of the second option is that the capital is finite and will eventually be depleted. The same is true of the environment. We are living off both the interest and the capital, leaving nothing in the bank for future generations. In other words we are mortgaging the welfare of future generations to finance our luxuries, and we are not that concerned with paying off the mortgage because we will be long dead. Perhaps the

Algonquin peoples can teach us something about our relationship with creation. They consider themselves part of nature and participants of a reciprocal agreement in which they take only what they need and replace all that they can. We take far more than we need and replace very little.

One writer commented,

> In an era of scarcity, colonial New Englanders were said to exhort their children: "Use it up, wear it out, make it do, or do without." That is a far cry from the reported philosophy of a current auto-making executive: Planned obsolescence is another word for progress. This decadence by design in the auto industry amassed unparalleled profits, to be sure, but it transmuted personal wastefulness into a virtue. The slightly old became slightly disreputable, the conspicuously new became fashionable and prestigious.[25]

A simple life-style may involve harder work, a slower pace, but in the end a more satisfying life. Henry David Thoreau recognized that a satisfying life is qualitative, not quantitative: "Most of the luxuries and many of the so-called comforts of life are not only not indispensable, but positive hindrances to the elevation of mankind."[26]

Practice True Spirituality

Nature is usually omitted from our thoughts about true spirituality. Spirituality is variously understood. The following views have been adapted from Bowman's *Beyond the Modern Mind*.[27] First, in the vein of Catholic mystics of the Middle Ages, spirituality meant a mode of perception beyond the five senses attained through deep prayer and meditation. This may be called contemplative spirituality. In this state one may perceive a mystical union with Christ or with the cosmos as a whole. The latter represents much of the spirituality in environmentalism.[28] Second, many in the church define spirituality as the renunciation of the world, flesh, and devil, meaning by this the denial of the physical aspect of life. Seekers advance up the spiritual ladder as they distance themselves from the world and draw nigh to God. Bowman called this "neoplatonic spirituality," for it reflects the neoplatonic concept of the great chain of being. Third, another form of spirituality recognizes the presence and power of God in our mundane daily affairs of life. Everything one does is done in the power of God and for God's glory. One may commune with God throughout the day in a variety of activities. Bowman called this "mundane spirituality."

There is a sense in which all three are correct, provided the flesh and the world are understood in Pauline usage. We may define spirituality as that state of being in close communion with and submission to God through prayer, meditation, devotion, and duty. It is a proximity to the divine that issues in godliness in every thought and action. Since the essence of spirituality is being perfectly at one with God, we cannot be spiritual if we are out of sorts with God. Just as we cannot be truly spiritual if we love God yet hate our brothers, we cannot be spiritual if we love God and brother, but harbor a low regard for God's creation. Therefore, spirituality involves living in harmony with God, others, and nature.

Spirituality also involves being obedient to God's laws or principles of the universe. Consistent obedience, however, can only come through the power of the Spirit. It is contingent on being submissive to the Holy Spirit who enables us to live above our demonic nature and thus in harmony with others in the cosmic community. One could say that spirituality means being in spiritual tune with the Creator, thinking as He thinks, seeing as He sees, acting as He would, loving as He loves, and appreciating all that He has made. We may call this a "theocentric spirituality." As we manifest this kind of spirituality, we will be spreading by word and deed the creative, redeeming, and transforming love of Christ and, in a limited way, seeing a new creation in all that we touch.

It is only with the above understanding that we could speak of a creation spirituality. It would, however, be radically different from Matthew Fox's version. Fox's panentheistic model of spirituality begins with the blessing of creation (God in people) rather than with the fall (people needing God), which he claims is the starting point for most Christian spirituality. He envisions four stages of spiritual growth: (1) affirming the blessing of creation (God dwells in creation), (2) emptying oneself of preconceived ideas, (3) mystically perceiving and cultivating the indwelling divinity, and (4) restructuring a new creation of peace and harmony by setting in motion the image of God.[29] Sin is defined as the refusal to journey further in a particular stage rather than rebellion against a transcendent God.

Both the fall-redemption model of spirituality and the creation-spirituality model begin where they perceive humans to be on their path to God. The fall-redemption model begins with the sinner in need of salvation through Christ and then in need of the Spirit to achieve victory over the sin nature. As believers progress on this path, they will be able to reflect the image of God and thereby have a transforming influence on the world around them. The creation-spirituality model begins with a panentheistic notion of God in all things (the original blessing). People stand in need of recognizing through mystical meditation that God dwells within and then nurturing the indwelling presence so it will have a transforming influence on themselves, society, and creation.

The creation-spirituality model suffers from its denial of a transcendent God. This denial produces a weak view of sin, that in turn affects the person and mission of Christ. The Cosmic Christ is defined simply as "the pattern that connects."[30] Jesus is viewed as simply one of many enlightened mystics who incarnated the Cosmic Christ, something all are expected to do before healing can take place.[31] Salvation then is corporate, not individual, and is achieved through a mystical awakening. In denying the sin nature and stressing an original blessing, creation-spirituality virtually affirms a form of panentheistic Pelagianism. Since it fails to present a realistic view of humanity, it also fails to be a viable option for environmentalists, for to reject humanity's innate disposition toward sin is to court ecological disaster. Traditional Christianity affirms human inability and dependence on God for total healing.

True spirituality derives its strength from the Holy Spirit to enable one to rise above the sin that alienates and to manifest the love that heals. It is an extroverted spirituality that is concerned with self-giving service and love to others. Only this kind of spirituality can give hope to an ailing world. Healing cannot be achieved through mystical experiences but only through triumph over sin and reaching out to others. Thus, biblical spirituality seeks resolution of disharmony through the power of the Spirit, whereas creation spirituality seeks it through mystical union with the nebulous concept of a Cosmic Christ.

Exercise Redeeming Conduct

Everything in our lives should have a redemptive quality about it, whether our thoughts, speech, or actions. We want our relations with others to be free of arguing, envy, and boastful pride. In other words, we want our interpersonal relations to reflect a certain degree of peace and harmony, that is, to display a redeemed quality. To the extent that this is accomplished with all types of relations, the redeemed will reflect the peace and harmony of God's creation before sin entered the world.

The redemption of Christ is designed to redeem the entire creation from the effects of the fall. This activity began with Christ on the cross and continues through His followers as they spread the redeeming love of Christ in word and deed. It would be unthinkable for the redeemed not to seek the peace and harmony of the prelapsarian state in all their relations.

As we separate our trash, start a compost pile, grow our own vegetables for ourselves and to share, and reduce our consumption, we will be living more in harmony with nature. Our relationship with creation will have a redeeming quality about it, one that reflects a little more the harmony of the original creation. There are many things everyone can do to help the environment as witnessed by the plethora of books on the topic that came out in connection with Earth Day 1990. These contain helpful ideas, but they should not limit our creativity for a redeeming life-style.

Our redemption should be manifest in our choice of cars and dwellings as well. Churches could even construct solar buildings as a testimony to creation harmony and the peace that Christ can give to all. Granberg-Michaelson cited a study conducted in 1980 that estimated only about twenty churches in this country were designed to use solar energy. He commented, "If we are to have buildings in which to worship, then let them speak of the new creation brought about by Christ. Let them be structures that cherish the gifts of creation."[32]

Another area of a redeemed life concerns reducing the quantity of trash we produce. The easiest way to reduce our trash is not to buy so much and to recycle what we do accumulate. God set up the earth to decompose and recycle the remains of all the debris of plant and animal life. Everything is recycled. If this principle is part of God's creative order, then the redeemed should strive to live in harmony with it as much as possible. We should realize that we are living in God's house, and God's house does not have a trash can. Everything we want to dispose of remains to clutter up the house. Yet, we persist in turning God's beautiful creation into an ugly trash heap full of our thoughtless creations. We should mimic nature by recycling and reprocessing our wastes.

Redeeming conduct also includes spreading the message of personal redemption through Christ. As we broaden our theological understanding of the universe and raise our environmental awareness, our concern for evangelism will grow correspondingly. Since the root problem of disharmony in God's creation is human sin, the only lasting solution is to be found in Christ's victory over sin on the cross. Finding better ways to dispose of our wastes or reducing some of the pollution will bring a measure of success, but they are merely superficial remedies. Unless the problem is confronted at the root level, it will continue regardless of efforts to the contrary. The true Christian approach to the environment is the most radical and potentially the most effective. Sin must be dealt with, and it can only be dealt with through a personal encounter with Jesus Christ. The winning of souls to Christ actually becomes a key element of an ecological reclamation project.

Evangelists should incorporate the larger vision of peace in their gospel presentation. The gospel is not simply the good news of human salvation but the good news of total healing. It is designed to mend all sorts of broken relationships and to show the way for us to relate to God, others, self, and nature through victory over sin. A gospel witness that embodies such a broadened concept has an incredible evangelistic appeal, for this is exactly what people today are seeking. Let us not forget that a gospel witness accompanied with redeeming acts in the social, ecological, and political arenas makes people much more willing to listen to the only message that can bring the healing and peace which they desire.

Conclusion

We began our study with a survey of the critics who cast blame on Christianity for the present environmental problems, mentioning among others the article by Lynn White. The arguments White and other early critics raised are still being voiced by ardent anti-Christian environmentalists. The alarming observation is that much of what the critics say is correct when understood as relating to Christendom and how the church has interpreted the Scriptures, rather than to the Scriptures themselves. It is very easy to vindicate the Scriptures, for they are rich in ecological wisdom. The difficult task is to change the thought and practice of those sectors of the church steeped in traditionalism. Hopefully, in the context of interacting with the objections sorting the wheat from the chaff solid groundwork has been laid for correcting the problem in the church.

Even though our critics' arguments are misguided at times, we still owe them a debt not only for calling attention to our weaknesses but also for provoking a Christian response. Before White's article, there were very few Christian writings on environment. His article has brought the environmental issue onto the theological agenda, challenging scores of theologians to examine Christian traditions, the Scriptures, and theological models to uncover ecological motifs and begin work on a theology of nature. "Thanks largely to Lynn White, the liberation of nature is now unavoidably before us as a theological theme."[33]

In summary, the environmental crisis is the natural consequence of a "dysfunctional civilization."[34] Our civilization no longer functions as it should because it has cut itself off from its roots—it has forsaken God and renounced its communality with the earth. Vincent Rossi correctly observed that "it was only when western civilization 'liberated' itself from Christianity and its traditional doctrinal restraints that the door was opened for the ecological disasters of the present day."[35] By asserting its autonomy, our civilization has severed the cosmic harmony and plunged creation into disarray. Humans now stand confused, stunned by their own wanton behavior, lost in an abnormal world, and estranged from God, themselves, others, and their environment. They have deserted the only feasible approach to righteous living, the only true source of healing, and the only hope for restoration.

The radical affirmations of the Christian faith offer the only hope for total healing of the environment. "Our help," as the psalmist wrote, "is in the name of the Lord, the Maker of heaven and earth" (124:8). The Jewish prophets envisioned that God would heal their broken land when the people repented of their sins and returned to God: "If my people, who are called by my name, will humble themselves and pray and seek my face and turn from their wicked ways, then will I hear from heaven and will forgive their sin and will heal their land" (2 Chron. 7:14).

Early in 1991 I conducted a survey to evaluate the environmental attitudes among Christian fundamentalists. Attitudes will vary considerably within Christendom, depending on the theological leanings of the group. Fundamental Christianity, as expected, stood firm in the traditional, dominant theology of Western Christianity with a very strong theanthropocentric stance and a very strong mastery-over-nature orientation. The survey consisted of four statements and four possible responses for each, ranging from strongly agreeing to strongly disagreeing.

The first statement was taken from Shaiko's study so that my results could be compared with his.[1] In response to the statement, "I believe that plants and animals exist primarily for man's use," 79.9 percent agreed. This is a significant deviation from Shaiko's figures (see table 1). Shaiko drew upon the data from two previous surveys. One sampled the attitudes of those belonging to environmental groups and the other of the general public.

Percent who agreed with the statement, "I believe that plants and animals exist primarily for man's use."		
	Belonging to an Environmental Group	General Public
Unchurched	8.6	26.0
Protestant	24.6	54.5
Catholic	30.8	54.5
Jewish	8.7	---

The breakdown of my survey was as follows: 46.5 percent strongly agreed, 33.4 percent somewhat agreed, 11.2 percent somewhat disagreed, and 8.9 percent strongly disagreed. Ranking these responses on a 4 to 1 scale, with 4 representing strongly agreeing and 1 representing strongly disagreeing, the mean for fundamentalists was 3.2. In Shaiko's study, the mean for those belonging to environmental groups and with no religious affiliation was 1.6, Jewish 1.7, Protestant 2.0, Catholic 2.1. This finding partially substantiates White's statement that it is a "Christian axiom that nature has no reason for existence save to serve man." It certainly appears to be an axiom of fundamental Christianity.

The second statement evaluates the strength of the received tradition within fundamental circles, especially in regard to the

283

understanding of the mission of Christ and the meaning of salvation. In response to the statement, "I believe that Christ's redemptive act pertains only to humans, not to plants or animals," 81.2 percent agreed. Many commented that plants and animals cannot be saved because they lack souls. This implies that nature is reduced to the status of a backdrop for the drama of human salvation or in some way peripheral to the Christian message. The responses were as follows: 74.3 percent strongly agreed, 6.9 percent somewhat agreed, 7.9 percent somewhat disagreed, and 10.9 percent strongly disagreed. On a 4 to 1 scale, the mean was 3.5. Several of those who did not strongly agree made reference to Romans 8:19-21.

The third statement, "I believe that Christians have a God-given responsibility to become involved in environmental causes," probably would have been answered differently twenty years ago. Nevertheless, 92.0 percent agreed. This may look encouraging, but not in view of the anthropocentric responses to the first two statements. The fourth statement will also qualify what is meant by this involvement. The results of the third statement were as follows: 39.9 percent agreed, 52.1 percent somewhat agreed, 6.3 percent somewhat disagreed, and 1.7 percent strongly disagreed. The mean was 3.3.

The last statement qualifies what was meant by environmental involvement. An astounding 98 percent agreed with the statement, "I believe that stewardship of the environment means the proper management of natural resources for the good of all people." The results were: 75.2 percent strongly agreed, 22.8 percent somewhat agreed, 1.7 percent somewhat disagreed, and only .3 percent strongly disagreed. The mean on a 4 to 1 scale was 3.8. Stewardship then is not viewed as caring for creation for the sake of creation, but for the sake of humanity.

Summary of the results					
4	Strongly Agree	46.5	74.3	39.9	75.2
3	Somewhat Agree	33.4	6.9	52.1	22.8
2	Somewhat Disagree	11.2	7.9	6.3	1.7
1	Strongly Disagree	8.9	10.9	1.7	.3
	Mean	3.2	3.5	3.3	3.8

It appears that fundamentalists would have difficulty justifying environmental involvement except where it served human interests or the evangelization of the lost. The difficulty to fit environmental concerns into a theological agenda has led to a silence from the pulpits and inactivity from the laity.

Chapter 1

[1] Lynn White, Jr., "The Historical Roots of Our Ecologic Crisis," *Science* 155 (March 10, 1967): 1205-6.

[2] Ibid, 1206.

[3] Carl F. H. Henry, "Stewardship of the Environment," *Applying the Scriptures*, ed. Kenneth S. Kantzer (Grand Rapids: Zondervan, 1987), 477.

[4] John Passmore, *Man's Responsibility for Nature: Ecological Problems and Western Traditions*, 2d ed. (London: Duckworth & Co., 1980), 20.

[5] Ibid., 13.

[6] Arnold Toynbee, "The Religious Background of the Present Environmental Crisis," in *Ecology and Religion in History*, eds. David Spring and Eileen Spring (New York: Harper & Row, 1974), 141-3. First published in *International Journal of Environmental Studies 3* (1972).

[7] Ian L. McHarg, *Design with Nature* (Garden City, N.Y.: The Natural History Press, 1969), 26.

[8] Joseph Campbell with Bill Moyers, *The Power of Myth*, ed. Betty Sue Flowers (New York: Doubleday, 1988), 32.

[9] Toynbee, 149.

[10] White, 1207.

[11] Leo Marx, "American Institutions and Ecological Ideals," *Science* 170 (November 27, 1970): 948.

[12] Clarence J. Glacken, "Man against Nature: An Outmoded Concept," *The Environmental Crisis: Man's Struggle to Live with Himself*, ed. Harold W. Helfrich, Jr. (New Haven: Yale University Press, 1970), 129-30.

[13] Richard A. McCormick, "Notes on Moral Theology: April- September, 1970," *Theological Studies* 32 (March 1971): 97.

[14] White, 1205.

[15] Tom Morton, "Groups Disagree on Approach to Nature," *Colorado Springs* [Colorado] *Gazette Telegraph*, April 21, 1990, NewsBank, ENV 33: C8.

[16] Toynbee, 145.

[17] White, 1205.

[18] Ibid., 1206.

[19] Harvey Cox, *The Secular City*, rev. ed. (Toronto: Macmillan, 1966), 21.

[20] Toynbee, 144.

[21] Ibid., 146.

[22] Paul R. Ehrlich, *The Population Bomb*, rev. ed. (Rivercity, Mass.: Rivercity Press, 1971), 156.

[23] White, 1207.

[24] Roger Sorrell argued that White (Ibid., 1206) is incorrect in interpreting Francis as despising man's monarchal position over creation and seeking to establish a "democracy of all God's creatures." Francis maintained that man was a special agent of God and occupied a superior place in creation. There was still a hierarchy within the community of creatures of which man was a part. Roger D. Sorrell, *St. Francis of Assisi and Nature: Tradition and Innovation in Western Christian Attitudes Toward the Environment* (New York: Oxford University Press, 1988), 6, 47.

[25] Stanley L. Jaki, *The Road of Science and the Ways to God* (Chicago: University of Chicago Press, 1978), 34-49.

[26] Jacques Ellul, *The Technological Society* (New York: Alfred A. Knopf, 1973), 33.

[27] Ludwig Feuerbach, *The Essence of Christianity*, trans. George Eliot (New York: Harper and Brothers, 1957), 287.

[28] Kenneth L. Woodward, "A New Story of Creation: It's the season for a theology of ecology," *Newsweek*, June 5, 1989, 71.

[29] Matthew Fox, *The Coming of the Cosmic Christ: The Healing of Mother Earth and the Birth of a Global Renaissance* (San Francisco: Harper & Row, 1988), 148-9.

[30] Michael E. Zimmerman, "Quantum Theory, Intrinsic Value, and Panentheism," *Environmental Ethics* 10 (Spring 1988): 24. Zimmerman (p. 25) commented, "Fortunately, the Judeo-Christian tradition can be interpreted panentheistical." He offered such a reinterpretation as a corrective to the dualism inherent in the Judeo-Christian tradition.

[31] Wendell Berry, "A Secular Pilgrimage," *The Hudson Review* 23 (Autumn 1970): 403.

[32] Ibid., 403-4.

[33] See Wesley Granberg-Michaelson, *A Worldly Spirituality: The Call to Redeem Life on Earth* (San Francisco: Harper & Row, 1984), 106-9.

[34] A survey of the literature since Lynn White's article can be found in Joseph K. Sheldon, "Twenty-one Years After 'The Historical Roots of Our Ecologic Crisis': How Has the Church Responded?" *Perspectives on Science and Faith* 41 (September 1989): 152-8.

[35] Alfred North Whitehead, *Science and the Modern World* (New York: Macmillan, 1925).

[36] Ian G. Barbour, ed., *Earth Might Be Fair: Reflections on Ethics, Religion, and Ecology* (Englewood Cliffs, N.J.: Prentice-Hall, 1972), 9.

[37] John B. Cobb, Jr., "Process Theology and an Ecological Model," in *Cry of the Environment: Rebuilding the Christian Creation Tradition*, eds. Philip N. Joranson and Ken Butigan (Santa Fe, N.M.: Bear & Co., 1984), 330.

[38] Periodical literature that applies process theology to environmental concerns includes Delwin Brown, "Respect for the Rocks': Toward a Christian Process Theology of Nature," *Encounter* 50 (Autumn 1989): 309-21; Clifford Cain, "'Regarding Nature as Thou: A Reorientation toward Eco-justice," *Encounter* 52 (Winter 1991): 21-32; John B. Cobb, Jr., "Process Theology and Environmental Issues," *Journal of Religion* 60

(October 1980): 440-58; Jerry K. Robbins, "The Environment and Thinking about God," *Encounter* 48 (Autumn 1987): 401-15.

[39] Fox, 27.

[40] Ibid., 144.

[41] Ibid., 67, 145.

[42] Ibid., 70.

[43] Ibid., 151.

[44] Ibid.

[45] Ibid., 140.

[46] Thomas Berry, *The Dream of the Earth* (San Francisco: Sierra Club Books, 1988), 80.

[47] Ibid.

[48] Ibid., 207.

[49] Ibid., 87.

[50] Ibid., 195.

[51] Ibid., 46.

[52] Compare Eugene C. Hargrove, ed., *Religion and Environmental Crisis* (Athens: University of Georgia Press, 1986).

[53] *Earthkeeping: Christian Stewardship of Natural Resources*, by the Fellows of the Calvin Center for Christian Scholarship, Calvin College, Peter De Vos, et al. (Grand Rapids: Wm. B. Eerdmans, 1980), 104.

[54] Lynn White, Jr., "Continuing the Conversation," in *Western Man and Environmental Ethics*, ed. Ian G. Barbour (Reading, Mass: Addison-Wesley Publishing Co., 1973), 61.

[55] White, "Historical Roots," 1207.

[56] Wesley Granberg-Michaelson, ed., *Tending the Garden: Essays on the Gospel and the Earth* (Grand Rapids: Wm. B. Eerdmans, 1987), 2-3.

[57] Ronald G. Shaiko, "Religion, Politics, and Environmental Concern: A Powerful Mix of Passions," *Social Science Quarterly* 68 (June 1987): 250-1.

[58] See the appendix for the results of a study I conducted.

[59] H. Paul Santmire, in commenting on the need for a theology of nature after twenty years of discussion, commented, "As anyone familiar with the discussion knows, it has been uncertain and episodic at best. After more than 20 book-length studies and scores of articles directed to the topic, one can justly ask what has really been said. It is symptomatic of the disjointed state of the discussion that books and articles continue to appear under the rubic [sic] 'Toward a New Theology of Nature' which show little or no acquaintance with the fact that a significant international discussion has been underway for 20 years." H. Paul Santmire, "Toward a New Theology of Nature," *Dialog* 25 (Winter 1986): 44.

[60] Regarding philosophical endeavors, Passmore (p. 215) said, "The working out of such a metaphysics [suited to the environmental problem] is, in my judgment, the most important task which lies ahead of philosophy."

[61] Jürgen Moltmann, *God in Creation: An Ecological Doctrine of Creation*, The Gifford Lectures, 1984-1985, trans., Margaret Kohl (London: SCM Press Ltd., 1985), 53.

[62] George S. Hendry, *Theology of Nature* (Philadelphia: Westminster Press, 1980), 11-12.

[63] Ibid., 12-14.

[64] Some question this whole enterprise. John Passmore (p. 184) remarked, "For my part I more than doubt whether Christian theology can thus reshape itself without ceasing to be distinctively Christian, whether it can bring itself to deny, in the light of its central theology, either that man is *metaphysically* unique—as a soul to be saved—or that in the end his survival is *metaphysically* guaranteed. Only if men see themselves, I should rather argue, for what they are, quite alone, with no one to help them except their fellow-men, products of natural processes which are wholly indifferent to their survival, will they face their ecological problems in their full implications. Not by the extension, but by the total rejection, of the concept of the sacred will they move towards that somber realisation."

Chapter 2

[1] Lynn White, Jr., "Continuing the Conversation," in *Western Man and Environmental Ethics*, ed. Ian G. Barbour (Reading, Mass.: Addison-Wesley Publishing Co., 1973), 57.

[2] See Eugene C. Hargrove, ed. *Religion and Environmental Crisis* (Athens: University of Georgia Press, 1986), ix-xix.

[3] Eiseley commented, "Man has always had two ways of looking at nature, and these two divergent approaches to the world can be observed among modern primitive peoples, as well as being traceable far into the primitive past. Man has a belief in seen and unseen nature. He is both pragmatist and mystic. He has been so from the beginning, and it may well be that the quality of his inquiring and perceptive intellect will cause him to remain so till the end." Loren Eiseley, *The Firmament of Time* (New York: Atheneum, 1960), 3-4.

[4] Stephen J. Pyne, "Firestick History," *The Journal of American History* 76 (March 1990): 1132-41.

[5] John B. Cobb, Jr., *Is It Too Late?* (Beverly Hills, Calif.: Bruce, 1972), 42.

[6] René Dubos, *A God Within* (New York: Charles Scribner's Sons, 1972), 41.

[7] Alluded to in Thomas S. Derr, "Religion's Responsibility for the Ecological Crisis: An Argument Run Amok," *Worldview* 18 (January 1975): 41.

[8] F. B. Welbourn, "Man's Dominion," *Theology* 78 (November 1975): 564.

[9] McHarg asserted, "Whatever the earliest roots of the western attitude to nature it is clear that they were confirmed in Judaism. The emergence of monotheism had as its corollary the rejection of nature; the affirmation of Jehovah, the God in whose image man was made, was also a declaration of war on nature;" p. 26.

[10] For treatments of Jewish attitudes toward the environment, see David Ehrenfeld and Philip J. Bentley, "Judaism and the Practice of

Stewardship," *Judaism* 34 (Summer 1985): 301-11; Jonathan Helfand, "The Earth Is the Lord's: Judaism and Environmental Ethics," in *Religion and Environmental Crisis*, ed. Eugene C. Hargrove (Athens: University of Georgia Press, 1986), 38-52; and Dvora Waysman, "Ecology Began in the Bible," *Israel Digest* 21 (November 17, 1987): 12.

[11] R. H. Charles, trans. *The Apocrypha and Pseudepigrapha of the Old Testament in English*, vol. 2 (London: Oxford at the Clarendon Press, 1963), 596.

[12] Nina Jidejian, *Byblos through the Ages* (Beirut: Dar El-Machreq Publishers, 1968), 137; see also 17, 82, 86-88.

[13] Dubos, 159.

[14] John A. Moore, "Science as a Way of Knowing—Human Ecology," *American Zoologist* 25 (1985): 547.

[15] Yi-Fu Tuan, "Discrepancies between Environmental Attitude and Behavior: Examples from Europe and China," in *Ecology and Religion in History*, eds. David Spring and Eileen Spring (New York: Harper & Row, 1974), 107-10. First published in *The Canadian Geographer* 12 (1968): 176-91.

[16] Dubos, 160.

[17] Yi-Fu Tuan, "Our Treatment of the Environment in Ideal and Actuality," *American Scientist* 58 (June 1970): 247. Dubos (p. 160) concurred, saying "The Chinese attitude of respect for nature probably arose, in fact, as a response to the damage done in antiquity."

[18] Stephen Vincent Bentét, *Western Star* (New York: Farrar & Rinehart, 1943), prelude, line 12.

[19] Lynn White, Jr., remarked that our daily habits "are dominated by an implicit faith in perpetual progress which was unknown either to Greco-Roman antiquity or to the Orient. It is rooted in, and is indefensible apart from, Judeo-Christian teleology." "The Historical Roots of our Ecologic Crisis," *Science* 155 (March 10, 1967): 1205.

[20] Aeschylus, *Prometheus Bound* 436-506.

[21] Sophocles, *Antigone* 332-52.

[22] Clarence J. Glacken, *Traces on the Rhodian Shore: Nature and Culture in Western Thought from Ancient Times to the End of the Eighteenth Century* (Berkeley and Los Angeles: University of California Press, 1967), 118.

[23] Plato, *Critias* 111.

[24] Dubos, 160.

[25] Aristotle, *Politics* 1.8 [1256b.15].

[26] Lucretius, *On the Nature of Things* 5.195-234.

[27] Richard Wright, "Responsibility for the Ecological Crisis," *Christian Scholar's Review* 1 (1970): 38.

[28] Yi-Fu Tuan has noted many dysfunctions between religious beliefs and ecological practices of its people. See Tuan, "Discrepancies," 91-113; and "Our Treatment of the Environment," 244-49. In the latter article, Tuan (p. 244) remarked, "A Culture's publicized ethos about its environment seldom covers more than a fraction of the total range of its attitudes and practices pertaining to that environment. In the play of

forces that govern the world, esthetic and religious ideals rarely have a major role."

[29] Santmire commented, "As a theological construct, nature has been in travail throughout most of Western history. At times it has appeared as if the theology of nature has been at the point of joyful birthing. At other times the theology of nature has never really emerged in its own right. On some occasions, indeed, it would appear that theology was stillborn. This is the ambiguous ecological promise of Christian theology." H. Paul Santmire, *The Travail of Nature: The Ambiguous Ecological Promise of Christian Theology* (Philadelphia: Fortress Press, 1985), 11. Santmire identified two theological motifs in Western thinking relevant to the ecological discussion: (1) a spiritual motif, in which the object of theological reflection is God and the soul, or God and humankind, and (2) an ecological motif, in which the interrelationship between God, humanity, and nature are appreciated and reflected on. *Travail*, 9.

[30] Ibid., 48. The earliest of which was Nemesius, bishop of Emesa in Syria of the late fourth century. In his *On Human Nature*, he incorporated the concept of the great chain of being and emphasized man's applying reason and judgment "to whatever he will" in the pursuit of virtue and godliness. There is no thought in his writing of absolute dominion over nature. George Huntston Williams, "Christian Attitudes Toward Nature," *Christian Scholar's Review* 2.1 (1971): 23-24.

[31] *1 Clement* 20.11.

[32] Dionysius, *Concerning Nature* 3.

[33] Arnobius, *Against the Heathens* 1.12.

[34] Origen, *Contra Celsum* 4.74.

[35] Tertullian, *On the Resurrection of the Flesh* 5.7.

[36] John Passmore, *Man's Responsibility for Nature: Ecological Problems and Western Traditions*, 2d ed. (London: Duckworth and Co., 1980), 17, 27, 112.

[37] Philo, *De Opificio Mundi* 77.

[38] Philo, *Quaestiones et Solutiones in Genesin* 1. 94.

[39] Philo, *Quod Deus Immutabilis sit* 47.

[40] David Jobling, "'And have Dominion . . .' The Interpretation of Genesis 1,28 in Philo Judaeus," *Journal for the Study of Judaism* 8 (January 1977): 56.

[41] Augustine, *Soliloquies* 1.7.

[42] Augustine, *City of God* 12.4.

[43] Augustine, *Confessions* 23.33.

[44] Santmire, *Travail*, 217. See also H. Paul Santmire, "St. Augustine's Theology of the Biophysical World," *Dialog* 19 (Summer 1980).

[45] Cited in A. Cohen, *The Teachings of Maimonides* (London: G. Routledge & Sons, 1927), 49.

[46] Moses Maimonides, *The Guide for the Perplexed* 3.13.

[47] Passmore, 12.

[48] Cited by Robin Attfield, *The Ethics of Environmental Concern* (Oxford: Blackwell, 1983), 34-5.

[49] Cited in Vladimir Lossky, *The Mystical Theology of the Eastern Church* (Crestwood, N.Y.: St. Vladimir's Seminary Press, 1976), 110-11, from *Mystic Treaties*, ed. A. J. Wensinck, 341.

[50] A. M. Allchin, "The Theology of Nature in the Eastern Fathers and among Anglican Theologians," *Man and Nature*, ed. Hugh Montefiore (London: William Collins Sons & Co., 1975), 146.

[51] Cited in and translated by Lawrence S. Cunningham, *Saint Francis of Assisi* (Boston: Twayne Publishers, 1976), 58-9. Cunningham (p. 55) commented, "The *Canticle of Brother Sun* must be read against the whole background of the stories of Francis preaching to the birds, exhorting the flowers in the field to praise God, redeeming lambs being taken to the slaughterhouse, taming the wolf of Gubbio, insisting that his friars cut wood in the forest in such a way as to let the trees live."

[52] Cited in Hugh Montefiore, *Man and Nature* (London: William Collins Sons & Co., 1975), 48, from Eloi Leclerc, *Le Cantique des Creatures, ou les Symboles de l'Union* (Paris, 1971), 28.

[53] Williams, 25-6.

[54] Cunningham, 55.

[55] Passmore, 112-13.

[56] White, "Historical Roots," 1207.

[57] Derr argued that it would not be beneficial to adopt Francis' "mystic reimmersion" into nature. He agreed with Dubos that Francis' "'romantic and unworldly attitude'. . . is largely irrelevant today." Derr, "Religion's Responsibility," 43-44.

[58] Dubos, 168-70.

[59] Richard Woods, "Environment as Spiritual Horizon: The Legacy of Celtic Monasticism," *Cry of the Environment: Rebuilding the Christian Creation Tradition*, eds. Philip N. Joranson and Ken Butigan (Santa Fe, N.M.: Bear & Co., 1984), 78.

[60] Aquinas, *Summa Theologica* 1, Quest. 96, Art. 1.4.

[61] Aquinas, *Summa Contra Gentiles* 3.112.13.

[62] Passmore, 113.

[63] John Calvin, *Genesis*, ed. and trans. John King, vol. 1 (Edinburgh: Banner of Truth Trust, 1965), 125.

[64] Calvin, *Institutes* 1.16.6.

[65] Cited by Glacken, *Traces on the Rhodian Shore*, 481, from Sir Matthew Hale, *The Primitive Origination of Mankind* (London: Printed by W. Godbid for W. Shrowsbery, 1677), 370. Also cited by John Black, *The Dominion of Man: The Search for Ecological Responsibility* (Edinburgh: Edinburgh University Press, 1970), 56; and Passmore, 30.

[66] Martin Luther, *Lectures on Genesis: Chapters 1-5*, trans. George V. Schick, in vol. 1 of *Luther's Works*, ed. Jaroslav Pelikan (St. Louis: Concordia Publishing House, 1958), 71.

[67] Santmire, *Travail*, 122.

[68] Ibid.

[69] Ibid., 132.

[70] Julian Huxley, *A Religion without Revelation* (New York: Harper & Brothers, 1957), 239.

[71] Wesley Granberg-Michaelson, *Worldly Spirituality* (San Francisco: Harper and Row, 1984), 41.

[72] Pascal, *Pensées* 4.277.

[73] See H. Paul Santmire, "Reflections on the Alleged Ecological Bankruptcy of Western Theology," *Anglican Theological Review* 57 (April 1975): 137-38.

[74] George S. Hendry, *Theology of Nature* (Philadelphia: Westminster Press, 1980), 54.

[75] Ibid., 55. Hendry made reference to 2 Corinthians 4:4; Ephesians 2:2; and the Legend of Faust.

[76] Ibid., 55-6.

[77] Ibid., 56.

[78] Bacon, *Novum Organum* 1.3.

[79] Ibid., 1.129.

[80] Ibid.

[81] Ibid.

[82] Descartes, *Discourse on Method* 4.

[83] See Glacken, "Man Against Nature," 129, 131.

[84] See Hendry, 71-2.

[85] Pascal, *Penses* 2.94.

[86] Sherrard spoke of the "desanctification of nature," which he defined as "that process whereby the spiritual significance and understanding of the created world has been virtually banished from our minds." Philip Sherrard, *The Eclipse of Man and Nature: An Enquiry into the Origins and Consequences of Modern Science* (West Stockbridge, Mass: Lindisfarne Press, 1987), 90.

[87] See Glacken, *Traces on the Rhodian Shore*, 494-5.

[88] Glacken, "Man Against Nature," 130.

[89] James Barr, "Man and Nature: The Ecological Controversy and the Old Testament," *Ecology and Religion in History*, eds. David Spring and Eileen Spring (New York: Harper & Row, 1974), 73. First published in *Bulletin of the John Rylands Library* 55 (Autumn 1972).

[90] White, "Historical Roots," 1206.

[91] Sherrard (p. 15) argued that "the worldview of modern science, which assumed a definite shape in the seventeenth century, has its roots in certain prior developments in Christian theology that partially eclipsed the full Christian understanding of man and his destiny."

[92] Thomas Berry, *The Dream of the Earth* (San Francisco: Sierra Club Books, 1988), 80.

[93] Barth commented, "Its understanding of God's creation is 'anthropocentric' to the extent that it follows the orientation prescribed for it by the Word of God; the orientation on man." Additionally, "The universe was created for the sake of God's gracious plan. Hence its goal and center is man." Karl Barth, *The Doctrine of Creation*, part 2, eds. G. W. Bromiley and T. F. Torrance *Church Dogmatics*, vol. 3, (Edinburgh: T. & T. Clark, 1960), 12,14.

[94] Barth said that creation is "a theatre on which it [the covenant of grace] can be enacted and unfolded. The created cosmos . . . is this the-

atre of the great acts of God in grace and salvation." *The Doctrine of Creation*, part 3, 48.

[95] Emil Brunner, *Revelation and Reason*, trans. Olive Wyon (Philadelphia: Westminster Press, 1946), 33-4, n. 4.

[96] Santmire, "Reflections," 143.

[97] Santmire, *Travail*, 137-8.

[98] Paul B. Sears, "The Injured Earth," in *This Little Planet*, ed. Michael Hamilton (New York: Charles Scribner's Sons, 1970), 42.

[99] Robert Runcie, Norman Lear, and Carl Sagan, "God Is Green, So Is Science," *New Perspectives Quarterly* 7 (Spring 1990): 70.

Chapter 3

[1] It is commonly said that the German zoologist Ernst Heinrich Haeckel coined the word *ecology* in 1866, but the Oxford English Dictionary cites Thoreau as using it in 1858. Haeckel defined as ecology "the oecology of organisms, the knowledge of the sum of the relations of organisms to the surrounding outer world, to organic and inorganic conditions of existence; the so-called 'economy of nature,' the correlations between all organisms living together in one and the same locality, their adaptation to their surroundings, their modification in the struggle for existence, especially the circumstances of parasitism, etc." Cited in J. Black, *The Dominion of Man: The Search for Ecological Responsibility* (Edinburgh: Edingburgh University Press, 1970), p. 2, from E. Haeckel, *The History of Creation* (London: King, 1876).

[2] Barry Commoner, *The Closing Circle: Nature, Man, and Technology* (New York: Alfred A. Knopf, 1971), 33-46. The four laws are reiterated in his *Making Peace with the Planet* (New York: Pantheon Books, 1990), 8-15.

[3] Paul E. Lutz, "Interrelatedness: Ecological Pattern of the Creation," *Cry of the Environment: Rebuilding the Christian Creation Tradition*, eds. Phillip N. Joranson and Ken Butigan (Santa Fe, N.M.: Bear & Co., 1984), 254-55.

[4] Commoner, *Closing Circle*, 39.

[5] Ibid., 41.

[6] Ibid., 44.

[7] Ibid., 46.

[8] Henlee H. Barnette, *The Church and the Ecological Crisis* (Grand Rapids: Wm. B. Eerdmans, 1972), 12.

[9] See William K. Stevens, "New Eye on Nature: The Real Constant Is Eternal Turmoil," *New York Times*, July 31, 1990, C1.

[10] Bill McKibben, *The End of Nature* (New York: Random House, 1989).

[11] George S. Hendry, *Theology of Nature* (Philadelphia: Westminster Press, 1980), 197.

[12] This is an oversimplification, as Glacken observed, "Frequently, the 'Western' concept of dominance or opposition has been contrasted with 'Eastern' concepts of harmony and union with nature, but I believe this contrast oversimplifies matters. Like all other great civilizations,

Western civilization is not monolithic in its summations, and it has nourished all sorts of different ideas." Clarence J. Glacken, "Man Against Nature," *The Environmental Crisis*, ed. Harold W. Helfrich, Jr. (New Haven: Yale University Press, 1970), 127.

[13] R. Buckminster Fuller, *Critical Path* (New York: St. Martin's Press, 1981), 27-8, 276.

[14] Pierre Teilhard de Chardin, *The Phenomenon of Man*, trans. Bernard Wall (London: Collins, 1955), 64-6, 72, 271-72.

[15] The members of the Findhorn community believe that "behind all the forces and forms of nature there were invisible Beings of great power and intelligence. These Beings, called *Devas* from the Sanskrit meaning 'Shining Ones,' embodied the energies of growth, life and formation; each species of plant was represented by a Deva, while there were also Devas of mountains, seas, of geographical locations, of natural forces such as wind and rain and of qualities such as sound and color." Members of the community are able to contact the Devas and receive information from them. David Spangler, *Revelation: The Birth of a New Age* (Middletown, Wis.: Lorian Press, 1976), 40-1.

[16] Joseph W. Meeker, *Minding the Earth: Thinly Disguised Essays on Human Ecology* (Alameda, Calif.: The Latham Foundation, 1988), 10, 13.

[17] Daniel B. Botkin, *Discordant Harmonies: A New Ecology for the Twenty-first Century* (New York: Oxford University Press, 1990), 7.

[18] What is implied by these thoughts is a need to formulate not merely a theology of nature but a theology of ecology which strives to interpret the systemic unity of the entire cosmos. For preliminary discussion along these lines, see Kenneth P. Alpers, "Starting Points for an Ecological Theology: A Bibliographical Survey," *Dialog* 9 (Summer 1970): 226-35; and James McPherson, "Towards an Ecological Theology," *Expository Times* 97 (May 1986): 236-40.

[19] See H. Richard Niebuhr, *The Responsible Self: An Essay in Christian Moral Philosophy* (New York: Harper & Row, 1963), 86-7.

[20] David Gosling, "Towards a Credible Ecumenical Theology of Nature," *Ecumenical Review* 38 (July 1986): 322.

[21] Joseph Sittler, "Ecological Commitment as Theological Responsibility," *Zygon* 5 (June 1970): 175.

[22] Wesley Granberg-Michaelson, *A Worldly Spirituality: The Call to Redeem Life on Earth* (San Francisco: Harper and Row, 1984), 82. Perhaps a three-dimensional prism with God at the apex and nature, humankind, and self as the three points of the base might offer a better model.

[23] See Jeanne Kay, "Human Dominion Over Nature in the Hebrew Bible," *Annals of the Association of American Geographers* 79 (June 1989): 214-32.

[24] Loren Wilkinson, "Redeemers of the Earth," in *The Environmental Crisis: The Ethical Delemma*, ed. Edwin R. Squires (Mancelona, Mich.: The AuSable Trails Institute of Environmental Studies, 1982), 42.

[25] Moltmann noted that *nephesh*, in addition to meaning life principle, also means "breath." Thus, humans are like all animals in that they have animated bodies and particularly like air-breathing animals that

are dependent on air (this excludes fish). Although this is true, it cannot be linguistically justified from the word *nephesh* in this context. See Jürgen Moltmann, *God in Creation* (London: SCM Press Ltd., 1985), 187.

[26] Frances Moore Lappé, *Diet for a Small Planet*, rev. ed. (New York: Ballatine Books, 1975), 3-7.

[27] Philip N. Joranson and Ken Butigan, eds., *Cry of the Environment: Rebuilding the Christian Creation Tradition* (Santa Fe, N.M.: Bear and Co., 1984), 1.

[28] Carl F. H. Henry, "Stewardship of the Environment," in *Applying the Scriptures*, ed. Kenneth S. Kantzer (Grand Rapids: Zondervan, 1987), 474.

[29] Moltmann, 187; see 6-7, 139, 285.

[30] Loren Wilkinson, "Cosmic Christology and the Christian's Role in Creation," *Christian Scholar's Review* 11 (1981): 39.

[31] John Passmore, *Man's Responsibility for Nature*, 2d ed. (London: Duckworth and Co., 1980), 214.

[32] Hendry, 190.

[33] G. W. H. Lampe, "The New Testament Doctrine of *Ktisis,*" *Scottish Journal of Theology* 17 (December 1964): 461.

[34] David Ehrenfeld, *The Arrogance of Humanism* (New York: Oxford University Press, 1978), 177.

[35] Ron Elsdon, *Bent World: A Christian Response to the Environmental Crisis* (Downers Grove, Ill.: Inter-Varsity Press, 1981), 110.

[36] Granberg-Michaelson, 74, 79.

Chapter 4

[1] Lynn White, Jr., "The Historical Roots of our Ecologic Crisis," *Science* 155 (March 10, 1967): 1206-7; Thomas Berry, *The Dream of the Earth* (San Francisco: Sierra Club Books, 1988), 136.

[2] Joseph W. Meeker, "Prologue to an Environmental Ethic," *The North American Review* 258 (Summer 1973): 20.

[3] John Passmore, *Man's Responsibility for Nature: Ecological Problems and Western Traditions*, 2d ed. (London: Duckworth and Co., 1980), 207. See Gordon D. Kaufman, "A Problem of Theology: The Concept of Nature," *Harvard Theological Review* 65 (1972): 337-66; Richard Bauckham, "First Steps to a Theology of Nature," *Evangelical Quarterly* 58 (July 1986): 229-31.

[4] See Jürgen Moltmann, *God in Creation: An Ecological Doctrine of Creation*, The Gifford Lectures, 1984-1985, trans. Margaret Kohl (London: SCM, 1985), 3, 21, 38.

[5] Passmore, 5n.

[6] Daniel B. Botkin, *Discordant Harmonics: A New Ecology for the Twenty-first Century* (New York: Oxford University Press, 1990), 8, 12.

[7] Thomas Berry, 46.

[8] John B. Cobb, in *Is It Too Late?* (Beverly Hills, Calif.: Bruce, 1972), 41, quotes Erich Neumann, *The Origins and History of Consciousness*, 2 vols. (New York: Harper & Brothers Torchbook, 1954), 40, regarding the fear of primitive man: "Exposed to the dark forces of the world and the

unconscious, early man's feeling is necessarily one of constant endangerment. Life in the psychic cosmos of the primitive is a life full of danger and uncertainty; and the daemonism of the external world, with its sickness and death, famines and floods, droughts and earthquakes, is heightened beyond measure when contaminated with what we call the inner world."

[9] Cobb, 41-2.

[10] Hugh Montefiore, *Man and Nature* (London: William Collins Sons & Co., 1975), 70.

[11] Philip Sherrard, *The Eclipse of Man and Nature: An Enquiry into the Origins and Consequences of Modern Science* (West Stockbridge, Mass.: Lindisfarne Press, 1987), 93-4.

[12] Mircea Eliade, *The Quest: History and Meaning in Religion*, Midway reprint (Chicago and London: University of Chicago Press, 1969), preface.

[13] David Ehreneld, *The Arrogance of Humanism* (New York: Oxford University Press, 1978), 179-88.

[14] Ibid., 202.

[15] Ibid.

[16] Charles Hummel, "The Tyranny of the Urgent," *HIS* 26 (February 1966): 1-3.

[17] E. F. Schumacher, *Small Is Beautiful: Economics as if People Mattered*, Colophon ed. (New York: Harper & Row, 1973), 41.

[18] Clyde Y. Stewart, Jr., "Factors Conditioning the Christian Creation Consciousness," in *Cry of the Environment: Rebuilding the Christian Creation Tradition*, eds. Philip N. Joranson and Ken Butigan (Santa Fe, N.M.: Bear & Co., 1984), 123.

[19] Richard A. McCormick, "Notes on Moral Theology: April-September, 1970," *Theological Studies* 32 (March 1971): 98.

[20] Peter F. Drucker, *The New Realities* (New York: Harper & Row, 1989), 135.

[21] Robert Runcie, Norman Lear, and Carl Sagan, "God Is Green, So Is Science," *New Perspectives Quarterly* 7 (Spring 1990): 68-9.

[22] Gabriel Fackre, "Ecology and Theology," in *Western Man and Environmental Ethics*, ed. Ian G. Barbour (Reading, Mass.: Addison-Wesley, 1973), 122. First published in *Religion in Life* 40 (Summer 1971): 210-24.

[23] James A. Rimbach, "'All Creation Groans': Theology/Ecology in St. Paul," *Ecology and Life: Accepting our Environmental Responsibility*, ed. Wesley Granberg-Michaleson, (Waco, Tex.: Word, 1988), 166. First published in *Asia Journal of Theology* 1 (October 1987): 379-91.

[24] Francis A. Schaeffer, *Pollution and the Death of Man: The Christian View of Ecology* (Wheaton, Ill.: Tyndale House, 1970), 54.

[25] Norman L. Geisler, *Christian Ethics* (Grand Rapids: Baker Book House, 1989), 302.

[26] See A. R. Peacocke, *Creation and the World of Science, The Bampton Lectures, 1978* (Oxford: Clarendon Press, 1979), 304.

[27] L. Berkhof, *Systematic Theology*, 4th ed. (Grand Rapids: Wm. B. Eerdmans, 1941), 129.

[28] Montefiore, 26.

[29] Wim Rietkerk, "Pollution and the Christian View of Nature," (Lecture given at the Atlanta L'Abri Conference, July 29, 1989).

[30] Walter Brueggemann, *The Land: Place as Gift, Promise, and Challenge in Biblical Faith* (Philadelphia: Fortress Press, 1977), 154.

[31] Moltmann, xiii.

[32] Ibid., 6-7.

[33] Vincent Rossi, "The Eleventh Commandment," *Epiphany* 1 (Summer 1981): 15.

[34] Berry, 35.

[35] Aldo Leopold, *A Sand County Almanac with Other Essays on Conservation from Round River* (New York: Oxford University Press, 1966), x.

[36] Aquinas, *Summa Theologica* 2.1, Quest. 94, Art. 5.3.

[37] Ibid., 1, Quest. 98, Art. 1.3.

[38] See William J. Byron, "The Ethics of Stewardship," *The Earth Is the Lord's: Essays on Stewardship*, eds. Mary Evelyn Jegen and Bruno Manno (New York: Paulist Press, 1978), 46.

[39] Joseph A. Fitzmyer, "The Letter to the Romans," *The New Jerome Biblical Commentary*, eds. Raymond E. Brown, Joseph A. Fitzmyer, and Roland E. Murphy (Englewood Cliffs, N.J.: Prentice-Hall Media, 1990), 835.

[40] Robert P. Meye, "Invitation to Wonder: Toward a Theology of Nature," in *Tending the Garden: Essays on the Gospel and the Earth*, ed. Wesley Granberg-Michaelson (Grand Rapids: Wm. B. Eerdmans, 1987), 31.

[41] Plato, *The Republic* 7.514-516.

[42] Aristotle, *Metaphysics* 1.982b.

[43] Kant, *Critique of Practical Reason* 2.concl.

[44] Berry, 46.

[45] Glacken wrote, "To say of the earth that it has been designed by a Creator for the sake of all life is one thing; to say that it is made for man alone and to use as he sees fit is another. The anthropocentrism of the latter is narrow and crippling." Clarence J. Glacken, "Man Against Nature," in *The Environmental Crisis*, ed. Harold W. Helfrich, Jr. (New Haven: Yale University Press, 1970), 133.

[46] See Charles Birch and John B. Cobb, Jr., *The Liberation of Life: From the Cell to the Community* (Cambridge: Cambridge University Press, 1981), 151-2, 154.

[47] Calvin B. DeWitt, "The Price of Gopher Wood," *Faculty Dialogue* 12 (Fall 1989): 59-62.

[48] Paulos Mar Gregorios, "New Testament Foundations for Understanding the Creation," in *Tending the Garden: Essays on the Gospel and the Earth*, ed. Wesley Granberg-Michaelson (Grand Rapids: Wm. B. Eerdmans, 1987), 91.

[49] Schaeffer, 89.

[50] John Austin Baker, "Biblical Attitudes to Nature," in *Man and Nature*, ed. Hugh Montefoiore (London: William Collins Sons & Co., 1975), 96.

[51] John Black, *The Dominion of Man: The Search for Ecological Responsibility* (Edinburgh: Edinburgh University Press, 1970), 48.

[52] Joseph Wood Krutch, *The Voice of the Desert* (New York: William Sloane Associates, 1955), 200.

[53] Claus Westermann, *Creation*, trans. John J. Scullion (London: SPCK, 1974), 61.

[54] Ibid.

[55] Ludwig Koehler and Walter Baumgartner, eds., *Lexicon in Veteris Testamenti Libros*, vol. 1 (Leiden: E. J. Brill, 1951), 349.

[56] William J. Dumbrell, "Genesis 1-3, Ecology, and the Dominion of Man," *Crux* 21 (December 1985): 19.

[57] Delwin Brown, "Respect for the Rocks," *Encounter* 50 (Autumn 1989): 311.

[58] H. Paul Santmire, *Brother Earth: Nature, God and Ecology in Time of Crisis* (Camden, N.J.: Thomas Nelson, 1970), 120; Gerhard von Rad, *Genesis: A Commentary* (Philadelphia: Westminster Press, 1961), 59.

[59] Bernhard W. Anderson, "Creation in the Bible," in *Cry of the Environment: Rebuilding the Christian Creation Tradition*, eds. Philip N. Joranson and Ken Butigan (Santa Fe, N.M.: Bear & Co., 1984), 31.

[60] John W. Klotz, "A Creationist Environmental Ethic," *Creation Research Society Quarterly* 21 (June 1984): 6-7.

Chapter 5

[1] Wendell Berry, "A Secular Pilgrimage," *The Hudson Review* 23 (Autumn 1970): 403.

[2] Thomas Berry, *The Dream of the Earth* (San Francisco: Sierra Club Books, 1988), 113.

[3] Joseph Campbell with Bill Moyers, *The Power of Myth*, ed. Betty Sue Flowers (New York: Doubleday, 1988), 98.

[4] Jerry K. Robbins, "The Environment and Thinking About God," *Encounter* 48 (Autumn 1987): 403.

[5] See H. Paul Santmire, *Brother Earth: Nature, God and Ecology in Time of Crisis* (Camden, N.J.: Thomas Nelson, 1970), 94, 97.

[6] Loren Eiseley, *The Firmament of Time* (New York: Atheneum, 1960), 171.

[7] Ibid.

[8] Moltmann noted that "the trinitarian concept of creation binds together God's transcendence and His immanence" into a very positive ecological theme. Jürgon Moltmann, *God in Creation* (London: SCM, 1985, 98).

[9] Harvey Cox, *The Secular City*, rev. ed. (Toronto: Macmillan, 1966), 15-32.

[10] See Hugh Montefiore, *Man and Nature* (London: William Collins Sons & Co., 1975), 22-4; John Macquarrie, "Creation and Environment," *Expository Times* 83 (October 1971): 4-9.

[11] Jaroslav Pelikan, *The Spirit of Eastern Christendom (600-1700)*, *The Christian Tradition: A History of the Development of Doctrine*, vol. 2 (Chicago: University of Chicago Press, 1974), 248.

[12] See Robbins, "The Environment and Thinking About God," 404.

[13] Thomas Aquinas, *Summa Contra Gentiles* 3.112.9-3.113.3. For Aquinas, the inverse is true of rational beings, where God is more concerned with preservation of individuals.

[14] Teilhard de Chardin, *Le Milieu Mystique* (1917), excerpted in Appendix 2 of Henri de Lubac, *The Religion of Teilhard de Chardin*, trans. René Hague (New York: Desclee, 1967), 251.

[15] Author's translation, but versions that interpret the passage in this manner include the *Jerusalem Bible, The New Berkeley Version*, J. B. Phillips, *Revised Standard Version*, and *American Standard Version.*

[16] Joseph Sittler, "Ecological Commitment as Theological Responsibility," *Zygon* 5 (June 1970): 178.

[17] Calvin B. DeWitt, "Seven Degradations of Creation: An Urban Religious Response" (A lecture delivered at the Chattanooga Venture Environmental Forum, Chattanooga, Tenn., April 27, 1991).

[18] C. F. D. Moule, *Man and Nature in the New Testament* (Philadelphia: Fortress Press, 1967), 17.

[19] John Macquarrie in "Creation and Environment" (pp. 4-9) sets forth the organic model to understand God's relation to the world.

[20] Richard Bauckham, "First Steps to a Theology of Nature," *Evangelical Quarterly* 58 (July 1986): 239-240.

[21] Loren Wilkinson, "Cosmic Christology and the Christian's Role in Creation," *Christian Scholar's Review* 11 (1981): 18-40.

Chapter 6

[1] Frederick Elder, *Crisis in Eden* (Nashville: Abingdon Press, 1970), 13-22.

[2] Dostoyevsky *The Brothers Karamazov*, 4.11.4.

[3] Ian L. McHarg, *Design with Nature* (Garden City, N.Y.: The Natural History Press, 1969), 24.

[4] Lynn White, Jr., "The Historical Roots of Our Ecologic Crisis," *Science* 155 (March 10, 1967): 1205.

[5] William B. Badke, *Project Earth: Preserving the World God Created* (Portland, Oreg.: Multnomah Press, 1991), 72, 117, 153-54.

[6] Ibid., 54, 81.

[7] Thomas S. Derr, *Ecology and Human Need* (Philadelphia: Westminster Press, 1975), 17.

[8] Ibid., 54. Derr (p. 65) added, "Biblical anthropocentrism certainly does not make nature, by contrast to man, of no value whatever. The divine is both transcendent, the origin of all that is, and immanent, in that all things display their Creator. The 'reverence' we owe to nature is thus for God's sake."

[9] Passmore failed to recognize this distinction. He upheld the Old Testament as "uncompromisingly theocentric" but condemned the New Testament as teaching a human arrogance toward nature. John Passmore, *Man's Responsibility for Nature: Ecological Problems and Western Traditions* (London: Duckworth and Co., 1980), 12.

[10] H. Paul Santmire, *Brother Earth: Nature, God and Ecology in Time of Crisis* (Camden, N.J.: Thomas Nelson, 1970), 111.

[11] See René Dubos, *A God Within* (New York: Charles Scribner's Sons, 1972), 45.

[12] Santmire, 81.

[13] Hans Schwarz, "Eschatological Dimension of Ecology," *Zygon* 9 (December 1974): 331.

[14] Vincent Rossi, "Theocentrism: The Cornerstone of Christian Ecology," *Epiphany Journal* 6 (Fall 1985): 9-10.

[15] Schwarz, 330.

[16] H. Richard Niebuhr, *The Meaning of Revelation* (New York: Macmillan, 1941), 31.

[17] Dubos, 180.

[18] John Carmody, *Ecology and Religion: Toward a New Christian Theology of Nature* (New York: Paulist Press, 1983), 117.

[19] John B. Cobb, *Is It Too Late?* (Beverly Hills, Calif.: Bruce, 1972), 100.

[20] Rossi, 13.

[21] Jürgen Moltmann, *God in Creation*, The Gifford Lectures 1984-1985 (London: SCM Press, Ltd., 1985), 197.

[22] Thomas Berry, *The Dream of the Earth* (San Francisco: Sierra Club Books, 1988), 30.

[23] David Oates, *Earth Rising: Ecological Belief in an Age of Science* (Corvallis: Oregon State University Press, 1989), 3.

[24] Arnold Toynbee remarked, "If I am right in my diagnosis of mankind's present-day distress, the remedy lies in reverting from the *Weltanschauung* of monotheism to the *Weltanschauung* of pantheism, which is older and was once universal." See "The Religious Background of the Present Environmental Crisis," in *Ecology and Religion in History*, eds. David Spring and Eileen Spring (New York: Harper & Row, 1974), 148.

[25] Berry, 35.

[26] Bill Devall and George Sessions, *Deep Ecology* (Salt Lake City: Gibbs M. Smith, 1985), 67.

[27] Rossi, 13.

[28] Ibid.

[29] Robert H. King, "The 'Ecological Motif' in the Theology of H. Richard Niebuhr," *Journal of the American Academy of Religion* 42 (June 1974): 340.

[30] Rossi, 13.

[31] Ibid., 14.

[32] H. Paul Santmire, "Reflections on the Alleged Ecological Bankruptcy of Western Theology," *Anglican Theological Review* 57 (April 1975): 150.

[33] Moltmann, 31.

[34] Rossi, 14.

Chapter 7

[1] Gerhard von Rad, *Genesis: A Commentary* (Philadelphia: Westminster Press, 1961), 78.

[2] Bruce C. Birch, "Nature, Humanity, and Biblical Theology: Observations Toward a Relational Theology of Nature," in *Ecology and Life: Accepting Our Environmental Responsibility*, by Wesley Granberg-Michaelson (Waco, Tex.: Word Books, 1988), 147. First published in *The Predicament of the Prosperous*, by Bruce C. Birch and Larry L. Rasmussen (Philadelphia: Westminster Press, 1978).

[3] Cited by Joseph Campbell, *Myths to Live By* (New York: Bantam Books, 1972), 96, from Daisetz T. Suzuki, "The Role of Nature in Zen Buddhism," in *Eranos-Jahrbuch 1953*, ed. Olga Fröbe Kapteyn (Zurich: Rhein-Verlag, 1954), 294.

[4] See William J. Dumbrell, "Genesis 1–3, Ecology, and the Dominion of Man," *Crux* 21 (December 1985): 22.

[5] *Earthkeeping in the Nineties: Stewardship of Creation*, rev. ed., by the Fellows of the Calvin Center for Christian Scholarship, Calvin College, Peter De Vos, et al. (Grand Rapids: Wm. B. Eerdmans, 1991), 290.

[6] Wesley Granberg-Michaelson, *A Worldly Spirituality* (San Francisco: Harper and Row, 1984), 80.

[7] G. W. H. Lampe, "The New Testament Doctrine of *Ktisis*," *Scottish Journal of Theology* 17 (December 1964): 458.

[8] Bernhard W. Anderson, "Creation and the Noachic Covenant," in *Cry of the Environment: Rebuilding the Christian Creation Tradition*, eds. Philip N. Joranson and Ken Butigan (Santa Fe, N.M.: Bear and Co., 1984), 52. The *New International Version* interprets "all flesh" as people, "for all the people on earth had corrupted their ways" (Gen. 6:12).

[9] Anderson, 53.

[10] Joseph Campbell with Bill Moyers, *The Power of Myth*, ed. Betty Sue Flowers (New York: Doubleday, 1988), 99.

[11] See Grandberg-Michaelson, 197-203; Dumbrell, 19-21; Wilkinson, "Cosmic Christology," 36; E. C. Rust, "The Christian Understanding of and Attitude to Nature," *Issues in Christian Ethics*, ed. Paul D. Simmons (Nashville: Broadman Press, 1980), 171-72.

[12] See Dumbrell, 16-26.

[13] The question whether plants died before the fall is rather difficult. It could be argued that eating the fruit of the tree does not kill the tree. Yet eating parts of a plant does involve the death of plant cells. Klotz argued that plants are not alive in the same sense that people and animals are and that the "death" of plant cells does not constitute death in the biblical sense. His argument is based on the difference in cell construction and methods of propagation. John W. Klotz, "Is the Destruction of Plants Death in the Biblical Sense?" *Creation Research Society Quarterly* 16 (March 1980): 202-203.

[14] Alfred Tennyson, *In Memoriam* 56.4.

[15] See Francis A. Schaeffer, *Genesis in Space and Time, The Complete Works of Francis A. Schaeffer: A Christian Worldview*, vol. 2, *A Christian View of the Bible as Truth* (Westchester, Ill.: Crossway Books, 1982), 68;

Forrest W. Schultz, "The Ecological Dimension of Human Vicegerency," Th.M. thesis (Philadelphia: Westminster Theological Seminary, 1971), 112-13. The vision of a perfect ecosystem without death infers that there might have been anatomical and physiological differences in carnivorous animals before the fall to enable them to eat and digest plant life.

[16] C. F. D. Moule, *Man and Nature in the New Testament* (Philadelphia: Fortress Press, 1967), 15-16, 18-20.

[17] John Calvin (*Institutes*, 2.1.5) maintained that Adam's sin "perverted the whole order of nature in heaven and earth."

[18] Some, such as Matthew Fox (*The Coming of the Cosmic Christ* [San Francisco: Harper and Row, 1988], 151), totally rejected the concept of individual salvation, arguing instead that biblical salvation pertained to healing of the entire earth as a corporate entity.

[19] E. S. Feenstra, "The Spiritual vs. Material Heresy," *Journal of the American Scientific Affiliation* 21 (June 1969): 45.

[20] Jürgen Moltmann (*God in Creation* [London: SCM Press Ltd., 1985], 9) remarked, "According to the biblical traditions, all divine activity is pneumatic in its efficacy."

[21] Francis A. Schaeffer, *Pollution and the Death of Man* (Wheaton, Ill.: Tyndale House Publishers, 1970), 67.

[22] Ibid., 68.

[23] Ibid., 73.

[24] Granberg-Michaelson, 115. See H. Paul Santmire, *Brother Earth: Nature, God and Ecology in Time of Crisis* (Camden: N.J. Thomas Nelson, 1970), 109.

[25] Granberg-Michaelson, 115.

[26] Schulz, 126.

[27] Santmire, 103.

[28] For a provocative discussion see Gordon Zerbe, "The Kingdom of God and Stewardship of Creation," *The Environment and the Christian: What Can We Learn from the New Testament*, ed. Calvin B. DeWitt (Grand Rapids: Baker Book House, 1991).

[29] The kingdom of God and the kingdom of heaven are equivalent terms, *heaven* being a circumlocution for *God* due to the Jewish aversion to using the name "God." This explains the near absence of "kingdom of God" in Matthew's Gospel, since it was addressed to a Jewish readership.

[30] George E. Ladd, *Crucial Questions About the Kingdom of God* (Grand Rapids: Wm. B. Eerdmans, 1952), 80.

[31] See Santmire, 104.

[32] Moltmann, 5.

[33] Hans Schwarz, "Towards a Christian Stewardship of the Earth: Promise and Utopia," *The Environmental Crisis: The Ethical Dilemma*, ed. Edwin R. Squires (Mancelona, Mich.: AuSable Trails Institute of Environmental Studies, 1982), 34.

[34] Ibid.

[35] Lynn White, Jr., "The Historical Roots of Our Ecologic Crisis," *Science* 155 (March 10, 1967): 1205.

[36] Hwa Yol Jung, "Ecology, Zen, and Western Religious Thought," *Christian Century* 89 (November 15, 1972): 1153-54.

[37] See Hans Schwarz, "Eschatological Dimension of Ecology," *Zygon* 9 (December 1974): 336.

Chapter 8

[1] Forrest W. Schultz, "The Ecological Dimension of Human Vicegerency," Th. M. Thesis (Philadelphia: Westminster Theological Seminary, 1971), 9.

[2] Ibid., 28.

[3] William J. Dumbrell, "Genesis 1-3. Ecology, and the Dominion of Man," *Crux* 21 (December 1985): 18.

[4] Norman L. Geisler, *Christian Ethics* (Grand Rapids: Baker Book House, 1989), 305.

[5] James Barr, "Man and Nature: The Ecological Controversy and the Old Testament," *Ecology and Religion in History*, eds. David Spring and Eileen Spring (New York: Harper and Row, 1974), 63-4.

[6] Jürgen Moltmann, *God in Creation*, The Gifford Lectures 1984-1985 (London: SCM Press Ltd., 1985), 224.

[7] Calvin B. DeWitt, "Ecological Issues and Our Spiritual Roots" (A paper presented at the Conference on Land, Ethics and Community Values, Elizabethtown College, Lancaster County, Pa., July 22, 1988), 5.

[8] Dumbrell (p. 22) suggested that in addition to the clear meaning in the present context of tilling the ground, there is the notion of man's serving "in what is clearly a sanctuary presence." However, fusing two nuances into a single passage is what James Barr labled "illegitimate totality transfer." James Barr, *The Semantics of Biblical Language* (Oxford: Oxford University Press, 1961), 218, 222.

[9] Robin Attfield, "Christian Attitudes to Nature," *Journal of the History of Ideas* 44 (July-September 1983): 374.

[10] For a more comprehensive survey of views of the *imago Dei*, see Claus Westermann, *Genesis 1-11: A Commentary*, trans. John J. Scullion (Minneapolis: Augsburg Publishing House, 1984), 147-58.

[11] Francis A. Schaeffer, *Genesis in Space and Time*, The Complete Works of Francis A. Schaeffer, vol. 2 (Westchester, Ill.: Crossway Books, 1982), 33.

[12] Barr, "Man and Nature," 61.

[13] Gerhard von Rad, *Genesis: A Commentary* (Philadelphia: Westminster Press, 1961), 56.

[14] Ibid., 57.

[15] Ibid., 58.

[16] Westermann, 158; compare, Claus Westermann, *Creation* (London: SPCK, 1974), 56.

[17] Joseph Sittler, "Ecological Commitment as Theological Responsibility," *Zygon* 5 (June 1970): 174; see also *Earthkeeping in the Nineties: Stewardship of Creation*, rev. ed., by the Fellows of the Calvin Center for Christian Scholarship, Calvin College, Peter De Vos, et al. (Grand Rapids: Wm. B. Eerdmans, 1991), 285.

[18] Keith E. Yandell, "Fundamentals of Environmental Ethics: East and West," *The Environmental Crisis: The Ethical Dilemma*, ed. Edwin R. Squires (Mancelona, Mich.: AuSable Trails of Environmental Studies, 1982), 96.

[19] Barr, "Man and Nature," 61.

[20] Richard Bauckham, "First Steps to a Theology of Nature," *Evangelical Quarterly* 58 (July 1986): 233.

[21] Thomas Berry, *The Dream of the Earth* (San Francisco: Sierra Club Books, 1988), 194.

[22] Frank Moore Cross, "The Redemption of Nature," *The Princeton Seminary Bulletin* 10 (1989): 103.

[23] Thomas S. Derr, *Ecology and Human Need* (Philadelphia: Westminster Press, 1975), 148.

[24] *Earthkeeping in the Nineties*, 288.

[25] Loren Wilkinson, "Redeemers of the Earth," *The Environmental Crisis: The Ethical Dilemma*, ed. Edwin R. Squires (Mancelona, Mich.: The AuSable Trails Institute of Environmental Studies, 1982), 44.

[26] Lynn White, Jr., "Historical Roots of Our Ecologic Crisis," *Science* 155 (March 10, 1967): 1205.

[27] Richard C. Austin, "Toward Environmental Theology," *Drew Gateway* 48 (1977): 8.

[28] David Ehrenfeld and Philip J. Bentley, "Judaism and the Practice of Stewardship," *Judaism* 34 (Summer 1985): 307-308.

[29] *Earthkeeping in the Nineties*, 292.

[30] Delwin Brown, "Respect for the Rocks," *Encounter* 50 (Autumn 1989): 312.

[31] Ibid.

[32] *Earthkeeping in the Nineties*, 292.

[33] Andrew Linzey, *Christianity and the Rights of Animals* (New York: Crossroad Publishing Co., 1987), 29.

[34] Vincent Rossi, "Theocentrism: The Cornerstone of Christian Ecology," *Epiphany Journal* 6 (Fall 1985): 12.

[35] Hans Schwarz, *Our Cosmic Journey* (Minneapolis: Augsburg Publishing House, 1977), 163-64.

[36] Ibid., 163.

[37] H. Paul Santmire, *Brother Earth: Nature, God and Ecology in Time of Crisis* (Camden, N.J.: Thomas Nelson, 1970), 150.

[38] See Hugh Montefiore, *Man and Nature* (London: William Collins Sons and Co., 1975), 34.

[39] Derr, 103.

[40] William J. Byron, "The Ethic of Stewardship," *The Earth Is the Lord's: Essays on Stewardship*, eds. Mary Evelyn Jegen and Bruno Manno (New York: Paulist Press, 1978), 45.

[41] Ibid.

[42] Ibid., 46.

[43] Montefiore, 67.

[44] Linzey, 130.

[45] William Dyrness, "Stewardship of the Earth in the Old Testament," in *Tending the Garden: Essays on the Gospel and the Earth*, ed. Wesley Granberg-Michaelson (Grand Rapids: Wm. B. Eerdmans, 1987), 64.

[46] Hans Schwarz, "Towards a Christian Stewardship of the Earth: Promise and Utopia," *The Environmental Crisis: The Ethical Dilemma*, ed. Edwin R. Squires (Mancelona, Mich.: AuSable Trails Institute of Environmental Studies, 1982), 35.

[47] "It is difficult to give so much primacy to the causal efficacy of ideas. It is much more likely that, for most men, the function of ideas is to legitimate—and thus to facilitate—actions and institutions which have a much more materialistic origin. It may well be that Western man . . . used suitably selected and interpreted biblical ideas to legitimate his new-found technological power—just as, some hundreds of years earlier, the Crusaders had legitimated their brigandage." F. B. Welbourn, "Man's Dominion," *Theology* 78 (November 1975): 561-62.

[48] Ehrenfeld and Bentley, 305.

[49] *Earthkeeping in the Nineties*, 292.

[50] Montefiore, 67.

[51] Ehrenfeld and Bentley, 309.

[52] Santmire, 30.

[53] Ibid.

[54] Peter Steinhart, "Fundamentals," *Audubon* 83 (September 1981): 14.

[55] C. F. D. Moule, *Man and Nature in the New Testament* (Philadelphia: Fortress Press, 1967), 1.

[56] Aldo Leopold, *A Sand County Almanac with Other Essays on Conservation from Round River* (New York: Oxford University Press, 1966), 220.

[57] D. Bryce-Smith, "Ecology, Theology, and Humanism," *Zygon* 12 (September 1977): 221.

[58] John Black, *The Dominion of Man: The Search for Ecological Responsibility* (Edinburgh: Edinburgh University Press, 1970), 44.

Chapter 9

[1] Dostoyevsky, *The Brothers Karamazov* 2.6.3.g.

[2] Douglas John Hall, *Imaging God: Dominion as Stewardship* (Grand Rapids: Wm. B. Eerdmans, 1986), 6.

[3] Calvin B. DeWitt, "Responding to Creation's Degradation: Scientific, Scriptural and Spiritual Foundations" (A paper based on address presented at the North American Conference on Christianity and Ecology, Epworth Forest, Ill., 19-22 August 1987), 4-8. I conducted a similar survey in my Biblical Ecology class with a similar result: greed, apathy, selfishness, secularism, and ignorance.

[4] See Hall, 7.

[5] B. F. Skinner, *Beyond Freedom and Dignity* (New York: Alfred A. Knopf, 1972), 200.

[6] C. S. Lewis, *The Abolition of Man* (New York: Macmilian, 1947).

[7] Skinner, 3-5.

[8] Ibid., 215.

[9] Shirley MacLaine, *Out on a Limb* (Toronto: Bantam Books, 1983), 347.

[10] Eric C. Rust, *Nature: Garden or Desert?* (Waco, Tex.: Word Books, 1971), 59.

[11] *The Confession of Faith: The Larger and Shorter Catechisms* (Publications Committee of the Free Presbyterian Church of Scotland, 1976), 139.

[12] D. Bryce-Smith, "Ecology, Theology, and Humanism," *Zygon* 12 (September 1977): 220.

[13] Al Gore, *Earth in the Balance: Ecology and the Human Spirit* (New York: Houghton Mifflin Co., 1992), 220.

[14] For relation between the natural realm and moral evil, see James Orr, *The Christian View of God and the World* (New York: Charles Scribner's Sons, n.d.), 165-99.

[15] See G. W. H. Lampe, "The New Testament Doctrine of *Ktisis*," *Scottish Journal of Theology* 17 (December 1964): 452.

[16] John Passmore, *Man's Responsibility for Nature: Ecological Problems and Western Traditions*, 2d ed. (London: Duckworth and Co., 1980), 187.

[17] Richard Wright, "Responsibility for the Ecological Crisis," *Christian Scholar's Review* 1 (1970): 39.

[18] Ibid., 40.

[19] E. F. Schumacher, *Small Is Beautiful: Economics as if People Mattered* (New York: Harper and Row, 1973), 28-9.

[20] C. S. Lewis, *The Discarded Image: An Introduction to Medieval and Renaissance Literature* (Cambridge: Cambridge University Press, 1964), 222.

[21] Douglas Daetz, "No More Business as Usual," *Dialog* 9 (Summer 1970): 172.

[22] Passmore, 19-20, 209.

[23] G. Tyler Miller, Jr., *Living in the Environment: An Introduction to Environmental Science*, 6th ed. (Belmont, Calif.: Wadsworth, 1990), 620.

[24] Cited in David Douglas, "God, the World and James Watt," *Christianity and Crisis* 41 (October 5,1981): 270.

[25] Barbara Ward and René Dubos, *Only One Earth: The Care and Maintenance of a Small Planet* (New York: W. W. Norton and Co., 1972), 218.

[26] Schumacher, 36.

[27] James M. Gustafson, "Interdependence, Finitude, and Sin: Reflections on Scarcity," *Journal of Religion* 57 (April 1977): 167.

[28] Charles Birch and John B. Cobb, Jr., *The Liberation of Life: From the Cell to the Community* (Cambridge: Cambridge University Press, 1981), 144.

[29] Lynn White, Jr., "Historical Roots of Our Ecologic Crisis," *Science* 155 (March 10, 1967): 1205.

[30] Lewis W. Moncrief, "The Cultural Basis for Our Environmental Crisis," *Science* 170 (October 30, 1970): 509.

[31] Passmore, x.

[32] George S. Siudy, Jr., "Stewardship and World Poverty," in *The Earth Is the Lord's: Essays on Stewardship*, eds. Mary Evelyn Jegen and Bruno Manno (New York: Paulist Press, 1978), 159.

Chapter 10

[1] Albert Schweitzer, *Out of My Life and Thought: An Autobiography* (New York: Holt, Rinehart and Winston, Inc., 1961), 158.

[2] Aldo Leopold, *A Sand County Almanac with Other Essays on Conservation from Round River* (New York: Oxford University Press, 1966), 218.

[3] John Black,*The Dominion of Man: The Search for Ecological Responsibility* (Edinburgh: Edinburgh University Press, 1970) , 117.

[4] Charles Birch and John B. Cobb, Jr., *The Liberation of Life: From the Cell to the Community* (Cambridge: Cambridge University Press, 1981), 142.

[5] D. Bryce-Smith, "Ecology, Theology, and Humanism," *Zygon* 12 (September 1977): 224.

[6] Ian G. Barbour, ed., "Attitudes Toward Nature and Technology," in *Earth Might Be Fair: Reflections on Ethics, Religion, and Ecology*, ed. Ian G. Barbour (Englewood Cliffs, N.J.: Prentice-Hall, Inc., 1972), 146.

[7] Po-keung Ip, "Taoism and the Foundations of Environmental Ethics," in *Religion and Environmental Crisis*, ed. Eugene C. Hargrove (Athens: University of Georgia Press, 1986), 103.

[8] E. F. Schumacher, *Small Is Beautiful: Economics as if People Mattered* (New York: Harper and Row, 1973), 87.

[9] Arthur F. Holmes, *Contours of a World View* (Grand Rapids: Wm. B. Eerdmans, 1983), 34.

[10] Statement by Krishnamurti from a radio interview with Michael Toms on the "New Dimensions" program (July 10, 1988).

[11] Douglas John Hall, *Imaging God* (Grand Rapids: Wm. B. Eerdmans, 1986), 129-30.

[12] George Edward Moore, *Principia Ethica* (Cambridge: Cambridge University Press, 1903).

[13] Peter Singer, *Animal Liberation* (New York: Avon Books, 1975), n.p.

[14] Leopold, 240.

[15] Harold K. Schilling, "The Whole Earth Is the Lord's: Towards a Holistic Ethic," in *Earth Might Be Fair: Reflections on Ethics, Religion, and Ecology*, ed. Ian G. Barbour (Englewood Cliffs, N. J.: Prentice-Hall, Inc., 1972), 109.

[16] The entire argument of David Oates in his book *Earth Rising* is based on such a confusion of categories. See pp. 3-4, 150-52.

[17] Carolyn Merchant, *The Death of Nature: Women, Ecology, and the Scientific Revolution* (New York: Harper and Row, 1980), 4.

[18] Ibid.

[19] Hall, 40-1.

[20] See Schumacher, 89.

[21] See Francis A. Schaeffer, *Pollution and the Death of Man: The Christian View of Ecology* (Wheaton: Tyndale House Publishers, 1970), 71-2.

[22] Lionel Basney, "Ecology and the Scriptural Concept of the Master," *Christian Scholar's Review* 3 (1973): 49-50.

[23] Henry Campbell Black, *Black's Law Dictionary*, 5th ed. (St. Paul, Minn.: West Publishing Co., 1979), 1189.

[24] Extracted in *Animal Rights and Human Obligations*, eds. Tom Regan and Peter Singer (Englewood Cliffs, N. J.: Prentice-Hall, Inc., 1976), 179, from Joseph Rickaby, *Moral Philosophy* (1901), "Ethics and Moral Law." The essay was not included in the second edition (1989) of Regan and Singer's *Animal Rights*.

[25] Anselm Atkins, "Human Rights Are Cultural Artifacts," *The Humanist* 50 (March/April 1990): 15.

[26] Joseph Wood Krutch, *The Voice of the Desert* (New York: William Sloane Associates, 1955), 199.

[27] Cited in Anna Bray, "The Wrongs of Animal Rights," *Campus* 2 (Spring 1991): 16.

[28] Kenneth L. Feder and Michael Alan Park, "Animal Rights: An Evolutionary Perspective," *The Humanist* 50 (July/August 1990): 6.

[29] C. S. Lewis wrote, "Once the old Christian idea of a total difference in kind between man and beast has been abandoned, then no argument for experiments on animals can be found which is not also an argument for experiments on inferior men. If we cut up beasts simply because they cannot prevent us and because we are backing our own side in the struggle for existence, it is only logical to cut up imbeciles, criminals, enemies or capitalists for the same reasons." C. S. Lewis, "Vivisection," *God in the Dock: Essays on Theology and Ethics*, ed. Walter Hooper (Grand Rapids: Wm. B. Eerdmans, 1970), 227.

[30] Irving M. Copi, *Introduction to Logic*, 2d ed. (New York: Macmillan, 1961), 191.

[31] See Richard Griffiths, *The Human Use of Animals* (Bramcote: Grove Books, 1982), 4-5.

[32] Ibid., 17.

[33] Jones argued that it is not the suffering itself that is wrong but the "lack of a good reason for the suffering. . . . We judge inflicting pain as right and wrong depending on our sense of the appropriateness or inappropriateness of the act in the situation in which it occurs." John D. Jones, "Humans and Animals: Compassion and Dominion," *Anglican Theological Review* 63 (July 1981): 264.

[34] See Griffiths, 17.

[35] Christopher D. Stone, *Should Trees Have Standing? Toward Legal Rights for Natural Objects* (Los Altos, Calif.: William Kaufmann, 1974), 52.

[36] Roderick Frazier Nash, *The Rights of Nature: A History of Environmental Ethics* (Madison: University of Wisconsin Press, 1989).

[37] Ibid., 11-2.

[38] Griffiths, 18.

[39] Atkins, 15.

[40] See Andrew Linzey, *Animal Rights: A Christian's Assessment of Man's Treatment of Animals* (London: SCM Press, 1976) and *Christianity and the Rights of Animals* (New York: Crossroad Publishing Co., 1987).

[41] Linzey, *Christianity and the Rights of Animals*, 112.

[42] Ibid., 72.

[43] Ibid., 141.

[44] Ibid., 76.

[45] Ibid., 124-25.

[46] Norman J. Faramelli, "Ecological Responsibility and Economic Justice," in *Western Man and Environmental Ethics*, ed. Ian G. Barbour (Reading, Mass.: Addison-Wesley Publishing Co., 1973), 194.

[47] Thomas S. Derr, *Ecology and Human Need* (Philadelphia: Westminster Press, 1975), 140.

[48] Ibid., 101.

[49] Ibid., 92.

[50] J. Black, 111.

[51] James M. Gustafson, "Interdependence, Finitude, and Sin: Reflections on Scarcity," *Journal of Religion* 57 (April 1977): 161, 165.

[52] See Derr, 96.

[53] Robin Attfield, *The Ethics of Environmental Concern* (Oxford: Blackwell, 1983), 95.

[54] Ibid., 93.

Chapter 11

[1] Mircea Eliade observed: "The different types of bipartition and polarity, duality and alternation, antithetical dyads and *coincidentia oppositorum*, are to be found everywhere in the world and at all stages of culture." *The Quest: History and Meaning in Religion* (Chicago: University of Chicago Press, 1969), 173.

[2] Philip N. Joranson and Ken Butigan, *Cry of the Environment* (Santa Fe, N.M.: Bear and Co., Inc., 1984), 7.

[3] Wendell Berry, "A Secular Pilgrimage," *The Hudson Review* 23 (Autumn 1970): 403.

[4] *The Confession of Faith: The Larger and Shorter Catechisms* (Publications Committee of the Free Presbyterian Church of Scotland, 1976), 145.

[5] *Douglas John Hall, Imaging God (Grand Rapids: Wm. B. Eerdmans, 1986), 54.*

[6] Ibid., 28.

[7] *Earthkeeping: Christian Stewardship of Natural Resources*, by the Fellows of the Calvin Center for Christian Scholarship, Calvin College, Peter De Vos, et al. (Grand Rapids: Wm. B. Eerdmans, 1980), 3.

[8] Wesley Granberg-Michaelson, *A Worldly Spirituality* (San Francisco: Harper and Row, 1984), 99.

[9] H. Paul Santmire, *The Travail of Nature: The Ambiguous Ecological Promise of Christian Theology* (Philadelphia: Fortress Press, 1985), 216-17.

[10] Bernhard W. Anderson, "Creation in the Bible," in *Cry of the Environment: Rebuilding the Christian Creation Tradition*, eds. Philip N. Joranson and Ken Butigan (Santa Fe, N.M.: Bear and Co., 1984), 34.

¹¹ Francis A. Schaeffer, *Pollution and the Death of Man: The Christian View of Ecology* (Wheaton: Tyndale House Publishers, 1970), 59.

¹² Andrew Linzey, *Christianity and the Rights of Animals* (New York: Crossroad Publishing Co., 1987), 8-9.

Chapter 12

[1] Lynn White, Jr., "Historical Roots of Our Ecologic Crisis," *Science* 155 (March 10, 1967): 1207.

[2] Paul Santmire, *Brother Earth: Nature, God and Ecology in Time of Crisis* (Camden, NJ: Thomas Nelson, 1970), 6-7.

[3] Texe Marrs, "Flashpoint: A Newsletter Ministry of Texe Marrs," audiotape message blurb, March 1990, 5.

[4] Constance E. Cumbey, *The Hidden Dangers of the Rainbow* (Shreveport, LA: Huntington House, 1983), 162-163; compare Cumbey, *A Planned Deception: The Staging of a New Age "Messiah"* (East Detroit, Mich.: Pointe Publishers, 1985), 37, 126.

[5] *Christian Stewardship of Natural Resources*, by the Fellows of the Calvin Center for Christian Scholarship, Calvin College, Peter De Vos, et al. (Grand Rapids: B. Eerdmans, 1980), 4.

[6] Cumbey, *Planned Deception*, 126.

[7] Cumbey, *Hidden Dangers*, 162-63.

[8] *Earthkeeping*, 236-37.

[9] Robert W. Lee, "Six 'Crises' All Leading to World Government," *The New American* 5 (November 20, 1989): 23-30.

[10] Kevin Clauson, "Environmentalism: A Modern Idolatry," *Antithesis* 1 (March/April 1990): 16.

[11] Fellows of the Calvin Center for Christian Scholarship, *Earthkeeping in the Nineties: Stewardship of Creation*, Peter De Vos, et al., rev. ed. (Grand Rapids: B. Eerdmans, 1991), 345.

[12] Calvin B. DeWitt, "Degradation of Creation's Integrity: A Judeo-Christian Ethical Response" (A paper based on address presented at the University of Wisconsin-Madison, October 8, 1988), 23.

[13] Forrest W. Schultz, *The Ecological Dimension of Human Vicegerency*, Th.M. Thesis (Philadelphia: Westminster Theological Seminary, 1971), 4.

[14] Thomas S. Derr, *Ecology and Human Need* (Philadelphia: Westminster Press, 1975), 140.

[15] E. F. Schumacher, *Small Is Beautiful: Economics as if People Mattered* (New York: Harper and Row, 1973), 55.

[16] Calvin B. DeWitt, "Seven Degradations of Creation: An Urban Religious Response" (A lecture delivered at the 1991 Chattanooga Venture Environmental Forum, Chattanooga, TN, April 27, 1991).

[17] George Wilhelm Freidrich Hegel, *Philosophy of History*, Great Books of the Western World, trans. J. Sibree (Chicago: Encyclopædia Britannica, 1952), 155 (intro. 2.2).

[18] Santmire, 182.

[19] Francis A. Schaeffer, *Pollution and the Death of Man: The Christian View of Ecology* (Wheaton: Tyndale House Publishers, 1970), 82.

[20] Schultz, 178.

[21] Ibid., 179.

[22] Dave Hunt, *Peace, Prosperity, and the Coming Holocaust* (Eugene, Oreg.: Harvest House Publishers, 1983), 258. Hunt made references to Jeremiah 17:9 and Matthew 15:19-20.

[23] John B. Cobb, Jr., *Is It Too Late?* (Beverly Hills, CA: Bruce Publishing Co., 1972), 58; and Frederick Elder, *Crisis in Eden* (Nashville: Abingdon Press, 1970), 144. Elder (p. 145) mentions three elements of this new asceticism: (1) restraint, (2) an emphasis upon quality existence, and (3) reverence for life.

[24] Ron Elsdon, *Bent World: A Christian Response to the Environmental Crisis* (Downers Grove, ILL: Inter-Varsity Press, 1981), 140.

[25] John R. Sheaffer and Raymond H. Brand, *Whatever Happened to Eden?* (Wheaton, ILL: Tyndale House, 1980), 112-13.

[26] Ibid., 111.

[27] Douglas C. Bowman, *Beyond the Modern Mind: The Spiritual and Ethical Challenge of the Environmental Crisis* (New York: Pilgrim Press, 1990), 49-56.

[28] Fritjof Capra and Charlene Spretnak wrote, "We feel that deep ecology is spiritual in its very essence. It is a world view that is supported by modern science but is rooted in a perception of reality that goes beyond the scientific framework to a subtle awareness of the oneness of all life, the interdependence of its multiple manifestations, and its cycles of change and transformation. When the concept of the human spirit is understood in this sense, as the mode of consciousness in which the individual feels connected to the cosmos as a whole, the full meaning of deep ecology is indeed spiritual." *Green Politics* (New York: E.P. Dutton and Co., Inc., 1984), 53.

[29] Matthew Fox, *Original Blessing: A Primer in Creation Spirituality* (Santa Fe, N.M.: Bear and Co., 1983). The four paths constitute the structure of the entire book.

[30] Matthew Fox, *The Coming of the Cosmic Christ* (San Francisco: Harper and Row, 1988), 133.

[31] Ibid., 67, 137, 145.

[32] Wesley Granberg-Michaelson, *A Worldly Spirituality* (San Francisco: Harper and Row, 1984), 167.

[33] H. Paul Santmire, "The Liberation of Nature: Lynn White's Challenge Anew," *Christian Century* 102 (May 22, 1985): 533.

[34] Al Gore, *Earth in the Balance: Ecology and the Human Spirit* (New York: Houghton Mifflin Co., 1992), 230.

[35] Vincent Rossi, "Theocentrism: The Cornerstone of Christian Ecology," *Epiphany Journal* 6 (Fall 1985): 8.

Appendix A

[1] Ronald G. Shaiko, "Religion, Politics, and Environmental Concern: A Powerful Mix of Passions," *Social Science Quarterly* 68 (June 1987): 251. The scale for the mean scores and percentages has been inverted to correspond to my scale of computation.

BIBILIOGRAPHY

1 Clement. Loeb Classical Library. *The Apostolic Fathers.* Translated by Kirsopp Lake. Cambridge: Harvard University Press, 1977.

Aeschylus. *Prometheus Bound.* Great Books of the Western World. Translated by G. M. Cookson. Chicago: Encyclopædia Britannica, 1952.

Allchin, A. M. "The Theology of Nature in the Eastern Fathers and Among Anglican Theologians." In *Man and Nature,* edited by Hugh Montefiore. London: William Collins Sons & Co., 1975.

Alpers, Kenneth P. "Starting Points for an Ecological Theology: A Bibliographical Survey." *Dialog* 9 (Summer 1970): 226-35.

Anderson, Bernhard W. "Creation and the Noachic Covenant." In *Cry of the Environment: Rebuilding the Christian Creation Tradition,* edited by Philip N. Joranson and Ken Butigan. Santa Fe, N. M.: Bear & Co., 1984.

__________. "Creation in the Bible." In *Cry of the Environment: Rebuilding the Christian Creation Tradition,* edited by Philip N. Joranson and Ken Butigan. Santa Fe, N. M.: Bear & Co., 1984.

Aquinas, Thomas. *Summa Contra Gentiles.* Book 3, *Providence.* Translated by Vernon J. Bourke. Notre Dame: University of Notre Dame Press, 1956.

__________. *Summa Theologica.* Great Books of the Western World. Translated by the Fathers of the English Dominican Province, revised by Daniel J. Sullivan. Chicago: Encyclopædia Britannica, 1952.

Aristotle. *Metaphysics.* Great Books of the Western World. Translated by W. D. Ross. Chicago: Encyclopædia Britannica, 1952.

__________. *Politics.* Great Books of the Western World. Translated by Benjamin Jowett. Chicago: Encyclopædia Britannica, 1952.

Arnobius. *Against the Heathens.* The Ante-Nicene Fathers: Translations of the Fathers Down to A.D. 325. Edited by Alexander Roberts and James Donaldson. 10 vols. Grand Rapids: Wm. B. Eerdmans, 1951.

Atkins, Anselm. "Human Rights Are Cultural Artifacts." *The Humanist* 50 (March/April 1990): 15-16.

Attfield, Robin. "Christian Attitudes to Nature." *Journal of the History of Ideas* 44 (July-September 1983): 369-86.

__________. *The Ethics of Environmental Concern.* Oxford: Blackwell, 1983.

Augustine. *City of God.* Great Books of the Western World. Translated by Marcus Dods. Chicago: Encyclopædia Britannica, 1952.

__________. *Confessions.* Great Books of the Western World. Translated by Edward Bouverie Pusey. Chicago: Encyclopædia Britannica, 1952.

__________. *Soliloquies.* Nicene and Post-Nicene Fathers, first series. Edited by Philip Schaff. 14 vols. Grand Rapids: Wm. B. Eerdmans, n.d.

313

Austin, Richard Cartwright. "Toward Environmental Theology." *Drew Gateway* 48 (1977): 1-14.

Bacon, Francis. *Novum Organum.* Great Books of the Western World. Chicago: Encyclopædia Britannica, 1952.

Badke, William B. *Project Earth: Preserving the World God Created.* Portland, Oreg.: Multnomah, 1991.

Baker, John Austin. "Biblical Attitudes to Nature." In *Man and Nature*, edited by Hugh Montefiore. London: William Collins Sons & Co., 1975.

Barbour, Ian G. "Attitudes Toward Nature and Technology." In *Earth Might Be Fair: Reflections on Ethics, Religion, and Ecology*, edited by Ian G. Barbour. Englewood Cliffs, N.J.: Prentice-Hall, 1972.

__________, ed. *Earth Might Be Fair: Reflections on Ethics, Religion, and Ecology.* Englewood Cliffs, N. J.: Prentice-Hall, 1972.

__________, ed. *Western Man and Environmental Ethics.* Reading, Mass.: Addison-Wesley, 1973.

Barnette, Henlee H. *The Church and the Ecological Crisis.* Grand Rapids: Wm. B. Eerdmans, 1972.

Barr, James. "Man and Nature: The Ecological Controversy and the Old Testament." In *Ecology and Religion in History*, edited by David Spring and Eileen Spring. New York: Harper and Row, 1974. First published in *Bulletin of the John Rylands Library* 55 (Autumn 1972): 9-32.

__________. *The Semantics of Biblical Language.* Oxford: Oxford University Press, 1961.

Barth, Karl. *Church Dogmatics.* The Doctrine of Creation. Edited by G. W. Bromiley and T. F. Torrance. Vol. 3, Edinburgh: T. & T. Clark, 1960.

Basney, Lionel. "Ecology and the Scriptural Concept of the Master." *Christian Scholar's Review* 3 (1973): 49-50.

Bauckham, Richard. "First Steps to a Theology of Nature." *Evangelical Quarterly* 58 (July 1986): 229-44.

Benét, Stephen Vincent. *Western Star.* New York: Farrar & Rinehart, 1943.

Berkhof, L. *Systematic Theology*, 4th ed. Grand Rapids: Wm. B. Eerdmans, 1941.

Berry, Thomas. *The Dream of the Earth.* San Francisco: Sierra Club Books, 1988.

Berry, Wendell. "A Secular Pilgrimage." *The Hudson Review* 23 (Autumn 1970): 401-24.

Birch, Bruce C. "Nature, Humanity, and Biblical Theology: Observations Toward a Relational Theology of Nature." In *Ecology and Life: Accepting Our Environmental Responsibility*, by Wesley Granberg-Michaelson. Waco, Tex.: Word Books, 1988. First published in *The Predicament of the Prosperous*, by Bruce C. Birch and Larry L. Rasmussen. Philadelphia: Westminster Press, 1978.

Birch, Charles, and John B. Cobb, Jr., *The Liberation of Life: From the Cell to the Community.* Cambridge: Cambridge University Press, 1981.

Black, Henry Campbell. *Black's Law Dictionary*, 5th ed. St. Paul, Minn.: West Publishing, 1979.

Black, John. *The Dominion of Man: The Search for Ecological Responsibility.* Edinburgh: Edinburgh University Press, 1970.

Botkin, Daniel B. *Discordant Harmonies: A New Ecology for the Twenty-first Century.* New York: Oxford University Press, 1990.

Bowman, Douglas C. *Beyond the Modern Mind: The Spiritual and Ethical Challenge of the Environmental Crisis.* New York: Pilgrim Press, 1990.

Bray, Anna. "The Wrongs of Animal Rights." *Campus* 2 (Spring 1991): 16-19.

Brown, Delwin. "'Respect for the Rocks:' Toward a Christian Process Theology of Nature." *Encounter* 50 (Autumn 1989): 309-21.

Brueggemann, Walter. *The Land: Place as Gift, Promise, and Challenge in Biblical Faith.* Philadelphia: Fortress Press, 1977.

Brunner, Emil. *Revelation and Reason.* Translated by Olive Wyon. Philadelphia: Westminster Press, 1946.

Bryce-Smith, D. "Ecology, Theology, and Humanism." *Zygon* 12 (September 1977): 213-31.

Byron, William J. "The Ethics of Stewardship." In *The Earth Is the Lord's: Essays on Stewardship*, edited by Mary Evelyn Jegen and Bruno Manno. New York: Paulist Press, 1978.

Cain, Clifford. "Nature as Thou: A Reorientation toward Eco-justice." *Encounter* 52 (Winter 1991): 21-32.

Calvin, John. *Genesis.* Translated and edited by John King. 2 vols. in one. Edinburgh: Banner of Truth Trust, 1965.

__________. *Institutes of the Christian Religion.* Translated by Henry Beveridge. Grand Rapids: Wm. B. Eerdmans, 1962.

Campbell, Joseph, with Bill Moyers, *Myths to Live By.* New York: Bantam Books, 1972.

__________. *The Power of Myth.* Edited by Betty Sue Flowers. New York: Doubleday, 1988.

Capra, Fritjof, and Charlene Spretnak. *Green Politics.* New York: E. P. Dutton, 1984.

Carmody, John. *Ecology and Religion: Toward a New Christian Theology of Nature.* New York: Paulist Press, 1983.

Charles, R. H., trans. *The Apocrypha and Pseudepigrapha of the Old Testament in English.* 2 vols. London: Oxford at the Clarendon Press, 1963.

Clauson, Kevin. "Environmentalism: A Modern Idolatry." *Antithesis* 1 (March/April 1990): 10-16.

Cobb, John B., Jr. *Is It Too Late?* Beverly Hills Calif.: Bruce, 1972.

__________. "Process Theology and an Ecological Model." in *Cry of the Environment: Rebuilding the Christian Creation Tradition*, edited by Philip N. Joranson and Ken Butigan. Santa Fe, N. M.: Bear & Co., 1984.

__________. "Process Theology and Environmental Issues." *Journal of Religion* 60 (October 1980): 440-58.

Cohen, A. *The Teachings of Maimonides.* London: G. Routledge & Sons, 1927.

Commoner, Barry. *The Closing Circle: Nature, Man, and Technology.* New York: Alfred A. Knopf, 1971.

__________. *Making Peace with the Planet.* New York: Pantheon Books, 1990.

The Confession of Faith: The Larger and Shorter Catechisms. Publications Committee of the Free Presbyterian Church of Scotland, 1976.

Copi, Irving M. *Introduction to Logic*, 2d ed. New York: Macmillan, 1961.

Cox, Harvey. *The Secular City*, rev. ed. Toronto: Macmillan, 1966.

Cross, Frank Moore. "The Redemption of Nature." *The Princeton Seminary Bulletin* 10 (1989): 94-104.

Cumbey, Constance. *The Hidden Dangers of the Rainbow*. Shreveport, La.: Huntington House, 1983.

__________. *A Planned Deception: The Staging of a New Age "Messiah."* East Detroit, Mich.: Pointe Publishers, 1985.

Cunningham, Lawrence S. *Saint Francis of Assisi*. Boston: Twayne Publishers, 1976.

Daetz, Douglas. "No More Business as Usual." *Dialog* 9 (Summer 1970): 171-75.

Derr, Thomas Sieger. *Ecology and Human Need*. Philadelphia: Westminster Press, 1975.

__________. "Religion's Responsibility for the Ecological Crisis: An Argument Run Amok." *Worldview* 18 (January 1975): 39-45.

Descartes, René. *Discourse on the Method of Rightly Conducting the Reason and Seeking for Truth in the Sciences*. Great Books of the Western World. Translated by Elizabeth S. Haldane and G. R. T. Ross. Chicago: Encyclopædia Britannica, 1952.

Devall, Bill, and George Sessions. *Deep Ecology*. Salt Lake City: Gibbs M. Smith, 1985.

DeWitt, Calvin B. "Degradation of Creation's Integrity: A Judeo-Christian Ethical Response" (A paper based on address presented at the University of Wisconsin-Madison, October 8, 1988).

__________. "Ecological Issues and Our Spiritual Roots" (A paper presented at the Conference on Land, Ethics and Community Values, Elizabethtown College, Lancaster County, Pa.: July 22, 1988).

__________. "The Price of Gopher Wood." *Faculty Dialogue* 12 (Fall 1989): 59-62.

__________. "Responding to Creation's Degradation: Scientific, Scriptural and Spiritual Foundations" (A paper based on address presented at the North American Conference on Christianity and Ecology, Epworth Forest, Ill. August 19-22, 1987).

Dionysius. *Concerning Nature*. The Ante-Nicene Fathers: Translations of the Fathers Down to A.D. 325. Edited by Alexander Roberts and James Donaldson. 10 vols. Grand Rapids: Wm. B. Eerdmans, 1951.

Dostoyevsky, Fyodor Mikhailovich. *The Brothers Karamazov*. Translated by Constance Garnett. Great Books of the Western World. Chicago: Encyclopædia Britannica, 1952.

Douglas, David. "God, the World and James Watt." In *Christianity and Crisis* 41 (October 5, 1981): 258, 269-70.

Drucker, Peter F. *The New Realities*. New York: Harper and Row, 1989.

Dubos, René. *A God Within*. New York: Charles Scribner's Sons, 1972.

Dumbrell, William J. "Genesis 1-3, Ecology, and the Dominion of Man." *Crux* 21 (December 1985): 16-26.

Dyrness, William. "Stewardship of the Earth in the Old Testament." In *Tending the Garden: Essays on the Gospel and the Earth*, edited by Wesley Granberg-Michaelson. Grand Rapids: Wm. B. Eerdmans, 1987.

Earthkeeping: Christian Stewardship of Natural Resources. By the Fellows of the Calvin Center for Christian Scholarship, Calvin College. Peter De Vos, et al. Grand Rapids: Wm. B. Eerdmans, 1980.

Earthkeeping in the Nineties: Stewardship of Creation, rev. ed. By the Fellows of the Calvin Center for Christian Scholarship, Calvin College. Peter De Vos, et al. Grand Rapids: Wm. B. Eerdmans, 1991.

Ehrenfeld, David. *The Arrogance of Humanism*. New York: Oxford University Press, 1978.

__________, and Philip J. Bentley. "Judaism and the Practice of Stewardship." *Judaism* 34 (Summer 1985): 301-311.

Ehrlich, Paul R. *The Population Bomb*, rev. ed. Rivercity, Mass.: Rivercity Press, 1971.

Eiseley, Loren. *The Firmament of Time*. New York: Atheneum, 1960.

Elder, Frederick. *Crisis in Eden*. Nashville: Abingdon Press, 1970.

Eliade, Mircea. *The Quest: History and Meaning in Religion*. Midway Reprint. Chicago and London: University of Chicago Press, 1969.

Ellul, Jacques. *The Technological Society*. New York: Alfred A. Knopf, 1973.

Elsdon, Ron. *Bent World: A Christian Response to the Environmental Crisis*. Downers Grove, Ill.: Inter-Varsity Press, 1981.

Fackre, Gabriel. "Ecology and Theology." In *Western Man and Environmental Ethics*, edited by Ian G. Barbour. Reading, Mass.: Addison-Wesley Publishing Co., 1973. First published in *Religion in Life* 40 (Summer 1971): 210-24.

Faramelli, Norman J. "Ecological Responsibility and Economic Justice." In *Western Man and Environmental Ethics*, edited by Ian G. Barbour. Reading, Mass.: Addison-Wesley Publishing Co., 1973.

Feder, Kenneth L., and Michael Alan Park. "Animal Rights: An Evolutionary Perspective." *The Humanist* 50 (July/August 1990): 5-7, 44.

Feenstra, E. S. "The Spiritual vs. Material Heresy." *Journal of the American Scientific Affiliation* 21 (June 1969): 44-46.

Feuerbach, Ludwig. *The Essence of Christianity*. Translated by George Eliot. New York: Harper and Brothers, 1957.

Fitzmyer, Joseph A. "The Letter to the Romans," *The New Jerome Biblical Commentary*. Edited by Raymond E. Brown, Joseph A. Fitzmyer, and Roland E. Murphy. Englewood Cliffs, N. J.: Prentice-Hall, 1990.

Fox, Matthew. *The Coming of the Cosmic Christ: The Healing of Mother Earth and the Birth of a Global Renaissance*. San Francisco: Harper & Row, 1988.

__________. *Original Blessing: A Primer in Creation Spirituality*. Santa Fe, N. M.: Bear & Co., 1983.

Fuller, R. Buckminster. *Critical Path*. New York: St. Martin's Press, 1981.

Geisler, Norman L. *Christian Ethics*. Grand Rapids: Baker Book House, 1989.

Glacken, Clarence J. "Man against Nature: An Outmoded Concept." In *The Environmental Crisis: Man's Struggle to Live with Himself*, edited by Harold W. Helfrich, Jr. New Haven: Yale University Press, 1970.

__________. *Traces on the Rhodian Shore: Nature and Culture in Western Thought from Ancient Times to the End of the Eighteenth Century*. Berkeley and Los Angeles: University of California Press, 1967.

Gore, Al. *Earth in the Balance: Ecology and the Human Spirit.* New York: Houghton Mifflin, 1992.

Gosling, David. "Towards a Credible Ecumenical Theology of Nature." *Ecumenical Review* 38 (July 1986): 322-31.

Granberg-Michaelson, Wesley. *Ecology and Life: Accepting Our Environmental Responsibility.* Waco, Tex.: Word, 1988.

__________, ed. *Tending the Garden: Essays on the Gospel and the Earth.* Grand Rapids: Wm. B. Eerdmans, 1987.

__________. *A Worldly Spirituality: The Call to Redeem Life on Earth.* San Francisco: Harper and Row, 1984.

Gregorios, Paulos Mar. "New Testament Foundations for Understanding the Creation." In *Tending the Garden: Essays on the Gospel and the Earth,* edited by Wesley Granberg-Michaelson. Grand Rapids: Wm. B. Eerdmans, 1987.

Griffiths, Richard. *The Human Use of Animals.* Bramcote: Grove Books, 1982.

Gustafson, James M. "Interdependence, Finitude, and Sin: Reflections on Scarcity." *Journal of Religion* 57 (April 1977): 156-68.

Hall, Douglas John. *Imaging God: Dominion as Stewardship.* Grand Rapids: Wm. B. Eerdmans, 1986.

Hamilton, Michael, ed. *This Little Planet.* N. Y.: Charles Scribner's Sons, 1970.

Hargrove, Eugene C., ed. *Religion and Environmental Crisis.* Athens: University of Georgia Press, 1986.

Hegel, Georg Wilhelm Friedrich. *Philosophy of History.* Great Books of the Western World. Translated by J. Sibree. Chicago: Encyclopædia Britannica, 1952.

Helfand, Jonathan. "The Earth Is the Lord's: Judaism and Environmental Ethics." In *Religion and Environmental Crisis,* edited by Eugene C. Hargrove. Athens: University of Georgia Press, 1986.

Hendry, George S. *Theology of Nature.* Philadelphia: Westminster Press, 1980.

Henry, Carl F. H. "Stewardship of the Environment." In *Applying the Scriptures,* edited by Kenneth S. Kantzer. Grand Rapids: Zondervan, 1987.

Holmes, Arthur F. *Contours of a World View.* Grand Rapids: Wm. B. Eerdmans, 1983.

Hummel, Charles. "The Tyranny of the Urgent." *HIS* 26 (February 1966): 1-3.

Hunt, Dave, *Peace, Prosperity, and the Coming Holocaust.* Eugene, Ore.: Harvest House, 1983.

Huxley, Julian. *Religion without Revelation.* New York: Harper & Brothers, 1957.

Ip, Po-keung. "Taoism and the Foundations of Environmental Ethics." In *Religion and Environmental Crisis,* edited by Eugene C. Hargrove. Athens: University of Georgia Press, 1986.

Jaki, Stanley L. *The Road of Science and the Ways to God.* Chicago: University of Chicago Press, 1978.

Jegen, Mary Evelyn, and Bruno Manno, eds., *The Earth Is the Lord's: Essays on Stewardship.* New York: Paulist Press, 1978.

Jidejian, Nina. *Byblos Through the Ages.* Beirut: Dar El-Machreq Publishers, 1968.

Jobling, David. "'And have Dominion . . .': The Interpretation of Genesis 1, 28 in Philo Judaeus." *Journal for the Study of Judaism* 8 (January 1977): 50-82.

Jones, John D. "Humans and Animals: Compassion and Dominion." *Anglican Theological Review* 63 (July 1981): 259-72.

Joranson, Philip N., and Ken Butigan, eds. *Cry of the Environment: Rebuilding the Christian Creation Tradition.* Santa Fe, N. M.: Bear & Co., 1984.

Jung, Hwa Yol. "Ecology, Zen, and Western Religious Thought." *Christian Century* 89 (November 15, 1972): 1153-56.

Kant, Immanuel. Great Books of the Western World. *Critique of Practical Reason.* Translated by Thomas Kingsmill Abbott. Chicago: Encyclopædia Britannica, 1952.

Kaufman, Gordon D. "A Problem of Theology: The Concept of Nature." *Harvard Theological Review* 65 (1972): 337-66.

Kay, Jeanne. "Human Dominion over Nature in the Hebrew Bible." *Annals of the Association of American Geographers* 79 (June 1989): 214-232.

King, Robert H. "The 'Ecological Motif' in the Theology of H. Richard Niebuhr." *Journal of the American Academy of Religion* 42 (June 1974): 339-43.

Klotz, John W. "A Creationist Environmental Ethic." *Creation Research Society Quarterly* 21 (June 1984): 6-8.

__________. "Is the Destruction of Plants Death in the Biblical Sense?" *Creation Research Society Quarterly* 16 (March 1980): 202-203.

Koehler, Ludwig, and Walter Baumgartner, eds., *Lexicon in Veteris Testamenti Libros.* 3 vols. Leiden: E. J. Brill, 1951.

Krutch, Joseph Wood. *The Voice of the Desert.* New York: William Sloane Associates, 1955.

Ladd, George E. *Crucial Questions About the Kingdom of God.* Grand Rapids: Wm. B. Eerdmans, 1952.

Lampe, G. W. H. "The New Testament Doctrine of *Ktisis.*" *Scottish Journal of Theology* 17 (December 1964): 449-62.

Lappé, Frances Moore. *Diet for a Small Planet,* rev. ed. New York: Ballantine Books, 1975.

Lee, Robert W. "Six 'Crises' All Leading to World Government." *The New American* 5 (November 20, 1989): 23-30.

Leopold, Aldo. *A Sand County Almanac with Other Essays on Conservation from Round River.* New York: Oxford University Press, 1966.

Lewis, C. S. *The Abolition of Man.* New York: Macmillan, 1947.

__________. *The Discarded Image: An Introduction to Medieval and Renaissance Literature.* Cambridge: Cambridge University Press, 1964.

__________. *God in the Dock: Essays on Theology and Ethics.* Edited by Walter Hooper. Grand Rapids: Wm. B. Eerdmans, 1970.

Linzey, Andrew. *Animal Rights: A Christian's Assessment of Man's Treatment of Animals.* London: SCM Press, 1976.

__________. *Christianity and the Rights of Animals.* New York: Crossroad, 1987.

Lossky, Vladimir. *The Mystical Theology of the Eastern Church.* Crestwood, N. Y.: St. Vladimir's Seminary Press, 1976.

Lubac, Henri de. *The Religion of Teilhard de Chardin.* Translated by René Hague. New York: Desclee, 1967.

Lucretius. Great Books of the Western World. *On the Nature of Things.* Translated by H. A. J. Munro. Chicago: Encyclopædia Britannica, 1952.

Luther, Martin. *Luther's Works.* Edited by Jaroslav Pelikan. 30 vols. St. Louis: Concordia Publishing House, 1958.

Lutz, Paul E. "Interrelatedness: Ecological Pattern of the Creation." In *Cry of the Environment: Rebuilding the Christian Creation Tradition,* edited by Philip N. Joranson and Ken Butigan. Santa Fe, N. M.: Bear & Co., 1984.

MacLaine, Shirley. *Out on a Limb.* Toronto: Bantam Books, 1983.

Macquarrie, John. "Creation and Environment." *Expository Times* 83 (October 1971): 4-9.

Maimonides, Moses. *The Guide for the Perplexed,* 2d ed. Translated by M. Friedländer. London: George Routledge & Sons, 1947.

Marx, Leo. "American Institutions and Ecological Ideals." *Science* 170 (November 27, 1970): 945-52.

McCormick, Richard A. "Notes on Moral Theology: April-September 1970." *Theological Studies* 32 (March 1971): 66-122.

McHarg, Ian L. *Design with Nature.* Garden City, N. Y.: The Natural History Press, 1969.

McKibben, Bill. *The End of Nature.* New York: Random House, 1989.

McPherson, James. "Towards an Ecological Theology." *Expository Times* 97 (May 1986): 236-40.

Meeker, Joseph W. *Minding the Earth: Thinly Disguised Essays on Human Ecology.* Alameda, Calif.: The Latham Foundation, 1988.

__________. "Prologue to an Environmental Ethic," *The North American Review* 258 (Summer 1973): 16-22.

Merchant, Carolyn. *The Death of Nature: Women, Ecology, and the Scientific Revolution.* New York: Harper and Row, 1980.

Meye, Robert P. "Invitation to Wonder: Toward a Theology of Nature." In *Tending the Garden: Essays on the Gospel and the Earth,* edited by Wesley Granberg-Michaelson. Grand Rapids: Wm. B. Eerdmans, 1987.

Miller, G. Tyler, Jr. *Living in the Environment: An Introduction to Environmental Science,* 6th ed. Belmont, Calif.: Wadsworth, 1990.

Moltmann, Jürgen. *God in Creation: An Ecological Doctrine of Creation,* The Gifford Lectures, 1984-1985. Translated by Margaret Kohl. London: SCM Press Ltd., 1985.

Moncrief, Lewis W. "The Cultural Basis for Our Environmental Crisis." *Science* 170 (October 30, 1970): 508-12.

Montefiore, Hugh, ed. *Man and Nature.* London: William Collins Sons & Co., 1975.

Moore, George Edward. *Principia Ethica.* Cambridge: Cambridge University Press, 1903.

Moore, John A. "Science as a Way of Knowing—Human Ecology." *American Zoologist* 35 (1985): 483-637.

Moule, C. F. D. *Man and Nature in the New Testament.* Philadelphia: Fortress Press, 1967.

Nash, Roderick Frazier. *The Rights of Nature: A History of Environmental Ethics.* Madison: University of Wisconsin Press, 1989.

Niebuhr, H. Richard. *The Meaning of Revelation.* New York: Macmillan, 1962.

__________. *The Responsible Self: An Essay in Christian Moral Philosophy.* New York: Harper and Row, 1963.

Oates, David. *Earth Rising: Ecological Belief in an Age of Science.* Corvallis: Oregon State University Press, 1989.

Origen. *Contra Celsum.* The Ante-Nicene Fathers: Translations of the Writings of the Fathers Down to A.D. 325. Edited by Alexander Roberts and James Donaldson. 10 vols. Grand Rapids: Wm. B. Eerdmans, 1951.

Orr, James. *The Christian View of God and the World.* New York: Charles Scribner's Sons, n.d.

Pascal, Blaise. *Pensées.* Great Books of the Western World. Translated by W. F. Trotter. Chicago: Encyclopædia Britannica, 1952.

Passmore, John. *Man's Responsibility for Nature: Ecological Problems and Western Traditions,* 2d ed. London: Duckworth & Co. Ltd., 1980.

Peacocke, A. R. *Creation and the World of Science,* The Bampton Lectures, 1978. Oxford: Clarendon Press, 1979.

Pelikan, Jaroslav. *The Christian Tradition: A History of the Development of Doctrine.* Vol. 2, *The Spirit of Eastern Christendom* (600-1700). Chicago: University of Chicago Press, 1974.

Philo. *De Opificio Mundi.* Loeb Classical Library. Translated by F. H. Colson and G. H. Whitaker. Cambridge: Harvard University Press, 1929.

__________. *Quaestiones et Solutiones in Genesin.* Loeb Classical Library. Translated by Ralph Marcus. Cambridge: Harvard University Press, 1953.

__________. *Quod Deus Immutabilis sit.* Loeb Classical Library. Translated by F. H. Colson and G. H. Whitaker. Cambridge: Harvard University Press, 1930.

Plato. *Critias.* Great Books of the Western World. Translated by Benjamin Jowett. Chicago: Encyclopædia Britannica, 1952.

__________. *The Republic.* Great Books of the Western World. Translated by Benjamin Jowett. Chicago: Encyclopædia Britannica, 1952.

Pyne, Stephen J. "Firestick History." *The Journal of American History* 76 (March 1990): 1132-41.

Regan, Tom, and Peter Singer, eds. *Animal Rights and Human Obligations.* Englewood Cliffs, N. J.: Prentice-Hall, 1976.

Rimbach, James A. "'All Creation Groans': Theology/Ecology in St. Paul." In *Ecology and Life: Accepting our Environmental Responsibility,* by Wesley Granberg-Michaelson. Waco, Tex.: Word, 1988. First published in *Asia Journal of Theology* 1 (October 1987): 379-391.

Robbins, Jerry K. "The Environment and Thinking About God." *Encounter* 48 (Autumn 1987): 401-415.

Rossi, Vincent. "The Eleventh Commandment: Toward an Ethic of Ecology." *Epiphany* 1 (Summer 1981): 2-19.

__________. "Theocentrism: The Cornerstone of Christian Ecology." *Epiphany* 6 (Fall 1985): 8-14.

Runcie, Robert, Norman Lear, and Carl Sagan. "God Is Green, So Is Science." *New Perspectives Quarterly* 7 (Spring 1990): 68-70.

Rust, Eric C. "The Christian Understanding of and Attitude to Nature." In *Issues in Christian Ethics,* edited by Paul D. Simmons. Nashville: Broadman Press, 1980.

__________. *Nature: Garden or Desert?* Waco, Tex.: Word Books, 1971.

Santmire, H. Paul. *Brother Earth: Nature, God and Ecology in Time of Crisis.* Camden, N. J.: Thomas Nelson, 1970.

__________. "The Liberation of Nature: Lynn White's Challenge Anew." *Christian Century* 102 (May 22, 1985): 530-33.

__________. "Reflections on the Alleged Ecological Bankruptcy of Western Theology." *Anglican Theological Review* 57 (April 1975): 131-52.

__________. "St. Augustine's Theology of the Biophysical World." *Dialog* 19 (Summer 1980): 174-85.

__________. "Toward a New Theology of Nature." *Dialog* 25 (Winter 1986): 43-50.

__________. *The Travail of Nature: The Ambiguous Ecological Promise of Christian Theology.* Philadelphia: Fortress Press, 1985.

Schaeffer, Francis A. *Genesis in Space and Time.* In The Complete Works of Francis A. Schaeffer: *A Christian Worldview.* Vol. 2, *A Christian View of the Bible as Truth.* Westchester, Ill.: Crossway Books, 1982.

__________. *Pollution and the Death of Man: The Christian View of Ecology.* Wheaton, Ill.: Tyndale House, 1970.

Schilling, Harold K. "The Whole Earth Is the Lord's: Towards a Holistic Ethic." In *Earth Might be Fair: Reflections on Ethics, Religion, and Ecology,* edited by Ian G. Barbour. Englewood Cliffs, N. J.: Prentice-Hall, 1972.

Schultz, Forrest W. "The Ecological Dimension of Human Vicegerency," Th.M. Thesis. Philadelphia: Westminster Theological Seminary, 1971.

Schumacher, E. F. *Small Is Beautiful: Economics as if People Mattered.* Colophon ed. New York: Harper and Row, 1973.

Schwarz, Hans. "Eschatological Dimension of Ecology." *Zygon* 9 (December 1974): 323-38.

__________. *Our Cosmic Journey.* Minneapolis: Augsburg Publishing House, 1977.

__________. "Towards a Christian Stewardship of the Earth: Promise and Utopia." In *The Environmental Crisis: The Ethical Dilemma,* edited by Edwin R. Squires. Mancelona, Mich.: AuSable Trails Institute of Environmental Studies, 1982.

Schweitzer, Albert. *Out of My Life and Thought: An Autobiography.* New York: Holt, Rinehart and Winston, 1961.

Sears, Paul B. "The Injured Earth." In *This Little Planet,* edited by Michael Hamilton. New York: Charles Scribner's Sons, 1970.

Shaiko, Ronald G. "Religion, Politics, and Environmental Concern: A Powerful Mix of Passions." *Social Science Quarterly* 68 (June 1987): 244-62.

Sheaffer, John R., and Raymond H. Brand. *Whatever Happened to Eden?* Wheaton, Ill.: Tyndale House, 1980.

Sheldon, Joseph K. "Twenty-one Years After 'The Historical Roots of Our Ecologic Crisis': How Has the Church Responded?" *Perspectives on Science and Faith* 41 (September 1989): 152-58.

Sherrard, Philip. *The Eclipse of Man and Nature: An Enquiry into the Origins and Consequences of Modern Science.* West Stockbridge, Mass.: Lindisfarne Press, 1987.

Singer, Peter. *Animal Liberation.* New York: Avon Books, 1975.

Sittler, Joseph. "Ecological Commitment as Theological Responsibility." *Zygon* 5 (June 1970): 172-81.

Siudy, George S., Jr. "Stewardship and World Poverty." In *The Earth Is the Lord's: Essays on Stewardship*, edited by Mary Evelyn Jegen and Bruno V. Manno. New York: Paulist Press, 1978.

Skinner, B. F. *Beyond Freedom and Dignity*. New York: Alfred Knopf, 1972.

Sophocles. *Antigone*. Great Books of the Western World. Translated by Sir Richard C. Jebb. Chicago: Encyclopædia Britannica, 1952.

Sorrell, Roger D. *St. Francis of Assisi and Nature: Tradition and Innovation in Western Christian Attitudes Toward the Environment*. New York: Oxford University Press, 1988.

Spangler, David. *Revelation: The Birth of a New Age*. Middletown, Wis.: Lorian Press, 1976.

Spring, David, and Eileen Spring, eds. *Ecology and Religion in History*. New York: Harper and Row, 1974.

Squires, Edwin R., ed. *The Environmental Crisis: The Ethical Dilemma*. Mancelona, Mich.: AuSable Trails Institute of Environmental Studies, 1982.

Steinhart, Peter. "Fundamentals." *Audubon* 83 (September 1981): 5-14.

Stewart, Claude Y., Jr. "Factors Conditioning the Christian Creation Consciousness." In *Cry of the Environment: Rebuilding the Christian Creation Tradition*, edited by Philip N. Joranson and Ken Butigan. Santa Fe, N. M.: Bear & Co., 1984.

Stone, Christopher D. *Should Trees Have Standing? Toward Legal Rights for Natural Objects*. Los Altos, Calif.: William Kaufmann, 1974.

Teilhard de Chardin, Pierre. *The Phenomenon of Man*. Translated by Bernard Wall. London: Collins, 1955.

Tertullian. *On the Resurrection of the Flesh*. The Ante-Nicene Fathers: Translations of the Fathers Down to A.D. 325. Edited by Alexander Roberts and James Donaldson. 10 vols. Grand Rapids: Wm. B. Eerdmans, 1951.

Toynbee, Arnold. "The Religious Background of the Present Environmental Crisis." In *Ecology and Religion in History*, edited by David Spring and Eileen Spring. New York: Harper and Row, 1974. First published in *International Journal of Environmental Studies* 3 (1972): 141-46.

Tuan, Yi-Fu. "Discrepancies Between Environmental Attitude and Behaviour: Examples from Europe and China." In *Ecology and Religion in History*, edited by David Spring and Eileen Spring. New York: Harper and Row, 1974. 91-113. First published in *The Canadian Geographer* 12 (1968): 176-91.

__________. "Our Treatment of the Environment in Ideal and Actuality." *American Scientist* 58 (June 1970): 244-49.

Von Rad, Gerhard. *Genesis: A Commentary*. Philadelphia: Westminster Press, 1961.

Ward, Barbara, and René Dubos. *Only One Earth: The Care and Maintenance of a Small Planet*. New York: W. W. Norton & Co., 1972.

Waysman, Dvora. "Ecology Began in the Bible." *Israel Digest* 21 (November 17, 1987): 12.

Welbourn, F. B. "Man's Dominion." *Theology* 78 (November 1975): 561-68.

Westermann, Claus. *Creation*. Translated by John J. Scullion. London: SPCK, 1974.

__________. *Genesis 1-11: A Commentary*. Translated by John J. Scullion. Minneapolis: Augsburg Publishing House, 1984.

White, Lynn, Jr. "Continuing the Conversation." In *Western Man and Environmental Ethics*, edited by Ian G. Barbour. Reading, Mass.: Addison-Wesley Publishing, 1973.

__________. "The Historical Roots of Our Ecologic Crisis." *Science* 155 (March 10, 1967): 1203-1207.

Whitehead, Alfred North. *Science and the Modern World*. New York: Macmillan, 1925.

Wilkinson, Loren. "Cosmic Christology and the Christian's Role in Creation." *Christian Scholar's Review* 11 (1981): 18-40.

__________. "Redeemers of the Earth." In *The Environmental Crisis: The Ethical Dilemma*, edited by Edwin R. Squires. Mancelona, Mich.: AuSable Trails Institute of Environmental Studies, 1982.

Williams, George Huntston. "Christian Attitudes Toward Nature." *Christian Scholar's Review* 2 (1971): 3-35.

Woods, Richard. "Environment as Spiritual Horizon: The Legacy of Celtic Monasticism." In *Cry of the Environment: Rebuilding the Christian Creation Tradition*, edited by Philip N. Joranson and Ken Butigan. Santa Fe, N. M.: Bear & Co., 1984.

Woodward, Kenneth L. "A New Story of Creation: It's the season for a theology of ecology." *Newsweek* (June 5, 1989): 70-72.

Wright, Richard. "Responsibility for the Ecological Crisis." *Christian Scholar's Review* 1 (1970): 35-40.

Yandell, Keith E. "Fundamentals of Environmental Ethics: East and West." In *The Environmental Crisis: The Ethical Dilemma*, edited by Edwin R. Squires. Mancelona, Mich.: AuSable Trails Institute of Environmental Studies, 1982.

Zerbe, Gordon. "The Kingdom of God and Stewardship of Creation." In *The Environment and the Christian: What Can We Learn from the New Testament*, edited by Calvin B. DeWitt. Grand Rapids: Baker Book House, 1991.

Zimmerman, Michael E. "Quantum Theory, Intrinsic Value, and Panentheism." *Environmental Ethics* 10 (Spring 1988): 3-30.

Biographical Index

A

Abraham 234
Adam 41, 66, 69,
    71, 112, 137, 138,
    142, 143, 163, 168
Aeschylus 32
Anderson, Bernhard 97,
    141, 251, 274
Aquinas, Thomas . . 40,
    42, 89, 106
Aristotle 34
Atkins, Anselm 227
Attfield, Robin   164, 235
Augustine 36

B

Bacon, Francis 43,
    44, 45
Badke, William 118
Barbour, Ian . . .19, 209
Barney, Gerald 13
Barr, James . . 47, 162,
    165, 166
Barth, Karl   44, 49, 118
Basil 37
Bauckham, Richard 166
Benét, Stephen
    Vincent. 32
Bentley, Philip J. . . 178,
    179
Berkeley, George 57
Berkhof, L. 84
Berry, Thomas. . 17, 19,
    21, 48, 75, 77, 88, 92,
    99, 124, 166
Berry, Wendell. . 18, 99,
    241
Birch, Bruce 136
Birch, Charles. .19, 214
Black, John. . . 95, 180,
    208, 234
Bonaventure 39
Bonifazi, Conrad 19
Botkin, Daniel. 61
Bowman,
    Douglas C. 277

Brown, Delwin 97
Brueggemann,
    Walter 24, 87
Brunner, Emil . . 49, 118
Bryce-Smith, D. . . . 180,
    186, 209
Butigan, Ken 67

C

Calvin, John 40
Campbell, Joseph . . 12,
    100, 142
Carmody, John . . . 123
Christ . . 112, 113, 147,
    148, 154, 171, 220
Clement of Rome . . . 35
Cobb, John B. . . 19, 20,
    78, 214
Commoner, Barry . .52,
    61, 116
Copernicus 43
Cox, Harvey. . . 15, 103
Cross, Frank Moore 167
Cumbey, Constance 265

D

Daetz, Douglas. . . . 195
Derr, Thomas. 118,
    119, 123, 168, 272
Descartes, Réne . .43, 45
Devall, Bill 126
DeWitt, Calvin 93,
    163, 182, 268, 273
Dionysius the Great . .35
Dostoyevsky. . 116, 181
Drucker, Peter 82
Dubos, Réne . . .30, 31,
    33, 39, 123, 198
Dumbrell, William J. 161

E

Eckhart, Meister . . . 20
Ehrenfeld, David . . .81,
    178, 179
Ehrlich, Paul 15
Eiseley, Loren   103, 116
Elder, Frederick. . . 116

Eliade, Mircea . . 30, 80
Ellul, Jacques 16
Elsdon, Ron . . . 73, 276
Epicureans 34

F

Fackre, Gabriel. 83
Feder, Kenneth L. . . 224
Feuerbach, Ludwig. . 17
Fitzmyer, Joseph A. . 91
Fox, Matthew . . .17, 19,
    20, 77, 187, 214, 278
Francis of Assisi . . . 15,
    38, 62, 286
Fuller, Buckminster   59

G

Geisler, Norman L. . . 84
Glacken, Clarence J. 12,
    33, 46
Gore, Al 187
Granberg-Michaelson,
    Wesley. .24, 42, 151,
    280
Griffiths, Richard . . 226
Gustafson, James. . 199

H

Hale, Matthew 40
Hall, Douglas John   181
Hargrove, Eugene. . . 29
Hegel, Georg Wilhelm
    Friedrich 273
Hendry, George   27, 44
Henry, Carl 68
Hildegard of Bingen   20
Hobbs, Thomas 57
Holmes, Arthur. . . . 212
Holy Spirit 149
Hume, David 43
Hunt, Dave. 275
Huxley, Julian 42

I

Isaac the Syrian 38

J

Jaki, Stanley 15

Jesus 21
Jesus Christ 171,
      241, 281
Joranson, Philip N. . .67

K

Kant, Immanuel . . . 40,
      43, 91
Klotz, John 98
Krishnamurti 212
Krutch, Joseph
      Wood 95, 223

L

Ladd, George. 157
Leclerc, Eloi 39
Leibniz, G. W. 57
Leopold, Aldo 89,
      116, 180, 207, 214
Lewis, C. S. 194
Linzey, Andrew . . . 171,
      227, 252
Locke, John 43
Lovelock, James 60
Luther, Martin. 41

M

MacLaine, Shirley . .184
Maimonides, Moses. .37
Marrs, Texe. 265
Marx, Leo 12
McHarg, Ian . . .11, 116
McKibben, Bill. .55, 213
Meeker, Joseph. .60, 75
Merchant, Carolyn   214
Mill, J. S. 44
Moltmann, Jürgan . . 19,
      26, 157, 162, 274
Moncrief, Lewis 203
Montefiore, Hugh . . 78,
      176, 178
Moore, George
      Edward. 213
Moule, C. F. D. . . . 113,
      146, 179

N

Nash, Roderick 226
Newkirk, Ingred. . . .224
Newton, Isaac 43
Niebuhr, H. Richard 123
Noah. 92, 105,
      106, 234

O

Origen 36

P

Park, Michal Alan . . 224
Pascal, Blaise. . . 44, 46
Passmore, John 11,
      36, 39, 40, 71, 76,
      196, 203
Pelikan, Jaroslav . . 104
Philo 36
Pinchot, Gifford . . . 223
Plato 33, 91

R

Richardson, Herbert 116
Rickaby, Joseph. . . 222
Robbins, Jerry 100
Roosevelt, Theodore 223
Rossi, Vincent 87,
      122, 127, 128, 133,
      274, 282
Runcie, Robert. 82
Russell, Bertrand. . . 57

S

Sagan, Carl . . . 49, 269
Salk, Jonas 268
Santmire, H. Paul . .24,
      35, 36, 41, 49, 97,
      121, 129, 174, 179,
      262, 274
Schaeffer, Francis A. 83,
      94, 150, 165, 251,
      260, 275
Schilling, Harold K. . 19,
      214
Schultz, Forrest W. . . 160
Schumacher . . 81, 193,
      199, 211
Schwarz, Hans. . . . 122,
      123, 158
Schweitzer, Albert   207,
      214
Sessions, George . . 126
Shaiko, Ronald G. . . 283
Sherrard, Philip 79
Singer, Peter . . 214, 224
Sittler, Joseph 63,
      111, 166
Skinner, B. F. 184
Smith, Adam 44
Sophocles 33
Spinoza 57

Steinhart, Peter . . . 179
Stoics. 34
Stone, C. D. 225
Suzuki, D. T. 136

T

Teilhard de Chardin,
      Pierre. . . .19, 21, 59,
      106, 116, 265
Tertullian 36
Thoreau, Henry
      David. 277
Toynbee, Arnold .11, 12,
      14, 15, 30
Tuan, Yi-Fu 31, 32

V

von Rad, Gerhard . . 97,
      135, 165

W

Ward, Barbara 198
Watt, James . . 179, 198
Welbourn, F. B. 30
Westermann,
      Claus. 96, 165
White, Lynn 118
White, Lynn, Jr. .10, 12,
      13, 14, 15, 16, 21, 23,
      28, 34, 39, 47, 48, 75,
      123, 159, 168, 202,
      261, 281, 283
Whitehead, Alfred
      North. 19
Wilkinson, Loren 24, 69
Wittgenstein,
      Ludwig 214
Wright, Richard   34, 192

Y

Yandell, Keith E.. . . 166

Z

Zimmerman, Michael 17

SUBJECT INDEX

A

Accountability   129, 174
Alienation 56, 72,
    73, 78, 136
Amish 78, 235, 272
Animal rights. 222,
    223, 224, 227
Animals. 34, 37, 40,
    45, 66, 88, 105, 107
Animism 10, 14, 29,
    30, 78
Anthropocentrism . . . 13,
    31, 40, 41, 65, 92,
    115, 116, 117, 118,
    119, 121, 122, 123,
    137
Asceticism . . 35, 96, 241,
    244, 276
Autonomy . . . 65, 70, 80,
    122, 174, 255

B

Balance of Nature . . . 53
Biocentric ethic 210
Biocentrism. 22, 65,
    115, 124, 125, 126,
    127, 128
Biodiversity . . . 105, 106
Buddhism 57, 77

C

China 31
Christian duty 275
Christian environmental-
    ism. 7, 267
Coercion 199, 200
Commons 236
Continuing creation   114
Cosmic Community . . 62
Cosmic ecosystem . . . 73,
    113
Cosmic fall. 142
Cosmic law of
    harmony. . . . 74, 189
Cosmic salvation . . . 147,
    148
Creation 65, 76, 84

Creation spirituality . .20,
    278, 279
Crisis. 70
Critical thinking. . . .261,
    262
Critics 10, 261, 281
Crown of
    creation. 69, 129
Curse. 138
Cyclical concept
    of time. 158, 234

D

Death. 72, 142, 143
Death of nature 72
Death principle   153, 192
Deep ecology . . 210, 311
Deism 43, 100,
    101, 109, 110
Depravity 196
Desacralization
    of nature 14
Dispensationalism . . 156
Dominion. . . .12, 45, 137,
    160, 163, 166, 169
Dualism . . 16, 17, 44, 45,
    96, 238, 239, 240,
    249, 250, 253
Dualism of soul
    and body 242
Dualisms 96

E

Eastern Orthodoxy . . . 38
Ecojustice 231
Ecological crisis . .54, 70,
    192
Ecological triangle . . . 64
Ecology 51, 52
Ecosystem 53
Endangered Species
    Act 223, 226
Enlightenment . . .42, 46,
    119
Entropy 58, 59
Environmental crisis   49,
    52, 137, 182, 260, 281
Environmental
    ethics 207

Environmental
    retribution . . . 64, 140
Eschatological expecta-
    tions 17, 154
Ethics. 236
Evangelism. . . . 24, 257,
    258, 280
Evolution 223

F

Fall of humanity 136
Fallen nature 186
Findhord 60
Freedom . . 174, 200, 270
Fundamentalism. . . . 20,
    118, 283

G

Gaia hypothesis 60
Garden of Eden. 134
Globalism. 265, 266
Gnosticism 238
God's ownership 86
Goodness of Creation   96
Gospel 281
Great chain of
    being . . . 36, 277, 290
Greece 33
Greed 63, 193,
    194, 254

H

Hierarchical systems   217
Hinduism . . .57, 58, 106
Holy Spirit   188, 278, 279

I

Idolatry. 256
Image of God . . 68, 164,
    183, 240
Imago Dei   164, 165, 166,
    187, 204, 208, 240
Immanence of
    God 101, 104
Incarnation. . . . 113, 171
Integrity of Creation . .62
Intrinsic value. 82,
    98, 219

Intrinsic value
of nature. 84
Intrinsic value
to nature. 251

J

Judgment and blessing
motifs 113

K

Kingdom . . 156, 157, 158
Kingdom of God. . . . 270

L

Lamp. 72
Laws of thermo-
dynamics 58, 78
Linear time scale . . . 158
Love 70, 90,
170, 212, 246

M

Manichaeism . . 238, 244
Materialism . . . 192, 193,
194, 195, 253, 254
Mennonites 272
Millennial
expectations 154
Miracles 103, 113
Mission of the
church 257
Monism. 57
Monotheism. 14, 15,
30, 300
Mother Earth. . . . 21, 77,
101

N

Native Americans. . . . 29
Natural evils . . . 65, 146
Natural theology 26
Nature. 76, 77, 273
Nature religions 14,
256, 264
Neoplatonic
spirituality 277
Neoplatonism. 35
New creation 150
Noahic Covenant . . . 105

O

Objectification of
nature 44, 80

P

Panentheism 19, 77

Pantheism . . 77, 79, 100,
110, 125, 159, 183,
184, 210, 234, 267,
300
Pantheistism 106
Paradise. 135
Pelagianism . . . 196, 279
Pietism. 243
Pollution . . 192, 208, 264
Population 13
Population growth . . 167,
199
Poverty. . . 232, 233, 272
Private ownership 88, 89
Process Theology 19
Process theology. . . . 286
Progress. . . 32, 159, 289
Purpose in creation . . 89
Purpose of nature. . . 252

R

Reconciliation. 149
Redemption 47, 148, 279
Reformation 40
Religion 56
Renaissance. . . . 43, 119
Restoration 151
Restoration of nature 252
Resurrection . . 148, 153,
243
Rights 45, 221, 270
Romanticism . . . 83, 215

S

Sabbath. . . . 69, 87, 105
Sacredness
of nature 14, 76
Salvation . . . 63, 64, 147,
247, 252, 271
Santmire 246
Science and tech-
nology. . . . 15, 38, 47
Secular ethic 209
Secular humanism. . 184
Secular humanists . . 182
Secularism. 46
Secularization . . . 41, 46
Secularization of nature .
46, 47, 80, 102
Self-centeredness . . . 254
Sentiency. 224
Shalom 73, 136
Sin. . . 63, 136, 185, 186
Speciesism. 222
Spirituality. . . . 277, 279
Standard of living. . . 272

Stewardship . . . 68, 129,
172, 173, 174, 175,
176, 177
Stoics 36
Substantial healing 150
Sustainability . . 64, 109,
229
Syntropy. 59

T

Taoism 77, 210
Theanthropocentrism 49,
118, 121, 274
Theistic evolution . . . 96,
142, 143
Theocentric
spirituality 278
Theocentrism 116,
122, 128, 129, 130,
131, 137, 274
Theology of nature . . 26,
274, 287
Transcendence
of God . . 99, 102, 240
Transcendent 65

U

Uniqueness of
humanity. 240
Unity of creation . . . 251
Universalism. 148
Utilitarian value of
nature 75, 80, 81

V

Value of nature . . 82, 251
Vegetarianism. 67

W

Wealth . . . 195, 232, 271
World 153
Worldview shift 137
Worldview thinking . . 262
Worldviews 76, 125,
210, 211, 262, 263

Y

Year of Jubilee 106

Z

Zoroastrianism 238, 244

Scripture Index

Old Testament

Genesis 71
Gen. 1:1 84
Gen. 1:2 111
Gen. 1:4,10,12,
  18,21,25 96
Gen. 1:11-12,20-21,
  24-25 101
Gen. 1:20-21 67
Gen. 1:22 167
Gen. 1:24-31 66
Gen. 1:26 . . . .164, 178
Gen. 1:26-27 164
Gen. 1:26-28 156,
  178, 240
Gen. 1:27 . . . . . .66, 68
Gen. 1:28 . . 12, 13, 16,
  36, 41, 88, 160, 161,
  163, 167, 169, 178
Gen. 1:29 . . . .162, 174
Gen. 1:29-30 . . . 67, 97,
  135, 143, 144, 217
Gen. 1:30 67
Gen. 1:31 . . . . . 96, 97,
  143, 251
Gen. 2:4-5 163
Gen. 2:5 . . . . . . 66, 69,
  162,163
Gen. 2:5,15 68
Gen. 2:7 66
Gen. 2:8 135
Gen. 2:8-9 69
Gen. 2:9 . . . . . .66, 134
Gen. 2:9-10 151
Gen. 2:15 . . . . 40, 135,
  162, 163, 164
Gen. 2:17 . . . .138, 142
Gen. 2:19-20 71,
  144, 168
Gen. 3 136
Gen. 3:17 139
Gen. 3:17-19 . . .71, 139
Gen. 3:19 143
Gen. 3:19, 23 66
Gen. 3:21 71,
  144, 217, 228

Gen. 3:23 71,
  135, 163
Gen. 3:3 138
Gen. 3:5 138
Gen. 3:8 103
Gen. 4:1-5 228
Gen. 4:2 163
Gen. 4:8 71
Gen. 4:10-12 . . 71, 191
Gen. 4:12 163
Gen. 4:23 71
Gen. 5:3 . . . . . 66, 165
Gen. 5:28-29 140
Gen. 6 141
Gen. 6:5 71
Gen. 6:5-13 189
Gen. 6:7 146
Gen. 6:11-12 141
Gen. 6:12 301
Gen. 6:17 141
Gen. 6:19 106
Gen. 6:19-20 92
Gen. 8:17 167
Gen. 8:22 64
Gen. 9:1-3 . . . 72, 217
Gen. 9:1-7 160,
  161, 162
Gen. 9:1,7 167
Gen. 9:2-3 144
Gen. 9:3 . . . . 135, 228
Gen. 9:6 165
Gen. 9:8-17 105
Gen. 9:9 234
Gen. 9:10 105
Gen. 9:11-12 105
Gen. 11:6-9 97
Gen. 17:7 234
Gen. 26:12 191
Gen. 27:27-28 191
Gen. 38:7-10 13
Gen. 38:9-10 168
Gen. 41:35 163
Ex. 3:12 163
Ex. 5:18 163
Ex. 9:29 86
Ex. 10:13 113
Ex. 14:21 113

Ex. 15:26 163
Ex. 18:21 172
Ex. 19:5 . . . . . 86, 163
Ex. 20:4 256
Ex. 20:10 105
Ex. 20:17 . . . 195, 254
Ex. 21:2-6 163
Ex. 22:7,10 163
Ex. 22:21-24 232
Ex. 23:5 170
Ex. 23:10-12 106
Ex. 23:12 105
Ex. 26:14 228
Ex. 32:26 256
Ex. 34:26 79
Ex. 40:9 79
Lev. 18 190
Lev. 18:24-25 190
Lev. 19:9-10 232
Lev. 19:18 170
Lev. 19:23-25 107
Lev. 19:25 107
Lev. 23:22 232
Lev. 25 105
Lev. 25:1-5 170
Lev. 25:1-7 . . . 106, 188
Lev. 25:4 106
Lev. 25:11 106
Lev. 25:16 86
Lev. 25:18-19 87
Lev. 25:23 . . .87, 88, 174
Lev. 25:43, 46, 53. . 162
Lev. 26:1 256
Lev. 26:34-35 107
Lev. 26:17 162
Num. 3:13 79
Num. 4:37,41 163
Num. 16:37-38 79
Num. 32:22,29 161
Num. 35:33-34 189
Deut. 5:14 . . . 105, 170
Deut. 5:21 195
Deut. 7:9 234
Deut. 7:25 256
Deut. 8:12-14 254
Deut. 10:14 87
Deut. 11:13-17 190

Deut. 17:16-17 172
Deut. 17:18-19 172
Deut. 20:5. 234
Deut. 20:19. 170
Deut. 20:19-20 107
Deut. 22:4. 170
Deut. 22:6. 170
Deut. 22:6-7 106
Deut. 25:4. 105,
　　107, 170
Deut. 28:1-6 191
Deut. 28:15-68 113
Deut. 28:39. 163
Deut. 30:19. 256
Josh. 6:18-19 79
Josh. 7:11,20 189,
　　251
Josh. 10:13. 113
Josh. 10:24. 161
Josh. 18:1. 161
Josh. 24:15. 256
Judg. 2:11. 163
1 Sam. 15:23. 185
1 Sam. 17:20. 163
2 Sam. 8:11 161
2 Sam. 16:19. 163
2 Sam. 23:3 172
1 Kings 3:5-12. 172
1 Kings 4:24 162
1 Kings 5:6-7 31
1 Kings 5:13-14. 31
1 Kings 14:27 163
1 Kings 18:21 256
1 Kings 19:11-12. . .101
1 Kings 20:39 163
1 Kings 21:2-3. 88
2 Kings 6:6 113
1 Chron. 29:11 87,
　　132
1 Chron. 22:18 161
2 Chron. 28:10 161
2 Chron. 7:13-14. . .191
2 Chron. 7:14 262,
　　282
2 Chron. 8:10 162
2 Chron. 36:21 107, 188
Neh. 5:5 161
Neh. 9:6 . . . . . . .64, 84
Neh. 9:28 162
Esther 7:8. 161
Job 111
Job 4:19 66
Job 8:9 197
Job 9:5-7 64

Job 10:8-9 66
Job 14:4 187
Job 25:2 173
Job 26:7 84
Job 28:28 . . . 198, 253
Job 34:14-15. 110
Job 37:6 111
Job 37:9-10 111
Job 37:11 111
Job 37:12 111
Job 38:12-35. 64
Job 38:4 131
Job 38:26 . . . . 92, 131
Job 38:28-29 101
Job 39:1-4. 94
Job 39:5-8. 94
Job 39:9-12. 94
Job 39:13-18. 94
Job 39:19-25. 94
Job 39:26-30. 95
Job 40:15 66
Job 40:15-24. 95
Job 41:11 87
Job 41:1-34. 95
Psalms. 111
Ps. 8 137
Ps. 8:4. 182
Ps. 8:19a 90
Ps. 8:148 90
Ps. 19:1-2 91
Ps. 22:27-28 156
Ps. 22:28 173
Ps. 24:1 88
Ps. 24:1-2 87
Ps. 25:8 97
Ps. 34:8 97
Ps. 36:6 . . . . . . 64, 111
Ps. 45:7 170
Ps. 49:12, 20 68
Ps. 50:10-11 88
Ps. 51:10 114
Ps. 65:17-18 111
Ps. 65:9-13 111
Ps. 69:34 93
Ps. 72:1-2 172
Ps. 72:8 162
Ps. 78:69 152
Ps. 89 111
Ps. 89:5 93
Ps. 89:11-12 87
Ps. 89:12 93
Ps. 95:5 87
Ps. 96:10-13 110
Ps. 96:11-13 191

Ps. 96:11-13a. 93
Ps. 97:6-7. 91
Ps. 97:10 253
Ps. 98:7-9. 93
Ps. 100:2 163
Ps. 102:26 152
Ps. 103:14 66
Ps. 104. . . . . . . 92, 111
Ps. 104:5 152
Ps. 104:10-11. 92
Ps. 104:12 92
Ps. 104:13 101
Ps. 104:14 92
Ps. 104:14-15, 23. . .92
Ps. 104:16 92
Ps. 104:17 92
Ps. 104:18 92
Ps. 104:26 95
Ps. 104:27-30. 64
Ps. 104:29 66,
　　110, 111
Ps. 104:29-30. 66
Ps. 106:1 97
Ps. 107:33-34. 191
Ps. 110:2 162
Ps. 115:16b 137
Ps. 121:7 163
Ps. 124:8 282
Ps. 139:7-10. 104
Ps. 145:10,21. 93
Ps. 145:15-16. 111
Ps. 146:4 66
Ps. 147:8-9. 111
Ps. 147:16-17. 111
Ps. 147:16-18. 64
Ps. 148. . . . . 79, 93
Ps. 148:3-6. 152
Ps. 150:6 93
Prov. 3:19-20 94
Prov. 6:24. 163
Prov. 8:30-31 95
Prov. 11:26. 255
Prov. 12:10. 170
Prov. 12:11. 163
Prov. 14:16. 253
Prov. 14:31. 232
Prov. 16:18. 255
Prov. 21:4. 255
Prov. 23:20-21 255
Prov. 28:19. 163
Prov. 28:26. . . 198, 255
Eccl. 1:4. 152
Eccl. 3:18-20 68
Eccl. 3:18-21 66

Eccl. 3:20 66
Eccl. 5:10 254
Eccl. 11:5 197
Isaiah . . .140, 190, 197
Isa. 2:4 156
Isa. 3:14-15. 232
Isa. 5:8 232
Isa. 5:13 153
Isa. 5:21 255
Isa. 5:8-9 88
Isa. 8:1 84
Isa. 9:7 170
Isa. 11:6-9. .67, 68, 154
Isa. 11:9 156
Isa. 13:11 197
Isa. 24:1 190
Isa. 24:1-6. 65
Isa. 24:5-6. 190
Isa. 25:8 151
Isa. 29:16 66
Isa. 30:23-26. 154
Isa. 35:1-2. 154
Isa. 35:1-10. 156
Isa. 37:24 31
Isa. 40:6-8. 68
Isa. 41:17-20. 68
Isa. 41:18-19. 154
Isa. 41:18-20. 191
Isa. 41:2 162
Isa. 43:18-21. 68
Isa. 43:20-22. 93
Isa. 44:22-23. . .65, 191
Isa. 44:9-20. 101
Isa. 45:7 146
Isa. 45:18 84
Isa. 45:20 257
Isa. 46:10 84
Isa. 48:6-7. 114
Isa. 49:13 191
Isa. 51:3 153
Isa. 51:6 152
Isa. 55:12-13. 191
Isa. 55:13 154
Isa. 56:11-12. 254
Isa. 64:6 197
Isa. 65:17 68
Isa. 65:20 154
Isa. 65:25 154
Isa. 66:22 68
Jer. 10:11-13 112
Jer. 10:12-13 94
Jer. 16:18 191
Jer. 17:9. 187
Jer. 2:7 88

Jer. 2:7, 3:2 31
Jer. 2:8 88
Jer. 3:2-3. 189
Jer. 4:17-28. 191
Jer. 5:26-29. 232
Jer. 9:9-11. 191
Jer. 17:9 311
Jer. 23:23-24. . . . 104
Jer. 31:12-14. . . . 154
Jer. 31:22 114
Jer. 31:34 156
Jer. 31:35 112
Jer. 32:42-44. . . . 191
Jer. 34:11,16. . . . 161
Jer. 49:20 191
Jer. 51:15-16. . . . 112
Ezek. 16:49-50 . . . 232
Ezek. 27:5 31
Ezek. 29:15 162
Ezek. 34:1-6 . 162, 178
Ezek. 34:4 178
Ezek. 34:18-19 . . . 178
Ezek. 36:1-12 . . . 107
Ezek. 36:7 107
Ezek. 36:8-12 . . . 107
Ezek. 36:34 163
Ezek. 36:35 . . 153, 154
Ezek. 43:22-27 . . . 154
Ezek. 47:10 154
Dan. 4:35 132
Hosea 189
Hos. 2:3. 191
Hos. 2:18. . . . 149, 154
Hos. 2:18-20 68
Hos. 2:21-22 191
Hos. 4:1-3 . . . . 65, 189
Hos. 4:2-3 251
Hos. 8:4. 256
Hos. 14:9. 170
Joel 2:19-26 154
Amos 2:7 232
Amos 4:6-13 191
Amos 5:11-12 232
Amos 7:10 189
Amos 8:4-10 232
Obad. 4 255
Jonah 4:11 105
Mic. 2:1-2 88
Mic. 7:19 161
Nahum 112
Nahum 1:3 112
Nahum 1:4-6. 112
Nahum 1:7 97
Zeph. 2:15 255

Zech. 8:4 154
Zech. 9:15 161
Zech. 14:12-17. . . . 154
Mal. 1:11 156

New Testament

Matt. 4:8 245
Matt. 5:3-12. 272
Matt. 5:13-14. 275
Matt. 5:14 245
Matt. 5:20 258
Matt. 6:10 210
Matt. 6:11 276
Matt. 6:19-21 194,
     195, 254
Matt. 6:24 . . . 195, 254
Matt. 6:24-34. 195
Matt. 6:26 . . . 112, 219
Matt. 6:26, 28 64
Matt. 6:28 112
Matt. 6:33 . . . 132, 245
Matt. 8:8 139
Matt. 10:29 . . 106, 107
Matt. 10:31 219
Matt. 12:12 220
Matt. 12:32 247
Matt. 13:22 . . 195, 254
Matt. 13:38 245
Matt. 13:39-40. . . . 247
Matt. 13:49 247
Matt. 15:19-20. . . . 311
Matt. 16:25 . . 194, 256
Matt. 16:26 . . 247, 254
Matt. 19:11-12. . . . 167
Matt. 19:13 271
Matt. 19:16-24. . . . 195
Matt. 19:16-30. . . . 254
Matt. 19:17 97
Matt. 19:21-22. . . . 195
Matt. 20:25-28. . . . 171
Matt. 22:37-40. . . . 212
Matt. 23:12 . . 197, 255
Matt. 24:3 247
Matt. 24:14 248
Matt. 24:35 152
Matt. 25:14-30 173, 176
Matt. 25:34-40. . . . 155
Matt. 25:35-36. . . . 232
Mark 4:19 . . . 195, 271
Mark 5:1-20. 108
Mark 7:14-23. 187
Mark 7:15 252
Mark 8:34-37. 212
Mark 10:17-25 195

Mark 10:30 247
Mark 10:45 220
Mark 11:13-14,
    20-24 108
Mark 11:14,20-21 . . .139
Mark 12:30 243
Mark 16:15 245
Luke 2:1 248
Luke 6:32-34 185
Luke 8:14 195
Luke 9:2 258
Luke 12:6 106
Luke 12:15 . . 194, 254,
    255, 272
Luke 12:18-19 73
Luke 12:42-48 175
Luke 13:6-9 108
Luke 16:8 175
Luke 16:13 254
Luke 16:15 254
Luke 17:20-21 156
Luke 18:8 205
Luke 18:18-25 195
Luke 22:24-30 255
Luke 24:13-32 153
John 1:1-3 . . .113, 148
John 1:3 86
John 1:10 245
John 1:29 245
John 3:16 246
John 3:17 245
John 3:31 132
John 4:24 240
John 7:7 247
John 8:32-38 188
John 10:10 252
John 10:11 171
John 15:18 245
John 15:18-19 247
John 15:19 247
John 17:14-16 247
John 17:15 245
John 17:15-18 275
John 18:36 156
John 19:17 233
John 20:30-31 246
John 21:7-8 153
John 21:25 245
Acts 1:8 258
Acts 3:18-21 153
Acts 3:19-21 148
Acts 3:21 . . . . .151, 156
Acts 11:28 248
Acts 11:29 258

Acts 14:17 91
Acts 17:25,28 . .110, 112
Acts 17:26 248
Acts 17:27 104
Acts 17:29 257
Acts 17:31 248
Romans 132, 203
Rom. 1:8 245
Rom. 1:18-32 138,
    186
Rom. 1:20 66
Rom. 1:21-23 101
Rom. 1:23 256
Rom. 1:24-32 256
Rom. 2:14-15 208
Rom. 3:16-17 184
Rom. 3:19 245
Rom. 3:23 . . . 165, 186
Rom. 4:17 84
Rom. 5:7 185
Rom. 5:8 212
Rom. 5:12 142
Rom. 5:12-21 251
Rom. 5:17 142
Rom. 5:22 143
Rom. 6:12 253
Rom. 6:17-23 188
Rom. 6:23 144
Rom. 7 188
Rom. 7:7 254
Rom. 7:7-13 200
Rom. 7:14-25 185
Rom. 7:18 242
Rom. 7:24 150
Rom. 8:1-4 150
Rom. 8:2 188
Rom. 8:13 243
Rom. 8:18-21 148
Rom. 8:18-23 68
Rom. 8:19-21 . .120, 284
Rom. 8:20 139
Rom. 8:20-21 . .37, 140,
    147, 157, 252
Rom. 8:21 . . . .63, 156,
    240, 246, 271
Rom. 8:21-22 151
Rom. 8:22 . . . 141, 146,
    192
Rom. 9:14-21 227
Rom. 10:18 91
Rom. 11:36 90
Rom. 12:2 122,
    133, 203, 247, 263
Rom. 12:9 253

Rom. 13:9 254
Rom. 14:14 252
Rom. 14:17 . .156, 159,
    194, 235
1 & 2 Cor. 203
1 Cor. 3:12 239
1 Cor. 3:12-15 153
1 Cor. 4:2 173
1 Cor. 5:9-10 245
1 Cor. 7:7-8 167
1 Cor. 7:29-34 245
1 Cor. 7:31 152
1 Cor. 8:4 257
1 Cor. 8:6 132
1 Cor. 9:9 107
1 Cor. 9:10 107
1 Cor. 9:27 240
1 Cor. 10:6 253
1 Cor. 10:12 255
1 Cor. 10:26 88
1 Cor. 12:2 101
1 Cor. 12:26 251
1 Cor. 13:5 212
1 Cor. 13:12 197
1 Cor. 15 . . . . 143, 148
1 Cor. 15:25-26 . . . 151
1 Cor. 15:26 . .143, 154,
    192
1 Cor. 15:26,
    54-56 144
1 Cor. 15:28 156
1 Cor. 15:30-32 . . . 143
1 Cor. 15:31 243
1 Cor. 15:35-44 . . . 143
1 Cor. 15:35-49 . . . 153
1 Cor. 15:39-41 95
1 Cor. 15:54-57 . . . 147
2 Cor. 3:18 205
2 Cor. 4:4 16,
    241, 248, 292
2 Cor. 5:1-5 243
2 Cor. 5:17 114,
    150, 158
2 Cor. 5:18 149
2 Cor. 5:18-20 63
2 Cor. 8:13-14 232
2 Cor. 10:5 . . .122, 132,
    203, 263
2 Pet. 3:10-13 244
Gal. 1:4 . . .241, 244, 248
Gal. 2:10 258
Gal. 2:20 243
Gal. 3:5 243
Gal. 5:1 188

Gal. 5:16-18 239
Gal. 5:16-26 212
Gal. 5:19-21 242
Gal. 5:24 243
Gal. 6:3 255
Gal. 6:10 275
Gal. 6:14 . . . . 132, 243, 245, 247, 255
Eph. 1:10 . . . . 148, 156, 240, 252
Eph. 1:21 247
Eph. 2:10 255
Eph. 2:15 114
Eph. 2:2 292
Eph. 4:23-24 165
Philippians 203
Phil. 2:1-4 171
Phil. 2:5 . . . . 122, 132, 171, 203
Phil. 2:6 171
Phil. 2:6-11 171
Phil. 2:10 148
Phil. 2:12 63
Phil. 2:15 . . . .245, 275
Phil. 3:21 205
Phil. 4:1-3 171
Phil. 4:11 276
Phil. 4:19 195
Col. 1:6 245
Col. 1:13 156
Col. 1:16 . . .86, 90, 132
Col. 1:16-17 112
Col. 1:17 . . . . . .64, 145
Col. 1:20 . . 68, 142, 148, 149, 156, 240, 252
Col. 2:8 256
Col. 3:2 244
Col. 3:5 242
Col. 3:10 165
1 Thess. 5:22 253
1 Tim. 1:4 256
1 Tim. 3:3,8 254
1 Tim. 4:4 251
1 Tim. 4:7 256
1 Tim. 6:9 254
1 Tim. 6:10 . . 195, 232, 254
1 Tim. 6:15 132
1 Tim. 6:17 . . . . . 195, 254, 272
2 Tim. 3:1-5 204
2 Tim. 3:2 254
2 Tim. 3:13 205
2 Tim. 4:3 205

2 Tim. 4:4 256
Titus 1:7 175
Phil. 2:5-11 220
Phil. 3:21 243
Heb. 1:2 248
Heb. 1:3 . . 64, 112, 145, 170
Heb. 1:8 170
Heb. 1:10-12 60
Heb. 1:11-12 152
Heb. 2:8 . . . . 137, 178
Heb. 4:16 170
Heb. 7:9-10 251
Heb. 9:11 64
Heb. 9:26 247
Heb. 11:3 . . 84, 86, 139
Heb. 24 140
Heb. 24:1,5-6 140
Jas. 1:27 . . . . 247, 258
Jas. 1:9-11 232
Jas. 2:10 197
Jas. 2:1-13 271
Jas. 3:17 198
Jas. 4:4 . . 16, 244, 247
Jas. 5:1 195
Jas. 5:1-6 232
Jas. 5:3 272
Jas. 5:14 258
1 Pet. 3:11 253
1 Pet. 5:7 170
2 Pet. 1:4 245
2 Pet. 3:4 66
2 Pet. 3:3-13 105
2 Pet. 3:10 . . . 152, 153
2 Pet. 3:10-13 152
1 John 2:15 . . 195, 244
1 John 2:15-17 . . . 247
1 John 2:16 152
1 John 2:17 . . 152, 239
1 John 3:2 243
1 John 3:4 186
1 John 3:13 247
1 John 3:17 233
1 John 3:18 . . 233, 260
1 John 4:7-21 212
1 John 4:9 245
1 John 5:19 241
1 John 5:21 256
Rev. 1:5-6 156
Rev. 3:10 248
Rev. 3:14 66
Rev. 3:17 255
Rev. 4:11 84
Rev. 6-19 105

Rev. 15:3 170
Rev. 17:3-4 187
Rev. 18:3 187
Rev. 20:4 156
Rev. 21:1 152
Rev. 21:4 . . . . 135, 144
Rev. 22:1-5 151